JAPAN'S ROAD
to the PACIFIC WAR

Japan Erupts

Studies of the East Asian Institute—Columbia University

JAPAN'S ROAD
to the PACIFIC WAR

JAPAN ERUPTS

THE LONDON NAVAL CONFERENCE
and the MANCHURIAN INCIDENT,
1928–1932

Selected translations from
*Taiheiyō sensō e no michi:
kaisen gaikō shi*

Edited by JAMES WILLIAM MORLEY

Columbia University Press · New York · 1984

The Japan Foundation, through a special grant, has assisted the Press in publishing this volume.

Columbia University Press
New York   Guildford, Surrey

Printed in the United States of America

Library of Congress Cataloging in Publication Data
Main entry under title:

Japan erupts.

(Japan's road to the Pacific War) (Studies of the
East Asian Institute)
   Bibliography: p.
   Includes index.
   1. Japan—Foreign relations—1912–1945. 2. London
naval treaty, 1930. 3. Mukden Incident, 1931.
4. Manchuria (China)—History—1931–1945. 5. China—
Foreign relations—Japan. 6. Japan—Foreign relations—
China. I. Morley, James Williams, 1921–
II. Taiheiyō Sensō e no michi. III. Series.
DS885.48.J36   1984   327.52   83-27320

ISBN 0-231-05782-2

The East Asian Institute of Columbia University

The East Asian Institute is Columbia University's center for research, publication, and teaching on modern East Asia. The Studies of the East Asian Institute were inaugurated in 1962 to bring to a wider public the results of significant new research on Japan, China, and Korea.

Contents

Editor's Foreword

Not long after Japan had regained its independence from occupation following World War II, the Japan Association on International Relations (Nihon Kokusai Seiji Gakkai), which embraces Japan's leading scholars of international affairs, undertook an ambitious collaborative research project on the origins of the Pacific War from the 1920s to 1941. Under the leadership first of Kamikawa Hikomatsu,* professor emeritus of international politics at Tokyo University, and then of Tsunoda Jun, professor of diplomatic history at Kokugakuin University and head of the Shidehara Peace Collection of the National Diet Library, an impressive number of young, objective diplomatic and military historians were assembled. They were given access to a wide range of primary materials, including not only those of the International Military Tribunal for the Far East but also a mass of others hitherto unavailable from the former imperial army and navy, the Justice Ministry, and the Foreign Ministry. The private papers of Prime Ministers Konoe Fumimaro and Okada Keisuke, Ugaki Kazushige (who served as both army and foreign minister), Colonel Ishiwara Kanji, and others were opened. A number of leading participants in the events made themselves available for interview. Each scholar in the project was given personal responsibility to present the facts on a given subject as he saw them.

The result was a collection of essays of remarkably objective quality, designed not to fit an overall interpretation of events, an approach that was consciously rejected, but, as one researcher put it, "to provide clues and materials for future historians." Published in 1962–63 in seven volumes by the press of Japan's largest newspaper, the *Asahi shimbun*, under the title *Taiheiyō sensō e no michi: kaisen gaikō shi* (The Road to the Pacific War: A Diplomatic History of the Origins of the War), the series was immediately acclaimed as the most informative, factually based account of Japan's road to war.

---

*In accord with Japanese usage, Japanese names are given throughout this volume with the surname first.

Japan's Road to the Pacific War is a translation of selected parts of that work. The principle of selection has been to include those essays or portions of essays that focus primarily on the policy of Japan rather than other countries and use particularly materials of an unusual character. In each case as faithful a translation as possible has been rendered, but translation is not a mechanical process. With languages and cultures as different as the Japanese and the American, minor omissions, revisions, or insertions have occasionally been made to make the translated version more readily intelligible. In addition, for the convenience of researchers, footnotes have been clarified and occasionally changed to indicate the published location of sources originally used archivally. An effort also has been made to standardize spellings and identifications of the names of persons and institutions and the titles of documents. While each essay stands on its own authority, its value has been greatly enhanced by a brief introduction by its scholar-translator.

The maps are derived from those accompanying the original Japanese text; place-names are spelled according to the current usage of the National Geographic Society. Except for widely recognized romanizations, such as Nanking or Canton, Chinese and Mongolian place-names are romanized according to the modified Wade-Giles system, retaining only essential aspirants. Personal names are rendered in the romanized form preferred by their users insofar as we have been able to ascertain them; otherwise, standard orthographical principles have been followed: modified Wade-Giles for Chinese, modified Hepburn for Japanese, and modified Library of Congress for Russian.

It had been hoped when this project was begun that the translations could be produced more expeditiously than has been possible. In the intervening years much new research has been done and scholars on both sides of the Pacific have offered additional interpretations of these critical years. But the extraordinary richness of the factual data presented in the Japanese scholarship translated here has not been superseded. This work remains a fundamental source for any interpretation of the period and proves insights and implications that are still to be followed up.

Many have contributed to this painstaking editorial work, but particularly Shumpei Okamoto and Dale K. A. Finlayson. Ishihara Naoki and David Deck verified bibliographical and geographical data; Anita M. O'Brien prepared the index and readied the volume for the press.

Japan Erupts recounts the events surrounding the London Naval

Conference and the Manchurian Incident in the critical period from 1928 to 1932 when the "fleet faction" expansions finally wrested control of the Japanese Navy and the Kwantung Army plunged the country into a war in China from which there was to be no turning back. This volume is one of five in the series *Japan's Road to the Pacific War*. A list of the five volumes in the series is as follows:

Japan Erupts: The London Naval Conference and the Manchurian Incident, 1928–1932 (1984)

The China Quagmire: Japan's Expansion on the Asian Continent, 1933–1941 (1983)

Deterrent Diplomacy: Japan, Germany, and the U.S.S.R., 1935–1941 (1976)

The Fateful Choice: Japan's Advance into Southeast Asia, 1939–1941 (1980)

The Final Confrontation: Japan's Negotiations with the United States, 1941

J.W.M.

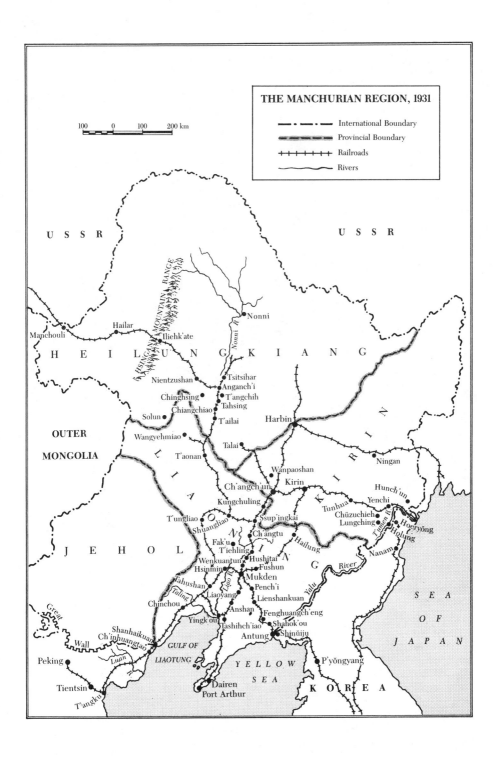

THE MANCHURIAN REGION, 1931

— ·· — ·· — International Boundary
████████ Provincial Boundary
+++++++++ Railroads
⌒⌒⌒⌒ Rivers

100 0 100 200 km

U S S R

U S S R

OUTER

MONGOLIA

H E I L U N G K I A N G

HSINGAN MOUNTAIN RANGE

Manchouli

Hailar

Iliehk'ate

Nonni

Nonni R.

Nientzushan

Tsitsihar
Anganch'i
T'angchih
Chinghsing
Tahsing
Chiangchiao
Solun
T'ailai
Harbin

Wangyehmiao

Talai

K I R I N

Ningan

T'aonan

Wanpaoshan
Kirin

Ch'angch'un
Kungchuling

Hunch'un
Yenchi

T'ungliao
Shuangliao

Ssup'ingkai

Tunhua
Chüzuchieh
Lungching

Tumen R.

Hoeryŏng

Holung

L I A O N I N G

Fak'u
T'iehling
Wenkuantun
Hsinmin
Hushitai
Fushun

Ch'angtu

Hailung

River

Nanam

J E H O L

Tahushan
Liaoyang
Chinchou

Mukden
Pench'i

Anshan

Lienshankuan

Fenghuangch'eng

Yalu

S E A

O F

J A P A N

Great

Wall

Shanhaikuan
Ch'inhuangtao

Luan

Taling

Liao R.

Yingk'ou
Tashihch'iao
Antung

Shahok'ou
Shinŭiju

P'yŏngyang

Peking

GULF OF

LIAOTUNG

YELLOW

Tientsin

T'angku

Dairen
Port Arthur

SEA

K O R E A

ONE

The London Naval Treaty, 1930

Introduction

ARTHUR E. TIEDEMANN

Nowadays, when world peace seems to hinge on strategic nuclear balances, it is difficult to appreciate that only fifty or sixty years ago naval disarmament conferences were major international events upon which were centered the interest and hopes of a worldwide public. In this respect the interwar naval disarmament conferences are to be compared with the postwar summit meetings or the SALT negotiations. Indeed, there is a direct line that runs from those naval conferences to the postwar arms limitation movement, and a historian perceives many analogues among the phenomena associated with each. The warships and the battle fleets that emerged in the late nineteenth and early twentieth century are the first of the sophisticated weapons systems based on advances in modern technology. Of course, in neither its firepower nor its consumption of national resources is yesterday's naval armament to be compared with today's intercontinental ballistic missiles and other nuclear weapons, but for both the governments and citizens of that day it represented a staggeringly large leap in destructive potential and financial costs.

Despite pious hopes for disarmament expressed by statesmen at Versailles, the immediate postwar years were marked by an escalation of plans for naval expansion and by the growing fear that clashing American and Japanese interests would bring on a Pacific war. By 1921 the public outcry in all the naval powers against the cost and danger of further arms increases had reached a crescendo, and this acutely brought home to many governmental and naval leaders the political wisdom of drawing back from their announced plans and taking action to satisfy the widespread clamor for disarmament. In November 1921 the Washington Conference was convened to work out the accommodations required for the acceptance by the five leading naval powers of a cap on the level of their naval forces.

A naval agreement was possible only if diplomatic tensions in the Pacific could be relaxed. During the years 1914–18 all the resources of the Western powers were concentrated on prosecuting the European war, and Japan had seized the opportunity presented by this absence of any countervailing forces to enlarge its position in China. In 1915 the Chinese government had been coerced by threats of military action into granting the Japanese numerous economic privileges, as well as transferring to them the German sphere of influence in Shantung province. In 1917 and 1918, its finances having been improved by its wartime export boom, Japan was able to shift to the softer weapon of money and extended its influence in north China through loans and military assistance to the warlord clique, which had established itself at Peking as the government of China. The collapse of the tsarist government also enabled Japan to occupy in 1918 Northern Sakhalin and large areas of Siberia. The Western powers, especially the United States, feared that Japan was carving out a paramount position in China and Siberia and that it intended to exclude them from the area politically and economically. In addition, the acquisition by Japan of the former German islands in the central Pacific was felt to have increased the military threat to America's Pacific possessions and even to California. Australia and New Zealand also were uneasy about these new, advanced Japanese positions to their north.

Since a naval agreement was contingent upon political detente, the arms conversations were paralleled by discussions on Chinese problems both within the conference proper and bilaterally between Japan and China. Out of these political discussions came the Nine-Power Treaty, which reasserted the territorial integrity of China and proclaimed equality of treatment in China for the economic undertakings of all nations. There emerged as well a Japanese agreement to evacuate Shantung and to allow the Chinese to buy back the Shantung railroad. The Japanese also gave private assurances that they would pull their forces out of Siberia. In general, the Japanese had, with the exception of the central Pacific islands, drawn back to the position they were in when the war broke out in 1914.

On the naval side, an accord was eventually reached on battleships and aircraft carriers but not on cruisers, destroyers, or submarines. Though the Japanese originally demanded a 70-percent ratio vis-a-vis American battleships, they were unable to wear down the adamantine American resistance, and they finally settled for 60 percent. The maximum battleship displacement was set at 35,000 tons and the maximum gun caliber was to be 16 inches. For a period of ten years there would be a "naval holiday" during which no battleships could be built, not even those needed to replace vessels that by the treaty's own definition had become "over-age" and therefore eligible for scrapping. Each nation was assigned an overall battleship tonnage: Japan 315,000, the United States 525,000, and Britain 525,000. Aircraft carrier tonnage was to be limited to 81,000 for Japan, 135,000 for the United States, and 135,000 for Britain. Maximum displacement for carriers was not to exceed 27,000 tons. Coupled with these limitations on naval armament was an agreement that in essence forbade Japan, the United States, and Britain to create new or enlarge existing fortifications and naval facilities in the area east of Singapore and west of Hawaii, except, of course, that Japan was free to do as it wished in its four home islands.

Without doubt the Washington Naval Treaty assured the security of the home territories of Japan and the United States. A 40-percent infe-riority in capital ships and carriers rendered it unlikely that the Japanese could successfully invade the eastern Pacific. On the other hand, the ab-sence of modern and large-scale facilities at Guam, Wake, the Philip-pines, and the Aleutians made United States operations in the western Pacific extremely difficult, given the then state of naval technology. The consensus of naval opinion was that these operational difficulties negated the superior American strength and that therefore the treaty gave the Japanese an unchallengeable control in East Asian waters. This Japanese naval hegemony in East Asian waters did not merely assure the security of the Japanese home islands from American attack. It also meant that the United States could not credibly threaten military intervention if Japan should fail to keep the agreements on China made at the Wash-ington Conference.

Secretary of State Charles Evans Hughes was well aware that adop-tion of his naval proposals would make it difficult to use military sanc-tions to control Japanese actions in China, but he undoubtedly believed that the same factors that had brought Japan to conclude the Washing-ton treaties could also be relied on to persuade it to keep them. Japan had not given up almost all its wartime gains in any fit of generosity or remorse. Japan had contracted its position in East Asia because its civil-ian and military leaders had become convinced they did not have the resources to maintain that expanded position in the face of a determined American opposition.

In 1921 Japan's economy was in a serious recession and was beset with many long-term problems. In 1919 the wartime export boom had ended and foreign trade had fallen off precipitously, partly because Europe and America reentered the market as suppliers and partly because the Japanese had been unable to match other nations in readjusting their prices downward from the wartime inflationary levels. Japan's industrial plant was outmoded, for the country had not kept up with the new technologies and fields of production that had emerged in the West under the pressure of war needs. If Japan were to compete successfully again in foreign markets, old industries would have to be extensively modernized and new industries would have to be introduced. That required capital, and in 1921 capital was very scarce in Japan. Gone was much of the large foreign exchange and specie balances accumulated during the war, drained away by political and military adventures in East Asia, as well as by a boom in conspicuous consumption. In 1921 Japan was looking to the United States, the one great postwar source of capital funds, for the loans that would help reconstruct its industries and develop its established colonial areas—Korea, Taiwan, and Manchuria. As a market that absorbed 40 percent of Japan's exports, the United States was also regarded as a key factor in the revitalization of Japan's foreign trade.

When the Washington Conference met, the Japanese well understood that Japan's floundering economy was presently incapable of supporting adventurism on the Asian continent or naval competition with the United States. They knew that to get that economy back on its feet and to expand further the nation's economic base they needed access to the American market and to American capital, an access they reasoned would be denied if Japan were not cooperative on China and arms limitation. They were fairly optimistic that once the home economy had been stabilized they would be able through purely economic means to achieve that control over Chinese raw materials and markets that they held so vital to the future of Japan. Meanwhile, it was an achievement to have been able to put a cap on American battleship strength and to have in being at no further financial cost 60 percent of that battleship strength. The challenge to Japanese dominance in East Asian waters had been averted, and Japan had preserved thereby an essential condition for keeping open alternative options to the mode of operation in China accepted at the Washington Conference.[1]

It seems inherently difficult for military leaders to rest easy with any margin of safety that is not absolute, and consequently, within months of the signing of the Washington Naval Treaty, the American, British, and Japanese naval staffs were planning construction in those categories for which the treaty had not established tonnage limits, namely cruisers, destroyers, submarines, and other auxiliary craft. The upsurge in construction activity became particularly marked in the cruiser category. The treaty had defined a battleship as any craft over 10,000 tons' displacement or mounting guns of more than 8-in. caliber. Conversely, those lower limits for the battleship now became the upper limits for the cruiser. Till this time cruisers had usually been between 4,000 and 6,000 tons and carried 6-in. guns. Naval designers now hastened to take advantage of these new expanded limits and created a new type of cruiser: the heavy cruiser or Washington Treaty cruiser, a high-speed, heavily armored craft of 10,000 tons' displacement armed with six to ten 8-in. guns and possessing a long cruising range. By the beginning of 1927 Japan had built or had abuilding eight of these heavy cruisers, and Britain had laid down fourteen.[2] Although Congress had in 1924 authorized eight of the 8-in. gun cruisers, the United States was slow off the mark and had by October 1926 started only the first two of these craft. A new style of naval competition had obviously begun, and under pressure from reluctant legislators and taxpayers the three great naval powers held a conference at Geneva in the summer of 1927 to see if an agreement could be reached on cruisers and other auxiliary craft.

Kobayashi's essay picks up the story at this point, the Geneva Naval Conference of 1927, and carries it forward through the ratification of the London Naval Treaty in the fall of 1930. His account centers largely on the struggle within Japan over the terms of the treaty and does not devote much space to the negotiations at London. For a general outline of events at London one can use Raymond G. O'Connor's *Perilous Equilibrium: The United States and the London Naval Conference of 1930*, though this book's value is limited by the fact that O'Connor was unable to use Japanese sources and did not have access to the British archival material.[3] O'Connor should be supplemented for the British material with the second volume of Stephan Roskill's *Naval Policy Between the Wars* and for the Japanese material with Horinouchi Kensuke's *Kaigun gunshuku kōshō fusen jōyaku*, although Horinouchi's study is pretty much confined to the formal record and fails to get into the internal policy discussions and the behind-the-scene maneuvering that underlay the final documents.[4]

Though Kobayashi's main emphasis is on the domestic scene, even here there is a certain narrowing of focus, and his analysis concentrates principally on the policy disputes over the treaty within the navy and on the maneuvers used by the Hamaguchi cabinet to sometimes appease, sometimes circumvent their naval opponents. A much fuller picture of how all the important political elements in Japan responded to the London Naval Treaty crisis will be found in Itō Takashi's magisterial work, *Shōwa shoki seiji shi kenkyū: Rondon kaigun gunshuku mondai o meguru sho seiji shūdan no taikō to teikei.*[5] It must also be said that in Kobayashi's handling of the quarrel within the navy there is somewhat of a bias in favor of the proponents of the treaty. This has come about mostly, I would suspect, because the sources available to him in his research were the Japanese Foreign Ministry materials and the records and testimony of members of the "treaty faction." Events are described as refracted through the prism of the "treaty faction," and so it is not surprising that Admiral Yamanashi Katsunoshin, who attended a session of the Study Group on the Causes of the Pacific War at which Kobayashi reported his findings, should have exclaimed at the end of the presentation, "That's just the way it happened!"[6]

One can imagine what Admiral Katō Kanji might have said if he had been present at that same session, for he has been accorded less than justice in being portrayed as a good-natured but not too bright old sea dog whose opposition to the treaty was an aberration brought about by the machinations of a wily subordinate (Admiral Suetsugu Nobumasa). There was more intellectual substance to Katō Kanji than that, and his criticism of the treaty reflected long-held opinions, opinions deeply rooted in a seriously pondered and coherent world view.[7] Moreover, Katō's technical objections to the treaty were not frivolous. During the long holiday in battleship construction initiated in 1922, naval designers had shifted their technological ingenuity to the improvement of the cruiser and the submarine. As a result these two craft had begun to emerge as ever more formidable weapons, even against battleships. Taking advantage of these new capabilities, naval planners like Admiral Suetsugu had evolved tactics that called for submarines and cruisers to wear down the United States fleet as it advanced westward across the Pacific toward Japanese waters and thus reduce the odds to the point where in the final fleet engagement the Japanese would have a reasonable hope of destroying the American fleet à la Battle of Tsushima. Once the United States navy had been eliminated, years would pass before the Americans could rebuild to mount another offensive. By then the Japanese would have been able to develop fully the resources of the region, and the Americans would resign themselves to the inevitable. Underlying this sense of the necessity of preparing for an impending clash with America was the conviction, which Katō shared with increasing numbers of his countrymen, that Japan would have to abandon the Washington Conference approach and adopt more forceful measures in China, since Japanese attempts to achieve their ends through purely economic means had foundered on Chinese nationalism.[8] To a person holding such views it seemed the height of folly to accept an agreement that allowed the Americans to increase their actual cruiser tonnage and required the Japanese to scrap one-third of their existing submarine tonnage. Katō's case may have been ill founded, but one cannot tell from Kobayashi's essay that he did have a case or why precisely his opponents felt that it was less dangerous for the interests of the nation to reject it than to accept it.

In calling attention to Kobayashi's inclination to see things from the viewpoint of the "treaty faction," I seek merely to convey a necessary caveat to the reader and intend in no way to diminish the importance of the contribution this essay makes to the study of "the road to the Pacific War." The wealth of detail and documentation brought together by Kobayashi enlarges considerably our understanding of an event that was a watershed between the cooperative diplomacy of the 1920s and the aggressive expansionism of the 1930s. The Hamaguchi cabinet was committed to the belief that Japan's future lay in a peaceful economic development based on a multidirectional expansion of foreign trade. The cabinet saw as its prime task a reorganization of the Japanese economy that would rid it of the problems previous cabinets had unsuccessfully grappled with since 1920 and would finally enable Japan to compete effectively in world markets. Believing that cooperation and material support from Western economic and political leaders was indispensable to accomplishing this goal, the cabinet was anxious to achieve an agreement at London not simply because the savings in naval expenditures would be useful but also, more importantly, because the good will thus generated would predispose the Westerners to aid in the solution of Japan's fundamental economic problems. For this larger goal the cabinet was willing to override the perhaps justified security concerns of the Navy General Staff and to accept the political risks this entailed.[9]

If larger events had not supervened, this gamble might have been carried off. However, before the cabinet's long-range economic measures could yield their fruit, the world depression spread to Japan and further intensified the economic hardships that had been the lot of so many Japanese during the 1920s. To this boiling domestic social discontent was added a growing public concern that Shidehara's China policy was a failure and would cost Japan its economic interests in China. In this atmosphere the Navy General Staff's charges against the Hamaguchi cabinet gained currency and became a central element in the great spurt in growth of ultranationalist organizations and propaganda that occurred in 1930. This agitation not only cost Hamaguchi his life but also laid the groundwork for the public's acceptance of the Kwantung Army's move in Manchuria a year later. The naval officers who opposed the treaty, the so-called "fleet faction," were able to drive the treaty supporters into retirement and eventually to reorganize the structure of the navy so as to shift the locus of control from the Navy Ministry to the Navy General Staff.[10] With their victory hope disappeared for any further naval agreements, for the emphasis of the "fleet faction" was on unrestricted construction and on expansion into Southeast Asia, two policies which could not but increase the probability of conflict with the Western powers.

ONE

The London Naval Treaty, 1930

KOBAYASHI TATSUO

Translated by
ARTHUR E. TIEDEMANN

The Geneva Conference

After the failure of the Washington Conference to establish limits for auxiliary vessels, competition in naval construction shifted from capital ships to auxiliary vessels. This trend was particularly conspicuous in submarines and in 10,000-ton, 8-in.-gun cruisers. If things were allowed to continue in this way, the progress made at the Washington Conference would be nullified. Table 1 shows the Japanese, American, and British strength in auxiliary vessels at the time of the Washington Conference and five years later. As early as December 1922 Senator William E. Borah of Idaho proposed an amendment to the naval bill then before Congress requesting the president to call an arms limitation conference. The essentials of his proposal were incorporated in the naval acts of 1923, 1924, and 1925.

The League of Nations had since its inception been wrestling unsuccessfully with the problem of arms limitation. In December 1925 the League decided to create a preparatory commission for a general arms limitation conference. The United States and Germany, though not League members, participated in this commission. The commission worked hard to achieve arms limitation, but there was no clear prospect of an agreement's being attained. At this point President Calvin Coolidge and Secretary of State Frank B. Kellogg decided to take a preliminary step toward general disarmament by holding an arms limitation conference among the five great naval powers. On February 10, 1927, they proposed to Britain, France, Italy, and Japan that a naval arms limitation conference

This essay originally appeared as "Kaigun gunshuku jōyaku (1921 nen–1936 nen)," in *Taiheiyō sensō e no michi*, vol. 1, part 1, sec. 3–5, pp. 47–160.

be held in March at Geneva. The letter of invitation stated that the American government thought the general principles of the Washington Treaty were a suitable basis for the discussions and that it was disposed to accept the application of the 5:5:3 ratio to auxiliary vessels.

On February 19 the cabinet of Wakatsuki Reijirō replied that Japan would be happy to participate in the conference in order that the work of the Washington Conference might be brought to completion. On February 28 Britain expressed its wholehearted approval. Japan, however, indicated a wish for the conference to be held after June 1. In addition, the Japanese answer explained that to assure the success of the conference it was necessary that each country act "guided by the spirit of mutual accommodations and helpfulness consistent with the defensive requirements of each nation."

By this statement Japan implicitly expressed its intention of opposing the 5:3:3 ratio. Britain's response hinted at an uncompromising attitude on the cruiser question. Adequate consideration, it said, must be given the needs imposed by the British Empire's geographic position, by its long lines of communication, and by the vulnerability of its food supplies.[1] Both France and Italy declined to join the conference and limited themselves simply to sending observers. Thus Japan, Britain, and the United States were the only powers attending the second Naval Arms Limitation Conference, which opened on June 20, 1927, in the League of Nations headquarters at Geneva. The representatives of the three countries were:

Japan:	Saitō Makoto (governor-general of Korea)
	Ishii Kikujirō (ambassador to France)
Britain:	William C. Bridgeman (First Lord of the Admiralty)
	Robert Cecil (chancellor of the Duchy of Lancaster)
	F. C. Field (deputy chief of the naval staff)
United States:	Hugh S. Gibson (ambassador to Belgium)
	Hilary P. Jones (rear admiral and member of the Navy General Board)

On April 17, just before Saitō's departure from Japan, the Wakatsuki cabinet fell and was replaced on the 19th by a cabinet headed by General Tanaka Giichi, who served concurrently as foreign minister. The new navy minister was Okada Keisuke, and Suzuki Kantarō was navy chief of staff.

The American representative, Hugh Gibson, served as chairman of the conference. Each delegation presented a draft proposal based on its country's position. Table 2 shows the auxiliary vessel strength possessed or under construction in each country as of February 10, 1927.

The American plan divided auxiliary vessels into three categories: cruisers, destroyers, submarines. It was based on the principle that the overall tonnage within each category should be determined by the 5:5:3 ratio. The British proposal emphasized the British empire's geographical position and needs. Each of the three American categories was divided by the British into subcategories of large and small vessels. The British confined the application of the 5:5:3 ratio to the 10,000-ton, 8-in.-gun heavy cruiser, the large-vessel subcategory of the cruiser category. They sought to attain naval arms reduction by decreasing the allowed size of each type of vessel and by extending their age limits. The Japanese objective was to avoid any increase in the actual existing strength of each power. They divided auxiliary vessels into surface vessels and submarines, and they aimed at a 70-percent ratio in surface vessels vis-a-vis the United States and Britain.

The American and Japanese views were opposed on the question of tonnage, while between the Americans and the British there arose a strong difference of opinion over cruisers. The British wished to limit severely the number of 10,000-ton, 8-in.-gun heavy cruisers but to be allowed large numbers of 7,000-ton, 6-in.-gun light cruisers. In contrast, the Americans were unyielding in their demand that there be an overall limit on cruiser tonnage and that within this overall limit the United States be allowed a large number of heavy cruisers. Japan endeavored to arrange a compromise and by July 18 had managed to work out a tentative agreement with Britain. However, the United States was unyielding, and the conference finally ended in failure as a result of the deadlock between Britain and the United States. To save face the three powers issued an announcement on August 4 stating that the conference was temporarily recessed. Table 3 sets forth the main points of the proposals made at the conference by each power.

The breakdown of the Geneva Conference was caused by the irreconcilable views of Britain and the United States. Britain desired a large number of light cruisers and the United States wanted a large number of heavy cruisers. Since Britain's territories were scattered around the world, its existence depended on the security of its widespread lines of sea communications. The possession of large numbers of light cruisers was necessary to Britain and, since it had naval bases everywhere, was also expedient. Consequently, Britain worked to reduce the numbers of heavy cruisers and wanted to limit the size of cruisers to 7,000 tons and their guns to 6 in. The United States, on the other hand, facing upon two oceans and its naval bases severely limited by the Washington Treaty, needed heavy cruisers with an extended range of action. The British emphasis on light cruisers was also relatively disadvantageous to the United States because, compared with 880,000 tons for the British, it had only 180,000 tons of high-speed merchant vessels that could be armed with 6-in. guns and easily converted into cruisers.[2] Both countries held uncompromisingly to their views, and the conference broke up over a difference in their demands of, so to speak, 2 in.

At the Geneva Conference Japan mediated between the United States and Britain, exerting every effort to make the conference a success. Economic and financial conditions in Japan after the Washington Conference showed the impossibility of a full-scale naval race with the United States and Britain. This was even more evident after the financial crisis that began in March 1927. However, Japan's adoption of a conciliatory attitude at the Geneva Conference is thought to be largely attributable to the views on national defense of the Japanese delegates. Saitō Makoto issued a warning to the "hard liners" among the naval officers accompanying the delegation:

> We have to consider what is the best thing to do from the viewpoint of our actual present national power, from the viewpoint of the national interest and the people's welfare, from the viewpoint of the armament necessary for our future expansion, and from the viewpoint of continuing to be ranked among the nations supporting peace. . . . Bluffing is inadvisable. It won't do. The only way to attain in the future both safety and expansion is to stick to our present position. Our nation's power will more and more increase; our economic strength, our industrial power, our sense of honor, our international morality will be increasingly understood and respected by the world. Gradually the nation's power will become strong. In other words, we must refrain from acting like automatons and trying to increase our naval strength by means of one or two international conferences. We will not get them to sit down at the desk and hurriedly write us out a promissory note.[3]

To succeed, a naval disarmament conference required peace and a settled international environment. On that score the times were by no

means against the Geneva Conference. In August 1924 the Dawes Plan
had been adopted and the German reparations deadlock finally resolved.
In December 1925 the Locarno treaties were signed and there was some
hope for a settlement of the security problem. Europe was at last re-
covering its stability. Why then did the Geneva Conference end in failure? The following reasons may be offered:

First, for the United States, the sponsor of the conference, circumstances differed from those of the Washington Conference. In auxiliary
vessels afloat and planned, especially in cruisers, the United States did
not have the overwhelming superiority over Japan and Britain it had had
at the Washington Conference. Second, the status of the civilians on the
American and British delegations was low. The technical opinions of the
professional officers dominated, and it was difficult to bring a wider political view into play. Third, the conference was held without preliminary negotiations among the three powers and therefore without a prior
adjustment of their views. Once each country had presented its position
in the official sessions, it was difficult afterward to make concessions and
compromises. Fourth, a common yardstick was lacking by which to cal-
culate the fighting power of the heavy cruiser and the light cruiser. Finally, the absence of France and Italy made concessions difficult for
Britain, which had to take the European situation into consideration.

The London Conference
and the Reed-Matsudaira Compromise

After the failure of the Geneva Conference, naval expansionism again
became prominent in the United States. In January 1928 the House of
Representatives received an immense naval authorization bill drawn up
by the Navy General Board. The bill called for the construction over a
nine-year period of 71 vessels at an expenditure of $740 million. In-
cluded were 25 heavy cruisers, 9 destroyer flotilla leaders, 32 submarines, and 5 aircraft carriers. Britain's response was to announce it would
eliminate one of the cruisers scheduled for construction in the 1928 budget, and this conciliatory attitude strengthened American public opinion
against the bill. Ultimately the bill was withdrawn and a new one substituted calling for 15 cruisers and 1 aircraft carrier. This substitute bill
passed the House of Representatives in March 1928. Another area of
competition between the United States and Britain was foreign trade.

American foreign trade was then running at about $9 billion a year and had reached Britain's level. This intensification of economic warfare between the two nations led to an emphasis on freedom of the seas as a reason for naval expansion.

After the Geneva Conference Britain adopted a policy of rapprochement with France, conducting as part of this policy secret disarmament conversations with France that led on July 28, 1928, to the conclusion of an agreement. Up to now the arms limitation method favored by France had been the assignment to each country of an overall tonnage that the country could freely distribute among the various vessel categories in accordance with its particular needs. In the new Anglo-French agreement France tentatively accepted the principle of limitation by categories, the categories being defined as capital ships, aircraft carriers over 10,000 tons, surface craft armed with 6- to 8-in. guns, and submarines over 600 tons. The tonnage allotted to each category could, within the overall tonnage limit, be transferred under a fixed ratio from one category to another. In return for France's recognizing the British desire for a large number of small cruisers, Britain agreed to the French wish to exclude from consideration already trained reserve soldiers when limitations on land forces came up for discussion.[4] When Japan, the United States, and Italy were notified of this agreement, Japan expressed approval but the other two opposed it. Since the American opposition was particularly strong, Britain and France had no choice but to allow the automatic expiration of their agreement.

Thus the difficulties over naval disarmament between the United States and Britain were not ended, and both nations worked hard to achieve a breakthrough. The signing of the Kellogg-Briand Pact on August 27, 1928, was a turning point toward the easing of Anglo-American tension. When in February 1929 the Senate passed the naval bill already approved the preceding spring by the House of Representatives, Britain expressed its desire to set to work on the disarmament problem. Action had been impossible until this point, since the British government feared any move would result in an accusation that it was interfering with the Senate's passage of the naval bill.[5]

On March 4, 1929, Herbert H. Hoover assumed the presidency and appointed Henry L. Stimson his secretary of state. In his inaugural address Hoover spoke of the advance in international ideals represented by the Kellogg-Briand Pact, and he emphasized that this treaty ought to

be the key to the attainment of arms reduction. On April 10 he designated former Vice President Charles G. Dawes ambassador to Britain
and by this act indicated his exceptional determination to pursue disarmament negotiations with Britain. Stimson also attached the greatest
importance to reestablishing American understanding with Britain.[6] On
April 22, at the sixth session of the League of Nations Disarmament
Preparatory Commission, Hugh S. Gibson, acting in accordance with
President Hoover's instructions, publicly stated America's position on
disarmament. What he said about naval disarmament may be summarized as follows:[7]

1. The United States would not abandon the present method of limitation within categories. It was, however, prepared to compromise and
accept as a basis for discussion the amendment of this principle so as to
allow the transfer of fixed percentages of tonnage among all categories except capital ships and aircraft carriers.

2. In comparing naval combat capacity, besides displacement the
United States was willing to consider taking into account age, gun caliber,
and other factors.

3. The United States recognized that in the work of disarmament a
time had been reached when the negative concept of arms limitation must
be abandoned and nations should press on positively toward really substantial reductions in armaments.

4. Disarmament must apply without exception to all categories of vessels.

In the midst of this gradual development of an international trend
toward disarmament, President Hoover delivered a speech at Arlington
National Cemetery in which he stressed the necessity of further progress in disarmament. Since the conclusion of the Kellogg-Briand Pact,
he said, all armament should be for defensive purposes only; the strength
required for a defensive navy must be determined on a relative basis;
and for the sake of achieving disarmament, a rational yardstick must be
discovered to measure the naval combat capacity of each country. In
Britain the Conservatives were defeated by the Labour Party in a general election held about this time, and on June 7 the second cabinet of
Ramsay MacDonald took office. Since the Labour Party had fought the
election on a platform that included pro-American and pro-disarmament
planks, the aims of the two new governments were in harmony and the
drive toward disarmament was intensified.

Ambassador Dawes arrived at his post on June 14. On the 16th he conferred with Prime Minister MacDonald, their discussion marking the beginning of the Anglo-American preparatory negotiations. Tanaka's Sei-yūkai cabinet was then still in power in Japan. On June 12 Matsudaira Tsuneo, the Japanese ambassador to Britain, had reported to Tanaka: "Judging from Hoover's temperament and the platform of the Labour Party, the disarmament issue will be thoroughly discussed. We must therefore be prepared to respond to every possible development related to this problem and to state our opinion at a moment's notice."[8]

Dawes arranged to talk with Matsudaira early on the morning of June 17. He explained to Matsudaira that the Geneva Conference had failed because of procedural mistakes, and therefore there had to be a change in methods to ensure the success of the next conference. Dawes said he would set all this forth in a speech on the 18th, and he read Matsudaira a draft of the speech. Matsudaira expressed his gratitude for Dawes' frank attitude and his hope that there would be close liaison in the future also. Dawes replied: "I received special instructions from the president that when I came to Britain I must arrange to cooperate with Japan and maintain as close a liaison with the Japanese as I do with the British. From this day forward I will exchange views with you in complete frank-ness."[9]

At a welcoming banquet the following day, Dawes pointed out that the method of negotiating for disarmament had to be changed. "Each government," he suggested, "might separately obtain from their respec-tive naval experts their definition of the yardstick and then the inevita-ble compromise between these differing definitions, which will be ex-pressed in the final fixation of the technical yardstick, should be made by a committee of statesmen of the nations. . . . The Committee from the Governments which met at Geneva . . . was a mixed commission of statesmen and naval technicians . . . and that was the reason for its fail-ure."[10] MacDonald also on June 17 announced that his emphasis was on cooperation with other countries. He would not, he promised, settle the problem in bilateral negotiations with the United States and then try to force the arrangement on other nations.

As the Anglo-American conversations continued, their progress was communicated to Matsudaira by both MacDonald and Dawes. On July 24 MacDonald announced to the House of Commons that he had ac-cepted the principle of parity between Britain and the United States.

He further stated that work would be suspended on two heavy cruisers. By previous arrangement Hoover announced on the same day that the United States would postpone laying down three cruisers. That very day Japan's ratification of the Kellogg-Briand Pact was deposited with the American secretary of state and the treaty went into effect. The British and American announcements had made the most of the opportunity this afforded.

The Anglo-American conversations were carried on for about three months and then at long last their results were revealed. On September 3, at the plenary session of the League of Nations tenth General Assembly, MacDonald proclaimed that there were good prospects for an Anglo-American agreement. An agreement had more or less been reached, for there remained to be settled only three of the twenty points that had been at issue.[11] Of the points settled, the five most important were:

1. The Kellogg-Briand Pact was the starting point for arms reduction.
2. The principle of naval parity between Britain and the United States was accepted.
3. A naval holiday for capital ships would be considered.
4. Submarines would be abolished or drastically limited.
5. Britain would have a cruiser tonnage of 339,000 tons, of which 140,000 tons would be 15 8-in.-gun cruisers and 192,200 tons would be 35 6-in.-gun cruisers. The United States would have a cruiser tonnage of 315,500 tons, of which 210,000 tons would be 21 8-in.-gun cruisers and 105,500 tons would be 15 6-in.-gun cruisers.

The three points still in dispute were:

1. Whether the United States' 21 8-in.-gun cruisers should be reduced to 18.
2. The problem of a yardstick to compare the combat capacity of 8-in. and 6-in.-gun cruisers.
3. Whether the destroyer tonnage of the two countries should be 150,000 tons or 200,000 tons.

On October 4 MacDonald went to the United States, bearing these results of the preliminary negotiations. On the 5th he saw Hoover at Rapidan and confirmed the provisional agreement he had reached with Dawes. There thus came into existence what was afterwards called the Rapidan Agreement. On the 10th a joint communiqué was issued stating that all problems would be negotiated with the Kellogg-Briand Pact as a fundamental premise and on the assumption that there could never be a war between Britain and the United States. While MacDonald was in the United States the British government, acting on his instructions, issued to Japan, the United States, France, and Italy in the name of Foreign Secretary Arthur Henderson an invitation to attend a third naval conference at London starting early in the third week of January 1930.

During the Anglo-American preliminary conversations, the Tanaka cabinet had to resign on July 2 in the wake of the assassination of Chang Tso-lin, the Manchurian warlord. On the same day a new cabinet was organized with Hamaguchi Osachi, president of the Minseitō, as prime minister. In the cabinet were Shidehara Kijūrō as foreign minister, Inoue Junnosuke as finance minister, Ugaki Kazushige as army minister, and Takarabe Takeshi as navy minister. Shidehara diplomacy and Inoue finance were the twin pillars of the Hamaguchi cabinet. On July 9 the cabinet announced it had decided upon a ten-point program. The ten points were: (1) just government, (2) enhancement of the national spirit, (3) enforcement of official discipline, (4) reform of China policy, (5) encouragement of arms reduction, (6) adjustment and retrenchment in finance, (7) a no-loan policy and reduction of the national debt, (8) lifting of the gold embargo, (9) establishment of a social policy, and (10) reform of education. Point 5 made clear the government's willingness to grapple with the disarmament problem. The announcement elaborated this point as follows:

> When it comes to the problem of armament reduction, at this time we must, in cooperation with the other powers, determinedly promote the establishment of an international agreement. The object of this agreement should not be restricted merely to the limitation of arms but should include substantial reductions in arms. . . . It is believed that on the present occasion the consummation of this great world undertaking will not be difficult if each power approaches this matter in a spirit of mutual conciliation and, taking into consideration the special situation of each country, provides equally for the security of all.

When the Hamaguchi cabinet came to power, the national treasury was in extremely poor condition as a consequence of the financial depression that had begun in 1927. It was a time, as Finance Minister Inoue said, of national economic crisis. Immediately after taking office, the cabinet adopted on July 5 a policy of rigorous retrenchment, which it applied both in revising the Tanaka budget for fiscal 1929 and in drawing up its own budget for fiscal 1930. The cabinet decided to postpone expenditures for all new programs, and in the revised working budget for fiscal 1929 there were reductions or postponements in expenditure totaling ¥90.47 million in the general account and ¥57.15 million in the special accounts. Arms reduction was an indispensable prerequisite to improving government finance and to lifting the gold embargo. With regard to Point 6 (adjustment and retrenchment in finance) of the ten-point program the cabinet explained, "To achieve an adjustment of finances, even the expenditures for the army and navy will be adjusted and reduced to as great an extent as possible without creating impediments to the national defense."

The Anglo-American preliminary negotiations had begun, of course, during Tanaka's premiership. On June 28, just before its resignation, the Tanaka cabinet approved two documents related to the anticipated naval conference. One was entitled "Measures To Cope with the Arms Limitation Problem," and the other, "The Empire's Arms Limitation Policy." The latter document concluded that in naval armaments "Japan asserts the necessity of an auxiliary vessel strength equivalent to at least 70 percent of that of the world's largest navy." It established that, "with regard to specific distribution within categories, this ratio should be emphasized for large vessels such as 20-cm.-gun cruisers and above, but in the case of submarines and small vessels such as light cruisers and below the principal consideration ought to be the strength each nation itself feels to be necessary."[12] This standard of a 70-percent ratio vis-a-vis the United States was inherited by the Hamaguchi cabinet. On July 19 the new cabinet approved telegraphic instructions to Ambassador Matsudaira regarding the naval armament reduction question. These instructions ordered Matsudaira to inform Dawes and MacDonald at a suitable opportunity that "Japan desires an overall ratio of 70 percent" and told him to exert himself to obtain their consent to this.[13] Instructions to Matsudaira approved by the cabinet on August 20 specified in more detail that Japan required 70 percent of the United States' heavy cruiser strength, 70 percent of its light cruiser strength, and 80,000 tons in submarines.[14]

Matsudaira had already seen Dawes on July 4 and told him that, "considering Japanese public opinion, it would not be possible to accept an application of the 5:5:3 ratio to any category other than capital ships and emphasized that Dawes must thoroughly understand this point be-

forehand."[15] On August 27 Matsudaira had an interview with Mac-
Donald during which he explained that "the Japanese government would
require a 70-percent ratio in auxiliary vessels vis-a-vis Britain and the
United States." He expressed the hope that, "in view of the past relationship between Japan and Great Britain, the prime minister would wish
to lend his assistance."[16]

Meanwhile, the Anglo-American preliminary negotiations had pro-
gressed to the point where the only remaining difficulty was how many
heavy cruisers the United States should have. The United States wanted
21; Britain would consent only to 18. On September 20 the cabinet approved instructions to Matsudaira urging him to intensify his efforts to
get the British and Americans to lower their tonnage in heavy and light
cruisers and thus translate disarmament into a reality. The instructions
expressed the desire as follows:

> Should it be decided to give the United States the 21 cruisers for which
> it is asking, our country will have to build about another 40,000 tons.
> Considering what the real aim of disarmament is supposed to be, it is
> very difficult to give our consent to this. Moreover, our 8-in.-gun cruiser
> tonnage will exceed parity with regard to Britain, and this will give rise
> to serious difficulties. . . . If it is unavoidable, . . . we would like you
> to take measures to stave off any plan giving the United States 21 8-in.-
> gun cruisers and hold it to 18 and Britain to 15.[17]

The October 7 invitation of the British government reported that a
tentative agreement had been reached between it and the American
government with regard to the following four principles:

> 1. They would make the Kellogg-Briand Pact the starting point for any
> agreement.
> 2. They would adopt the principle of parity between themselves in all
> categories of vessels and would achieve the said parity by December 31,
> 1936.
> 3. They would approve reconsideration of the capital ship replace-
> ment schedule established by the Washington Treaty.
> 4. They hoped for total abolition of the submarine.[18]

The Japanese government's reply to the British invitation was decided by the cabinet on October 15 and delivered by Matsudaira to Foreign Secretary Henderson on the 16th. In giving its complete approval
to the idea of holding a conference, the Japanese government expressed

the earnest desire "that the informal conversations between the British Government and the Japanese ambassador on questions of special moment will be carried on and completed before these questions are presented to the conference for final adjustment." In addition, it hoped that the conference would not confine itself to arms limitation but would succeed in actually reducing armaments. [19]

On October 18 the delegates to the conference were appointed: Wakatsuki Reijirō, a former prime minister; Takarabe Takeshi, the navy minister; Matsudaira Tsuneo, ambassador to Britain; and Nagai Matsuzō, ambassador to Belgium. Admiral Abo Kiyokazu was chosen as adviser and Vice Admiral Sakonji Seizō as chief technical adviser.

On November 26 the Hamaguchi cabinet decided on Japan's basic demands at the London Conference; these came to be called the "three basic principles." The aim was to secure the minimum strength necessary "(1) to preserve the safety of our national territory by resisting in the western Pacific the naval forces employed by a certain country; (2) to protect the sea communications our special national circumstances have made vital to our national existence." The "three basic principles" were as follows:

> 1. The standard for our auxiliary vessel strength should be the actual amount we will possess at the end of fiscal 1931, and the ratio of our forces to those of the United States should be overall at least 70 percent.
> 2. We should have a 70-percent ratio vis-a-vis the United States, particularly in the category of 20-cm.-gun heavy cruisers.
> 3. Submarine tonnage should be the actual amount we will possess at the end of fiscal 1931. [20]

The actual strength Japan would have at the end of fiscal 1931 was 108,400 tons in heavy cruisers (12 ships), 98,400 tons in light cruisers, 132,495 tons in destroyers, and 78,497 tons in submarines. [21]

The Japanese delegation departed Tokyo on November 30 and arrived in London on December 27. At the invitation of the American government the journey had been made by way of the United States. While in the United States Wakatsuki communicated to Hoover Japan's intention of requesting a 70-percent ratio vis-a-vis America; he also spoke publicly to this effect. On January 9 Wakatsuki, accompanied by Takarabe and Matsudaira, called on MacDonald at 10 Downing Street and began informal Anglo-Japanese negotiations.

The American and European delegates to the London Conference were:

Britain: Prime Minister Ramsay MacDonald
                Foreign Secretary Arthur Henderson
                First Lord of the Admiralty Albert Victor Alexander
United States: Secretary of State Henry L. Stimson
                Secretary of the Navy Charles Francis Adams
                Ambassador to Britain Charles G. Dawes
                Ambassador to Belgium Hugh S. Gibson
                Ambassador to Mexico Dwight Morrow
                Senator David Reed (Republican, Pennsylvania)
                Senator Joseph T. Robinson (Democrat, Arkansas)
France: Prime Minister André Tardieu, Chief Delegate
Italy: Foreign Minister Count Dino Grandi, Chief Delegate

On January 21, 1930, the opening ceremony of the five-nation conference was held in the presence of King George V in the Royal Gallery of the House of Lords. MacDonald was elected chairman. After the other chief delegates had spoken, Wakatsuki addressed the conference, saying that Japan wished to go beyond a mere limitation of armaments to an actual reduction in arms, that Japan was interested in having forces capable of defending itself but not sufficient to attack others. That morning London was wrapped in an impenetrable fog. However, the mist had largely cleared by the time the opening ceremony ended at one o'clock. It seemed an intimation of what the future of the conference would be.

The highest decision-making body in the conference's organization was the plenary session. Then there was the First Committee, which consisted of all the delegates. Next was the Second Committee, which consisted of the chief delegates and came to be called the Chief Delegates Committee. The First Committee was principally concerned with considering the details of the treaty text, and when necessary it set up technical committees. The Second Committee met only occasionally and had the task of expediting the work of the conference as a whole. The public meetings of these various bodies were not the really important part of the conference. The more important and difficult negotiations were conducted in informal conversations among the delegates of the countries concerned.[22]

Since the United States and Britain had in the main arrived at an agreement, the disputes at the conference were naturally either between Japan and the United States or between Britain and France. Particularly vexatious was the question of what method of limitation should be used. Britain adhered firmly to the principle of limitation by categories, while France demanded limitation by overall tonnage exclusively. In the end a compromise plan was adopted. It was agreed to allow a 10-percent transfer of tonnage between light cruisers and destroyers but not between any other categories. The American-Japanese dispute revolved around the 70-percent ratio. Japan insisted on its "three basic principles," but the U.S. response was to propose a 60-percent ratio. Both countries held to their views unyieldingly, and negotiations came to a complete halt. In the midst of this chaotic situation France submitted a plan in which it demanded an overall strength of 724,400 tons. Whereupon Italy also claimed the same tonnage on the basis of its principle of parity with France. The conference was confronted with a crisis, and the rumor was that it would collapse. Just at that point there was a political contretemps in France, and on February 17 the Tardieu cabinet fell. In these circumstances the conference could not function; therefore MacDonald announced a one-week recess, from February 19 to 26.

Parallel with the discussions on auxiliary vessels, negotiations were also being conducted with regard to capital ships. The outcome of these negotiations was the following agreement, based on a proposal put forth by the United States:

> 1. The capital ship construction holiday provided for in the Washington Treaty would be extended until 1936.
> 2. The limit of 15 ships for Britain, 15 for the United States, and 9 for Japan scheduled for 1942 under the Washington Treaty would be achieved immediately through the scrapping of 5 ships by Britain, 3 by the United States, and 1 by Japan.

Since Japan, the United States, and Britain could not reconcile their views on the reduction of the size of capital ships or of gun calibers on capital ships, there were no changes in these aspects of the Washington Treaty.

In the matter of submarines, Britain and the United States advocated the abolition of this category, but this was vigorously resisted by Japan and France. An agreement was finally concluded among the five powers limiting the use of the submarine and making 2,000 tons the maximum permissible displacement.

On February 26 a meeting of the Chief Delegates Committee decided, at MacDonald's suggestion, to facilitate the negotiations by dividing the conference into a Pacific Section (Japan, United States, Britain) and a European Section (Britain, France, Italy). Under the new procedure there were to be created two-man committees that would carry on free bilateral conversations without in any way binding their respective delegations. The American-Japanese negotiations were conducted by Matsudaira and Reed; the Anglo-Japanese negotiations by Robert L. Craigie, head of the American Division of the Foreign Office, and Saitō Hiroshi, chief of the Public Information Division of the Foreign Ministry.

Although the Matsudaira-Reed talks had rough going, both men continued to work very hard to break the deadlock. Parallel talks were also carried on by Wakatsuki and Stimson. As a result of these free American-Japanese conversations the distance between the demands of the two sides gradually narrowed. On March 12 Wakatsuki visited Stimson at his hotel, the Ritz, to confer with him and Reed. At this conference they worked out the Japanese-American compromise plan, set out in table 4. Under this plan the overall Japanese ratio was 69.72 percent. In addition, the United States promised not to lay down the sixteenth, seventeenth, and eighteenth of its heavy cruisers until 1933, 1934, and 1935 respectively, and not to complete them before 1936, 1937, and 1938. Consequently the Japanese heavy cruiser ratio would be 72.26 percent in 1935, 67.8 percent in 1936, 63.8 percent in 1937, and 60.2 percent in 1938. Japan, the United States, and Britain were to have parity in submarine tonnage, which was set at 52,700 tons, but Japan was to be permitted to keep its existing 78,500 tons and, by not constructing replacements for scrapped overage submarines, was to reduce its tonnage to the proper amount by 1936, the year the treaty reached full term.[23]

The following day, the 13th, Reed went to Wakatsuki and communicated requests for a few changes made by the American naval experts. After additional discussion they arrived at the compromise plan given in table 5. Under this plan the overall Japanese ratio was 69.75 percent vis-a-vis the United States and 67.9 percent vis-a-vis Britain. Reed told Wakatsuki that any concessions beyond these would be absolutely impossible. On March 14 the four Japanese delegates conferred on the compromise plan. They decided to send the plan to Tokyo over all their signatures and take the occasion to seek new instructions from the Japanese government.

In his memoirs Wakatsuki recalls, "Even though there were slight differences in form from the plan we had sent, the return instructions I received from the government in general met our needs, and I thought it was all right to sign the treaty." The degree of his determination is shown by his saying, "If the government had not sent its approval or if it had sent its approval with substantial amendments or demands appended, I was absolutely resolved, quietly and without threats, to resign from the delegation."[24]

The Japanese Government's Reply to the Compromise Plan

After his March 12 talk with Stimson, Wakatsuki reported the outcome of the discussion to Shidehara, concluding his telegram with these words: "My impression from today's conversation is that this kind of wrangling between Japan and the United States has for the moment no prospect of bringing any further advantage to Japan."[25] On March 14 the delegation's request for instructions was telegraphed to Shidehara.[26] The telegram arrived at the Foreign Ministry on the morning of the 15th. At 1:30 P.M. that afternoon Shidehara brought the telegram to Hamaguchi and discussed it with him at great length. At 5:00 P.M. Hamaguchi summoned Yamanashi Katsunoshin, the navy vice minister, handed him the telegram, and ordered him to coordinate the formulation of navy opinion regarding the instructions to be sent back to the delegates.

The delegates' telegram implicitly asked for the government's consent to the Japanese-American compromise plan and beseeched the government to act with prudence:

> The Americans have already accepted the principle of a de facto overall 70-percent ratio. Although it is true that the ratio falls short by two hundredths of a percent, this shows that great pains have been taken to meet Japan's desires, while at the same time the Americans avoid the criticism of having knuckled under completely to our demands. Our demand with regard to heavy cruisers has not been met, but it can be seen that until the next conference we will in fact have a strength in excess of 70 percent. Though it is regrettable that our submarine tonnage is less than we asked for, it can be regarded as a concession that they have reduced their submarine strength and suggested parity with us. As we see the situation, short of new circumstances developing, it will be difficult to force any further concessions from the Americans. Setting aside a sit-

uation in which on account of the French problem the conference ends in a failure to achieve a five-nation agreement, careful consideration must be given to the many important consequences there will be for us in various areas should it appear that the conference was ruined by Japan's attitude.

The arrival of the telegram began a pitched battle over the London Treaty that was without precedent in the history of naval disarmament.

During Takarabe's absence, Hamaguchi served as acting navy minister, following the precedent established at the time of the Washington Conference. Under him the important leaders in the Navy Ministry were Vice Admiral Yamanashi Katsunoshin, the vice minister; Rear Admiral Hori Teikichi, the chief of the Naval Affairs Bureau; and Captain Koga Mineichi, the chief Navy Ministry adjutant. These men came to be known as the Navy Ministry "trio." In the midst of the noisy confusion to come, this "trio" and Admiral Okada Keisuke made the greatest contribution to the bitter and wearisome struggle to formulate a prudent reply to the delegates' request for instructions. The leaders of the Navy General Staff were Admiral Katō Kanji, the chief of staff; Vice Admiral Suetsugu Nobumasa, the vice chief of staff; and Rear Admiral Katō Takayoshi, chief of the First (Operations) Division of the Navy General Staff.

Yamanashi was a clear-headed man, thoroughly discrete and with a strong sense of responsibility.[27] He was evaluated in the following terms by Home Minister Adachi Kenzō, who belonged to the chauvinistic wing of the cabinet: "Yamanashi was a smart, honest fellow who was clever at perceiving opportunities. Moreover, he had an accurate view of our future national defense problems, and he had the ability to control his ministry."[28] Hori was said to be a genius throughout his studies at the Naval Academy, and he had the reputation of having the best brain in the Navy Ministry.[29] Katō Kanji was impulsive and hot blooded. Suetsugu was a resourceful schemer.[30]

Generally speaking, Yamanashi, Hori, and Koga were disciples of Katō Tomosaburō. Their mental horizons were wide and flexible. Katō Kanji and Suetsugu were their complete antithesis: they were rigid and adhered to a purely technical point of view. As naval specialists both Yamanashi and Hori also hoped to achieve the "three basic principles." In that there was no difference between them and the men of the Navy General Staff. However, though they thought that something close to these demands would probably be obtained in the conference, they were aware of the wider situation and had the mental suppleness to grasp that there were other parties to these negotiations and that therefore the "three basic principles" were an ideal goal for diplomatic bargaining, and not a fixed absolute.[31] In contrast, Katō and Suetsugu believed that these principles were unchangeable and that not a single concession could be made even if failure to do so meant the conference would break up.

In later years Katō put together his reminiscences of the London Treaty problem in the form of a diary entitled "Katō Kanji ikō" (The Literary Remains of Katō Kanji).[32] According to this diary, Katō spoke to Shidehara about the disarmament negotiations on October 11, 1929, and stressed to him that "70 percent is the absolute minimum figure."[33] On November 18 Katō also told Hamaguchi that 70 percent "is the absolutely lowest ratio and is a matter of life and death for our navy. If an agreement for that ratio is not secured, we must resolutely break off negotiations."[34] On January 29, 1930, Katō sent to Makino Nobuaki, the lord privy seal, a memorandum entitled "Views on Disarmament."[35] In this he again emphasized the absolute nature of the "three basic principles." In the midst of the difficulties at London Katō sent a letter, dated February 5, to Admiral Abo, the adviser to the delegation:

> If they turn a deaf ear to the small 10 percent more that Japan is requesting and thus break up the conference, Japan will gain the sympathy of the world. Because of the Kellogg Pact the United States will perhaps be in the impossibly awkward position of feeling too ashamed to undertake any large naval expansion in the future. Even if it builds the "top fleet" and expands its navy to many times that of Japan . . . the effect will be that Britain and Japan will draw together and the United States will become another Germany.
>
> We cannot say that out of these difficulties some fortunate result may not come. For instance, suppose Japan does not yield one inch in its just demands but breaks up the conference with an attack upon America's violation of the spirit of the Anti-war Pact. If that were to happen, the puritans and pacifists in America would appreciate Japan's character. They would wish to cooperate with Japan and repress the imperialists.[36]

Imperial Prince Fushimi Hiroyasu, a member of the Supreme War Council, and Fleet Admiral Tōgō Heihachirō aligned themselves with the uncompromising approach of Katō and his vice chief Suetsugu. On March 16 Katō visited Tōgō and explained the plan sent by the delegates. Tōgō expressed the following opinion:

We have already yielded 30 percent. If they do not concede to us in this very important matter of the heavy cruisers, we can only give the conference up as hopeless and return home. Even if we are defeated, there will be no big naval expansion. Therefore there is nothing to worry about fiscally. We have adopted the position that without 70 percent we cannot feel secure in our national defense. Consequently, petty bargaining over one or two percentage points is useless. If they will not accommodate our demands, the only thing to do is resolutely to withdraw from the conference.[37]

On March 23 Prince Fushimi complained about Shidehara's weak diplomacy to Admiral Okada, who had called at his residence. "If we retreat one step at this conference, the future of the nation will be uncertain. If it comes to the worst, I am determined to request an audience with the emperor to tell him this." Okada requested the prince to be prudent and went to visit Tōgō, who also let Okada know that he was greatly dissatisfied with the delegation's plan.[38]

Leaving aside whether Fushimi and Tōgō's hard-line position was their own idea or had been influenced by the opinions of Katō and his group, neither of these two men can have had a concrete plan or clear view of how to deal with the situation that would develop if the conference failed. In short, what they said amounted to nothing more than a verbal show of strength. Still, it was no small problem for the Navy Ministry "trio" to contend with this attitude on the part of these two old gentlemen, of whom one was a member of the imperial family and the other a deified hero.

Along with the telegram from the delegation requesting instructions, Shidehara received a top-secret telegram from Matsudaira, which read as follows:

Mr. Wakatsuki has requested that the following message be limited to yourself alone.

Telegram 208 from the delegation has requested return instructions from the government. In point of fact, the details of the situation have been explained. Now is really the time we must finally make up our minds. The only thing for us to do is to conclude the conference on the basis of the Japanese-American negotiations reported in recent messages. Although I had wished to make clear in the request for instructions that we have no option other than this, it was necessary to word that request in such a way that this was not spelled out because there was one delegate who did not want to have the full particulars explained. . . . Wakatsuki's telegram asking for instructions is the final request for instructions that he will send the government. Therefore I ask you to settle the issue with my above point fully in mind.[39]

The delegate "who did not want to have the full particulars explained" was Takarabe. Indeed, Wakatsuki later said that Takarabe and the majority of the naval entourage were dissatisfied with the compromise plan.[40] Takarabe's situation was quite anomalous. As a naval expert he found unsatisfactory the strength allotted Japan under the Japanese-American agreement. On the other hand, as a cabinet colleague he felt he should cooperate with the Hamaguchi cabinet. He did not at all have the kind of commanding influence exercised by Katō Tomosaburō, the navy minister and delegate to the Washington Conference. Nor, being a straightforward man, was he very good at subterfuge. As a result he could not repress the discontent within the navy.

Before he left Japan, Takarabe had himself advocated a hard-line approach, and this further limited his range of action. At the August 5 Prefectural Governors Conference, Takarabe had asserted that both technically and practically the slightest compromise with regard to the 70-percent ratio was absolutely impossible.[41] Before his departure he had definitely assured Prince Fushimi and Admiral Tōgō that he would not retreat one inch on the "three basic principles."[42] It was these statements opponents of the treaty had in mind when they later criticized Takarabe for being "double-tongued." But Takarabe, who had been trained by Katō Tomosaburō, was by no means a man of limited vision. Though he himself was caught in the crossfire, nevertheless he went through agony working to discover some means of bringing the situation under control and thus avoid a collision between the government and the navy.

In a telegram sent on March 23 Admiral Sakonji reported that fundamentally it was difficult for Takarabe to consent to the American proposal as it then stood. But Takarabe, he said, planned to effect several final compromises that the navy should be able to endure temporarily. If the government did not adopt those compromises or if it took the attitude that it had to consent to the American plan, "this would lead to a very serious disturbance. It is this point that most worries the minister, and his mind is constantly seeking solutions to this problem."[43]

In another telegram sent on March 25 Sakonji set forth Takarabe's policy:

He is wondering whether one way of dealing with the present situation might not be to use . . . the failure to obtain a five-power agreement
. . . as a stratagem to force the suspension of the conference. As navy
minister, who combines in himself the heavy responsibility of both controlling the navy and carrying out the present cabinet's important mission, he concludes, after carefully considering the various international
and domestic circumstances, that the situation compels this move. [44]

On the ground that the delegation could be reproached for sending
a telegram that asked for instructions but did not fully explain the situation, Wakatsuki sought Takarabe's consent for a new telegram to the
foreign minister in which the course of the past negotiations would be
set forth in detail. Since Takarabe had both a different viewpoint and a
different estimate of the situation, it was arranged that a telegram would
be sent in Wakatsuki's name alone. Takarabe was to send a separate
telegram after coming to an understanding with Wakatsuki and showing
him its text. [45]

Wakatsuki's telegram was sent on March 26. It explained at great
length the circumstances surrounding the request for instructions and
asserted that there was absolutely no prospect of any further concessions. If Japan caused the conference to fail, he could not, Wakatsuki
said, find it in his heart really to enumerate the disadvantages and woes
the nation must incur. He then warned:

> If Japan offers a plan that gives us more advantageous conditions but
> they turn it down, we must be resolved to withdraw from the conference
> altogether. Let us say we continue the negotiations without having taken
> that resolution. Then if they do not respond to our overtures and we in
> the end accept the compromise plan, the empire's prestige will be com-
> pletely lost. This is what worries me the most. [46]

That day Takarabe also sent a telegram, his being addressed to Vice
Minister Yamanashi. In it he said it would be premature to conclude that
the United States and Britain were absolutely unwilling to entertain any
new proposals from Japan. If Japan were willing to run the risk of the
three-power agreement's falling through, there was still some room for
negotiation. He understood, Takarabe wired, the view of the navy chief
of staff, and it was extremely difficult for him to approve acceptance of
the Reed-Matsudaira compromise. Takarabe then went on to explain the
way he thought the situation should be handled:

I would suggest the following as a plan that will give us a successful conference and will eliminate any chance of our encountering the disadvantageous situation of having to leave the conference because we cannot gain their consent to our proposals. Let us use the failure of the five-power agreement as an opportunity . . . to recess the conference. Let us express our determination to withdraw and say that we wish to wait patiently until the time is ripe for a five-power agreement. If they then show that they are sincere in their wish to establish a three-power agreement, we will confront them at that time with our final proposal. We will demonstrate the substantial nature of our concessions and will determine our course of action on the basis of their reaction to our terms. If we handle it this way, we will surely not have very much to fear from the conference's breakdown.[47]

In a telegram sent to Yamanashi on March 29 Admiral Abo reported the following details of Takarabe's final proposal:

Japan will not abandon the three important points of its settled policy. However, there is no objection to accepting the following items as measures to be in effect until 1936, i.e., through the term of the present treaty:
1. The construction of 18 8-in.-gun cruisers by the United States is agreed to, with the understanding that Japan will hold to its present 12 cruisers until the sixteenth American cruiser has been constructed and that Japan will lay down a 10,000-ton class vessel when the United States lays down its seventeenth cruiser.
1. Japan will be allowed 70,000 tons in submarines.
3. In auxiliary vessels, Japan will have an overall ratio of 70 percent vis-a-vis the United States.

At the end of his telegram Abo reminded the vice minister that Takarabe thought the return instructions must represent a consensus of the views of the government and the navy.[48]

Even if Takarabe's telegram was a last desperate measure, it still took too optimistic a view of the situation and was quite inconsistent with the telegram that the whole delegation had sent and he had signed. Hamaguchi commented to Harada Kumao, "What he says doesn't seem to make any sense. I think it's very queer."[49]

Perhaps even Takarabe himself did not have any confidence in his final plan. In a telegram sent on March 16 to Yamanashi and Suetsugu, Sakonji noted, "The plan is not regarded as really being worth much consideration." However, he went on to say that if the government's return instructions were not backed by a willingness to break up the con-

ference, "the navy minister admits with distress that it will be very difficult to obtain a settlement more advantageous than the private plan
proposed by the Americans."[50] In another telegram the following day
Sakonji further warned, "It is considered that it is almost impossible to
attain all of Japan's demands, and this will be the truer if we flatly break
up the conference in this way. . . . The return instructions . . . must
clearly state the government's final decision."[51] Thus Sakonji indirectly
suggested that the choice was either to swallow the Matsudaira-Reed
compromise or to break up the conference.

Takarabe's contradictory behavior may have been a device to persuade the navy hard liners that they had to accept the Matsudaira-Reed
compromise. It was only natural that on account of this behavior he was
afterward accused of having lied. Indisputably, his conduct in itself became one of the factors that created confusion within the navy.

In conformity with its public commitment, the Hamaguchi cabinet
announced on November 21, 1929, that it would lift the gold embargo.
The embargo was removed on January 11, 1930, and in the general election of February 20 the government won an absolute majority of 273 out
of 466 seats. It was placed, therefore, in the best possible position for a
showdown on the disarmament issue. Hamaguchi was of the opinion that
the naval disarmament conference must absolutely not end in failure. This
belief was a natural consequence of his cabinet's twin policies of financial
retrenchment and cooperative diplomacy. The government had approved in cabinet the "three basic principles," but it had taken great pains
to avoid any definitive statement that would finalize the mathematics of
the ratio and limit the government's freedom of action.

When the Diet came back from recess on January 21, 1930, Inukai
Tsuyoshi, the president of the Seiyūkai, made an address in which he
asserted that the 70-percent ratio was the minimum required for Japan's
national defense. Would the government, he asked, hold out for this demand to the very last? In his answer Hamaguchi avoided any pronouncement on the 70-percent ratio and merely said he was resolved to
maintain the minimum naval strength needed to ensure that Japan neither threatened any other country nor was threatened by any other
country. Seeking in an underhanded way to tie down the government,
the Seiyūkai then introduced a resolution reading, "The House of Representatives recognizes that the government's claims at the London Naval Conference are the desire of the Japanese people as a whole." How-

ever, the opposition of the government and the Minseitō prevented anything from coming of this.

To afford time for the navy chief of staff's anger to cool, Hamaguchi decided to delay settling the return instructions for as long as possible.[52] But he never wavered in his determination to bring the conference to a successful conclusion. On March 25 he told Yamanashi that the government had made up its mind it could not run the risk of the conference's failing: "Though I lose the prime ministership, though I lose the Minseitō, though I lose my life itself, this decision is unshakable and I cannot go back on it."[53]

Hamaguchi was supported in his resolve by the last genrō Prince Saionji Kimmochi and other court officials: Lord Privy Seal Makino Nobuaki, Imperial Household Minister Ichiki Kitokurō, and Grand Chamberlain Suzuki Kantarō. All of these men took the view that the overall situation required the conclusion of a treaty at London. Senior navy leaders such as Yamamoto Gonnohyōe and Saitō Makoto, the governor-general of Korea, were also of this opinion. Saionji explained his position as follows:

> Looking at the question in its broader aspects, no matter how strong you say you are, the mere saying so does not mean you will actually be able to fight on to the very end and win the ultimate victory. Judging from our national strength, that sort of thing is, after all, still difficult for us. A nation begins to have strength with real staying power only when its armaments are kept within the bounds permitted by its finances. No matter what reckless plans you may make, flash-in-the-pan armaments are almost the same as having no strength. If Japan steps forward and by accepting a 60-percent ratio leads this conference to a successful agreement, then the powers will recognize, especially in view of the present circumstances, that Japan is sincerely working to further international peace. If Japan takes the lead in making this conference a success, our future international position will be raised even higher. To march out in front chanting, "We must have 70 percent come what may," will not get us what we want. . . . Right now we have both the United States and Britain grabbing for the leader's baton. Precisely because of that situation we can step in between the two and gain appropriate advantages for ourselves. What profit is there in completely estranging ourselves from them?[54]

Saionji's view dominated opinion among the court officials, who both publicly and privately backed up the Hamaguchi cabinet. Saionji's private secretary Harada Kumao circulated untiringly among them and coordinated their activities.

The emperor also keenly desired the treaty to be concluded. When he discussed the disarmament problem with Hamaguchi on March 27, the emperor told him that for the sake of world peace he must endeavor to conclude the treaty quickly. In consequence, Hamaguchi became immovable in his determination to accept the plan set forth in the delegates' request for instructions.

On March 15, the day the delegates' request for instructions arrived, Admiral Okada Keisuke was at Hiratsuka in Kanagawa, where at 8:00 P.M. he received a telegram from Yamanashi asking him to return to Tokyo.[55] The next day Okada went to Tokyo and began to take an energetic part in settling the treaty problem. At the time Okada was simply a member of the Supreme War Council, a position with relatively light duties. Since Okada was a former navy minister and a senior fellow provincial of the navy chief of staff, Yamanashi counted on him for assistance in handling Katō.[56] Okada was committed to the position that the London Conference must be a success. He explained his view of disarmament as follows:

> Generally there is no limit to armaments. No matter how many arms are piled up, there never comes a point of saying, "That's enough, with that much we are safe." . . . It would be fine if we were well enough prepared to engage in a contest; but no matter how dogged our efforts, that sort of thing is impossible for a country like Japan whose national resources are inferior to those of the major powers. If it is impossible, then it would be better to go easy.[57]

A resourceful man of common sense and infinite tact, Okada was ideally suited to play the role of a troubleshooter. In his diary he speaks of his activities as follows:

> When I was running around as a peacemaker for the London Conference, my object was imperceptibly to ease everyone into an acceptable solution and as far as possible to avoid a violent confrontation. In dealing with opponents of the treaty, I would sometimes adroitly carry things off by silently nodding in agreement as if I supported their ideas. With the pro-treaty people, I would do things like expressing opinions that smacked of the "hard line." In short, because they were all men of common sense, common sense was my *point d'appui*. In the most exciting human being there is some remnant of common sense and you try to establish contact with that. Then you just flee, that's my tactic.

Katō Kanji and his group were very passionate in their opposition to the treaty. However, since there was only one honest course to take, it was easy for me to make my choice. Katō was a simple-hearted, rather nice fellow. Compared to him, the really sly fox was his scheming subordinate Suetsugu. In view of this, the only thing I could do was to take on Suetsugu as my opponent.[58]

Through mediation conducted with this kind of flexible approach, Okada greatly assisted the government to settle the problem of the return instructions without the numerous clashes with the navy people's erupting into a full-scale confrontation between the navy and the government. When Captain Koga went to meet Takarabe at Harbin on behalf of Yamanashi, he carried a message in which the vice minister said, "Admiral Okada has performed all manner of services, and I am grateful to him. I have done my share of the work unsatisfactorily, and it is entirely due to the admiral that the affair has ended as well as it has."[59]

At 5:00 P.M. on March 15 Hamaguchi gave Yamanashi the delegates' telegram requesting instructions. Earlier that day at 10:30 A.M., important navy leaders had met in the chief of staff's office to discuss the policy the navy should adopt toward the Japanese-American compromise as it had been reported in Wakatsuki's telegram of March 12. At the meeting were: Katō Kanji, Suetsugu, Yamanashi, and Koga; First Division chief Katō Takayoshi, and Second Section chief Noda Kiyoshi under him; Kobayashi Seizō, chief of the Navy Ministry's Naval Construction Division; Andō Masataka, chief of naval aviation; and Captain Shimomura Shōsuke, deputizing for Naval Affairs Bureau chief Hori Teikichi, who was on sick leave.

At this meeting Kobayashi ventured the opinion that it would be all right to make some concessions on large cruisers and submarines. "It is not advisable for the navy and the navy alone to persist in Japan's original demands and thereby wreck the conference," he said. "Upon thinking the matter over a little, wouldn't it be advantageous to move to an agreement?" Suetsugu and Andō opposed any concessions, and Yamanashi told the meeting he wished to delay the sending of instructions until the following week, since there was still scope for further consideration of their content. Before the meeting broke up, Katō Kanji remarked, "I expect another important telegram to arrive today. I would like us to decide our policy in the light of that telegram." It was about this time that a secret telegram arrived from Abo for the navy chief of staff, so the important telegram to which Katō referred was probably this one. This telegram reads:

> As a result of exhaustive discussions among the four delegates, instructions have now, March 14, been requested from the government. If by some chance the five-power conference falls through and this becomes a three-power conference, it is difficult to expect that this will in any way improve our situation. If we are to bring this conference to a successful conclusion, my impression is that at worst we will have to accept until 1936 an overall ratio of 70 percent with 60,000 tons in submarines (parity) and 18 American 8-in.-gun cruisers (15 completed) to our present 12. My opinion is that you should sound out the views of the government and try to decide on countermeasures for the future. The situation is now fairly tense. Please consider the implications carefully.[60]

Abo's telegram arrived at 10:00 A.M. on the 15th. Between 11:00 and 11:30 A.M. the telegram section chief gave it to Kasuya Sōichi, the Navy General Staff adjutant, but somehow or other it was not circulated to the Navy Ministry. The ministry became aware of its existence only in mid-August as the result of an investigation undertaken when on his return to Japan Abo mentioned having sent it.[61] Thus, quite early in the game the strange behavior on the part of the Navy General Staff had already commenced.

After the arrival of the delegates' request for instructions important conversations continued for several days between the Navy Ministry and the Navy General Staff. On March 17 Yamanashi visited Okada to consult with him on what ultimately would be the very best way to handle the delegates' request. Okada replied:

> If unavoidable, we will in the end have to swallow the proposal just as it stands. With the strength allowed under the agreement we can have an effective national defense. We must not be responsible for breaking up the conference, but we should still try once or twice more to get what we want. Also, we must telegraph the navy minister and ask him what on earth his opinion really is.[62]

On the evening of March 17 the newspapers carried the full text of "A Statement by the Naval Authorities," which Suetsugu had without authorization supplied to newspaper reporters. It contained the following assertion:

The American plan is only a superficial concession. The essentials of the plan still adhere closely to the original American position. Either because this fact is not clear to them or because they are dispensing self-serving propaganda, there are people who are spreading the fabrication that the United States has accepted Japan's claims. They are seriously misleading the people of the nation. The navy cannot possibly accept this kind of proposal from the United States.[63]

When this press release was reported in the British and American press, it created quite a stir. The London *Times* of March 18 said that this statement was strong evidence of a serious difference of opinion between the government and the navy. On the 19th the *Times* made this ironical comment:

> Readers abroad may find it difficult to believe that officers can indulge in such "politics" and retain their posts if the views they publish are not in fact those of the Government or, at least, of the Navy Ministry, but public opinion in Japan is accustomed to see the Army and Navy go to great lengths in advocating their own views, even in opposition to the Government.[64]

On March 19 Katō went to the prime minister's official residence to see Hamaguchi, who, it will be remembered, was acting navy minister. He spent more than an hour explaining why, as a person responsible for national defense planning, he could not possibly consent to the American proposal. Throughout this controversy the Navy General Staff persisted in calling the compromise proposal either the American plan or America's final offer. The government and the delegates, on the other hand, referred to it as the Japanese-American compromise. Wakatsuki in London insisted that the proposal he had telegraphed was not America's final offer but was a venture mutually agreed upon by the Japanese and American delegations.[65]

About this time the American, British, and French ambassadors in Tokyo all began to take actions aimed at influencing Japan's decision. On March 14 Castle called on Shidehara and read him a telegram from Stimson and Reed. The message in the telegram was that the United States was inclined to conclude some sort of agreement with Britain even if Japan were excluded but that they continued to hope earnestly for Japan's participation.[66] On March 17 the French chargé d'affaires proposed to Shidehara that Japan should persist in its demand to be allowed to retain its existing submarine tonnage.

On the morning of the 18th the British ambassador confidentially showed Shidehara a telegram from MacDonald saying that Britain felt there was absolutely no room for any concessions beyond those in the Japanese-American compromise. That afternoon the American ambassador called on Vice Foreign Minister Yoshida Shigeru and told him that Stimson feared the French recommendation to Japan on the submarine issue was nothing more than an attempt by France to maintain its own position while getting Japan blamed for breaking up the conference.[67]

On March 20 Naval Affairs Bureau chief Hori received from First Section chief Katō a statement of the Navy General Staff's views in a document entitled "Policy Toward the Delegates' Request for Instructions." The American plan, it claimed, sought to impose the original American demands even though the proposal was cleverly disguised as a concession. The General Staff therefore desired the following changes:

1. The transfer to the 20-cm.-gun cruiser category of 17,600 tons from the overall 205,950 tons in light cruisers and destroyers allowed Japan under the American plan.
2. When the United States lays down its sixteenth 20-cm.-gun cruiser, Japan will lay down its thirteenth heavy cruiser out of the transferred tonnage provided for in point 1. When the United States completes its eighteenth cruiser, Japan will complete its fourteenth cruiser.
3. Japan's submarine tonnage should be 65,500 tons; 12,350 tons will be transferred from the overall light cruiser and destroyer tonnage.
4. If the transfer of tonnage to submarines is not accepted, then this should be conditioned on the exclusion of submarines under 8,700 tons from the limitation placed on submarine tonnage, and our submarine tonnage should be reduced to 72,000 tons.[68]

After he had considered the opinion of the Navy General Staff, Hori prepared a statement on March 22 that formally summed up his bureau's position on the instructions to be sent the delegates. He forwarded this statement to Hotta Masaaki, chief of the Foreign Ministry's Europe-America Bureau. Hori pointed out that the American proposal accepted one of Japan's desires almost in its entirety, but at the same time it greatly departed from Japan's wishes in the matter of heavy cruisers and submarines. Therefore, it was not possible for the navy readily to approve the plan. Hori's document listed four points that had been agreed upon in bargaining among the navy men and expressed the hope that these points would be adopted as Japan's final proposal and suitably negotiated at London.

1. Based on the American proposal of February 5 (option), the number of American 20-cm.-gun cruisers should be set at 15 vessels (150,000 tons); but in this case American tonnage in 15-cm.-gun or below light cruisers should be 173,500 tons.
2. Japan will make the following concessions with regard to submarines and destroyers:
   a. Japan's submarine tonnage will be 65,500 tons.
   b. Japan's destroyer tonnage will be reduced to 92,700.
3. Based on Gibson's statement at the sixth session of the League of Nations Disarmament Preparatory Commission, tonnage transfers among all categories of auxiliary vessels will be recognized (with no prejudice to using an appropriate yardstick), the limitation on transferable tonnage to be 20 percent of the tonnage of the class into which the transfer is made.
4. In making tonnage transfers into the 20-cm.-gun cruiser category, Japan will yield precedence to the United States and will make such transfers after the United States has done so.[69]

Yamanashi explained this plan to a meeting of the naval members of the Supreme War Council on March 24 at the navy minister's official residence. The plan was approved by all the councillors. At that meeting Prince Fushimi asked what Japan's situation would be if the London Conference collapsed. Chief of Staff Katō replied lightly that it was nothing to be greatly concerned about.[70]

On March 25 Yamanashi advised Hamaguchi that it was impossible for the navy to accept the American plan in its original form. Hamaguchi explained that the government emphatically desired the conference to succeed and that it would be a very serious matter to risk breaking it up. On the 26th leaders of the Navy Ministry and General Staff—Okada, Katō Kanji, Yamanashi, Suetsugu, Hori, and Parliamentary Vice Minister for the Navy Yabuki Shōzō—discussed the policy the navy was to adopt toward arms reduction. Their decision was embodied in a document entitled "Future Policy," which stated:

1. The American plan cannot be accepted. The navy's draft of the return instructions represents the greatest extent to which we may yield on Japan's original demands. It is earnestly desired that the necessary steps

be taken to have the delegates now exert themselves to attain the demands set forth in the navy draft.

2. It is impossible for the navy to submit an intermediate compromise plan which is not accompanied by the determination to break off negotiations if the plan is not accepted. To prevent the failure of the conference, an intermediate plan must be a one-and-only final plan which clearly indicates our determination. In the view of the technical experts, we therefore cannot construct an intermediate plan which is unaccompanied by such a determination.

3. When the government has settled on a policy, we would like the acting navy minister (accompanied by the foreign minister if necessary) to explain the policy to the navy leaders responsible.

4. No matter what the circumstances of the government's decision, the navy vice minister should answer the questions of the acting navy minister with regard to the various technical matters on which we wish the delegates to make special efforts, i.e., those points in the American plan that are most disadvantageous to us and those points that require changes.

5. Even though the government does not heed the navy's policy (or rather, strictly speaking, the opinions of officers attending various discussions), the naval agencies have, of course, no right to go beyond the proper boundaries of state and military matters. They will, of course, follow official regulations and do the best they can within the limits set by government policy.[71]

During the meeting Suetsugu suggested that point 5 need not be included, since what it said could be assumed to be the duty of a naval officer. However, Katō argued that it was better to include the point to avoid any possibility of a misunderstanding. In the end it was arranged that Yamanashi would present Hamaguchi with a written memorandum on the first three points but make an oral statement on the last two. Yamanashi saw Hamaguchi that same day and explained to him the policy the navy leaders had adopted.[72]

Subsequently Katō and Suetsugu were to claim that a decision on military strength was a matter for joint advice to the emperor by the cabinet and the military command agencies. It infringed the right of military command, they said, when the government adopted return instructions in opposition to the opinion of the navy chief of staff. Nevertheless, the facts of the March 26 meeting clearly show that both Katō and Suetsugu agreed at the time to follow the government's decision even if it were contrary to the navy's opinion. In other words, they acknowledged that the right to decide military strength lay with the government.

Okada and Katō called on Hamaguchi on March 27 to advise him about the navy's policy. Hamaguchi explained his position to them as follows:

> Since I am both prime minister and acting navy minister, I have been pondering this treaty policy from the standpoint of the nation's overall situation. I feel that as a general policy I would like to conclude an agreement on the basis of the plan sent by the delegation and avoid the breakup of the conference.[73]

After the interview Katō made a remark to Okada that implied he had consented to the Japanese-American compromise plan. "This time," he said, "I have made up my mind. After all, if we concentrate on airplanes, we can maintain our national defense."[74]

On March 28 Okada asked Yamanashi to come to his home for a conference. He gave Yamanashi this warning:

> We will have to swallow the delegates' plan. But only on the condition that we make the government promise measures to offset the deficiencies we feel the American plan imposes on us with regard to both our overall tonnage and the distribution of that tonnage among the various categories of vessels. We must force the government to put its consent to these measures in the form of a cabinet memorandum. Also, it would be risky to hold a meeting of the members of the Supreme War Council, for there would be opposition to the government. There must be no such meeting.[75]

The following day Prince Fushimi summoned Okada. Despite his regret that the navy's demands had not been attained, the prince acknowledged the need to accept Hamaguchi's decision. Should there not now be a meeting of the Supreme War Council?[76]

Okada discussed Fushimi's proposal with Yamanashi, then went to tell Katō there must be no meeting of the council. Katō confided to Okada that he intended to submit an address to the emperor. Okada cautioned that this could not be done before the prime minister advised the emperor on the return instructions.[77]

By March 30 the Navy Ministry had completed a memorandum on the supplemental plan that Yamanashi was to present to the cabinet detailing the countermeasures to remedy the defects in national defense that would arise from the proposed London agreement. The memorandum was based on a draft prepared by Hori and was presented by Yamanashi to Suetsugu, who passed it on to Katō for perusal. Yamanashi next obtained Hamaguchi's and Shidehara's approval for the plan and on the following day the consent of Finance Minister Inoue.

In the memorandum Yamanashi explained that while the American plan fulfilled the condition of giving Japan an overall ratio of 70 percent in auxiliary vessels, it fell short of the navy's desires with respect to heavy cruisers and submarines. He expressed the hope that in the formulation of the return instructions sufficient consideration would be given to these shortcomings. If it were decided to send return instructions that exactly followed the delegates' proposals, he would like the following points considered:

> To mitigate the difficulties in implementing national defense plans that will inevitably arise as a result of the arms limitation agreement, there must be improvements both in matériel and in technical skills. With regard to matériel, the following must be borne in mind: the maintenance and improvement of the capabilities of our existing vessels; full provision for air power; the promotion and development of experimental research installations; the improvement of defense facilities; the full provision of special types of surface vessels; the maintenance of construction skills and productive capacity; the adoption of suitable measures to prevent unemployment in the shipbuilding and related industries. With regard to the improvement of technical skills, the following must be borne in mind: the improvement of various educational facilities; the rigorous implementation of every kind of training exercise; the improvement of the conditions of life in the service, etc. Consequently, full consideration must be given to funds for every kind of operating cost, for maneuvers, and for remodeling as well as repairing vessels. In the past there has been a tendency to hold such appropriations tightly down in order to divert money to ship construction.[78]

Yamanashi's memorandum was based on the premise that the navy was going to accede to the government's draft of the return instructions, in other words, the delegates' plan. This is shown by the phrase, "if at this cabinet meeting this draft of the return instructions is adopted as it now stands." Likewise, the approval of the memorandum by naval leaders logically implied acceptance of the government's draft. Moreover, Suetsugu had said to Yamanashi that he would be grateful if the government approved the memorandum.[79]

The draft of the government's return instructions was completed on the evening of March 31 and thus was ready for presentation at the regularly scheduled cabinet meeting of April 1. To secure the navy's approval prior to the cabinet meeting, early on the morning of the 1st Hamaguchi requested Okada, Katō, and Yamanashi to see him. Okada and Katō gave careful consideration to what should be said to Hamaguchi. According to Okada's diary, he tried to leave the talking to Katō. However, Katō demurred, saying, "I can't say it. You say it." To make doubly sure, Okada said to him, "Since I am going to speak, I want your consent." Katō promised, "I won't say a thing. I'll be silent."[80]

At 8:45 A.M. Okada, Katō, and Yamanashi met with Hamaguchi at the prime minister's official residence. Hamaguchi explained his view of the domestic and international situations and affirmed that he was resolved to settle the matter at the coming cabinet meeting largely on the basis of the delegates' plan. In arriving at his decision he had given full consideration to the opinions of the technical experts, and in particular had attached great importance to the views of Navy Minister Takarabe. He then handed Yamanashi the draft of the return instructions.

Okada responded:

> I fully understand your decision. I think it is unavoidable that you submit the draft to the cabinet meeting. The navy made certain demands from the technical experts' viewpoint, and these demands are still unchanged. I request that you arrange for Vice Minister Yamanashi to explain all this later at the cabinet meeting. If the cabinet should adopt this draft, the navy will do everything in its power to devise means of adjusting to the decision.

Katō muttered rather vaguely, "From the standpoint of strategic operations, the American plan creates problems . . . from the standpoint of strategic operations. . . ." Hamaguchi asked the two admirals to inform Tōgō of the outcome of the conversation. The interview ended with Hamaguchi's consenting to Yamanashi's request that the draft not be presented to the cabinet until the navy had completed consideration of it.[81]

During this meeting Katō had said merely that there were difficulties from a purely military point of view. Not only had he not said that he was opposed to the draft of the return instructions, but he had not denied that what Okada said represented the official navy position. In later days Katō unilaterally claimed he had clearly affirmed his opposition. However, no matter how one looks at his actual words, it is difficult to interpret them in that way. Considering the context in which they were uttered, it is not a forced interpretation to regard what he said as giving a kind of passive consent to the draft.

At 9:35 A.M. Yamanashi returned to the navy minister's official residence and reported the situation to his waiting colleagues from the ministry and the staff, showing them the draft. The ensuing discussion resulted in a decision to request the following three amendments:

1. With respect to 20-cm.-gun cruisers there is a reservation freeing Japan from treaty restraints after 1936. This reservation must without question apply to submarines, and it is necessary that it also be extended to all auxiliary vessels.
2. Although it is anticipated that there will be an increase in submarine tonnage as a result of the French and Italian positions on the question, it is equally necessary to consider a situation in which Britain and the United States increase submarine tonnage for other reasons.
3. From the viewpoint of maintaining naval construction skills and industrial capacity, it is necessary that exceptions to the agreed replacement age limits be acknowledged in every category, but especially in the submarine category.[82]

In the course of the meeting Yamanashi read his memorandum aloud three times. No one present objected to it, and one said the memorandum was not necessary. It scarcely needs repeating that the decision by the group on this memorandum and on the three suggested amendments was premised upon the acceptance of the government's draft of the return instructions.

At 11:00 A.M. Yamanashi saw Hamaguchi and Shidehara at the prime minister's official residence and reported to them on the amendments. At noon the cabinet meeting was opened. First Hamaguchi stated his opinion, then Shidehara gave a detailed explanation to the situation. After two or three questions had been answered, Yamanashi read his statement. The draft of the return instructions was then unanimously approved. At 3:45 P.M. Hamaguchi went to the palace to advise the emperor to approve the instructions. After being notified by Hamaguchi that the emperor had given his sanction, Shidehara at 5:00 P.M. telegraphed the instructions to the delegates in London. The next day Shidehara visited Army Minister Ugaki Kazushige, who had been absent from the cabinet meeting on account of illness, explained to him the return in-

structions, and secured his countersignature for them. Meanwhile, Yamanashi had called on Admiral Tōgō after the cabinet meeting and had
given him an account of the events leading to the cabinet's adoption of
the return instructions. Tōgō's response was:

> Since the matter has been definitely decided, we have to go along with
> it. Now that things have reached this stage, it's silly to grumble. In this
> situation we must work to unify the navy. In a cheerful spirit we must
> develop harmony and cooperation among all ranks. We must pour our
> energy into three things: the provision of matériel, improving morale, and
> rigorously training our personnel. It is important to raise our quality, to
> concentrate with religious dedication upon the intrinsic mission of the
> navy.[83]

While these events were occurring, Prince Fushimi was traveling in
the Kansai region. Sawamoto Yorio, chief of the First Section of the Naval Affairs Bureau, was dispatched to bring the prince up to date. Upon
hearing Sawamoto's report, Fushimi commented:

> Since the decision has already definitely been made by the cabinet,
> agitation by the navy can only redound to the navy's disadvantage. There-
> fore I hope that we will strive to supplement the defects created by the
> treaty and that we will speed up the implementation of plans to bring
> about the fullest development possible within the provisions of the treaty.[84]

Meanwhile, at 7:00 P.M. on March 31 Yamanashi had telegraphed a
last appeal to Takarabe, who was still agonizing over his decision. The
essential part of his telegram read as follows:

> The government believes disruption of the conference by us would
> profoundly affect Japan's future. It is conjectured that the government will
> adopt return instructions based in general upon the plan submitted in the
> delegates' request for instructions. If this is the position taken by the gov-
> ernment, it is feared that in the event you should take actions differing
> from Wakatsuki's, there will develop a grave situation regrettable both
> domestically and internationally for Japan's future. I earnestly beg you to
> act on this occasion from the standpoint of the overall situation of the na-
> tion. I implore you to prudently bear with these difficulties and to fulfill
> your duty as a delegate.

Yamanashi ended his telegram with these words:

I truly fear that what I have said above oversteps the bounds of my position. However, confronted by this serious situation and considering the general state of affairs within the country, I have been so bold as to forget the respect which is due you, and I have revealed my inmost thoughts. I hope you will make allowance for these circumstances.[85]

Before Yamanashi sent this telegram, he showed it to Katō and obtained the chief of staff's seal. He next showed it to Okada, who suggested that the last sentence was unnecessary and that Yamanashi should simply say that Okada and he were of like mind. Yamanashi thereupon deleted this sentence from the final version and substituted, "Admiral Okada is in agreement with the above views." Katō did not see this revision.

Takarabe's answer arrived at the Navy Ministry on April 2 at 6:10 P.M. The reply read:

I also have given deep consideration to the points raised in your telegram. On this occasion I will not err with respect to the greater work of the nation through reckless insistence on my own narrow views. I will refrain from behavior that may create problems for the future. I am resolved to do everything in my power to meet my heavy responsibility. I particularly desire your understanding on that point. I would like the above passed on to both Admiral Okada and the navy chief of staff.[86]

It is quite plain that this message fell in with Yamanashi's opinion and expressed an intention to approve the delegates' plan. Yamanashi showed Takarabe's telegram to Katō, who signed his name to it. After Katō had submitted his April 2 address to the emperor, he personally composed the following answer to Takarabe and requested Adjutant Koga to send it off:

I have been informed of the contents of your telegram to the vice minister. At this time, when both the domestic and the foreign situation are very serious, I feel greatly reassured to hear of your excellency's determination and to envisage your resolute attitude. Since we still today have before us the coming problem of ensuring the reservation with respect to the 70 percent heavy cruiser ratio as well as agreements on other things important to the imperial navy's future, I earnestly pray that you will take good care of your health. Today, April 2, after my audience with the emperor, I issued the press release quoted below. Please do not worry about it.[87]

In the press release Katō expressed confidence that in the matter of the return instructions the navy would not act rashly but would respond prudently to the changed situation. The Navy General Staff, he said, as a matter of conviction could not agree to the strength proposed in the American plan. Both out of duty and out of conviction the Navy General Staff was resolved to exert every effort to prevent the national defense's being endangered.

When Katō's telegram is read in the light of Yamanashi's and Takarabe's, there would seem to be no interpretation other than that, at this time at least, Katō too intended to approve the government's return instructions. In fact, Takarabe later said that when he received the telegram, his reaction was, "Katō opposed the treaty at first, but now in the end he has given in."[88] At a cabinet meeting on May 30 Shidehara inquired whether it could not be asserted in the presentation before the Privy Council that the navy chief of staff had consented to the instructions. Takarabe affirmed that it could and exhibited as evidence his own and Katō's telegrams.[89]

On July 16, after Katō had resigned as navy chief of staff, General Staff Adjutant Kasuya Sōichi turned over to Koga Mineichi, the Navy Ministry adjutant, a five-volume collection of materials labeled "Materials Related to Events at the Time of the Issuance of the Government's Decision on the Return Instructions." When these documents were given to Koga, they had affixed to them the official seal of the navy chief of staff and were addressed to the navy minister. They were dated June 4, before Katō resigned. Since Koga had doubts about this procedurally, on July 22 Kasuya redelivered them, readdressed as material sent from the Navy General Staff adjutant to the Navy Ministry adjutant.[90]

In these documents it was stated with regard to Katō's prior reading of Yamanashi's memorandum that "there was, of course, no special significance to this act beyond the mere fact of reading." Concerning Katō's affixing his seal to Yamanashi's March 31 telegram before it was dispatched, it was said, "The affixing of his seal to this telegram by the navy chief of staff had no meaning other than to signify he had read it. This is shown by the fact that at the end of the telegram there is only 'Admiral Okada is in agreement with the above views,' and it is not noted that the navy chief of staff approved any point at all."

The documents also asserted that Katō's April 2 telegram to Takarabe "was not sent in order to indicate approval of the government's return instructions." With respect to Katō's failure at the navy leaders' meeting on the morning of April 1 to insist that the return instructions be opposed, the documents explained, "Since the Navy General Staff had already declared that it did not approve the plan, there was no reason why the Navy General Staff should have discussed the matter." All these interpretations, of course, knowingly twisted the truth.

On March 31 Katō decided to address the emperor on the subject of the return instructions. At 10:00 A.M. he sent Kasuya to the office of the emperor's chief aide-de-camp to inquire when it would be convenient for the emperor to receive him. An imperial aide named Imamura Nobujirō came to the General Staff headquarters to inform Katō that the emperor would be engaged until about 5:30 P.M., adding that the grand chamberlain would like to see him before he presented his address. At 1:45 P.M. Katō called on Suzuki at his private residence. Suzuki explained that it would not be seemly for the navy chief of staff to have an audience prior to the prime minister when both were presenting addresses on the same subject. Katō accepted this and withdrew his request for an audience.[91] When the next day he renewed his request, the emperor's schedule was too full, and the audience was put off until the following day. On April 2 at 10:30 A.M. Katō went to the palace and submitted his address.

The tonnage called for by the "three basic principles," Katō declared, was the absolute minimum strength necessary for Japan's self-defense. The American plan contained provisions that, it was feared, would create serious operational deficiencies for the imperial navy. Therefore that plan, or any other agreement that materially reduced the ratio or tonnage originally claimed by Japan, would lead to important changes in the operational plans that had been prepared in accordance with the national defense policy approved by the emperor in 1923. Consequently, he, Katō, believed that this matter required the most careful consideration.[92]

Upon returning from the palace to the Navy General Staff headquarters, Katō issued his press release.

On April 21, the day before the treaty was to be signed, Noda Kiyoshi brought to Hori the following document:

Memorandum Regarding the London Naval Treaty Plan
The Navy General Staff cannot consent to the London Naval Treaty,

since the auxiliary vessel tonnage allotted to our country under the treaty is not sufficient to provide the minimum naval strength required for our country's defense.[93]

Hori refused to accept delivery of the memorandum, but Adjutant Koga took it to Yamanashi. Concerned about how to dispose of it, Yamanashi enlisted Okada's aid in getting the Navy General Staff to take back the communication. When Okada saw Katō on April 22 and recommended that the statement be withdrawn, Katō answered, "This time it is necessary to make the matter very clear. In addition, the statement was delivered to the Navy Ministry the day before the treaty was signed. That fact is very important." Katō suggested, however, that the communication be shown to no one until Takarabe returned to Japan. It should, he said, be placed in the Navy Ministry safe and shown to Takarabe immediately on his return. After a bit more discussion Okada decided that any further effort was useless and left.[94]

Just before this, Katō had personally signed a telegram of thanks to Takarabe drafted on April 19 and sent jointly in the names of the navy vice minister and the navy chief of staff. This telegram, which was actually dispatched on April 21, read:

> Since your departure from this country you have for a long time been engaged in difficult negotiations. You have throughout continued to fight bravely, for which we are extremely and sincerely grateful. Now that the conference is drawing to a close and the treaty will be signed in a few days, we pray from afar for your health. Please pass this message on to Delegate Wakatsuki also.[95]

Katō was later to insist that from beginning to end he had consistently opposed the government's draft of the return instructions, and he charged that the government's action had infringed the right of military command. However, as the events detailed above clearly demonstrate, such a claim is in complete contradiction to the facts. When the return instructions were being decided, Katō may not have given positive assent, but he did give tacit consent or at least did not raise an objection. In considering his contradictory and schizoid behavior after March 26, it is often difficult to determine what his true intention was. As a simple-hearted but quick-tempered man, he was probably divided in his feelings on the question. In his diary Harada observed: "When Suetsugu isn't around, Katō is very quiet; but when Suetsugu puts in an appearance, Katō again becomes troublesome. In the final analysis, Suetsugu is manipulating Katō."[96] That may have been the truth.

The London Treaty and Public Opinion

The government's return instruction reached the delegates on the evening of April 1, London time. At 3:00 P.M. the next day the heads of the delegations met in St. James's Palace. There Wakatsuki announced that with only one or two reservations Japan accepted the Matsudaira-Reed compromise. This was done, he said, out of consideration both for the advancement of international peace and friendship and for the spirit of cooperation and conciliation displayed by Britain and the United States. Prime Minister MacDonald expressed his deep appreciation for the cooperation and friendship of the Japanese delegation and the Japanese government.

On April 3 the delegates of the three nations discussed the Japanese reservations, which for the most part were acceded to by the United States and Britain. The main reservations were: (1) that the present treaty should in no way limit Japan's freedom of action at the next conference; (2) that the replacement age for submarines, destroyers, and light cruisers should be lowered so as to maintain construction skills and capacity; (3) that submarine parity should be maintained with the United States and Britain. Concerning the first point, the government's instructions explained, "Although this point is almost self-evident, it is believed that a reiteration and clarification will be useful in dispelling somewhat the anxiety of the Japanese public." In other words, this point was essentially a matter of domestic policy.

The negotiations among the three European powers—Britain, France, and Italy—ultimately fell through. France and Italy adhered to the London Treaty in three respects only: (1) the agreement on capital ships and aircraft carriers; (2) the agreement on the replacement of auxiliary vessels and the limitation of submarine types; (3) the agreement limiting the use of submarines. Thus only Japan, Britain, and the United States subscribed to a treaty limiting auxiliary ship tonnage. It was provided that if developments between France and Italy required it, the three signatories could increase their tonnage without controverting the basis of the treaty, the so-called "escape clause." The new treaty, officially called the "London Naval Treaty of 1930," was signed at St. James's Palace at 10:30 A.M. on April 22. The closing of the conference was referred to as an adjournment rather than a termination, in order that the door might be kept open for later French and Italian participation. Table 6 shows the treaty's effect on the naval strength of each country.

In addition to promoting international peace and good will, a declared objective of the London Conference was the reduction of the tax burden borne by the people of each country. On April 11 President Hoover issued a statement on the conference that explained this point in the following terms. At the Geneva Conference Britain had asked for an overall strength of 1.5 million tons. To match this the United States would have had to spend from $1.4 billion to $1.64 billion. Under the London agreement Britain's overall tonnage was only 1,136,000 tons a reduction of 364,000 tons from its Geneva demands. Not only had the United States been able to achieve the parity with Britain denied at the Washington Conference, but it had saved $1 billion on what the Geneva tonnage figures would have cost. The savings over the Geneva costs amounted for all three countries to more than $2.5 billion.[97]

Speaking in the House of Commons on May 15, Prime Minister MacDonald announced that under the London Treaty Britain could by 1936 save £54 million on battleships and another £13 million on other categories of vessels.[98]

When Hamaguchi spoke to Okada, Katō, and Yamanashi on April 1, he gave them this view of Japan's fiscal situation:

> If this conference on auxiliary vessels collapses, construction of capital ships will immediately start up. If we had not had this conference, from fiscal 1931 to fiscal 1936 we would have had to spend ¥820 million, of which ¥340 million would be for capital ships and ¥480 million for auxiliary vessels. . . . Let us move on to consider the problem of competitive building. The United States has already obligated itself by law to build 23 heavy cruisers. Since 70 percent of that is 161,000 tons, we would need an additional 52,600 tons. We would have to build 5 new 10,000-ton cruisers, and this would cost about ¥145 million.[99]

Comparing Japan's construction costs until 1936 under the treaty with those entailed by the full implementation of Japan's "three basic principles" yields the following results. Under the treaty ¥328,575,000 was needed if replacement building was moved ahead of schedule to maintain construction capacity; if this was not a consideration, the cost would be ¥106,165,000. To implement the "three basic principles" ¥334,091,300 was needed if replacement building was speeded up, ¥199,916,000 if it were not.[100] However, these figures for the "three basic principles" are purely hypothetical. If Japan had stubbornly insisted upon the "three basic principles," the conference would have broken up and competitive building would have begun. Far greater amounts of construction funds would have been required, and a financial collapse would have been inevitable. If fear of financial disaster had caused the government to hold construction funds down to a safe level, then the ratio vis-a-vis the United States would have become even lower than that established by the London Treaty. If the financial aspects are disregarded and it is assumed that it was possible to achieve the strength called for by the "three basic principles," then table 7 shows how Japan's actual tonnage compared with that allowed under the treaty. In heavy cruisers and submarines the treaty tonnage fell below the desired levels, but in light cruisers and destroyers it exceeded desired levels. From a technical naval standpoint there may have been some diminution in combat capacity. Nevertheless, to have immediately decided this constituted a national defense crisis would seem to be a display of great oversensitivity.

The American Senate Foreign Relations Committee began its treaty hearings on May 12. The admirals and the "big navy" proponents in the Senate were intensely dissatisfied with the treaty. Above all they vigorously attacked the heavy cruiser concession and the acceptance of a 70-percent ratio for Japan. Appearing before the Foreign Relations Committee on the 15th, Rear Admiral Hilary Jones scathingly denounced the treaty. He expressed his firm belief that, given the current situation of American naval bases and territories, a 60-percent ratio actually gave Japan the equivalent of a 70-percent-plus ratio. The next day Rear Admiral Mark Bristol told the committee the treaty did not give parity with Britain. He criticized the failure to attain a 5:3 ratio with Japan and insisted that 21 heavy cruisers were the minimum American requirement. That same day Jones was explaining in great detail to the Naval Affairs Committee why America's geographical position vis-à-vis the Orient necessitated 8-in.-gun cruisers. On May 20 Rear Admiral Jehu Valentine Chase expressed to the Foreign Relations Committee his disapproval of the failure to have amended in the slightest way the Washington Conference's disadvantageous fortification agreement. Since that agreement was retained, there was, he claimed, no justification for raising the Japanese ratio. Only Admiral William V. Pratt expressed satisfaction with the treaty for reasons of international friendship and naval efficiency and costs.[101]

Meanwhile, on May 13 Stimson had explained to the Foreign Relations Committee that the treaty gave the United States parity with Britain in every category. Moreover, with the exception of capital ships there had been a reduction in tonnage as compared with the Geneva Conference figures. With regard to Japan, he summarized the situation in this way. At the Geneva Conference the United States and Britain had received with good will the Japanese request for a near-70-percent ratio in auxiliary vessels. When the present conference opened, the United States actually had in the water two 8-in.-gun cruisers compared with Japan's eight. In 6-in.-gun cruisers the United States had 70,000 tons compared with Japan's 98,000 tons. Over the six-year life of the treaty the United States was to be allowed to raise its strength to fifteen 8-in.-gun cruisers in the water and on top of that was to be permitted to bring near to completion another three 8-in.-gun cruisers. During this same period Japan would hold itself to the twelve 8-in.-gun cruisers it already had in the water or abuilding when the conference began. In 6-in.-gun cruisers the United States was authorized to expand its present 70,000 tons to 143,000 tons while Japan would add only 2,000 tons. (See table 8 for the tonnages allowed Japan in comparison with its original demands and the tonnages allowed the United States.)

In Japan there was, Stimson told the committee, a very active campaign by the "big navy" party. The Navy General Staff had the right of direct access to the emperor and was not subordinate constitutionally to the cabinet. At the conference the Japanese delegation and the Japanese government had therefore faced a harder problem than any other nation. For this reason the entire American delegation came away from the conference with a greater admiration than ever before for the Japanese delegation and the Japanese government. Stimson concluded his remarks by saying:

> A government that had the courage to go into a treaty tying itself to stand still while another built past it and put itself into a far better position in case the treaty should not be continued after 1936, has a very hard problem, and no amount of argument could minimize that problem. No country is so poor that it cannot be frightened into competitive building. I take my hat off to the Japanese Government in this treaty.[102]

In Japan the treaty's opponents deliberately twisted Stimson's tribute into a sneer at the Japanese government and found in it excellent ammunition with which to attack the treaty. Thus there arose the "I take my hat off" problem. Of course, if the whole speech had been read through and not just these few words picked out of context, Stimson's remark could not possibly have been interpreted as a sneer at the Japanese government. Also, it ought to have been taken into consideration that his speech was designed to deal with the situation in the American Senate.

In a radio broadcast on June 12 Stimson pointed out that in all three countries there was opposition from the extremists among the military but that ordinary public opinion supported the treaty overwhelmingly. In each country, he said, the treaty opponents claimed their country was placed at a disadvantage. This was proof enough that the treaty was fair to all three countries.[103]

On July 21 the Senate finally approved the treaty by a vote of 59 to 9. A *New York Times* editorial on the 23rd commented that no country had won a diplomatic victory at the London Naval Conference.[104] This is probably a reasonable evaluation.

Even in Britain the navy gave strong opposition to the treaty. The reduction from 70 cruisers to 50 came under especially severe criticism in both houses of parliament on the grounds that it lowered naval strength below the minimum required for the defense and safety of the British empire. William C. Bridgeman, the former First Lord of the Admiralty, as well as Admirals David Beatty and Earl John R. Jellicoe, were among the critics. Winston Churchill also rose to attack the treaty. It gave, he charged, merely paper equality with the United States. In actual combat strength Britain had fallen to second place when one took into account the reduction in the cruisers so necessary to protect British trade routes in wartime and the fact that the United States would now possess a large number of new vessels.

On June 2 MacDonald argued in the House of Commons that the treaty was clearly fair to all three countries in spite of the expressions of discontent on the part of bigots in each country. First Lord of the Admiralty Albert Victor Alexander also stated that it was the unanimous opinion of the Admiralty that the treaty could be expected to place the defense of the nation on a secure foundation. That same day the Conservative Party introduced a motion in the Commons for the appointment of a special eleven-man committee to consider the treaty, but the motion failed by a vote of 201 to 282.[105]

On April 23 the editorial pages of the British press had uniformly rejoiced at the signing of the London Naval Treaty. The London *Times* was representative of the tone of the press when it said that the conference marked an important stage on the road to arms reduction even though it was regrettable that a full five-power agreement had not been possible.[106]

What attitudes toward the treaty were displayed by the Japanese public? Here we will confine ourselves to describing briefly the press comment and the opinions of right wing organizations. The discussions in the Diet and the Privy Council will be taken up later.

At the beginning of the London Conference all the Japanese newspapers expatiated on the reasonable nature of Japan's "three basic principles" and called on the United States to reconsider its position. But it is worth noting that in the midst of this the *Ōsaka Asahi shimbun* stated that it was necessary to be wary of attaching importance only to the opinions of the naval men. National defense plans were very dangerous, the newspaper explained, when drawn up only by technical experts who made one single country the hypothetical enemy and did not give the slightest thought to the problem of the neutrality of other powers.[107]

After the arrival of the delegates' request for instructions, the press divided into two groups. One group argued that some agreement or other ought to be concluded on the basis of the plan sent home by the delegates. The other insisted that Japan must persist in its demands without the slightest compromise to the bitter end. This group also believed the breakup of the conference was inevitable.

The majority of the larger newspapers tended to be in the first group. The *Ōsaka Asahi* said it was essential to avoid the rupture of this conference over which everyone had taken so much trouble; it expressed the hope that Hamaguchi would on this occasion formulate his return instructions in terms of the overall situation.[108] The *Jiji shimpō* argued that in general Japan's demands had been accepted, since an overall 70-percent ratio was secured and there would be a 70-percent ratio in cruisers until 1936.[109] The *Ōsaka Asahi* further said that armaments and diplomacy were the two wheels of the chariot of national defense and that it was very dangerous for the military to control foreign policy.[110] But while the *Ōsaka Asahi* and the *Jiji shimpō* exhibited an affirmative attitude, the *Tōkyō Nichi nichi* and the *Ōsaka Mainichi* had doubts about the compromise plan.[111]

After the return instructions had been sent, the more influential newspapers commented favorably on the government's action, although they varied in the degree of their support. The *Jiji shimpō* said it believed the general public would approve the conciliatory spirit in which Japan had cooperated to bring about an agreement.[112] The *Ōsaka Asahi* argued that the answer given the United States and Britain was a true expression of the real opinion of the Japanese people; that Japan's acceptance of the compromise plan was in no sense a servile capitulation; that the concessions were more than compensated for by the good impression given the American and British peoples; that, moreover, the action of the Japanese government made very good sense when one considered how great would be the benefits of reducing the tax burden of the people.[113] This atmosphere is reflected in a telegram sent to the delegates on April 2 by Nagai Ryūtarō, the parliamentary vice minister for foreign affairs: "Sensible people in accord with you. Issue already settled. Unbearably moved by and appreciative of each delegate's hard work."[114]

In contrast, ultranationalist groups had been calling all along for the full attainment of the "three basic principles": such groups as the Yūshū-kai (headed by Admiral Arima Ryōkitsu), Yōyōkai (Admiral Tochinai Sojirō, president), Kaikōkai (Admiral Ōi Shigemoto, president), Gunshuku Kokumin Dōshikai (People's League on the Disarmament Question, led by Tōyama Mitsuru), Kokuryūkai (Amur River Society), Seikyōsha (Society for Political Education), Kenkokukai (National Founding Society), Aikokusha (Patriotic Society), Kōkoku Gikai (Righteous Society for Reviving the Nation), and Gakusei Kōkoku Remmei (Students League for Reviving the Nation). After the delegates telegraphed for instructions, the activities of these groups became even more intense. Not one concession must be made, they cried, even if it should mean the breakup of the conference. They distributed printed materials and delivered lectures in various parts of the country. Claiming to speak for prefectural or national "people's rallies," they telegraphed or sometimes directly handed to the government authorities previously prepared resolutions of fiery protest.

For example, the directors of the Gunshuku Kokumin Dōshikai met on March 25 and issued the following statement, which they sent to Shidehara: "If our original minimum demands are not accepted, we must proclaim at home and abroad the justice of our position and immediately withdraw from the conference."[115] On the 27th the Kōkoku Gikai sent this petition to Shidehara: "We demand that the Japanese government firmly reject the fraudulent American compromise and that the Japanese government boldly fulfill our people's commitment to the 70-percent heavy cruiser ratio."[116]

On March 27 all the newspapers carried a pronouncement from the Seiyūkai, in the form of an interview with Mori Kaku, the party's secretary general: "We must adamantly reject a compromise that makes us feel our national defense is threatened. Even if it should mean the collapse of the conference, we must be strong in our resolve to secure our minimum national defense requirements."[117]

After the government had decided upon its return instructions, the Gunshuku Kokumin Dōshikai held a rally in Shiba Park on April 3, when the following declaration and resolution were passed and sent to Wakatsuki and to the chief American and British delegates.

Declaration
The return instructions are an abject surrender to the American plan. They thoughtlessly abandon our three basic demands and sacrifice the safety of our national defense.

Resolution
The Japanese people absolutely oppose the return instructions and believe these instructions endanger our national defense.[118]

In the midst of this agitation, no voices were raised in support of the return instructions, and it might have been thought that the whole country was solidly opposed to the London Treaty. The real feelings of the people were revealed, however, when Wakatsuki and Takarabe returned to Japan and were met with unprecedentedly tumultuous receptions. Under the violently agitated surface eddies was the deep, slow current of true public opinion.

The Right of Military Command Controversy

In the debate over the formulation of the return instructions, the point emphasized by the government's opponents, including the military, had been that the strength allowed Japan under the compromise plan was not sufficient for the nation's defense. Nothing at all had been heard about the right of military command. In his April 2 report to the emperor, for example, Katō had confined himself to saying that careful consideration was required since "the American plan included provisions that, it was feared, would create serious disadvantages for the navy's operations." Even the navy's "big two," Admiral Tōgō and Prince Fushimi, had stated that the government's decision must be followed once it was made.

The right of military command controversy arose suddenly after the 58th Diet session was opened on April 21. Katō again abruptly changed his position and began to assert that the government's decision had infringed upon the right of military command. Overnight the right of military command became a major political issue.

The right of military command was unquestionably the cancer of Japanese constitutional government, and the need to resolve this problem had long been recognized. Nevertheless, right down into the Taishō and Shōwa periods it had been handled in an indecisive way because of political considerations. The problem originated in an interpretation of Articles 11 and 12 of the Meiji Constitution, which established a dual structure of "state affairs" (kokumu) and "military command" (tōsui). By this interpretation Article 11 placed the command of the army and navy outside the area in which ministers of state were to advise the emperor. Here "command" is to be interpreted as the operational direction of military units. The reasoning behind this arrangement is rooted in the special functional requirements of military units. Article 12 assigned to the imperial prerogative the determination of the organization and peacetime standing of the military forces, but this power was considered to be an item of state affairs. Military organization is related in numerous ways to military command, and therefore Article 12 became a point of contention between those responsible for state affairs and those responsible for military command. The military adopted the broadest interpretation of military command and expanded the concept to include Article 12.[119] As indicated previously, the determination both of national defense policy and of the military strength required for national defense was actually made by the military command agencies. This fact undeniably added weight to the interpretation holding that military strength was to be determined by the military.

The military repeatedly overthrew or sometimes aborted cabinets by means either of national defense policy or of the requirement that army and navy ministers be military officers on active service. Because of such experiences, the cabinet of Yamamoto Gonnohyōe in June 1913 abolished the rule that the army and navy ministers had to be military officers on active service. To prevent the infiltration of party men the army responded to this change with an agreement between the Army Ministry and the Army General Staff that restricted the personnel assignment authority of the army minister. It was arranged that assignments of general officers would be decided jointly by the army minister, the army chief of staff, and the inspector-general of military education, i.e., the army "big three." As the influence of the political parties increased, the beleaguered military sought in the right of military command a weapon with which to counter the offensive of the political parties.

When Navy Minister Katō Tomosaburō left Japan to attend the Washington Conference, Prime Minister Hara Takashi sought, with the consent of the navy, to become acting navy minister. This action was opposed by the army, which feared that the appointment of a civilian prime minister as acting navy minister would be the first step toward appointing civilians as army and navy ministers. Ultimately, following the mediation of the former army minister Tanaka Giichi, Army Minister Yamanashi Hanzō consented to the arrangement, but only after a memorandum was drawn up saying, "The prime minister . . . has no intention of venturing to disregard the army minister's view and opinion by trying to apply to the army the navy's interpretation of this matter."[120]

On January 31, 1922, after the fall of the Hara cabinet, Egi Tasuku, a member of the Kenseikai, raised a question in the House of Peers about the responsibility of ministers of state under Articles 11 and 12. The premise of his question was that the organization of the army and navy was legitimately a matter of state affairs and that logically ministers of state were responsible for advising the emperor in this regard. As acting navy minister, Prime Minister Takahashi Korekiyo must, Egi said, be regarded as acting for the navy minister in connection with matters not only of naval administration (*gunsei*) but also of naval command (*gunrei*). Therefore was it intended, Egi asked, to transfer to ministers of state responsibility for the determination of the army's and navy's organization and peacetime standing or for state affairs related to military command? Did the army too, he wanted to know, accept the idea of an acting minister?

Prime Minister Takahashi evasively replied, "I think I would like to avoid making a statement here and now about the propriety of transferring to the responsibility of ministers of state all state affairs related to military command." Army Minister Yamanashi responded:

> There are points of difference in the way the army and the navy conduct their business. On this occasion it has been convenient for the navy to have an acting minister during the absence of the navy minister. However, the allocation of responsibility is different in the army, and some matters related to military command (*gunrei*) must be carried out mainly by the army minister. The army minister directly advises the emperor with regard to such matters and then carries them out. Consequently, though it may be possible for the navy conveniently to use a civilian as acting minister, I think it is impossible for the army to do so.

When Egi went on to ask why the army was different, Takahashi replied in the following not entirely precise terms:

> In the case of the Navy General Staff, the navy chief of staff reports directly to the emperor. With the army all that is done through the army minister. It's in this way I think there is a difference. However, as a temporary measure it is allowable under Article 9 of the Cabinet Regulations for another minister of state to be ordered temporarily to act as a substitute when it is impossible for the navy minister to discharge his functions. The qualifications for appointment as navy minister are another matter.[121]

In 1925 during the 50th Diet session Hanai Takuzō asked in the House of Peers about the relation between the right of military command embodied in Article 11 and the right of military organization embodied in Article 12. On March 22 the Katō cabinet's Legislative Bureau chief Tsukamoto Seiji gave this answer:

> The government believes the right of military command embodied in Article 11 is outside the area of responsibility to advise the emperor placed by Article 55 on each minister of state. There are, indeed, some matters related to military command that are closely connected with matters for which ministers of state do bear the responsibility to advise the emperor. Insofar as such matters are connected with state affairs, ministers of state participate in planning them and bear responsibility for advising the emperor with respect to them.
> The right of military command embodied in Article 11 is the so-called right of direct access to the emperor, and it is interpreted as not includ-

ing the powers embodied in Article 12. Of course, the powers embodied in Article 12 are closely connected with the powers embodied in Article 11. Consequently, the exercise of the powers in Article 12 is contingent upon the operation of the right of military command embodied in Article 11.[122]

Thus, questions were raised about the right of military command. However, Seiyūkai and Kenseikai cabinets alike, in short the political party forces, feared to irritate the military. They therefore proceeded stealthily and avoided making any clear intepretation of the constitution. Under the Hamaguchi cabinet this problem suddenly became the crucial point of contention in the London Treaty controversy, and the issue masked a plot to overthrow the cabinet. An inescapable showdown was forced on the political parties.

The facts of the situation show not the slightest basis for the controversy over the infringement of the right of military command that sprang up in connection with the London Treaty. The issue was raised by the Seiyūkai as a device for overthrowing the cabinet and was used to attack the government in the Diet. The newspapers reported these attacks in the most sensational manner and thereby sparked an explosion of discontent from the military. Right wing groups immediately joined in, and among the public there was created a mood of doubt about whether the right of military command had not in fact been infringed.

In the domestic background of this controversy was political party corruption and a serious economic depression; in the international background was the impasse in Manchuria and Mongolia. The agitation implanted among the military an acute sense of crisis and led them to repudiate party government. The seeds were sown for many ominous later incidents, and the dispute exerted an incalculably important influence on the course taken by Japan in both domestic politics and international relations.

The direct cause of the controversy was probably the Seiyūkai policy of sticking at nothing in its efforts to pull down the cabinet. However, as already pointed out, from a legal point of view the controversy arose out of the interpretation given Articles 11 and 12 of the Meiji Constitution. Let us therefore now examine the opinions of the government and the military on the subject of who had the power to determine military strength.

The Hamaguchi cabinet held that determining the military strength required for national defense was a matter on which the emperor was advised by the cabinet. The theoretical bases for the cabinet's position were the constitutional doctrines of Minobe Tatsukichi, professor of constitutional law at Tokyo Imperial University.[123] It was Minobe's opinion that "the Navy General Staff is part of the emperor's military establishment and by planning assists him in the exercise of his prerogative. It is sufficient if the government simply treats the Navy General Staff's opinion as one of the important materials to be used in reaching a decision. The Navy General Staff has not the slightest legal right to decide the matter."[124]

In the Tokyo Imperial University newspaper (*Teikoko Daigaku shimbun*) of April 21 Minobe published an article entitled "The Naval Treaty Negotiations and the Military's Right of Direct Access: A Criticism of the Military's *Ultra Vires* Action."[125] In it he developed his argument along the following lines. The right to command the military forces must be distinguished from the right to organize the military forces. "The determination of the army's and navy's organization, especially the decision about what their general strength should be, is a matter that is intimately related to the country's foreign policy and finances. It falls, of course, into the political category, and the cabinet alone should bear the responsibility for advising the emperor with regard to it. It is not a matter that should be determined by the exercise of the prerogative of military command." According to Minobe, the right to command the military forces is the right to direct the activities of the military forces; the right to organize the military forces is the right to establish the military forces, and the military forces are established by the nation. Thus, while he accepted that the activities of the military forces established by the nation should be controlled by their own internal organization with no participation therein of the nation, the establishment of the military forces in itself was an act of the nation and a matter for which the cabinet alone had the responsibility of advising the emperor.

"Even if," Minobe argued, "the cabinet had opposed the opinion of the military in the London Treaty matter and advised the emperor to approve acceptance of the compromise plan, this action would not have infringed the ordinances regulating governmental structure, let alone have violated the constitution." The function of the Navy General Staff or the Supreme War Council was to make national defense plans strictly for the military alone. "For the nation these plans are only one among many materials to be used in arriving at a decision." The degree to which these plans should be adopted as the will of the nation was something to be studied from the standpoint of foreign policy, finance, and other state matters. And it was the official responsibility exclusively of the cabinet.

The cabinet would, of course, have the greatest respect for the opinions of the technical experts, Minobe continued, but it would never be unconditionally bound by them. "The function of advising the emperor with regard to the organization of the military forces, i.e., national defense, is the cabinet's alone. It is not the joint responsibility of the cabinet and the Navy General Staff, and it is most definitely not the exclusive responsibility of the Navy General Staff." Once a treaty was signed, it had no connection with the prerogative of military command. The Privy Council alone had the duty to answer an imperial query for advice on ratification. Therefore, the Navy General Staff acted *ultra vires* when in connection with the ratification of the London Treaty it requested the emperor to ask for the opinion of the Supreme War Council.

Minobe used the same line of reasoning in a series of articles entitled "The Naval Treaty Negotiations and the Right of Military Command," published by the *Tōkyō Asahi* and the *Ōsaka Asahi* early in May.[126] Another professor of constitutional law, Sasaki Sōichi of Kyoto Imperial University, wrote a series of articles for the *Ōsaka Mainichi* called "The Controversial Right of Military Command: The Government and the Determination of Military Strength." Sasaki argued that in the present matter the government was not bound by the Navy General Staff's opinion and had not infringed the right of military command when it made a decision about the navy's strength.[127]

Despite this support from the scholars, Hamaguchi's approach remained cautious. "From the standpoint of the emotions of the military," he remarked, "it isn't a very good idea to declare one's opinions as candidly as Professor Minobe does. Since this matter has bearing on the army, I will try to avoid hardening the atmosphere and will simply say that the opinions of the military were adequately considered."[128]

The Navy Ministry and the Navy General Staff took different views on the controversy over the right of military command. In the navy the authority of the chief of staff had from the first not been as great as that of the army chief of staff. Even when the navy chief of staff advised the emperor on a matter coming under the Article 11 right of military command, he invariably secured the prior approval of the navy minister. After such matters had been sanctioned by the emperor, it was customary to entrust their implementation to the navy minister. Insofar as he thought their implementation to be reasonable and practicable, the navy minister approved the plans of the navy chief of staff. In addition, matters subsumed under the Article 12 right of military organization were, as a rule, handled in all respects as a responsibility of the navy minister, and to the greatest possible degree these matters were treated in accordance with the usages of ordinary political administration.[129]

At the time of the London Treaty it was the opinion of officials in the Navy Ministry that there was not the slightest impropriety in the way the government dealt with the matter. The Navy Ministry, whose function it was to represent the overall navy position, had carefully listened to the technical opinion of the Navy General Staff with regard to the military strength required by national defense strategy. They had incorporated this opinion into their negotiations with the government. Since it had proved difficult to gain acceptance of Plan One, the Navy Ministry had put forward Plan Two as the second best policy. The Navy General Staff had not only not raised any objection to this second plan but had actually on its own initiative expressed approval of the plan. The government had accepted Plan Two as the solution to the problem.

The government's return instructions also had not been forced through without consultation with the navy chief of staff. The instructions had been worked out in his presence and with his participation. Moreover, he had not raised the slightest objection to them. This was the way those in the Navy Ministry understood what had happened, and this was the correct version of the events.

The Navy General Staff, on the other hand, interpreted the Article 12 right of military organization to be a matter for the joint advice of the cabinet and the military command agencies. It claimed that the consent of the navy chief of staff was necessary to the decision on the return instructions and charged that the cabinet had disregarded the Navy General Staff and determined the matter on its own authority alone. This procedure, the Navy General Staff held, infringed the right of military command. In a meeting on May 28 Katō sought Takarabe's approval for the following memorandum:

> Military strength and organization, which are subsumed under the imperial prerogative embodied in Article 12 of the constitution, are mat-

ters for joint advice by the navy minister (army minister) (and through him in turn the cabinet) and by the navy chief of staff (army chief of staff) and are not matters that can be decided unilaterally.[130]

In his June 10 address to the emperor, Katō expressed this concept as follows:

> The prerogative embodied in Article 12 is related to that embodied in Article 11. It is always contingent upon the operation of the right of military command, and it is not permitted in the slightest degree to function independently. In this present matter of the return instructions to the London Conference delegates, a person with the duty of advising Your Majesty in State affairs, a person prejudiced in favor of his own policy, has unilaterally advised Your Majesty on the important question of changing the peacetime standing of the military forces without consulting those responsible for military planning. Behavior of this kind obstructs the exercise of Your Majesty's prerogative of military command as commander-in-chief. It undermines the very basis of military operations and opens the way for national defense policy to become the constant plaything of the vagaries of political change. The command of the military forces will be reduced to utter confusion. There truly can be no greater peril for the nation than this.[131]

When it handed over to the Navy Ministry on July 22 the "Materials Related to Events at the Time of the Issuance of the Government's Decision on the Return Instructions," the Navy General Staff explained the point as follows: Matters covered by Article 12 were not purely matters of military administration (*gunsei*) but included also matters of military command (*tōsui*). The determination of the organization and peacetime standing of the army and navy could not be separated from strategic requirements. In his *Commentaries on the Constitution of the Empire of Japan* Prince Itō had remarked, "Although it can be said that this right is exercised with the advice of the responsible ministers, yet it belongs to the prerogative of the emperor in the same way as does the right of military command, and there should be no interference in it by the Diet." Prince Itō meant, according to the Navy General Staff, that matters covered by Article 12 "cannot be said to be reserved exclusively to the advice of the responsible ministers. They are, on the contrary, intimately related to the Article 11 right of military command and must involve advice from the military command agencies." If one looked at actual practice, continued the memorandum, the Navy General Staff and the Army

General Staff worked out the level of forces required by national defense policy, and the cabinet was allowed simply to look over the document. In the present controversy the real issue was that there had not been a consensus of views between the navy chief of staff and the cabinet and that "despite the clearly expressed opposition of the navy chief of staff the prime minister had in the end proceeded to issue return instructions whose content had not been approved by the navy chief of staff."[132]

It must be remembered that the opinions expressed in the July 22 document were opinions formed after the return instructions had been decided upon. From the previously noted March 26 document entitled "The Navy's Future Policy" it can be inferred that the Navy General Staff had no such opinions at the time the return instructions were being formulated. Moreover, in May 1929 Katō had expressed the following view to the leaders of both the Navy Ministry and the Navy General Staff:

> In today's circumstances it is quite difficult for national defense problems to be settled by the military alone. . . . I think it is absolutely impossible to achieve a true national defense unless the nation has first been allowed to determine the goals of naval armament and the navy has then been ordered to carry out these goals.[133]

In its interpretation of Articles 11 and 12 the view of the army was identical to that of the Navy General Staff.

On April 22, for the purpose of coordinating responses to the questions expected in the coming Diet session, Chief Cabinet Secretary Suzuki Fujiya met at the prime minister's official residence with the vice ministers, parliamentary councillors, and appropriate bureau chiefs of the Army, Navy, and Foreign ministries. There the Navy Ministry laid out its position. The decision on the strength agreed to in the London Treaty was a matter falling under the Article 12 organization and peacetime standing of the military forces; it did not infringe the right of military command dealt with in Article 11. Consequently, it was inappropriate to discuss the decision in terms of an infringement of the right of military command. The prerogative embodied in Article 12 involved the overall structure of military armament, in other words, matters that would affect the national budget. Thus, it was to be distinguished from the right of military command, which involved the internal organization of the military forces, matters unconnected with the budget.

In contrast to the view expressed by the Navy Ministry, the Army Ministry believed the right of military command had clearly been infringed. The government, it argued, had pushed aside the Navy General Staff's claim that the American plan made it difficult, from a strategic standpoint, to ensure the safety of the national defense. The government had acted on its own and decided the issue at a cabinet meeting from which both the army minister and the navy minister were absent. If the government were able in this manner to decide national defense plans at its own discretion, the future would hold grave problems for the national defense, and the effects would not be limited to the navy alone.[134] The attitude of the Army Ministry was a reflection of the fact that in many respects the Army Ministry was dominated by the Army General Staff. The truth of the matter is that the Army General Staff was strongly opposed to the Japanese-American compromise plan and had offered its support to the Navy General Staff. In particular, the Army Generals Staff's opposition was stiffened by what it interpreted as a disregard of the military in the April 1 decision on the return instructions, and it was apprehensive of the consequences this act might have for the land disarmament question.

When Minobe's article appeared in the Tokyo Imperial University newspaper, the Army General Staff asked the Navy General Staff for its opinion of Minobe's position. Up to that point the Navy General Staff had considered the issue solely a navy problem and had turned aside the Army General Staff's previous offers of assistance. Now its attitude changed and it formed a united front with the Army General Staff. On April 25 Katō got together with Army Chief of Staff Kanaya Hanzō, and the two agreed they must take strong cooperative action. Hata Shunroku, chief of the Army General Staff's Operations Division, visited his naval counterpart Katō Takayoshi and worked out with him a common approach on the right of military command controversy.[135]

The government insisted it had the right to determine military strength where a treaty was involved. But in consideration of its delicate relations with the military, it adopted three guidelines for answering questions in the Diet:

1. The opinion of the military had been given respectful consideration.
2. The government bore the responsibility for national defense insofar as the Diet was concerned.

3. There was no necessity to respond to constitutional arguments or to questions about the internal decision-making processes used in connection with the return instructions.[136]

In all probability an arrangement along these lines was arrived at between the government and the Army Ministry.

On May 1 Sugiyama Gen, the chief of the Military Affairs Bureau, reported to Ninomiya Harushige, chief of the Army General Staff's General Affairs Division, that, as a result of the entreaties of the Navy Ministry and the Legislative Drafting Bureau, the Army Ministry would not disclose its own view but would cooperate with the prime minister on the matter of his Diet answers regarding the right of military command controversy. However, if in the House of Peers or elsewhere the prime minister expounded the reasoning by which he justified his actions, the Army Ministry was firmly resolved to proclaim its own position on the question. In view of this intention on the part of the Army Ministry, Sugiyama requested Ninomiya to arrange that the Army General Staff make no moves in the matter. Nevertheless, the discontent felt among the members of the Army General Staff did not disappear. They saw no reason why they and the Army Ministry should join with the political parties to commit double suicide over the right of military command controversy.[137]

On April 2, the day after the decision on the return instructions, Seiyūkai Secretary General Mori Kaku, after consulting with Inukai Tsuyoshi, issued this statement:

Properly speaking, national defense must not be looked upon as an ordinary affair of state. Within the navy the Navy General Staff is the agency responsible for directly advising the emperor with regard to national defense. Within the army it is the Army General Staff. This can be acknowledged by everyone. The situation is this: ministers of state who have no direct responsibility have imprudently decided an important national defense matter in knowing disregard of the strong opposition of the Navy General Staff, which does have direct responsibility. It must be recognized that this action entails a fearful political responsibility both as regards the present and as regards the future.[138]

In Mori's statement appears the first glimmer of the charge that the right of military command has been infringed. Of course, the groundwork had been laid in Suetsugu's April 21 memorandum to Yamanashi, which declared that the Navy General Staff could not agree to the treaty proposals. This can be inferred from the fact that the next day, just one day before the treaty was to be signed, Katō stressed the document's significance by insisting on forwarding it to the Navy Ministry despite Okada's request for its withdrawal.

Authentic historical materials are available by which it can be determined when and to what extent the Seiyūkai connived with the Navy General Staff. Mori thought that if American influence were not driven from China, it would be absolutely impossible for Japan to become paramount in that country. In his view a 70-percent ratio vis-a-vis the United States was absolutely essential in order to secure Manchuria and Mongolia. To prevent the conclusion of the London Treaty, Mori set to work chiefly on Army Minister Ugaki and members of the Navy General Staff. He also maneuvered by means of public rallies to block the treaty and overthrow the cabinet. Kuhara Fusanosuke, Uchida Shinya, and others who accepted Mori's ideas sought to influence the Privy Council.[139] Okada recorded that Yamamoto Jōtarō, Kuhara Fusanosuke, Suzuki Kisaburō, and other Seiyūkai leaders visited him in May and June and tried every conceivable means to get him to have the navy say the national defense was unsafe. The fact that Mori had foreknowledge of Katō's June 10 address to the emperor is clear evidence that the Seiyūkai was behind the Navy General Staff's sudden change of position.[140] In later years Takarabe himself answered a friend's query about the controversy with the remark, "That was mischief-making committed by the Seiyūkai."[141]

The 58th Diet was convened on April 21, the day before the treaty was to be signed. The opening ceremonies took place on April 23, and the session ended on May 14. The strength of the political parties in the lower house was: Minseitō 271, Seiyūkai 173, Kokumin Dōshikai 6, Kakushin Kurabu 3, Shakai Minshūtō 2, Taishūtō 2, Rōnōtō 1, independents 7. The Hamaguchi cabinet controlled an absolute majority. For the first time since it had come to power, the cabinet had an opportunity, in this Diet, to lay its principles and policies before the people.

After Hamaguchi had delivered his policy statement, Shidehara took the rostrum. He expressed pleasure that through the mutual concessions and friendly cooperation of the powers concerned the London Naval Treaty had been signed. He emphasized that the treaty's effects would not be limited to the material realm alone but that its moral influence would also be important. Among his remarks he said:

The total auxiliary vessel tonnage allotted to Japan under the treaty is about 50,000 tons less than we have at present. Nevertheless, both in 8-in.-gun heavy cruisers and in overall auxiliary vessels the tonnage we will actually have at the time of the 1935 conference will be almost identical with the tonnage we originally asked. Only in submarines has the tonnage been reduced sharply below what we had claimed. However, in that category we have maintained perfect parity with the United States and Britain, both of whom abandoned their original demand for the abolition of the submarine. Because of this treaty we will be able to economize on our military expenditures, and yet for at least the life of the treaty the security of our national defense is, I believe, completely assured. . . . The government considered fully the opinions of the naval technical experts and with firm faith took the resolve to join in the present treaty.

The world situation is constantly changing. The naval equipment on which we place special emphasis this year may not necessarily have the same value next year. Also, it may even be that what today seems not very necessary can some day be absolutely indispensable. Therefore we must reserve the freedom to present at the 1935 conference whatever claims are appropriate to the world situation existing at that time. That freedom is expressly acknowledged in the treaty's text. There are those who fear that the London Treaty will restrict our actions for eternity, and under this assumption they exhibit an excessively jittery attitude. I am compelled to say that this sort of attitude is not worthy of a self-confident people.

Speculation is reported among the gossips that Japan was coerced into this agreement by pressure from other countries. This is completely at variance with the truth, and I do not consider it worth refuting here in the Diet. We studied the comparative advantages and disadvantages of this treaty not only from the viewpoint of diplomacy but also from the viewpoint of military power, of economic and financial capacity, and of all the other national strengths upon which the national defense must rest. As a result of our study we were decisively persuaded that on this occasion the best policy for Japan was to participate in this treaty.[142]

Shidehara's speech expressed his opinions very logically and unequivocally, but he did not pay sufficient heed to the delicate and complicated atmosphere within the navy. Regrettably, the political sense usually characteristic of Shidehara was lacking in this speech. As was to be expected, Shidehara's remarks were extremely irritating to the Navy General Staff and placed the Navy Ministry leaders in a very awkward position. Katō noted in his diary: "Shidehara's April 25 foreign policy speech vomited irresponsible statements. From all sides there is an uproar of public criticism."[143]

Prince Fushimi summoned Okada on May 3 and told him:

> Shidehara's Diet speech is outrageous. It is absurd for him to say such things as that the government decides military strength. By heaven, is Yamanashi wearing a naval uniform? With the government saying anything it pleases, it is inexcusable for Yamanashi to be its cat's paw. Oughtn't he to resign as vice minister?[144]

The view expressed here is completely at odds with the statements Fushimi was making when the return instructions were being decided. In his diary Katō says that he was called in by Fushimi on May 1 and questioned about the right of military command controversy.[145] This raises the question of whether Fushimi's changed opinion was not simply the result of his having been influenced by Katō's strong views.

An incident that occurred in connection with Shidehara's speech illustrates the formalism so typical of the man. On the day before the speech was given, Hamaguchi, Shidehara, Yoshida Shigeru, Yamanashi, Hori, and others met at the prime minister's official residence for an article-by-article review of the London Treaty. After Hamaguchi left the meeting, Shidehara read the draft of the speech he was to deliver next day in the Diet. At Hori's suggestion he amended one or two phrases that seemed inexpedient. The Foreign Ministry representatives present thought this meant the speech had been approved by the Navy Ministry. The Navy Ministry people present, however, had no idea that their approval was being sought at that time and believed they would later be given an opportunity to read the document carefully. Next day when Yamanashi heard the speech being delivered to the House of Peers in this same version, he was greatly astonished. He explained to the Foreign Ministry that such a speech would not calm feelings within the navy, and he proposed that Shidehara revise it before he spoke to the House of Representatives. The Foreign Ministry representatives said they would exercise care in the future, but the text could not be changed for the lower house once it had been delivered in the House of Peers. Thus exactly the same speech was made to the House of Representatives.[146]

In the "Materials Related to Events at the Time of the Issuance of the Government's Decision on the Return Instructions" there is also an expression of indignation at Shidehara's speech:

> In matters that should first be judged with accuracy by the naval experts, the prime minister and the foreign minister have imposed a mistaken judgment that is in complete contradiction to the findings and opinions of the naval experts. Having done this, they then declare that the

national defense is safe. Such actions clearly disregard the legitimate authority of the Navy General Staff. These actions are *ultra vires* and must be recognized as an infringement of the right of military command.[147]

On April 26 Hamaguchi invited Yamanashi to his official residence and assured him that in future Diet answers he intended to mollify the discontent within the navy.[148]

When Inukai, speaking for the Seiyūkai, rose in the Diet to question Hamaguchi and Shidehara on their speeches, he charged that it was most doubtful that the safety of the national defense could be assured by the naval strength allotted to Japan under the American plan:

> The prime minister and the foreign minister have said the national defense is safe with this naval strength, but subsequent to the dispatch of the return instructions a statement was made by the navy chief of staff, the officer who bears the responsibility for the handling of the naval forces. In that statement, which was given out to the public, . . . he declared . . . that no matter what measures were taken, national defense was impossible with the naval strength allowed under the treaty. Now, the prime minister has said that he made his decision from the viewpoint of various factors such as politics, economics, etc., but . . . the national defense is impossible with that naval strength, says the Navy General Staff, which bears the complete responsibility for the handling of the naval forces. What is the truth? Has the Navy General Staff circulated this statement in order to mislead the public? This I will never believe. . . . The minister of state has said that he gave full consideration to the opinions of the naval experts. But if you say the opinions of the naval experts, surely the very heart of those opinions must be the Navy General Staff. And the Navy General Staff has issued a statement that it is absolutely opposed to the treaty. In such circumstances the people cannot rest easy.[149]

To this Hamaguchi replied:

> The government bears the responsibility for national defense insofar as the Diet is concerned. I assume the responsibility of asserting that Japan's national defense is very secure with the naval strength allotted under the present treaty.[150]

The second Seiyūkai blast against the treaty was fired by former Education Minister Hatoyama Ichirō. His denunciation pressed the government hard on the political responsibility it had incurred by determining the return instructions in disregard of the navy chief of staff's opinion:

The handling of naval forces is a technical matter. It should be entrusted to naval experts and left completely to their control. Meddling by outsiders is inexcusable. Since outsiders must not be allowed to meddle in the handling of the military forces, it logically follows that it is sensible to entrust national defense to the military experts and leave the matter entirely to them.

Are the employment of military forces and the making of national defense plans functions coming under the Article 11 right of military command? Since both of these matters are provided for in the Army General Staff Regulations and the Navy General Staff Regulations, they are, of course, indisputably among the functions covered by Article 11. If that is so, then it is truly a bold step for the government to have made a change in national defense plans in opposition to or in disregard of the opinion of the navy chief of staff. The navy chief of staff and the army chief of staff are the two agents who directly advise the emperor with regard to national defense plans. In spite of the existence of agents directly responsible to the emperor for the exercise of the right of military command, an individual has come butting in who is not an agent responsible for advising the emperor in these matters. That individual has overridden the opinions of the responsible agent and has changed the national defense plans. This is perfectly outrageous behavior. I think it is the most risky political adventure of these times.[151]

Hamaguchi dismissed Hatoyama's interpellation out of hand, arguing that Hatoyama's charge against the government was premised on a constitutional argument based on assumed facts:

. . . the government is not the Navy General Staff alone. The technical opinions of the military were fully considered. Therefore it is not a fact that their opinions were disregarded. Since that is not a fact, there is no need to answer a constitutional argument that is based upon an error.[152]

In their questions Inukai and Hatoyama went beyond merely recognizing the military's supremacy over the government. They actually championed the military's supremacy. They deserted their principles as party politicians who had for many years fought the military, urged economy in armament, and advocated disarmament. The arguments they presented were unquestionably suicidal. We have here a perfect instance of the irony of history. The controversy they provoked over the infringement of the right of military command became ultimately the cause of the May 15 incident, which ended simultaneously both the life of Inukai and the existence of party politics.

Inukai's and Hatoyama's behavior was widely condemned in the Japanese press. The *Tōkyō Asahi* scathingly criticized their inconsistency:

> In connection with the London disarmament conference the Seiyūkai has bestowed its approval on the primacy of the Navy General Staff's right to advise the emperor directly. They have denied the cabinet's authority over and responsibility for national defense. It is to be expected that we would hear such opinions in the House of Peers or the Privy Council, but we must say that this is utterly incomprehensible behavior on the part of a political party, which ought to be advocating party government and responsible cabinets. The feeling of weirdness must be redoubled when these things are heard from the mouth of Mr. Inukai, who has a history of battling the military in order to establish party government; and from the mouth of Mr. Hatoyama, who should have custody of the Seiyūkai's future. Mr. Hatoyama has questioned the government's political responsibility for having reached a decision on national defense plans in opposition to the navy chief of staff's opinion. The ground for his accusation is that decisions on armament levels should be entrusted to the military and not meddled in by outsiders. We think it strange that a party politician does not understand the meaning of constitutional government.[153]

A *Hōchi shimbun* editorial also denounced the Seiyūkai position as being "plainly logical suicide with regard to the advocacy of party cabinets and the principle of responsible cabinets."[154] On May 1 the *Tōkyō Asahi* again attacked the inconsistencies in the Seiyūkai's attitude. It pointed out that, as president of the Kokumintō, Inukai had preached disarmament and introduced in the Diet a resolution advocating changes in the administrative regulations that would permit civilian army and navy ministers. Merely for the sake of snatching political power, the newspaper commented, "it is an act of exceptionally shortsighted foolishness to betray past positions and to raise to greater heights those obvious barriers that will confront them on future occasions when they themselves are in power."[155] A *Tōkyō Nichi-nichi* editorial scolded Inukai and Hatoyama "for extraordinarily fallacious arguments."[156] The *Jiji shimpō* characterized the Seiyūkai position as "shameless to a fault" and in a sharp comment pitied "the frivolity and stupidity of these men who in a desperate search for a political weapon will today serve the army but who tomorrow will be complaining that they have been bitten by an ungrateful dog."[157]

Hamaguchi had said that the opinions of the military had been fully considered and that the government bore the responsibility for national defense. At the Budget Committee meeting on April 30 Maeda Yonezō (Seiyūkai) inquired to what extent the military's opinions had been considered and whether the decision about the disarmament ratio was based on Article 11 or Article 12. The government's reply sidestepped the issue by saying that there was no need for it to answer the question. That evening the Seiyūkai released this statement over the name of Mori Kaku:

> Under the constitution ministers of state execute important matters of state appertaining to the emperor's prerogative. They should therefore accept their responsibility toward the Diet and make clear the constitutional authority for their acts. If a minister of state does not do this, can you call him anything other than a despotic politican who has repudiated the Diet? In this present affair Prime Minister Hamaguchi and his cabinet have disregarded the authority of the Diet and have thus treated with contempt the people's right to participate in the government. We can only conclude that they have declared in favor of despotic government and have thrown down the gauntlet to the people.[158]

The Tokyo newspapers consistently attacked the Seiyūkai's position, but they also denounced the evasive nature of the government's answers. The *Tōkyō Asahi* and the *Jiji shimpō* reproached the government for excessive timidity and for forgetting about "open politics."[159] The *Tōkyō Nichi-nichi* urged Hamaguchi to reflect whether he ought not to exert himself on this occasion to cut out the cancerous growth endangering constitutional government.[160] Perhaps it was in response to this kind of criticism that Hamaguchi replied at a House of Peers Budget Committee meeting on May 8 to a question from Inoue Kiyosumi (Kōseikai) about the determination of military strength. In his answer he clarified the government's position to the following extent:

> The technical opinions of the military, including the navy chief of staff, were listened to with the greatest respect. After they had been considered, the government then made the final decision.[161]

Before long the Seiyūkai grew weary of attacking the government for evasive answers on the treaty problem and sought to use the issue of an acting army minister as a device for cutting an opening through the cabinet's defenses and driving it from office. It happened that around this time Army Minister Ugaki was hospitalized with a middle-ear infection and was unable to attend Diet meetings. On April 28 Hanai Takuzō pointed out in the House of Peers that it was not permissible for the prime minister to answer questions in place of the army minister unless the necessary formalities for appointing him acting army minister had been effected. Hamaguchi replied that on state matters he would answer in his capacity as prime minister but that questions directed to the army minister on military command matters would be answered in writing by Ugaki himself.

The Seiyūkai immediately took this issue up in the House of Representatives. At a Budget Committee meeting on the afternoon of May 2 Yamazaki Tatsunosuke submitted a written question for the army minister: "When, as provided in Article 9 of the Cabinet Regulations, it is impossible for a minister of state to discharge his functions, is a temporary proxy or an acting minister appointed even if the minister of state in question is the army minister?"[162] At the time of the Washington Conference the army had strongly opposed Prime Minister Hara Takashi's becoming the acting navy minister; similarly, Ugaki had not been in favor of Hamaguchi's becoming acting navy minister during the London Conference. Therefore, in pursuing this problem the Seiyūkai was most likely trying to overthrow the cabinet by developing an internal rift between the army and the government.

Ugaki's written reply, delivered to the Budget Committee meeting the next afternoon, read: "There may be situations in which the provisions of Article 9 of the Cabinet Regulations apply also to the army minister. However, applicability should be determined in accordance with the circumstances prevailing at the time." The *Tōkyō Asahi* described the background of Ugaki's answer as follows:

> Since the present cabinet has appointed an acting navy minister, it is impossible for them to accept the principle that an acting army minister cannot be appointed. After repeated negotiations with the hospitalized Army Minister Ugaki and the Army Ministry authorities, a compromise was reached. It was settled that in principle an acting army minister could also be appointed, but the Army Ministry reserved the freedom to interpret the specific circumstances in which this could be done. In consequence of this arrangement, Ugaki issued the reply he did.[163]

At the May 3 Budget Committee meeting Ugaki's reply elicited from Yamazaki a further question, to which the army minister responded in writing as follows: "In view of the scope and special nature of the army minister's official business, I do not think it is at present suitable to appoint a nonmilitary minister of state as a temporary proxy or acting army minister."[164] When Yamazaki asked Hamaguchi's views on Ugaki's reply, the prime minister said he was of the same opinion.

Ugaki's answer acknowledged in principle but denied in substance that a civilian could be acting army minister. In explanation of why there could not be a civilian acting army minister though there could be a civilian acting navy minister, the Army Ministry advanced the following argument. In the case of the navy, Article 3 of the Navy General Staff Regulations said that the navy chief of staff made plans for the national defense and the employment of forces and that after securing the emperor's approval he transmitted these plans to the navy minister for implementation. After the navy chief of staff had obtained the emperor's approval, the plans were transmitted to the navy minister for implementation just as they stood. In the army's case, however, the procedure was different. After the army chief of staff had given his advice to the emperor, the army minister gave additional advice to the emperor about implementation and only subsequent to that did the army minister actually implement the decision. Over and above his responsibility for advising the emperor as a minister of state, the army minister, as compared with the navy minister, had a great many purely military command functions. Thus there would be difficulties if he were not a military officer.[165]

This was the same line of argument they had advanced at the time of the Washington Conference. Peculiarly enough, from the viewpoint of the division of functions between the ministry and the staff the navy minister was much more powerful than the army minister, and so the argument should have probably been just the reverse. The army really opposed an acting army minister because it feared this would lead to the appearance of civilian ministers for the military services. The government equivocated with respect to the right of military command problem and the acting army minister problem because it feared a forthright interpretation would make the Army Ministry hostile to it. It felt the chief result would be to invite the disruption of the cabinet's unity, especially since there was a strong feeling in the Army Ministry that Ugaki should resign on account of his illness.[166] When a short time later Ugaki's illness did in fact lead him to try to resign, political considerations forced the government to do its utmost to persuade him to stay. The government managed to prevent his resignation by on June 17 appointing Lieutenant-General Abe Nobuyuki minister of state without portfolio and acting army minister.

Despite its failure in the matter of the acting army minister, the Sei-yūkai had a second go at trying to split the army from the cabinet. At the May 5 meeting of the Budget Committee's Fourth Subcommittee (Army and Navy Appropriations), Uchida Shinya submitted two written queries for Ugaki. One read: "Did Army Minister Ugaki agree with Prime Minister Hamaguchi's statement that the government bore the responsibility for determining military strength?" The second read: "Is the concurrence of the army chief of staff necessary in decisions on military strength?" That same afternoon at the full Budget Committee meeting Uchida was handed a written reply:

1. As army minister I have no objection to the prime minister's statement that in connection with the London Treaty the determination of military strength was a matter for the government.
2. There is no compulsion for me to explain what internal negotiations are conducted with the army chief of staff in connection with the determination of military strength.[167]

Uchida wished to ask the further question: "Is there or is there not any objection to the interpretation that the determination of the army's strength is a matter for the government?" Military Affairs Bureau chief Sugiyama, who was present, stated that Ugaki would not reply, since at present this problem had not actually arisen. Though Uchida persisted in demanding a prompt written answer, Ugaki refused to answer on the grounds there was no necessity to do so.[168] Rumor had it that the Army General Staff's reaction to Uchida's question was one of strong opposition to the idea that the peacetime standing of the military forces could be determined without the concurrence of the army chief of staff.[169]

At the May 7 plenary session of the House of Peers Ikeda Nagayasu (Kōseikai) quoted the statement made in 1925 by Tsukamoto Seiji and then asked if the Hamaguchi cabinet accepted the interpretation of the Katō cabinet, which had contained several members of the present cabinet, namely, Ugaki, Takarabe, Shidehara, and Hamaguchi. He requested that his query be answered not only by the prime minister but by the army minister as well. Hamaguchi's reply was: "It is not possible to give a definite answer, such as that the present cabinet rejects the answer of the cabinet of that day or that this cabinet affirms in its entirety the answer of that cabinet." After Ugaki had consulted with his vice minister and Military Affairs Bureau chief Sugiyama, he decided not to answer the question on the principle that with regard to the right of military command controversy he would absolutely give no answer to abstract questions unconnected with substantive issues.[170]

As the right of military command became a serious issue in the Diet, a movement to protect constitutional government developed, its participants drawn from all the political parties. In a statement to the press on May 9 Tomita Tsunejirō, the Minseitō secretary-general, charged that the Seiyūkai was collaborating with a group of military intransigents in a plot to use the right of military command controversy to overthrow the cabinet. This was, he said, as foolish an undertaking as spitting up into the sky. If the Seiyūkai would think seriously about the future of parliamentary government, it would unhesitatingly cooperate with everyone else to achieve a fundamental solution to this problem and thereby further the progress of parliamentary government.[171]

There was even an important group of Seiyūkai members who met privately in the Diet building on May 10 and reached the unanimous conclusion that it was very bad for the party's future to create the false impression the Seiyūkai was supporting the military. On this occasion the Seiyūkai, they argued, should not be swayed by short-term gains or losses but, in order to establish the principle of responsible cabinets, should take the momentous decision to cooperate with the Minseitō and even, when the situation demanded, to form a united front with the government. By thus clarifying the party's true position, the misapprehensions of the people would be swept away. The ideas developed at the meeting were communicated to the party managers, who were urged to take action along these lines. However, the party managers did nothing, claiming that it was a serious problem and they were in the midst of making a careful study.[172]

When party President Inukai addressed the Seiyūkai caucus on May 16, he adopted a position contrary to that suggested by those present at the May 10 meeting. The government, he charged, had disregarded the Navy General Staff. In the determination of military strength one must rely on the knowledge of the experts, and the experts were saying that the national defense was endangered. The people, Inukai said, were being deluded by the government's propaganda that the savings from disarmament would be used for tax reductions or social programs.[173]

The 58th Diet, plagued from beginning to end by the right of military command controversy, came to a close on May 14. A few days later the Tōkyō Nichi-nichi published what was probably a fair evaluation of the proceedings:

> Debate in the Diet tended to be mainly formalistic and legalistic. There was almost no discussion of any serious content or of such subjects as the treaty's connection with the people's tax burden and its influence on the entire range of international relations. But in the American and British legislatures . . . the questions and answers, as well as the discussion, constituted an exchange of principled opinion regarding the consequences of the treaty for national defense or the effects of the treaty as seen from a higher and broader viewpoint. We are forced to conclude that in this point above all debate in our Diet leaves a great deal to be desired.[174]

The Diet debates on the right of military command were reported in a sensational manner by the newspapers, and what might be termed a "right of military command mood" was born. When the government deferred to the military and avoided discussing the internal decision-making processes followed in formulating the return instructions, this undeniably became a factor in creating among the public the impression that the cabinet had disregarded the navy chief of staff's opposition. Right wing groups had already been vociferous about deficiencies in military strength and the danger to national defense. Now they shifted and began to attack the government for infringing the right of military command. The earliest group to use the expression "infringement of the right of military command" (tōsuiken kampan) was probably the Gunshuku Kokumin Dōshikai, whose leader was Tōyama Mitsuru. The day following its April 3 "people's rally," when the resolution opposing the return instructions was passed, Dōshikai representatives went to the prime minister's official residence and had an interview with Suzuki Fujiya, the chief cabinet secretary. They presented him with their resolution and said they believed the imperial prerogative embodied in Article 11 had been clearly infringed when the government sent the return instructions without incorporating therein the opinion of the navy chief of staff.[175]

Thereafter right wing groups passed declarations and resolutions at "people's rallies" and lecture meetings and distributed fiery pamphlets screaming about the infringement of the right of military command and the danger to national defense.[176] On June 9, for example, the Kaikōkai, an association of reserve generals and admirals presided over by Admiral Ōi Shigemoto, passed the following resolution:

> The organization and strength of our army and navy should under no circumstances be determined unilaterally by the government and in disregard of the authority of the military command agencies. The London Treaty dealt primarily with tonnage levels and the combination of vessel types required for national defense and the effective employment of forces, in other words, with our navy's organization and strength. Despite this fact the government decided the matter on its own responsibility. This was an *ultra vires* act that disregarded the authority of the Navy General Staff. The result of this act has been to create confusion once again with regard to the division of authority between the agencies responsible for state affairs and the agencies responsible for military command matters. Thus this act has endangered the foundations of the national polity.[177]

On June 25 the following resolution was adopted and mailed to regional newspapers by the National League of Students Opposed to the Traitorous Treaty (Baikoku Jōyaku Hantai Zenkoku Gakusei Dōmei):

> Externally, this government has knuckled under to the United States and Britain and has made an agreement that throws away our national defense. Internally, this government has infringed the right of military command and has endangered the very foundations of our nation's military forces. . . . Great crimes have been committed by the Hamaguchi cabinet against the emperor and the nation. In the name of the loyal Japanese people we here proclaim the abrogation of the 1930 London Treaty and we demand the immediate resignation of the cabinet.[178]

Were these actions based on a satisfactory understanding on the part of the participants of the constitutional principles and practices involved? Or is it not the case that they had no such understanding or even the capacity for such understanding? Were they not rather acting solely under the intoxication of the public mood mentioned earlier? Prince Saionji deplored their activities in these words: "Uninformed young men will be stirred up when people such as admirals and vice admirals, people who are looked upon by the public as respectable men, act as if they really know what they are talking about and proclaim that the London

Treaty infringes the right of military command and is disadvantageous to the nation."[179] In recollecting these events, Kodama Yoshio, one of the right wing leaders, said: "The people may have castigated the government for weak diplomacy in connection with the London Treaty, but that did not mean they actually understood the provisions of the treaty."[180]

Meanwhile, Katō, irritated by Shidehara's Diet speech and by the whole controversy over the right of military command, became more inflexible than ever. Up to this point he had stressed the deficiencies in naval strength created by the treaty. Now he changed course. "The naval strength problem is a mere trifle," he averred. "The really serious issue is the right of military command."[181] To Harada Kumao, who visited him on May 3, he exclaimed indignantly: "When the government disregarded the Navy General Staff, it in effect disregarded the emperor's prerogative to command the military forces. I'll be damned if this is the way national defense is going to be decided." He then proceeded to disown party government: "Party cabinets are completely beyond redemption. Cabinets ought to be composed of career officials only. Now the only way to operate is by the emperor's personal decision."[182] On May 7 he subjected Okada to a similar tirade: "The right of military command issue is a serious matter. We must hold a meeting of the field marshals, admirals of the fleet, and the supreme war councillors so that we can correct the government's blunder. . . . This cabinet is leftist. If this problem is not cleared up, the navy too will have its 'grave affair.' "[183]

Harada believed that Suetsugu was manipulating Katō and that Suetsugu in turn was being manipulated by Hiranuma Kiichirō, the Privy Council vice president. Takarabe and Okada too saw the situation in this way.[184] Suetsugu was obliged to apologize to Hamaguchi on April 2 for his behavior and on the 16th received a caution from Katō. Nevertheless, he did not stop his secret maneuvers. Katō visited Hiranuma on April 27 for an exchange of views and was encouraged by Hiranuma to believe that the issues raised in Katō's address to the emperor ought to be resolved by the Privy Council, that Hiranuma regarded the London Treaty as a humiliation and was opposed to its signing.[185] Both men had been long acquainted through their association with the Kokuhonsha, and Harada's speculation about Hiranuma's influence may therefore be true. Decisive evidence is, however, lacking. It is more probable that the wire puller was Mori Kaku. Still, whoever the puppet master may have been, it is undeniable that Katō was wanting in the settled convictions appropriate to his high and responsible position.

The Diet debates had also caused Prince Fushimi and Admiral Tōgō to stiffen their positions. Nonchalantly switching their views for the third time, they changed to the "hard line" and began to drive Navy Ministry leaders wild with their demands that the treaty be abandoned because of the deficiencies in the military strength allowed under it. However, many see Fushimi's and Tōgō's hard-line opinions not as settled convictions of their own but rather as reflecting the views of Katō, Suetsugu, and Vice Admiral Ogasawara Naganari, a close associate of Tōgō.[186] On May 15 Takarabe told Harada: "Fleet Admiral Tōgō and Prince Fushimi are saying rather strong things. That's because Katō is visiting them just about every day to persuade them and to plant firmly his ideas in their minds. It's very troublesome."[187] Takarabe also told Harada that what Tōgō and Suetsugu were saying was exactly the same, almost to the very words, and that he was truly astonished at how pervasively and thoroughly Katō's and Suetsugu's own ideas had been infused into the two old men.[188]

Katō and Suetsugu made no attempt to resolve their differences with the Navy Ministry leaders by treating the latter as equals and debating with them fully and rationally. Instead, they picked up a member of the imperial family and a national hero and carried the two around on their shoulders like *mikoshi* or portable shrines. They sought to eliminate counterarguments by invoking the sacred authority of these two personages, an authority no one could openly set himself against. Fushimi's and Tōgō's hard-line position severely complicated the problem, despite the fact that it was due to their having been misled by their associates and displayed like *mikoshi*.

Controversy Between the Navy Ministry and General Staff

While the controversy over the right of military command was at its height in the Diet, Takarabe was on his way home by way of Siberia. Both before and after the decision on the return instructions Yamanashi carried on the fight with two major principles in mind: (1) not to reveal to the outer world any divisions of opinion within the navy; (2) not to allow the government's policy to be obstructed by the navy.[189] If Takarabe returned to Japan while the Diet was in session, Navy Ministry leaders feared there would be further complications in the right of military command controversy and the navy itself would be pulled into the political maelstrom. On April 30 Koga Mincichi sent a telegram to Arima Yutaka, the naval attaché in the USSR, instructing that the navy minister's return should be delayed:

> Please communicate to Minato, the minister's personal secretary, now in transit through Russia: "Treat this as extraordinarily secret. With regard to minister's arrival date, as I said in previous telegram, we (including therein the government) hope the minister will approve some date from the 17th on, since the Diet ends on the 14th. Please convey to the minister as my private opinion the recommendation that he consider breaking his journey en route and delaying his arrival in Tokyo if the Diet session should be further extended one or two days."[190]

Koga was afterward sent to Harbin to inform Takarabe of the political situation in Japan. With him he carried verbal messages given to him by various people: Okada on April 27; Hamaguchi, Yamanashi, and Harada on May 1; Shidehara and Katō on May 2. With the exception of Katō, who merely said to Koga, "Well, please give the minister my regards," all requested Takarabe to be prudent in his behavior and not to accede to advice that he resign. Yamanashi conveyed his own intention to withdraw from office, and Harada assured Takarabe of Prince Saionji's great satisfaction at the signing of the treaty.[191]

Takarabe's party arrived at Manchouli on May 7. With Vice Admiral Sakonji sitting nearby, Takarabe was interviewed in the station waiting room by Fukuoka Seiichi, chief of the Foreign Bureau of the Shimbun Rengōsha (Associated Press). Under a May 7 dateline, Fukuoka recorded the following statement by Takarabe:

> Since in view of the overall situation the decision was taken that to sign this treaty was the right thing to do, I was happy to affix my signature. National defense is, of course, important, but state affairs are not limited simply to national defense. They include finance, economics, foreign policy, and other matters. We responded to the general trend toward world peace and signed this treaty in a spirit of international cooperation. From the wider national point of view I do not think it was detrimental to Japan for us to have done so. On the contrary, I firmly believe that there are many ways in which the treaty will contribute to our national progress. We did not achieve all our demands, so there is

bound to be some dissatisfaction with the terms of the treaty. However, since the terms will not be fully implemented until 1936, I think that gives us time to study the matter thoroughly and prepare for the conference.[192]

At midnight on May 8 a further telegram from Fukuoka was delivered to Iwanaga Yūkichi, the managing director of the Associated Press, saying: "Not only Takarabe's but also Sakonji's attitude is clear. They appear in no way anxious to trouble the political situation." That same day Iwanaga sent copies of the interview and the subsequent telegram to Vice Foreign Minister Yoshida.[193] Wakatsuki has conjectured that Takarabe changed in favor of the treaty after he had sounded out the views of Governor-General Saitō in Seoul,[194] but Takarabe had made up his mind before then.

Takarabe reached Harbin on May 7 and immediately upon entering the South Manchuria Railway offices had a 45-minute private conference with Koga. Under the pretext of having become ill on the Trans-Siberian Railway, Takarabe remained at the South Manchuria Railway offices for several days, purportedly to convalesce under the care of a naval doctor named Sugawara. He then proceeded to Seoul, where on May 16 between 3:00 and 4:00 P.M. he had a private conversation with Saitō that attracted intense interest. Saitō had around this time expressed to a reporter the following opinion on the London Treaty:

> I don't think it in any way infringed the right of military command for our country to have participated in the disarmament conference and given approval to the London Treaty on the grounds that it was necessary from the viewpoint of international relations. I think it exceedingly disagreeable that this kind of problem was used as a political weapon. Isn't the real mistake what those fellows themselves have done? Bringing up the issue that an important agency of the nation has been disregarded and at this late hour provoking a controversy among the military about a treaty which the government signed as a compromise? Also, looking at the contents of the treaty, I do not consider that this agreement creates any deficiencies in the national defense before 1936. There are no limits to national defense, but even an amateur can tell by one glance at the figures that the agreement creates no deficiencies in our national defense.[195]

It is not known what was said at the Takarabe-Saitō conference, but it can be inferred from the above statement. The Ōsaka Mainichi gave this report on the conference:

According to the governor-general the London Conference was on the whole a success. The controversy over the right of military command was not a matter which from its nature should have become a problem. The much more important problem for the navy minister is how from this point on to develop to its fullest potential the naval strength allowed us under the treaty. Saitō reassured the navy minister and said that he now wished Takarabe to sweep aside conflicting public criticism and meet the present situation with ever greater prudence. This must be done for the sake of both the nation's overall situation and the navy's future. The navy minister understood what Saitō had in mind and promised he would not take the wrong course of action. . . . This balm from the governor-general is regarded as having greatly strengthened Takarabe's spirits and brightened his journey back to Tokyo.[196]

Takarabe's party disembarked at Shimonoseki on May 18 and, traveling overland, reached Tokyo Station at 8:30 A.M. on the 19th. The *Tōkyō Nichi-nichi* gave this description of the tumultuous reception at the station:

> The instant Delegate Takarabe's right foot touched down from the train onto the concrete of the station platform, enthusiastic shouts of *banzai* arose. Over the heads of the pushing and jostling masses countless bouquets were flying through the air in the delegate's direction but frequently did not reach him. . . . When he began to move toward the reception room for distinguished guests, the wildly excited crowd surged forward, blocking his path and paying no attention to the attempts of the police to control them.[197]

Wakatsuki had arrived at Tokyo Station the day before, and his welcome was reported as follows in the *Tōkyō Asahi:*

> Waving banners of welcome, the citizens gathering to see the delegate's arrival rushed into Tokyo Station one after another. The Metropolitan Police tried to maintain control by distributing about 400 policemen between the platform and the plaza before the station. . . . As soon as the train pulled in, cries of *banzai*, sounds of clapping, shouts of joy arose and spread like waves. In the midst of all this there appeared from a rear carriage the familiar tall, slim figure of the delegate. . . . Delegate Wakatsuki politely returned individual salutations to the large number of officials and friends who were on hand to greet him. The entire time he was doing this, the cries of *banzai*, the clapping, the shouts continued without interruption, swelling and ebbing like waves.[198]

Until this moment all that had echoed and reechoed throughout Japan had been the vehement voices denouncing the infringement of the right of military command and opposing the traitorous treaty. The voices of the voiceless had not been heard in public, but these scenes at the station surely expressed the true will of the nation.

After he had conferred with Takarabe, Hamaguchi told Harada: "He appears to be already splendidly firm in his determination. . . . Yamanashi has also worked very hard on this matter, and I am sincerely grateful to him. His recent proposal to resign probably comes from the foresighted wish to use his own resignation to get the vice chief of staff to reflect on how he has been behaving, and also ultimately to force the chief of staff to resign."[199]

Takarabe visited the palace on May 25 and reported privately to the emperor on his activities as a delegate. Takarabe was deeply moved when the emperor said to him: "Thank you for your hard work. Continue your efforts so that the treaty can be ratified."[200] But a thorny road filled with tribulations lay before Takarabe. It began as early as his disembarkation at Shimonoseki, when a Nō actor tried to stab him. During his arrival at Tokyo Station handbills were distributed describing him as "Takarabe, the betrayer of his country." On May 20 near Fuji station on the Tōkaidō line, Lieutenant Commander Kusakari Eiji, an officer on the Navy General Staff, committed hara-kiri in a sleeping car of a train traveling toward Tokyo, a suicide that particularly shocked the public. The reason for it is not certain, but treaty opponents claimed Kusakari had killed himself in anger at the London Treaty, and they set him up as a hero who had died for his country.[201]

After his return to Japan, Takarabe met with the cabinet in special session and then held a conference with Katō. At that time Katō gave Takarabe the text of an address to the emperor and requested that he transmit it to the emperor. Since it contained phrases that amounted to an impeachment of the government, however, Takarabe held on to the document and did not forward it. In the address Katō gave his interpretation of Articles 11 and 12, then impeached the government for having infringed the emperor's prerogative of military command. He charged that the government had placed the nation in grave danger when it gave advice to the emperor about the return instructions on its own authority and without negotiating with the military command agencies. Katō went on to say that the mismanagement of this affair must be laid at his door, since he was the person charged with the grave responsibility of advising the emperor with regard to national defense and the employment of naval forces. In view of this and "reflecting on my heavy responsibility as Your Majesty's adviser, I respectfully and humbly tender Your Majesty my resignation."[202]

On May 20 Okada saw Katō and urged him to withdraw the address. Katō would not comply and said that if the navy minister would not transmit the address, he would himself present it directly to the emperor. Persisting in his effort to get Katō to change his mind, Okada argued that if the issue were the right of military command, there were other ways to solve that problem. He also pointed out that a document such as this could make difficulties for Katō in the future.[203]

Opposition to Takarabe had become very pronounced among officers of flag rank on the navy reserve list. The Seiyūkai was persistent in its attempts to win Okada's support against ratification of the treaty. Right wing groups were drumming up opposition to the "traitorous treaty." According to Katō's memoirs, he and Vice Admiral Ogasawara were incessantly exchanging visits from this time on.

Katō's rigid stand on the right of military command distressed naval leaders. Okada conferred again and again with Takarabe, and between them they exhausted every possible argument. But they did not succeed in persuading Katō to withdraw his address. Vice Admiral Yamamoto Hidesuke, the commander of the Combined Fleet, also recommended to Katō that he compromise with the navy minister, but Katō declined Yamamoto's advice. On May 25 Okada visited Katō's home and once again urged him to withdraw his address. Katō fumingly replied: "The emperor's errors must be corrected by his subjects. The people around the emperor are not good people." When Okada still urged reconsideration, Katō said, "I wish you would think it over, though your mind is already inclined toward withdrawal. Well, please wait, because I too will think it over carefully."[204] But in the end Okada's attempts at persuasion were wasted effort. Katō had already on May 8 told Suetsugu and Vice Admiral Nakamura Ryōzō that he had made up his mind to present the address. Katō records that both of them agreed with his decision and that Suetsugu requested him "to be unshakable in my determination once my resignation had been submitted."[205] Does not this incident too suggest that Suetsugu was behind Katō's obstinate attitude?

During the meeting between Takarabe and Katō on May 28, it was

agreed that the right of military command issue and the problem of Katō's resignation should be handled separately. Katō then gave Takarabe
his memorandum on military strength and organization and their relation to the imperial prerogative (see above), in response to which Hori
drafted for the Navy Ministry the following document:

> It is plainly stated in the Navy Ministry Regulations that the minister
> controls naval administration *(kaigun gunsei)* and that as part of its duties
> this ministry is in charge of naval armaments and other matters related to
> general naval administration. The Navy General Staff Regulations estab-
> lish that the navy chief of staff should draft plans for the national defense
> and the employment of naval forces. Also, according to Item 7 of the Rules
> for the Conduct of Business Between the Ministry and the General Staff,
> there should be a mutual exchange of opinions between the ministry and
> the general staff regarding changes in naval strength. Therefore, there
> should be an agreement of views between the minister and the chief of
> staff whenever *the minister* [author's italics] makes a decision about a na-
> val armament matter that involves a change in naval strength.

> Notes: 1. There are unclear points concerning the way in which mat-
>   ters were handled when the return instructions were sent to
>   the delegates. The prime minister was serving as acting navy
>   minister and under the circumstances these unclear points
>   were inevitable.
>   2. In the general debate over the right of military command,
>   that is, over the compass of Articles 11 and 12, even among
>   scholars there is no agreement. Therefore, a suitable proce-
>   dure would be to make case-by-case decisions as actual sit-
>   uations arise that involve this issue.[206]

Later that day Takarabe visited Prince Fushimi and Admiral Tōgō
to explain the background of this memorandum and obtain their approval of it. On the same day Katō himself spoke to Prince Fushimi. On
the 29th there was a gathering at the navy minister's official residence of
the naval members of the Supreme War Council. The navy minister
presented the Navy Ministry memorandum to the councillors for their
approval. In opposition to this, Katō offered the Navy General Staff
memorandum. Okada spoke in favor of adopting the ministry memorandum, arguing that it was clear while the General Staff document was
vague. No particular opposition to his view was expressed.[207]

On the 30th Takarabe told Hamaguchi and Shidehara the results of the previous day's meeting of the naval councillors. In the afternoon he saw Fushimi and Tōgō and gave them the memorandum the councillors had accepted. Both of them wished to delete the third reference to "the minister" (italicized), but Takarabe elicited their consent to the document as it stood when he explained that it was too late to make any changes once the memorandum had been approved by the councillors.

That same morning Katō had been to visit Fushimi. When Takarabe returned to his official residence, Katō came to him and suggested that the third reference to "the minister" be eliminated. Takarabe refused, and a quarrel broke out between the two men. "If this is the way things are," said Katō, "Then that's that. The chief of staff will have to do what he has said he will do. Please act as quickly as possible on the resignation I gave you the other day." Then he left. Katō's entries in his diary for May 29 and 30 probably refer to this incident: "Clash between myself and the navy minister over the memorandum. Have broken off relations. Visited His Imperial Highness [Fushimi] and the fleet admiral [Tōgō] to report same."[208]

When Koga related these events to Okada, the latter deplored them, exclaiming, "It was absolutely outrageous behavior for the chief of staff to go running to see His Imperial Highness ahead of the navy minister. It's truly shameful to have this kind of business from a man supposed to be a navy admiral." Okada then advised that the chief and vice chief of staff be changed, and he discussed the choice of successors.[209]

From May 30 on the attitude of the Navy General Staff became more and more inflexible. On June 1 Suetsugu visited Katō and explained the need to maintain close liaison with the Army General Staff. On the 3rd Prince Fushimi switched his position for the fourth time: he announced his determination to visit the palace and speak to the emperor about the right of military command issue. On the 5th Ogasawara came to see Katō. But Fushimi's proposal to submit a contrary opinion to the emperor incurred Hirohito's displeasure.[210]

While all this was going on, Takarabe, Okada, and Yamanashi were working to get the situation under control. On June 2 Okada decided, in consultation with Takarabe, that Katō's resignation should be accepted and that he should be replaced at an opportune time by Admiral Taniguchi Naomi, commander of the Kure Naval Base. Meanwhile, Vice Admirals Yamamoto Hidesuke and Ōsumi Mineo had undertaken to mediate between the ministry and the General Staff the difference of opinion concerning the phrasing of the memorandum. On June 2 the right of military command controversy was for the nonce settled when Takarabe and Katō agreed to an amended text drawn up by these two officers.

With the right of military command controversy settled, the next development was a great quarrel on June 6 between Takarabe and Katō over Suetsugu's resignation. Katō finally acquiesced to Suetsugu's departure. Then arose the problem of the changeover in the position of chief of staff. Takarabe suggested that Katō leave office peacefully and not elaborate on his reasons for resigning. If he and Katō did not act properly now, Takarabe explained, they would, without having any desire to do so, produce factions within the navy on which the political parties would capitalize. In view of the immoderate tone of Katō's address to the emperor, it could not, Takarabe insisted, be transmitted in its present form. Katō replied that the tendering of his resignation did not mean he wanted to be put into some sinecure; it meant he wished to be dismissed from service permanently. He was resigning, Katō said, out of remorse. He should have realized when he took his resolute action on April 1 that it would probably end in this way. Katō then asked that the memorandum be referred for advice to all the members of the Supreme War Council, army and navy alike. Their decision could then be taken to the government for negotiation.[211]

On June 10 the navy vice minister and the vice chief of the Navy General Staff were replaced by Vice Admiral Kobayashi Seizō, previously chief of the Navy Construction Bureau, and Vice Admiral Nagano Osami, commandant of the Naval Academy, respectively. At 11:00 that morning Katō had an audience with the emperor to report on the navy grand maneuvers. After making his report, he read aloud a previously prepared statement on the right of military command controversy and submitted his resignation. He had risen from his bed at 5:00 A.M. and performed purificatory ablutions. He had then gone to the Meiji Shrine to pray for the success of the day's project.

When Katō returned from the palace, he remarked, "I have just returned today from presenting my resignation to the emperor. His Majesty should understand the written statement I left behind, since Suetsugu explained all this to him several days ago."[212] Okada conjectured that Katō had somehow been inveigled into this action by others and that it probably did not represent his true feelings.[213]

At 4:30 that afternoon Takarabe had an audience with the emperor. The emperor handed him Katō's address with the remark that he was doing so because proper procedure had not been followed. He was entrusting Takarabe, he said, with the disposition of the matter. The navy minister then asked the emperor to appoint Katō a member of the Supreme War Council and to replace him as chief of staff with Admiral Taniguchi. The emperor did not consent immediately to Taniguchi's appointment but asked what Taniguchi's position was on the question of naval strength. When Takarabe replied that Taniguchi held very sound views and believed everyone should cooperate to make do with the strength allowed under the treaty, the emperor nodded approval and said, "Good." At 10 o'clock that evening Takarabe received a telephone call from General Nara Takeji, the emperor's chief aide-de-camp, communicating the emperor's approval.[214]

The following day Taniguchi's appointment was announced. When Okada sounded out the views of the new chief of staff a few days later, Taniguchi told him: "My own belief is that the national defense is safe with the naval strength allowed under the London Treaty. Moreover, the treaty must be ratified. Still, I am now the navy chief of staff, and I must take into account the position of the Navy General Staff."[215]

On June 23 Takarabe showed Okada, Katō, and Taniguchi the final draft of the memorandum on the right of military command and obtained their approval of it. He also communicated it unofficially to Fushimi and Tōgō and received their assent. Thereafter a formal meeting of the Supreme War Council was held in the Higashi Ni-no-ma of the palace, with Admiral Tōgō presiding. The memorandum was passed without objection, and Tōgō had an audience to request the emperor's approval. The final text as presented to the emperor read as follows:

> It has been decided that matters related to naval strength will be dealt with in accordance with pertinent laws and regulations and also in accordance with the following principle:
> Matters related to naval strength will be dealt with in accordance with traditional practice and in this case are considered to be matters about which there must be agreement between the navy minister and the navy chief of staff.
> Reason: It is clearly provided in the Navy Ministry Regulations that the minister is in charge of naval administration and that, as part of the duties of the ministry, he administers naval armament and other matters related to general naval administration. It is provided in the

Navy General Staff Regulations that the navy chief of staff make plans for the national defense and for the employment of forces. Since matters related to naval strength are included among the matters under the charge of both the Navy Ministry and the Navy General Staff, it is necessary on this occasion to make even more explicit the traditional practice with regard to relations between the two agencies.[216]

Taniguchi's first problem as navy chief of staff was to persuade the Supreme War Council and the Board of Field Marshals and Admirals of the Fleet (Gensuifu) to approve the London Naval Treaty. That approval partly depended on winning over Fushimi and Tōgō. Prince Fushimi was unhappy with the London Treaty. However, he had changed his mind for the fifth time and softened his position to the extent that he considered ratification appropriate if the government would adopt a suitable plan for offsetting the anticipated deficiencies the treaty would cause. Admiral Tōgō, out of the obstinacy of age, had become extremely inflexible in his opinion and would not yield on his demand that the treaty be rejected. His animosity toward Takarabe was intense. At this time anti-Takarabe feeling was running high in navy circles. By nature Takarabe did not resort to artifices or make excuses. He did not have much knowledge of the inner workings of the world or pay much attention to ulterior motives. Consequently, he was frequently misunderstood and disliked.[217] For instance, the fact that he took his wife along with him to the London Conference is said to have aroused the enmity of many within the navy and to have deeply offended Tōgō's susceptibilities.[218] As a result, when Taniguchi tried to win Tōgō's support by pleading that he would otherwise have to resign as navy chief of staff, Tōgō did not succumb to the argument. "It is a great failure in one's duty," Tōgō said, "to do something that gets you through your present situation but that causes irreparable harm in the future."[219] Taniguchi bewailed Tōgō's attitude, remarking, "that old fellow no longer has to carry out policy."[220]

Tōgō's hard-line position is thought to have been due in large measure to the influence of Ogasawara and Katō. That Takarabe thought this to be true was shown by his going to Ogasawara's home on June 27 in an attempt to win him over. During that visit Takarabe told Ogasawara, "You must seriously consider what the upshot may be when from motives of self-interest a godlike hero is incited to take action on behalf of fellows with all sorts of ideas whirling around in their heads." He explained to Ogasawara how very grave would be the effect if Tōgō and Tōgō alone blocked the disarmament for which the nation's people were longing. But Ogasawara did not respond.[221] Evidence of Katō's influence on Tōgō's position is to be found in Katō's *Diary*, where he relates conversations between himself and Tōgō about this time.

On July 2, having exhausted every other recourse, Taniguchi and Okada decided they must enlist the aid of Katō. When Taniguchi consulted Katō on the 3rd, Katō demanded the immediate resignation of the navy minister and said there was absolutely no other way of breaking the deadlock.[222] Through Takarabe's good offices Katō had been given the important position of war councillor even though he was guilty of submitting his resignation to the emperor by an irregular procedure. At that time Katō had said to Takarabe, "Despite having committed an act that evaded your authority as minister, I have received generous treatment from you. For this I truly am very grateful. Henceforth, no matter to what post I am transferred, I will never fail to accept the minister's authority nor do anything that will cause him trouble."[223]

It was Okada who ultimately undertook the task of advising Takarabe to resign. Having extracted from Katō a promise that he would cooperate in persuading Tōgō if Takarabe consented to resign, Okada went to see Takarabe at 7:30 P.M. on July 4. He explained that there was no alternative, and he asked Takarabe to inform Fushimi and Tōgō that he would resign when the treaty had been ratified. Late that night Takarabe revealed to Taniguchi his intention to resign, and it was arranged that Taniguchi and Okada would communicate this decision to Fushimi and Tōgō. On the 5th the two men visited Tōgō together and announced Takarabe's intention to him. The same news was passed on to Fushimi by Taniguchi. Both Fushimi and Tōgō demanded that Takarabe resign immediately, without waiting for the treaty to be ratified.[224]

Takarabe went to Tōgō early on the morning of July 6 and expressed his intention to resign. At the request of Takarabe, Okada, and Taniguchi, Katō called on Tōgō that same day to persuade him to accept a delay in the resignation. Katō explained, "There is apprehension that the navy will not exhaust every means to fulfill its duty just because there are some deficiencies in strength." But Tōgō replied, "There is no need to talk now about making up for deficiencies," and refused to listen to him.[225] In his diary, Katō reported Tōgō's words as follows:

It doesn't make sense for Takarabe to resign after the ratification. Since I don't want the treaty ratified, I can never accept the idea of using Takarabe's resignation as a means for getting the treaty through. Takarabe has said that His Majesty told him he wished the treaty ratified. But I told Takarabe that truly, with all due respect for His Majesty, one must remonstrate with His Majesty if one thinks a statement by His Majesty is not correct. . . . The sooner the minister is changed the better. . . . Okada has explained that there will be serious political repercussions if the minister leaves office immediately. Whether this trivial government falls or doesn't fall is not an issue worth the destruction of the Navy. . . . We can't imagine how much the navy would benefit if this rotten government were to be quickly replaced by a decent government.[226]

Tōgō also proposed to Katō that the Supreme War Council or the Board of Field Marshals and Admirals of the Fleet be asked their opinion of the treaty. When Okada, Takarabe, Taniguchi, and Katō met to consider this proposal, they unanimously agreed that by precedent the Board should deal with the matter but that the treaty could be referred to either body.

On July 8 Okada called on Tōgō and explained that if the navy minister were forced to resign at this time, the navy would become embroiled in a political problem and would make a certain group of gentlemen (i.e., court circles) enemies for a long time. Tōgō still would not yield, replying, "Telling the minister to resign with my own mouth would be mixing in politics, but would it become a political problem if the minister resigned on his own initiative?"[227]

The effort to persuade Tōgō to cease his opposition was thus completely deadlocked. On the evening of July 8 Takarabe secretly visited Hamaguchi to report on the situation, and the two conferred about what measures should be adopted for the future. Tōgō, for his part, was fully determined to go to the emperor and resign his rank of fleet admiral if his demands were not met.[228] According to Okada, the emperor commented to Grand Chamberlain Suzuki with regard to Tōgō's hard-line position, "The fleet admiral should take a far-sighted view in all matters. Besides we will have freedom of action at the 1935 conference."[229]

In these circumstances Takarabe, Okada, and Taniguchi conferred on the 8th to choose which body the London Treaty should be referred to for a military evaluation, the Board of Field Marshals and Admirals of the Fleet or the Supreme War Council. Since Fushimi and Tōgō considered either suitable, the three admirals selected the Board, on the basis of precedent, and began the procedures required to arrange a meeting of this body.

Previous to this decision the navy had already begun unofficial negotiations with the army for a meeting of the Board. On July 1 Navy General Staff Operations Division chief Oikawa Koshirō had called on his opposite number at the Army General Staff, Hata Shunroku, to sound out army opinion on such a meeting. That same day notice of this proposal had been given by Hori to Acting Vice Army Minister Sugiyama. The army's estimation of the situation within the navy was that the young officers on the Navy General Staff strongly supported a meeting of the Supreme War Council but that Navy Ministry leaders wished to avoid such a meeting for fear of the knotty issues likely to arise during debate in that body. After talking the matter over among themselves, the Army General Staff decided there was no objection to allowing the field marshals to attend a meeting of the Board. Acting Army Minister Abe Nobuyuki, however, disagreed, and on the morning of July 2 all concerned met to reexamine the question. The gathering concluded that it would be proper for the field marshals to participate, since the London Treaty involved changes in military strength related to the overall national defense, but they wished the agenda of the meeting to be arranged by consultations among all the military command agencies. This decision was verbally communicated to the navy.

The Army Ministry did not wish the field marshals to attend the meeting. Aware that Tōgō's group were maneuvering to have the treaty voted down by the Board, the Army Ministry feared the meeting would be used as a political weapon. The Army General Staff too was on guard against the possibility that the marshals would be plunged into the political maelstrom or that the army would find itself unwittingly committed to the expansion of the naval air force.[230] In 1930 the marshals were Oku Yasukata, who was ill, Imperial Prince Kan'in, and Uehara Yūsaku; the only fleet admiral was Tōgō. Uehara, who came from the same town as Takarabe (Miyako-no-jō), also feared that the meeting would be used as a political forum, and he believed that the meeting should be held after the treaty had been ratified.[231] According to Katō's *Diary*, Ogasawara visited Katō on June 16 to request that he persuade Kan'in to support Tōgō.

On July 7 Navy Vice Chief of Staff Nagano called on Army Vice Chief of Staff Okamoto Ren'ichirō to ask the army's opinion of a proposal Tōgō was making. Tōgō pointed out that the present issue regarding naval strength was a navy concern and involved many technical matters, yet there was only one naval member on the Board of Field Marshals and Admirals of the Fleet. In order to seek the opinions of naval technical experts, Tōgō proposed therefore holding a meeting of only the naval members of the Supreme War Council. That same day Navy Vice Minister Kobayashi saw Acting Army Vice Minister Sugiyama to communicate the same proposal. After consultations among themselves, the army officials involved agreed that if the navy so desired, the army would not object to a meeting of the naval war councillors alone, provided there were no changes in national defense plans or in the general plans for the deployment of forces.[232]

On July 9 Oikawa Koshirō went to the Army General Staff and communicated formally Tōgō's proposal that the Board meeting be dropped altogether and the matter handled solely by means of a Supreme War Council meeting attended only by naval members. The Army General Staff further studied the question and decided on the following three steps: (1) the chief of the Army General Staff would seek a detailed explanation of the navy's intentions from the chief of the Navy General Staff; (2) if there was nothing in the explanation to which exception was taken, there would then be a formal consultation; (3) after these formalities had been completed, the chief of the Army General Staff would secure the field marshals' consent to dropping the Board meeting and an answer would be sent to the navy. Umezu Yoshijirō, chief of the Army Ministry's Military Section, suggested, however, that if the army chief of staff sought too detailed an explanation and then consented to that explanation, the outcome could be undesirable if this consent were construed as support for the expansion of the naval air force. It was thereupon decided to seek the opinion of the Army Ministry. Just at that point, about 4:00 P.M., the Navy General Staff adjutant brought a message from Nagano asking that Tōgō's proposal be postponed. On the 10th Operations Division chief Hata checked this with Oikawa at the Navy General Staff and was told that since no decision had yet been reached concerning the Board and the Supreme War Council, it was desired to hold off initiating any action with regard to either.[233]

On July 12 Taniguchi called on Kanaya to request that the Board of Field Marshals and Admirals of the Fleet meet to consider the problem of military strength. The next day, however, he informed Kanaya that the navy now desired that the matter be discussed by the naval members of the Supreme War Council. The army people guessed that Tōgō's opposition had softened somewhat. Kanaya asked Taniguchi to assume the responsibility of affirming that the London Treaty would not change the national defense plans or the general plans for the deployment of forces, to which Taniguchi readily consented. On the 14th he handed Kanaya a memorandum to this effect. Army Vice Chief Okamoto thereupon drafted a memorandum detailing the reasons the participation of the field marshals was unnecessary. He orally explained these reasons to Prince Kan'in and Field Marshal Uehara and communicated them in writing to the military councillors.[234]

As the foregoing account has shown, the navy vacillated considerably in deciding its position. This was because Tōgō and his supporters wanted a meeting of the naval councillors while the leaders of both the ministry and the General Staff wanted a meeting of the Board. When Takarabe met with members of the Kōseikai, a House of Peers group, Baron Inoue Kiyosumi had asserted that the question of military strength ought to be left to the decision of the Supreme War Council. To this Takarabe had answered: "Legally a meeting of the Supreme War Council is, I think, permissible. However, I myself do not want it, because the right of military command problem would be debated at such a meeting, and this would agitate people's feelings to no useful purpose. There are also precedents for holding a meeting of the Board of Field Marshals and Admirals of the Fleet, and I would prefer to follow that course.[235]

The Tōgō group insisted on a meeting of just the naval councillors, arguing that the opinion of a wide range of naval experts would not be available at a Board meeting, but doubtless they also saw that a joint army-navy meeting would be to their disadvantage. As Katō explained to Tōgō on July 6: "It is absolutely essential that either the Board or the council be consulted, but I believe it would be better to have a meeting in which only the navy participates. At a meeting attended by both the army and navy we are at a disadvantage in the voting, since there will be those present who will not vote properly either from lack of comprehension or antipathy or for some other reason."[236] At a meeting of the Supreme War Council attended only by naval members, the voting would probably divide three in favor of the treaty (Takarabe, Okada, and Taniguchi) and three against (Fushimi, Katō, and Tōgō), and the matter would then be decided by Tōgō's extra vote cast in his capacity as chairman.

Okada too anticipated a minority-majority division of opinion in the Supreme War Council.[237] When on July 8 Taniguchi told Tōgō it would be appropriate to have a Board meeting, Tōgō insisted it was the Supreme War Council that must meet. Taniguchi suggested to Tōgō that at a Supreme War Council meeting only the naval members would be present and consequently Tōgō would become chairman; as chairman he would not have a vote and his side would be reduced to a minority. Tōgō rejoined that he would have one vote as a military councillor and that as chairman he would have the right to decide the issue if there were a tie vote. On investigation the Navy Ministry discovered that the presiding officer did have the voting privileges Tōgō had ascribed to him, a fact that Taniguchi duly reported to Tōgō.[238] Nonetheless, since Tōgō did not insist on a Supreme War Council meeting, it was decided to refer the treaty to the Board of Field Marshals and Admirals of the Fleet.

Okada had left Tokyo on the evening of July 8 for a special tour of inspection in northern Japan (Ōminato in Aomori) and did not return to Tokyo until the morning of the 14th. That day Taniguchi reported on what had happened during his absence. The navy vice chief of staff, he said, had conferred with the Army General Staff about referring the treaty to the Board, and he himself had talked with Chief of Staff Kanaya. The Army General Staff had postponed giving an answer until they had consulted with the Army Ministry. In the meantime, Taniguchi had thought it would do no harm to call on Tōgō and bring him up to date. After he had made his report to Tōgō, the admiral had said: "Last night I thought a great deal about this question of referring the treaty to the Board. That argumentative fellow Uehara is on the Board, so a Board meeting would be a very dreary affair. Isn't it possible to refer the treaty to the Supreme War Council?" Taniguchi had answered that he would arrange the matter and had gone immediately to Kanaya's private residence to make the request. Kanaya had replied that he would give an answer after consulting the Army Ministry but that he himself did not think there would be any difficulty. Later, the answer that there was no objection had been formally received.[239]

At their conference Okada and Taniguchi decided "not to try any stratagems but to move ahead on the changed basis."[240] Takarabe, Okada, Taniguchi, and Katō met at the navy minister's official residence to talk over the situation. Katō asked to be shown the draft of the reply to the emperor's query about the effect of the treaty on military plans, but Taniguchi declined to do so on the grounds the reply was still being worked out by the Navy General Staff. Katō then requested that at an informal meeting of the Supreme War Council an explanation be given of the supplementary measures to be taken to remedy the difficulties created for national defense plans by the treaty. This was agreed.[241] In his diary Katō says that at this meeting he got Takarabe to agree to put at the beginning of the text of the reply to the emperor the phrase, "There are defects in the national defense," and that both Takarabe and Okada consented to report this to Hamaguchi and request the prime minister's reaction to it.[242]

The following day, July 15, Taniguchi went to see Prince Fushimi at Karuizawa and came back with the report that he had obtained the prince's consent to the new arrangements. Takarabe, Okada, and Taniguchi worked ceaselessly to prevent Tōgō from being misled and placed in a compromising situation.[243] Takarabe was also troubled lest by participating in the vote Fushimi should arouse popular enmity against the imperial family. He cudgeled his brains seeking some method of preventing Fushimi from taking part in the proceedings.[244] Concerned that Tōgō should have two votes, Harada, at the behest of Hamaguchi, asked Ugaki, Kanaya, and Abe to do what they could to win acceptance of the interpretation that the chairman did not have a second vote in case of a tie. All three agreed, but in the end there was little they could do, since the army and navy had already reached agreement on the matter.[245] Okada was probably referring to this when he wrote in his diary that they had "decided not to try any stratagems but to move ahead on the changed basis."

With the situation thus confused and the outcome impossible to predict, Hamaguchi and Takarabe took counsel on July 14. The next day they brought Shidehara and Egi in on their discussions. On July 16 Kanaya visited the Navy General Staff and was told by Taniguchi: "The atmosphere has not improved, but the treaty cannot be abandoned. If the treaty is wrecked, the responsibility will be placed upon the military. Therefore we must make do with the strength allowed under the treaty. Navy Minister Takarabe is in a very tough position, and it's going to be very difficult during the next two or three days while waiting for the formal meeting of the council." When Kanaya asked what would happen if there were no agreement among those responsible for making a decision, Taniguchi indicated his determination that those responsible should push matters as far as they could. After that, the only thing to do was to inform the emperor that such and such were their opinions and to leave the matter to his decision.[246]

At 8:30 A.M. on July 21, Tōgō, Fushimi, Takarabe, Taniguchi, Okada, and Katō attended an informal meeting of the Supreme War Council at the navy minister's official residence. The items under discussion were the draft of the reply to the emperor and the supplementary measures to be adopted to offset the difficulties created for national defense plans by the London Treaty. Fushimi asked Takarabe what the prospects were for carrying out the supplementary measures, to which Takarabe replied: "That depends on the condition of the government's finances. The navy may say it needs such and such amount, but I cannot state that the government's financial situation will permit the entire program to be carried out." In the face of such a noncommittal answer the discussion took on a negative tone. Taniguchi thereupon proposed that at that point the meeting be ended for the day and that Takarabe make sure of the sincerity of the government's intentions. The meeting accordingly broke up at 3:00 P.M. Okada warned Takarabe that the sort of answer he had given meant trouble, and he asked Takarabe to state definitely that the program of supplementary measures would be unfailingly carried out. Taniguchi and Katō gave Takarabe the same advice.[247]

To discuss the answer the navy minister was to give at the next day's council meeting, Hamaguchi, Takarabe, Shidehara, and Egi met at the prime minister's official residence from 7:00 to 10:00 P.M. that night. Part way through they were joined by Home Minister Adachi Kenzō. The gathering decided that Takarabe would give the following answer, drafted by Egi:

> If there are shortcomings in the military strength needed to support and implement the operational plans drawn up in conformity with national defense policy, as navy minister I will, of course, consult fully with the navy chief of staff and make the best possible effort to ensure that compensations are made for such shortcomings.
>
> Moreover, when I asked the prime minister for his view on this matter, he gave his assurance in the following words: "If the investigations of the military authorities show it is necessary to supplement the military strength allowed under the treaty, it is my intention that the government too will, within the limits permitted by financial and other conditions, sincerely do its best to effect the necessary measures.[248]

At 8:30 A.M. on the 22nd the informal meeting of the Supreme War Council was reconvened. Before the meeting Takarabe showed Okada and Taniguchi the text of his reply. Okada warned him that the phrase "within the limits permitted by financial and other conditions" would become an issue at the meeting, and it was therefore decided to change the phrase to "adjusting as the occasion may demand to financial and other conditions."[249] After Takarabe had completed his explanation of the situation by reading his memorandum to the council, Tōgō urged that the reply to the emperor should conclude with a statement that there were defects in military strength. Okada stressed that the councillors would not be fulfilling their responsibilities as military men if the reply simply said there were defects but did not offer a plan for remedying these defects. Taniguchi and Katō supported Okada, and in the end both Tōgō and Fushimi accepted the draft of the reply, which was passed by the council at 9:00 A.M.[250]

That same day Taniguchi proceeded to the imperial villa at Hayama and advised the emperor to refer to the Supreme War Council the next day the question of "whether the strength allowed the imperial navy under the present London naval agreement does or does not give rise to difficulties with respect to national defense or the deployment of forces, and what measures should be adopted to deal with the situation." During the audience the emperor reminded Taniguchi, "This is probably not an arrangement that restricts our freedom of action at the 1935 conference."[251]

At 10:00 A.M. on July 23 the naval members of the Supreme War Council met within the imperial palace in the Higashi Ni-no-ma. Taniguchi explained in detail the report to the emperor, and the document was passed unanimously. There was a question-and-answer interchange between Takarabe and Katō on the right of military command problem, and then at 10:40 A.M. the meeting ended. The report to the emperor read as follows:

> The defense policy adopted by imperial decision in 1923 is the plan most appropriate to our present national condition. Acceptance of the present London Naval Treaty will cause shortcomings in the military strength required to support and implement the naval operational plans drawn up in conformity with the aforesaid established policy.
>
> Therefore, if the present treaty should come into existence, we must, until 1937, adopt the countermeasures listed below in order to hold these shortcomings to a minimum.
>
> 1. Complete utilization of the strength allotted under the agreement; the maintenance and improvement of the capabilities of existing vessels; full development of the categories of vessels upon which no limitations are placed by the treaty.

2. Full provision of the air strength necessary to support and implement operational plans.

3. Improvement of defense facilities; full development of experimental research agencies; improvement of educational facilities; rigorous implementation of every kind of training exercise; improvement and full development of personnel, matériel, amphibious equipment, arrangements for dispatching expeditionary forces, etc.

If the above countermeasures are adopted, we believe that under the circumstances presently existing the effects arising from the treaty's constraints can be mitigated, and there will be almost no difficulties with respect to national defense or the employment of forces.

However, from the standpoint of the intrinsic qualities of the armaments involved, there is an optimum distribution of strength among the various types of military forces. This distribution cannot automatically change in response to alterations in our national condition. Therefore, we would consider it very disadvantageous to our national defense if we were to be deprived of our freedom for a long time by this treaty. That is to say, as soon as this treaty expires, it is necessary immediately to perfect our national defense in accordance with the policies regarded as the best for our empire.

Submitted reverently and humbly.[252]

The phrase "will cause shortcomings in the military strength" near the beginning of the report mollified the hard-liners. But it was offset by the statement that if the proposed remedial countermeasures were adopted, "we believe . . . there will be almost no difficulties with respect to national defense or the employment of forces." As a whole the report affirmed the treaty and was the harvest of hard work on the part of Takarabe, Okada, and Taniguchi.[253] In all likelihood, however, the draft was the product of the intellectual exertions of Naval Affairs Bureau chief Hori Teikichi.

On the afternoon of July 23 Tōgō, accompanied by Taniguchi, journeyed to the imperial villa at Hayama and presented the emperor with the report. The emperor then summoned Taniguchi into his presence and was advised by the chief of staff to allow the prime minister to read the report. At the emperor's command aide-de-camp Nara called on Hamaguchi at 8 o'clock that evening and allowed him to read the report. On the 25th Hamaguchi informally presented the text of a reply to the emperor at a regular meeting of the cabinet, which gave its approval. The following day Hamaguchi traveled to Hayama and presented the following statement:

Your Majesty recently permitted me to read the report of the Supreme War Council regarding the London Naval Treaty. I have respectfully considered this report, and I will not neglect to provide fully for the empire's armaments. Since I believe the countermeasures proposed by the Supreme War Council are appropriate, I will endeavor to carry out these countermeasures after the London Naval Treaty is ratified and comes into effect. In implementing these countermeasures I will, of course, carefully discuss them with my cabinet colleagues, taking into account financial and other conditions and determining the suitability of the adjustments demanded by changes in circumstances. Furthermore, I will strive to obtain the consent of the Diet and bring these countermeasures to fruition. I pledge to do everything in my power to assist Your Majesty in carrying out the broad plans for the development of the nation.

Submitted in respectful and humble reverence by your subject Osachi.

July 26, 1930   Prime Minister Hamaguchi Osachi[254]

On July 22 Oikawa Koshirō had handed over to the Army General Staff a copy of Taniguchi's request to the emperor concerning the Supreme War Council. This version of Taniguchi's request differed substantially from that which Acting Army Minister Abe heard read at the July 25 cabinet meeting by Shidehara, who had borrowed it from the Navy General Staff. Then, on the 28th Taniguchi visited Kanaya and gave him a text of the Supreme War Council's report that did not contain the list of countermeasures. Taniguchi explained that the countermeasures were not included in the report, because they had been communicated orally to the emperor. As a result of these ambiguities the Army General Staff grew suspicious about the navy's behavior.[255]

The Privy Council Decides

After the report of the Supreme War Council had been accepted by the emperor, Hamaguchi asked the emperor to refer the treaty to the Privy Council for its advice. Immediately on his return to Tokyo Hamaguchi went to the private home of Privy Council President Kuratomi Yūzaburō and arranged with him the procedures for the examination of the treaty.

Although Kuratomi was Privy Council president, he was little more than a figurehead. The real power was held by Itō Miyōji, Vice President Hiranuma Kiichirō, and council secretary Futagami Heiji. These three, moreover, were strongly anti-Minseitō, primarily because of their dissatisfaction with Shidehara diplomacy. Hiranuma was president of the ultranationalistic Kokuhonsha (National Foundation Society) and had been a close friend of the Seiyūkai's Suzuki Kisaburō since the time they both served in the Justice Ministry. Itō Miyōji had set himself up as the guardian of the Constitution and had been the prime mover in the overthrow of the Wakatsuki cabinet. Futagami was an expert in laws, regulations, rules, precedents, customs, and usages. He was the man in the shadows who really ran the Privy Council.

The Privy Council's preliminary examination of the treaty involved six meetings held between July 26 and August 5. At these meetings Futagami gave notice of the Privy Council's antigovernment attitude by the exaggerated way in which he handled the problem of blurred printings and mistranslations in the treaty transcripts.

On the evening of August 4 Kuratomi came to Hamaguchi and requested that the report of the Supreme War Council be forwarded to the Privy Council for reference. Hamaguchi tactfully declined to do so, explaining that he had been specially allowed to read the report privately and thus had no copy to transmit to the Privy Council. He suggested that Kuratomi might take the necessary steps to secure the emperor's permission to read the report privately.[256] On August 6 Hamaguchi called on Kuratomi and gave a formal refusal to the request. Early on the morning of the 7th Kuratomi again visited Hamaguchi and pressed him to make available the council's report. Hamaguchi once more refused.

On August 11 the membership of the council's committee of inquiry was finally decided. Itō Miyōji was named chairman, the other members being Kaneko Kentarō, Kubota Yuzuru, Yamakawa Kenjirō, Kuroda Nagashige, Den Kenjirō, Arai Kentarō, Kawai Misao, and Mizumachi Kesaroku. Beginning with Ishii Kikujirō, the doyen of Japanese diplomats, every privy councillor who favored the treaty was excluded from the committee.

Hamaguchi's posture toward the Privy Council differed from that of Wakatsuki. From the beginning his attitude was quite firm. There were of course differences in the personalities of the two men as well, but Hamaguchi's firmness was based on the strong backing given to the return instructions by the genrō and senior court officials. Saionji at one point said to Harada, "I want the government to follow the path of logic to the very end. . . . If worst comes to worst and the Privy Council opposes the government with illogicalities, could not the prime minister, for the convenience of the government, use the powers of his office to dismiss the president and vice president and have the emperor's request for advice answered under a new president and vice president?"[257]

The committee of inquiry met thirteen times between August 18 and September 26. Its members wanted no officials below the rank of minister of state to attend, so only Hamaguchi, Shidehara, and Takarabe were present at the meetings. The exchange of questions and answers centered around such problems as the right of military command, shortcomings in the national defense, the memorandum on procedures to be used to determine military strength, a request for Katō Kanji to appear before the committee, the plan for supplementary measures, the tax reduction plan, and the request for transmittal of the Supreme War Council's report. The discussion of these issues was very heated.

At the second meeting (August 23) Hamaguchi described how the government had made its decision about the return instructions. He explained that the breakup of the conference would have invited serious diplomatic and financial consequences. Judging the matter coolly and calmly from the standpoint of the nation's overall situation, the following conclusion, he said, had been reached: even if the agreement had some unsatisfactory aspects in the light of Japan's original demands, the best policy for the nation was to accept in general the essential points of the compromise and, after attaching suitable reservations and desired conditions, to conclude the agreement. Shidehara explained the diplomatic point of view, and Takarabe compared the provisions of the treaty with the navy's original policy toward the conference. Takarabe stated that there was nothing in the treaty to cause uneasiness about the national defense during the life of the treaty. And while he acknowledged that from the technical viewpoint there were unsatisfactory points, from the overall situation of the national defense it was advantageous to have seized this opportunity and made an agreement.[258]

With the third meeting (August 26) the questioning began. Kaneko Kentarō began by criticizing the government's hostile attitude toward the Privy Council. He then asked whether the imposition of the treaty's detrimental conditions could not have been avoided if the government had cooperated at the conference with Italy and France and opposed the United States and Britain. He cited Stimson's "I take my hat off" speech and emphasized the disadvantages of the treaty. Shidehara responded with a detailed explanation of why Kaneko's view of the treaty was not correct.[259]

At the fifth (September 1) and sixth (September 3) meetings Kawai Misao (a former army chief of staff) and Kaneko hotly attacked the government on the right of military command issue.[260] Kawai inquired closely into why the navy chief of staff had been replaced, why Takarabe had communicated to the navy vice minister an opinion different from that in the delegates' request for return instructions, and why the navy chief of staff's dissenting opinion had been disregarded. In response, Hamaguchi detailed the circumstances at the time the return instructions were decided and said he believed the navy chief of staff had not opposed the return instructions. Takarabe read aloud Katō's April 2 telegram as evidence that Katō had approved the return instructions. Itō Miyōji asked that a copy of the telegram be submitted to the committee. When the navy minister declined to do so, Itō reprimanded him and characterized his position as "cowardly." There was a telegram in the committee's hands, Itō angrily exclaimed, which clearly showed the navy chief of staff's dissenting opinion. In the text of a telegram he was holding, Itō said, were the words, "I have opposed the return instructions. I am resolved also to address the emperor on the matter."[261]

From Kaneko Kentarō came a detailed exposition of constitutional theory. He censured as improper and indecent the government's action in disregarding the opinion of a military command agency and in arbitrarily deciding the return instructions at a cabinet meeting. Hamaguchi refuted this by saying, "The prerogatives are all united in the emperor. How can one prerogative infringe upon another prerogative? It is impossible to conceive of such a thing."[262]

Kawai asked the meaning of Hamaguchi's statement that in the Diet the government bore the responsibility for national defense. Hamaguchi replied that the command agencies of the military were institutions that must be hidden within their own structure and that have no connection with the Diet. If a defense problem should become a topic of debate in the Diet, however, the government could not respond to questions by saying that such matters were the responsibility of the command agencies and no concern of the government; therefore he had answered that the government bore the responsibility. Kawai also asked the grounds for Hamaguchi's statement to the Diet that with the military strength allotted under the treaty the national defense was very safe. Hamaguchi responded that in deciding national defense problems consideration must be given to diplomatic, economic, and other conditions. When he had surveyed the total national defense picture and had taken all factors into consideration, he had judged that the national defense was safe.

Kawai next suggested that there was a discrepancy between the prime minister's telling the Diet that the opinion of the military had been considered and his telling the committee that the navy chief of staff had consented. When Kaneko asked the reason for this inconsistency, Hamaguchi answered, "What opinion did Navy Chief of Staff Katō hold? Was there or wasn't there unanimity of opinion between the government and a military command agency? Questions like these were not of a character that required statements in the Diet. Matters of internal relations are not, I think, things about which explanations have to be given. Thus I intentionally confined my answer to saying that the military's technical opinion had been fully considered, and I avoided any statement beyond that. There is no contradiction between my answer in the Diet and my choosing to explain fully at a Privy Council committee meeting the facts of the internal situation." [263]

Noting that there were discrepancies between the facts as presented by the government and the documentary evidence in the committee's hands, Itō Miyōji proposed that to clear up these points the government arrange for Katō to appear before the committee. Hamaguchi responded that this was a very important matter and he would consult with his colleagues before giving an answer. [264]

After discussing the request with Takarabe and Shidehara, Hamaguchi decided to return a written refusal. The text of the refusal (including the reasons therefor) was drafted collaboratively by the government and the navy. On the afternoon of the next day, September 4, a letter of refusal addressed to Itō as chairman was handed to a Privy Council secretary by a cabinet secretary. It read as follows:

> At yesterday's meeting of the Privy Council committee of inquiry you requested that I arrange the appearance before your committee of Admiral Katō, the former navy chief of staff. After careful consideration I regretfully find that I cannot accede to your desire. I hope you will understand my position and not take offense. [265]

Earlier, at 10:30 that morning, Hamaguchi had said to Harada, who had come to call on him: "Since I have refused this request, the Privy

Council may resort to some plot or other. In that event, the government is determined to take drastic measures. Consequently, I would like to get the prince's approval beforehand. I would like you to communicate this to him." Harada immediately went to Gotemba and gave the message to Saionji. Saionji emphatically agreed with Hamaguchi and told Harada to inform the prime minister that he wanted strong measures to be taken. Harada returned immediately and told Hamaguchi, who commented that he was very pleased and relieved.[266]

On the 5th Katō dropped in on Taniguchi and said he wished to communicate with the navy minister about arranging to appear before the Privy Council committee to explain the circumstances at the time the return instructions were decided. Taniguchi urged him to keep silence. On the 8th Katō suggested the same thing to Takarabe, who refused and explained why it was impossible.[267] It is not clear whether Katō's proposal was made by previous arrangement with the Privy Council.

At the seventh meeting of the committee (September 5) Kawai argued that after 1936 the national defense would be imperiled. There was the danger, he said, that some incident might occur in China or that the United States might take advantage of the reduction in the ratio and try to impose an American policy in the Far East. What, Kawai wanted to know, was the government's opinion of this risk. Hamaguchi explained that national defense could be construed in either a narrow or a broad sense. "If we make too much of military armament and do not conclude this treaty, then, contrary to what might be expected, we will be worse off in our military defense when it is considered in its broadest sense, in other words from the standpoint of our nation's strength and bringing the power of its people to its fullest development. Consequently, though for one or two years the treaty may cause us some difficulties in connection with our armaments, we signed it to bring to perfection our national defense conceived in its broad sense."

Kawai then asked him whether the government was keeping the China problem in view when it prepared its armaments. Hamaguchi assured him, "There are few countries in the world that devote as high a proportion of their budgets to military expenditure as does Japan. We need not dwell on the fact that the reasons for such an enormous military expenditure arise mainly from the importance we attach to the China problem."[268]

At the eighth meeting (September 8) Kawai advanced the proposition that it would have been impossible for the United States to undertake offensive operations against Japan if Japan had obtained the submarine tonnage it had originally asked. With a 60-percent heavy cruiser ratio, Japan, he claimed, did not stand a chance against the United States. If a naval race were to begin right now, Japan would not suffer, since the tonnage it now actually possessed was superior to that held by the United States. In six years the situation would be reversed and Japan would be in a very disadvantageous position. Takarabe countered this argument by saying that operational plans did not remain fixed forever, and he could not be as confident about submarines as Kawai was. As for the shortage of heavy cruisers, there was no reason why this could not be offset by light cruisers and destroyers. If a naval construction race began now, Takarabe continued, the navy would be in a position of considerable difficulty. If this treaty were not concluded, the navy calculated that it would take ¥870 million to maintain the level of strength presently possessed by Japan.[269]

At the ninth session (September 10) Arai, Mizumachi, Kaneko, and Yamakawa raised questions about the tax reduction plan and the supplementary plan for countermeasures. Takarabe laid out the main points of the supplementary plan. Then Hamaguchi compared the naval strength allotted under the treaty with that demanded by Japan's three basic principles. The difference between the two sets of figures in no way justified the recent public clamor. By adopting supplementary measures to offset the gap, it would be possible to guarantee the security of the national defense. He would not, however, be able at that moment to specify the amounts of money involved in the supplementary plan or the tax reduction plan, Hamaguchi concluded, since the government had not finished drawing up the next fiscal year's budget.[270]

From this meeting on the atmosphere in the committee became more stormy, and the government began to prepare tactically appropriate countermeasures. The newspapers predicted a head-on collision between the Privy Council and the government and spread the rumor that there would be a change in government. At the tenth meeting of the committee (September 12) Yamakawa asserted that it was obvious a Japanese-American war could not be avoided if the United States continued in its present aggressive attitude. The only way to prevent such a war was for Japan to be thoroughly prepared in its armaments and make the United States respect it. Kubota added that Japan had attained its present international position solely because of its powerful military forces. Even if national wealth were to increase, this would not carry weight in the world. The most important things were the cultivation of the people's spirit and the fullest possible development of armaments.[271]

At the eleventh meeting (September 15) Itō announced that he had a request to make of the government, which he explained as follows:

> In the matter of the right of military command problem there still remain doubts about whether or not the navy chief of staff consented to the return instructions. The government has refused our request that the former navy chief of staff appear before us. Also, the government has given no answer to our request to be supplied with a copy of the telegram sent to Navy Minister Takarabe by the former navy chief of staff. Prime Minister Hamaguchi has shifted his position from the answer he gave in the Diet and has acknowledged that the navy chief of staff's consent is required in determining military strength. We have now reached a situation where it is impossible to pursue our inquiry, since further discussion will make it impossible to avoid a head-on collision between the government and the Privy Council. Therefore, believing that the right of military command problem has worked itself out, we will end any further questioning on that matter.
>
> In the case of the supplementary plan we are told to trust the plan to the government's decision. However, that would be the same as rubberstamping the matter before us, and it would be difficult to fulfill our official responsibilities with an act like that. Therefore we again here ask that we be given the report of the Supreme Military Council.

To this Hamaguchi answered that the government's position on the right of military command had not been changed in the Privy Council. Since answers were being given in different places, there were variations in what was said, but their purport was consistent. The government was not asking the Privy Council to rubber-stamp the supplementary plan, but the plan could not be shown to the Privy Council, since it was not yet the time to settle the concrete details of the plan. It was impossible, Hamaguchi continued, to reveal the verbatim contents of the Supreme Military Council's report to the emperor. However, since the contents were just as had been explained in detail by the navy minister, he would like the privy councillors to form an opinion of the report on the basis of that amount of information. It would be difficult to arrange the transmittal of the report and at this late hour in the proceedings it was not open to consideration.[272] When Hamaguchi had finished his statement, it was arranged that the next meeting of the committee would be on September 17 and would be for privy councillors only.

After the meeting Hamaguchi said to Harada, "I don't know what move the Privy Council members will make, but I intend to handle them with unshakable determination. I would like you to report this situation to Prince Saionji."[273] The next day Hamaguchi sent Egi to Gotemba as his representative to report to Saionji as well and to seek the prince's approval for future measures.

Anticipating there would be a change in government, the Seiyūkai had once again become very active. "This cabinet will fall in four or five days," Mori Kaku spiritedly told Harada.[274] On the 16th the Seiyūkai held a special party convention at their headquarters, at which Inukai charged, "It clearly infringed upon the right of military command for the government to have sent the delegates return instructions on the London Treaty plan without the consent of the Navy General Staff." In the Diet, Inukai continued, Prime Minister Hamaguchi had said only that he had taken the military's opinion into consideration; he had not said he had obtained their consent. However, it was rumored that in the Privy Council he had answered it was his conclusion the navy chief of staff had given his consent. If this report was true, then this was a piece of chicanery that changed the answer he had given in the Diet, and Hamaguchi's conclusion had in itself corroborated the infringement of the right of military command. The government had acknowledged that the treaty created defects in the national defense and was now in the midst of drawing up a supplementary plan. The expenditures required for this plan were greater than had previously been needed and in financial terms were an expansion of armaments. There was no surplus of funds that could be used to reduce the people's tax burden. "This treaty plan, at least so far as our country is concerned, has ceased to serve the purpose for which it was negotiated."[275]

In contrast the entire Tokyo press editorially criticized the Privy Council's position. On September 17 the Tōkyō Nichi-nichi said, "The people unquestionably support the London Naval Treaty. When the Privy Council ventures to antagonize the people and public opinion, is it not an act of lawlessness? To the government we say: fight the Privy Council and struggle on wherever your convictions lead. We find it hard to understand the Seiyūkai's attitude."[276]

The twelfth meeting of the committee, attended only by privy councillors, opened at 1:00 P.M. on September 17. There was a desultory exchange of opinions among the councillors, and finally the chairman proposed the committee write its report along the following lines: "If the government does everything necessary both to achieve the treaty's objective of reducing the people's tax burden and to carry out a sound supplementary plan based on full cooperation with the military, then we think it will be suitable for Your Majesty to ratify this treaty."[277] Mizumachi told Harada that Itō explained this sudden change in direction as follows:

> If the committee postpones its inquiry into the treaty, the government will request an inquiry with a time limit. After that, if our inquiry proves impossible, we will have to send back to the emperor unanswered his request for advice on the treaty. If we reject the treaty, the government will probably nonetheless advise the emperor to disregard our advice. Whichever course we take, the result will be that the issue is left to the emperor's decision, and he will be distressed. Truly that would be an unbearably dreadful situation. Further, if we look at the state of affairs within the Privy Council, a resolution from this committee rejecting the treaty would not be unanimously approved by the full Privy Council. If the plenary session of the Privy Council does not approve our resolution, we will have to resign. In all events the situation is grave. In these circumstances we must completely change course and vote to recommend unconditionally that the emperor ratify the treaty. I would like you please to sympathize with my painful predicament and give your approval to the treaty.[278]

When the real powerholders changed direction, the other committee members fell into line. Privy Councillor Kubota lamented, "The maneuvers of two or three wily schemers among the privy councillors have injured our honor and destroyed the public's confidence in us."[279] The nub of the problem, however, was the lack of independence of most of the privy councillors. While they should have been appointed because of their wisdom and experience, in actuality they all too readily echoed the opinions of two or three schemers, who therefore dominated their decision-making.

At its thirteenth meeting on September 26 the committee of inquiry unanimously adopted a report based on Itō's proposed text. This cut the ground from under the Seiyūkai, whose maneuverings had already been scathingly criticized in a *Tōkyō Asahi* editorial on the 18th.

There truly has never been a more wretched farce than the Seiyūkai special convention of the 16th. Perhaps it was merely wishful thinking or perhaps they really were deluded into believing there would be a change of cabinets. In any event, the Seiyūkai departed from the path of constitutional government and rushed to join themselves with the Privy Council's iniquity. And together with the Privy Council the Seiyūkai has come a cropper. Ludicrous is not the word for this spectacle. As for those who are responsible for having led the party to play this wretched farce before the world, they must take the tonsure and apologize both to the party and to the world. In fact, this present affair is not only a defeat for the Privy Council. It is also a defeat for the Seiyūkai. Moreover, since the Seiyūkai went out of its way to bring this defeat upon itself, it must be called a most inept party. The Hamaguchi cabinet has won a double victory.[280]

The full Privy Council met at 10:25 A.M. on October 1 in the Higashi Tamari-no-ma of the imperial palace, with all the privy councillors and cabinet ministers present. The recommendation made by the committee of inquiry was unanimously approved and the Privy Council adjourned. The hour was 12:30 P.M.

At 2:35 P.M. on October 2 the emperor handed over the certificate of ratification of the London Naval Treaty. The next day Takarabe resigned his post and Admiral Abo Kiyokazu was appointed navy minister. Okada had selected Abo for the post in advance and on September 20 had ascertained that their views on the issue of naval strength were identical.[281]

Thus ended the stormy process of ratification of the London Naval Treaty. The Tōkyō Asahi of September 21 was probably accurate when it attributed Hamaguchi's firm stand to the widespread support of the public and to the backing of the genrō and senior court officials. The certificate of ratification left Yokohama on October 4 aboard the Hikawamaru, went via the United States, and was delivered to Ambassador Matsudaira in London on October 24. On the 27th the ceremony of depositing the ratification documents was held in the Locarno Room of the British Foreign Office. That same day Hamaguchi, Hoover, and Mac-Donald made radio broadcasts from their respective capitals celebrating the conclusion of the treaty. On December 31 Ireland deposited its certificate of ratification, and from that moment the 1930 London Naval Treaty came into effect.

Navy Minister Abo encountered difficulties in the negotiations with the government over the expenditures for the navy supplementary plan, but agreement was finally reached between Abo and Finance Minister Inoue at midnight on November 9. At the cabinet budget meeting on the 11th the navy supplementary plan was formally approved. Of the ¥508 million it was estimated would be saved in naval construction costs from fiscal 1931 through fiscal 1935, ¥374 million was to be devoted to the supplementary plan and the remaining ¥134 million used for tax reduction.[282]

TWO

The Manchurian Incident, 1931

Introduction
MARIUS B. JANSEN

With the Manchurian Incident, Professor Seki concludes, Japan entered on the road that would lead to the Pacific War. It did so in the name of "national defense," a term against which the twentieth century has provided few safeguards. Few events did more to shape the middle decades of this century. In Manchuria, Japan first demonstrated fatal weaknesses in its polity and policy, and the damage done there to the country's civilian decision-making apparatus found the country less adaptable and less flexible for the greater crises that lay ahead. In Manchuria Japanese nationalism, reformist and strident, came to resonate with Chinese nationalism, also reformist and strident. As a result, the land that had done so much by example and precept to encourage modernization and Asian consciousness among its neighbors ended by becoming the enemy against whom those neighbors' emotions were directed.

So important a milestone has naturally attracted the interest of many historians. For long the proceedings and records of the International Military Tribunal for the Far East constituted the principal source for evidence, and it was largely on this base that Takehiko Yoshihashi constructed his valuable *Conspiracy at Mukden: The Rise of the Japanese Military* (1963). The excellent work of Sadako N. Ogata, *Defiance in Manchuria: The Making of Japanese Foreign Policy, 1931–1932* (1964) added to this a coverage of the mass of documentation compiled for the National Defense Agency's Military History Office and had the benefit of much recent monographic work, including that of Professor Seki here translated. The diplomatic setting within which the Manchurian Incident fell has received persuasive treatment in Akira Iriye's brilliantly constructed *After Imperialism: The Search for a New Order in the Far East, 1921–1931* (1965). And James B. Crowley's *Japan's Quest for Autonomy: National Security and Foreign Policy, 1930–1938* (1966) has greatly advanced our comprehension of the thinking and the internal divisions of the military.

Despite areas of overlap, none of these studies fully share Seki's focus and concern. He is less concerned with Manchuria than Yoshihashi, less with diplomacy than Iriye and Ogata, and less with defense planning than Crowley. He addresses himself instead to the question, "How did the Manchurian Incident happen, and why?" and answers these questions in their immediate, and not in their ultimate, sense. The record he has compiled is tightly chronological, and he shifts his focus frequently as events crowd in upon the leading actors of the piece. Yet in its very narrowness of focus his account reproduces some of the feel of that era for activists who were, in the truest sense of the term, single minded. And for all his restraint in analysis and interpretation, Seki provides an abundance of material for anyone interested in the era and its people. His study becomes an important contribution to our knowledge of Japan and the Japanese, the Kwantung army and all militarism, specific fears and general fanaticism, specific bureau chiefs and all organization men.

This translation limits itself to Seki's middle and later sections, his action chapters. It is appropriate to preface these with a brief account of the setting drawn together from Seki's opening sections and from other sources.

The connotations of the term "national defense" for all decision makers, and especially for the members of the Japanese miitary, were formulated in terms of their perception of Japan's place and mission in the world. And those perceptions fell in a spectrum bounded at one extreme by the views of the Foreign Ministry under Baron Shidehara Kijūrō in the mid-1920s, and at the other by those of the Kwantung Army, the subject of Seki's monograph.

The decade between 1915 and 1925, between the years of World War I and Shidehara, brought Japan into a new kind of world. It was one for which the orderly imperialistic procedures of the Meiji genrō had provided little preparation. The sudden power vacuum created by fallen and falling empires—the Chinese, the German, the Russian—and the emergence of the United States as a new world power forced the replacement of the Anglo-Japanese alliance, whereby Japan had grown to world stature under the protection of the British navy, with the network of treaties concluded at the Washington Conference in 1922, which contemplated the development of a new and cooperative order in East Asia. Japan was now enabled, indeed forced, to engage in a kind of geopolitical and strategic thinking for which few of the old rules applied. The absence of a working international order made the more serious changes in the internal order. On every hand status relationships in domestic societies seemed to be challenged and questioned quite as much as were relationships in international life. Throughout East Asia, as also in Japan, the disadvantaged, the young, and the powerless were growing aware of new currents of thought and organization that seemed to require a restructuring of the polity. Revolutionary Russia and revolutionary China posed problems for policy makers who could no longer rely on the answers that had been worked out for dealing with Imperial Russia and Imperial China. And so it seemed that the values and procedures of Imperial Japan also required reconsideration and reform.

The Shidehara side of the spectrum of responses to these challenges represented the historical, philosophical, and often the lineal successors of the Meiji power elite. Western-oriented and internationalist in experience and inclination, they held a realistic, rather than a visionary, view of the world in which they lived. In their minds, Japan should maintain the attitudes of reliance and trust on the West that had brought it such success; it should maintain its membership in the circle of great powers, and jointly those powers should cooperate in measures described as designed to achieve the just aspirations of Asian peoples. Those aspirations, like those of modernizing Japan, were presumed to be middle class, commercial, and representative.

Shidehara had participated in the decisions reached at the Washington Conference, and he based his China policy on the twin points of economic advancement and nonintervention. During his first period of tenure as foreign minister, from June 1924 to April 1927, the Chinese civil war for national unification had only begun. In north China the challenges were still between rival warlords. Moreover, during the early stages of the "Northern Expedition" Chinese nationalism was directed principally against Great Britain, and it was politically prudent and economically advantageous to avoid excessive involvement in responding to those incidents. In the spring of 1927 the Nanking Incident, however, led to a powerful groundswell of criticism in Japan. Shidehara's refusal to join Britain and the United States in protective or punitive measures helped unseat the government in which he held office.

Economic advancement took the form of an emphasis on expanding exports to China. This emphasis naturally required the avoidance of political hostilities wherever possible, and it had as its logical corollary Japan's participation in international efforts and promises to relieve China from the worst burdens of the unequal treaties. Under Shidehara, Japan participated in a Special Tariff Conference that was convened in 1925, and he repeatedly expressed understanding and appreciation of the Chinese need for tariff autonomy. Yet the same emphasis on trade resulted in a tough and inflexible posture on details when it came to negotiations. Shidehara's obduracy on satisfaction in some form for the Nishihara loans (to northern warlords in 1918) and his insistence that the realization of China's "national aspirations" had to be paired with "temporary adjustments" for Japan in view of the "intimate and particular relations between Japan and China" left his coexistence and coprosperity "so defined," as Iriye phrases it, "as to leave little room for compromise." These elements of toughness in bargaining were, however, overshadowed by Japan's refusal to intervene, and since it was some time before the establishment of political stability in China gave meaning to the negotiations inaugurated in 1925—they bore fruit only in 1929—this side of the foreign minister's approach has received much less notice.

Shidehara's emphasis on the China trade overshadowed his policy on Manchuria. Here, again, his position in historical writing has benefited chiefly by the contrast it offers to that of the Japanese militarists. The stability of Manchuria was agreed by all to be of preeminent concern to Japan, and it was self-evident that it depended on keeping the civil war in the south out of Manchuria and developing and strengthening the three provinces to protect them from subversion by the Soviets. This in turn involved persuading the warlord Chang Tso-lin, or his replacement, to rely on Japanese assistance and guidance for Manchurian development of Manchuria, and keeping him out of the political maelstrom of revolutionary China. But under Shidehara the Foreign Ministry was not committed to Chang Tso-lin and recognized Manchuria as ultimately Chinese.

Baron Tanaka Giichi, who followed as prime minister in the spring of 1927, inherited the problems of revolutionary China and Manchurian policy. Since he had based much of his appeal on dissatisfaction with "Shidehara diplomacy" and the Nanking Incident in particular, he had limited his flexibility of action before taking office. Because he had come to power in good measure on China policy, he reserved for himself the Foreign Ministry post, with the result that the post of parliamentary vice minister of foreign affairs, normally quite unimportant, rose greatly in power. It was filled by the Seiyūkai politician Mori Kaku, who now strengthened a tendency that was already of long standing in his career to be a hard-line "mainland first" advocate. Tanaka himself was a political soldier of the sort produced by the Chōshū leadership of Meiji Japan. The last of that group in some respects, he had come to a position of importance as vice chief of the Army General Staff before the Siberian Intervention of 1918, an action that he supported warmly. During the same period in authority he had provided army backing for ill-starred and inadequately planned efforts to sponsor separatist regimes under Manchu and Mongol princes in Manchuria and Mongolia. Gradually his experience of politics and authority had produced a greater ability to accommodate himself to political reality. He gained the trust of the last genrō Saionji Kimmochi and became the choice of Seiyūkai politicians anxious to find a popular figure able to lead them back onto the paths of power after their long eclipse during the Katō-Shidehara Minseitō cabinets.

Tanaka's differences with Shidehara in terms of concrete policy were considerable, though not overwhelming. The contrast between the two in terms of style and image was very great. And the contrast between them in terms of their appraisal by historians has been, until recently, greater still. Yet the differences between them were neither deep nor principled, and neither proved able to restrain the proclivities of the Manchurian army activists. Tanaka, at least, managed in 1928 to keep things from going further, whereas Shidehara, in 1931, did not. It seems safe to say that this was largely because the tide of Chinese revolutionary nationalism had barely touched north China during Shidehara's first incumbency; it reached Manchuria during Tanaka's time in office, and during Shidehara's second period of service, which is treated by Seki's monograph, Manchurian problems were rapidly becoming inseparable from those of Kuomintang China.

Tanaka's first speech as foreign minister committed Japan to cooperation with the powers in China but stressed that Japan could not be indifferent to the spread of communist power in China. His first act was to reject a set of proposals on Manchuria and Mongolia directed to him by the revolutionary Wuhan government. On the other hand, he also rejected a British proposal to station more troops in north China; Japan's aims, he said, were restricted to the maintenance of treaty rights in that area. Personally and officially Tanaka favored highly the new leadership

Chiang Kai-shek showed after his break with the Chinese communists in the spring of 1927. But he favored him for China, not for Manchuria. He wanted Chiang to unify China south of the wall and to cooperate fully with a pro-Japanese Manchurian regime under Chang Tso-lin in Manchuria. That this did not accord with Chiang Kai-shek's ideas should have become clear in personal talks between Chiang and Tanaka in November 1927, during an interlude when Chiang had stepped down as head of the Kuomintang (in August), but both parties seem to have come away with a mistaken impression of the other's intentions and intensity.

If desire was one thing, implementation was quite another. The initial tone Tanaka gave to his China policy was set by his willingness to intervene to secure the safety of Japanese nationals. On May 24, 1927, this produced a decision to send a small force of Japanese troops to Shantung. Tanaka was persuaded on this score by Mori Kaku and other advisers who argued that his criticism of Shidehara's inaction in the face of danger to Japanese during the Nanking Incident left him no choice. On this occasion there was still no intention of interfering in China's unification, and Japanese troops were withdrawn early in September after the danger seemed to be past. Although the Chinese Nationalists felt betrayed by this intervention, and clarification of the reasons surrounding it constituted part of the reason for Chiang Kai-shek's visit to Tokyo, the international and diplomatic community drew few conclusions from it. The Kuomintang's extrication from communist influence was not yet fully clear, and the memory of Nanking and of the insecurity of foreign life was recent. Consequently the Western powers seemed less prepared even than Tanaka to credit the Kuomintang with good will and a promising future. No irreparable harm to Sino-Japanese relations had yet been done.

A more enduring legacy of Tanaka's period in office is the confusion that surrounds an "Eastern Conference" of leading civilian and military officials to discuss Japan's posture in the Chinese civil war. The conference met in Tokyo between June 27 and July 7, 1927. To it has been credited the spurious "Tanaka Memorial," a supposed blueprint of aggression in East Asia and a document whose use in wartime propaganda gave it such indestructability that it refuses to die.[1] The genuine record of the conference fails to unify the verdict of historians. Ogata writes that the conference saw "Tanaka's militaristic policy . . . explicitly announced," while Iriye, to whose work the conference is more central, concludes that the conference "officially recognized the strength of the Nationalist movement and reendorsed the policy of assistance to Kuomintang moderates. Both these points had characterized Shidehara's policy. The conference did not evolve any new 'positive' policy toward China."[2]

Toward China. But toward Manchuria the Tanaka line was more explicit, and consequently new, for it was a problem to which Shidehara had not had to address himself equally urgently. Seki brackets this new, explicitly "Manchuria-Mongolia first" position with the new emphasis on Japan's right to protect its nationals, a right that had already been expressed—and attacked—in the Shantung intervention. The intervention "right" was temporarily solved by the retirement of Chiang Kai-shek and the consequent interruption of the Northern Expedition. But the Manchuria-Mongolia emphasis was related to the China policy by Tanaka. As he explained to the representative he sent to the funeral of Chang Tso-lin in the summer of 1928,

. . . there is positively no need for us to sacrifice our ideas regarding Manchuria for the sake of promoting the unification [of China]. It is because I thought we would automatically come to the control of Manchuria that I helped the cause of China's unification for a long time.[3]

Yet by the time Tanaka made this statement he had already failed to reach his goal, for at the Eastern Conference he had also made clear, though not public, his decision to support Chang Tso-lin. "[T]he stabilization of Manchuria's political conditions," he said, "should best be left to the efforts of the Manchurian people. If an influential Manchurian should respect our special position . . . and sincerely devise means to stabilize political conditions there, the Japanese government would support him as it considers proper."[4]

These two requirements of sincerity in devising instruments of stability and respect for Japan's position were put to the test in a series of negotiations about Manchurian rights. These had as their purpose the resolution of infractions of Japanese rights, by competing or parallel rail lines and industries, and agreement on further construction projects along lines granted in the Twenty-one Demands of 1915. The negotiations were complicated by the fact that while Manchuria was not yet tied in with north China by nationalism, it was by prenationalist and anti-Kuomintang warlords. For Chang Tso-lin was temporary head of the government in Peking. He had derived courage from Tanaka's Shantung intervention and the talk of a "positive" Japanese policy to think that he had a chance of staying on in Peking. And this left Tanaka the choice of negotiating with Chang through Japanese Minister to China Yoshizawa Kenkichi, thereby granting Chang this north China legitimacy, or with local Manchurian authorities through Consul-General (and postwar prime minister) Yoshida Shigeru, or again at Peking through personal and private talks through Yamamoto Jōtarō, the head of the South Manchuria Railway. The details of the negotiations were complex and permit a variety of judgments on those who took part in them. At one juncture, as Iriye shows, the Japanese military attaché in Peking, Honjō Shigeru (who was to command the Kwantung Army in September 1931), was critical of Yoshida's high-handed and threatening bearing toward Chang Tso-lin. More important is the fact that personal and institutional jealousies brought the negotiations to a dead end. The Foreign Ministry succeeded in blocking arrangements Yamamoto had made with Chang Tso-lin, and the latter in turn procrastinated in implementing his agreements because of the political and nationalistic pressures to which he was increasingly exposed. Thus the combination of Shantung, the suspicious Eastern Conference, and the Manchurian negotiations with a shaky warlord government turned upon Japan the full force of Chinese nationalism. Chang Tso-lin, who was second to few in his own fears of communist subversion against his regime, had now the further threat of Japanese intervention to prevent the spread of communism in his area.

While matters stood at this unsatisfactory point during the winter months of 1927–28, Chiang Kai-shek came to Japan to visit Tanaka in November 1927. Upon his return to China he resumed command of the Kuomintang, whose armies continued the unification march toward Peking the following April. As the armies entered Shantung, the Japanese military again raised the question of the safety of Japanese residents and property during cabinet meetings in Tokyo. Tanaka sought to compromise by authorizing the dispatch of troops to the port of Tsingtao, but General Fukuda Hikosuke, the local commander, moved inland to the rail head of Chinan (Tsinan) in response to local pressure. Conflict with Kuomintang troops was avoided until May, but with the outbreak of violence between Nationalist and imperialist forces the matter quickly got out of hand. Soon 17,000 Japanese troops were committed to protect 2,000 Japanese civilians. Until January 1929 Japanese military government ruled the Chinan area with the help of Chinese hirelings. The harm this disastrous intervention did to Tanaka's cause in China was well-nigh irreparable. Japanese field commanders compiled an unenviable record of crudity and mendacity. The death of 13 Japanese opium smugglers, for instance, was reported and accepted in Tokyo as that of 300 Japanese citizens. Anti-Japanese agitation grew steadily, and boycotts hurt Japanese trade. Perhaps worst of all Chang Tso-lin, who had seemed amenable to an early return to Mukden where he could represent "Manchuria" under Japanese protection, drew further comfort from the Japanese confrontation with the Kuomintang for the prospects of lengthening his own stay in Peking.

The Japanese authorities did not leave Chang in this euphoric state very long. Consul-General Hayashi Kyūjirō, who replaced Yoshida in Mukden in April 1928, and who would still be in office in 1931, brought assurances from Tokyo that the military would not be allowed to take over Japan's China policy. It was also Tanaka's urgent desire to get Chang Tso-lin out of Peking at the earliest possible moment, before he could be attacked and replaced there by Feng Yü-hsiang, who was assumed to be amenable to Russian control, and before he had to retreat with a victorious Kuomintang army at his heel. But this left open the problem of whether he should be allowed to withdraw his troops into Manchuria or whether they should be dispersed at the pass in order to avoid their becoming a magnet for extension of the civil war into Manchuria. Kwantung Army opinion, strongly represented by Colonel Kōmoto Daisaku, the senior staff officer, was firmly against permitting any armed troops, Chang's or Chiang's, into Manchuria. Naturally the new security arrangements would be for Japan to devise. The government first decided to disarm all troops at the Shanhaikuan barrier and then changed its stand.

Tanaka reorganized his cabinet late in May 1928. He resisted army demands for greater troop strength at the Manchurian border, and he agreed with the Foreign Ministry that Chang Tso-lin's army should not be disarmed. Chang, in turn, satisfied himself about his inability to resist the Nationalist armies and prepared to retreat with his armies. Shortly after midnight on June 3 a special train pulled out of Peking for Mukden bearing Chang Tso-lin. Staff Officer Kōmoto had arranged an explosion the next morning at 5:23. It cost Chang his life and plunged Manchurian policy into the vortex of Japanese and international politics.

In contrast to General Fukuda's intemperate and atavistic insubordination in Shantung, Kōmoto's act in Manchuria was the product of important fissures in military generations, thinking, and tactics. On some issues, of course, the military could stand united. They resented the cutbacks in military spending of the postwar years. The Washington Conference had alarmed the navy, and the London Conference would confirm both services in their distrust of civilian governments. The army's disestablishment of four divisions in 1925 under Army Minister Ugaki Kazushige achieved technological reform and modernization at the cost of size. The sharp decrease in financial support for the armed services in the 1920s and the prospects of further cuts under the Minseitō government that followed Tanaka led some to think of direct action to make such cuts impossible. For many members of the military establishment these restrictions, accompanied as they were by widespread evidence of popular disesteem of soldiering, a rise in urban and intellectual liberalism, and fledgling tenant and labor movements, could be interpreted as part of a larger breakdown of devotion to the nation. And since, finally, all of this coincided with the apogee of political party governments and a new and greater visibility of a plutocracy as opposed to the regional cliques of the Meiji period, it seemed to suggest the need for a whole series of social, economic, and political reforms.

It was above all the army men, trained as they were in command of regional regiments and in reasonably close touch with a disadvantaged countryside, who furnished the motive power for changes they thought would constitute a new "Restoration." They had a natural pattern for organization through their class years in the military academy, and they had a lively, though often idiosyncratic, awareness of the challenges of their time. Some, like Araki Sadao, who had served in Russia during the Bolshevik upheaval, had experienced the effects of twentieth-century radicalism personally, but all of them feared communism as an ideological plague. And a good many were concerned that the growing differentiation between classes in a capitalist Japan, with the evidence of corruption in political party government, was preparing the way for communism among tenants and workers in Japan.

Strategically the army officers inherited the focus of their elders, who had never stopped expecting a Russian war of revenge after 1905. Tsarist Russia had gradually been drawn into a series of treaties and guarantees shortly before its fall, but Japan's subsequent participation in the intervention against the new Bolshevik regime left no reason to expect better relations with the revolutionaries. By the mid-1920s the evidence that the Washington Conference order was not going to work very well in protecting China was clear, and the great upheaval of that decade in China brought the dangers of communism and nationalism together in zones vital to Japanese interests. In warlord disorder and with an absence of a new international order, opportunity combined with danger for Japan. Attempts to seize opportunities, as in the Twenty-one Demands, had only increased the dangers. Issues surrounding the Twenty-one Demands remained to haunt Manchurian negotiations, thwarted the Foreign Ministry's nomination of Obata Yūkichi as minister of China in 1929, and led the new Kuomintang government's National Assembly to declare May 9 a Day of National Humiliation. And the unresolved and unproductive debts that Nishihara Kamezō had squandered on northern warlords blocked Shidehara's approach to customs reform, just as they had earlier helped spark the May 4 demonstrations in 1919. Japan also paid dearly in popularity for the Shantung holdings it had taken on so cheaply from the Germans in World War I.

There were also important fissures within the army. The Meiji military establishment had long been Chōshū dominated, and under the benign influence of Yamagata Aritomo it had gradually become an important, perhaps the principal, element of the political establishment. Yamagata himself, and Generals Katsura Tarō, Kodama Gentarō (had he lived), Terauchi Masatake, and now Tanaka all knew the top of the military, as well as of the political, hierarchy. Ugaki Kazushige, though not himself a Chōshū product, was a product of the Chōshū system, and his close cooperation with political party cabinets produced in him a willingness to defer to Shidehara diplomacy despite his personal hard-line views. Seen from the perspective of their younger subordinates, both Ugaki and Tanaka seemed to promise much and deliver little; both, indeed, represented the hope of the genrō Saionji to "control" the army, and both presided over new and more gross evidence of plutocratic control of government. Ugaki was army minister in a cabinet popularly considered to be Mitsubishi financed, and in Tanaka's time the use of money in elections, particularly that of 1928, the first to be conducted under the provisions of the manhood suffrage law of 1925, was more blatant than ever before.

Thus it was fitting that it was precisely these men who became the focus of intense pressure from a new breed of army officers. They were young enough to be unchastened by the Meiji memory of weakness, educated enough to be convinced of the need for sweeping technological and institutional changes to prepare Japan for the total war of the future, insular enough to be wholeheartedly committed to the doctrines of national purity and distinctiveness, and modern enough to be indignant over the evidence of continuing favoritism for Chōshū types and protégés. Many of these had reached field officer status by the mid-1920s, and they need to be recognized as among the most able men of their generation. Like many activists of the Meiji Restoration, they were by no means of humble status or rank, but like them also their zest for authority had been met by practical command without having been rewarded by ultimate power. The more able and important members of these groups came to dominate the section, division, and bureau desks of the bureaucratic pyramid, and in Seki's study we see them nearing the zenith of their ability and influence. We find among their number advocates of total mobilization like Nagata Tetsuzan, men committed to the establishment of a Manchuria severed from Chinese administration like Suzuki Teiichi, and others prepared to go a step farther and to deny the Chinese all sovereignty there, like Kōmoto Daisaku. In the mid-1920s a weekly discussion group included Nagata; Ishiwara Kanji, who figures so large in Seki's account; Okamura Yasuji; and Tōjō Hideki. The most influential of the officers' societies discussed by Seki, the Issekikai, included Kōmoto, Doihara Kenji, Nagata, Okamura, Tōjō, Suzuki, and Yamashita Tomoyuki, as well as Ishiwara and Itagaki Seishirō. There were many differences of temperament and timing among these men, but they were basically agreed on the need for a purification and militarization of Japanese society, as they were about Japan's opportunities on the Asian mainland. In 1928 their disappointment in Tanaka made Kōmoto's successful plot on the life of Chang Tso-lin much more than the act of an isolated fanatic.

It was inevitably the Kwantung Army that became their instrument. That army's mission was, as its name made clear, "east of the [Shanhaikuan] barrier," and the sharpness of its consciousness of a Manchurian task and entity was never in question. Neither was its institutional and administrative self-assertiveness. First formed as Japanese expeditionary forces faced the Russian armies in Manchuria, the army survived a number of attacks on its autonomy by Foreign Ministry and General Staff reformers who tried to regularize its status and place it under more usual channels of administrative control. These organizational changes ultimately resulted in a separation of military from administrative function. By 1931 the Kwantung Army was charged with the security of the Liaotung leasehold, for which it had a division, and the safety of the South Manchuria Railway system, from Port Arthur to Ch'angch'un, a distance along which it was permitted to station 15 men per kilometer. Its total strength was thus in the neighborhood of 10,000 men, a small force in the face of the enormous and expensive armies numbering around 250,000 men maintained by the Manchurian authorities. But the latter were neither well trained nor well equipped. The Japanese troops, the pride of the imperial army, were far better trained. Broken down into small detachments as they were along the length of the rail system, they were also equipped as mixed and independent units and thus constituted a far more versatile and flexible series of units than would have been true if the army had been stationed in one large base receptive to central command. The separation of military from administrative function had also had the effect of creating multiple levels and networks of command in Manchuria. The leased territory was administered by a governor appointed by the prime minister's office and had its own security police. The Foreign Ministry had a major consulate-general at Mukden and subsidiary consulates with consular police in settlements in other major cities in Manchuria. And the South Manchuria Railway, a semi-state-owned enterprise whose director-general was appointed by the prime minister, controlled an elaborate network of extractive industries (ores, coal at Fushun, forests) and warehouses in connection with its transport operations. It thus carried the brunt of the Japanese economic programs for Manchuria. The complexity of this administrative structure gave force to the frequent reminders, in the memoranda and schemes Seki describes, of the need to cultivate understanding and cooperation.

Manchuria itself, the arena in which the Kwantung army played its role, was of course Japan's true frontier. It was where the empire bordered on the Soviet Union and on communism. It was also a frontier of minerals and raw materials, materials recognized by all planners as essential to building a "national defense state," and materials that constituted Japan's one hope of building for itself an impregnable material position. And it was also agreed that the currents of revolutionary Chinese nationalism must under no condition be allowed to cross this frontier. The two decades during which the area had been under Japanese influence had constituted a period of relative political quiet, economic advance, and Chinese immigration. Koreans, too, partly in response to Japanese wish, partly out of a wish to escape Japanese control, had crossed their Manchurian border in large numbers into adjacent areas.

Thus there were many areas of friction suitable for exploitation. Anti-Japanese Koreans, affected by Russian and Chinese radicalism, made up one such. The Japanese insisted that they should be beneficiaries of concessions that had been made to Japan in 1915. And since they were also radicals, and beneficiaries as "Japanese" of extraterritoriality, Japanese consular police were sent in to investigate and control them. The Chinese insisted they were squatters and discriminated against them. The Japanese then played the role of defender. And so anti-Korean demonstrations in eastern Manchuria drew a response of anti-Chinese demonstrations in Korea, which in turn resonated with anti-Japanese protests in north China. The opportunities all this offered for malevolent design were endless. It comes as little surprise to read that extremist Japanese, anxious to channel hatred into military action, helped incite Koreans against Chinese in 1931, and that on the eve of the Manchurian Incident in 1931 Kōmoto was busily engaged in stirring up new riots against Koreans by Chinese settlers in the Chientao region of Manchuria in order to demand a Japanese response.

In this setting Kōmoto had decided in 1928 that the elimination of Chang Tso-lin would help to advance military control. Agreements between Tanaka and Chang had seemed to Kōmoto and his associates meaningless and mischievous private understandings among militarists. Some Kwantung Army men apparently thought that Chang Tso-lin's son, Chang Hsueh-liang, would not be affected by his father's dreams of power in Peking and would be prepared to cooperate with Japan if only the father were gone. Kōmoto himself, however, hoped to create a disorder sufficiently great to justify intervention by the Kwantung Army for the establishment of a new government. But he had not prepared with sufficient care. His associates in the Kwantung Army staff, not knowing his designs, had moved a brigade he had left stationed in front of the Mukden Yamato Hotel in order to have it at hand to receive the anticipated attack of Manchurian troops; and since those units had orders not to attack, nothing came of the plot. Inadequate preparation, planning, and follow-through: this was the meaning of the pleas made in the Kwantung Army's Port Arthur headquarters in 1931 not to let Ishiwara and Itagaki go the way of Kōmoto.

Prime Minister Tanaka's efforts to investigate and punish the murder of Chang Tso-lin, expressly commanded by the emperor, ran afoul of the factional bitterness and institutional strength of the anti-Chōshū, reform-minded military. The army, especially its middle ranks and key bureaucratic section and division heads, was in revolt against any thought of exposure and punishment. Kōmoto was reassigned, but only to be replaced by Itagaki Seishirō, a chief architect of the more successful incident of 1931. Tanaka's failure to carry out his purpose cost him his political leadership, his emperor's confidence, and in July 1929 his post as prime minister.

The murder of Chang Tso-lin did not mean that the Japanese would be at odds with his son Chang Hsueh-liang, but neither did it solve any of the problems outstanding. The young marshal, although he was not long in learning about his father's murderers, could ill afford to show resentment against Japan. He had a prior problem of establishing his personal authority in Manchuria, where his father's brother-in-law Chang Tso-hsiang and his father's Chief of Staff Yang Yü-t'ing had credentials for leadership as good as his own. Not until January 1929, when he had had the latter arrested and personally blew his brains out, was his internal position reasonably secure. In the meantime he announced, in July, that Manchuria had to reach some understanding with Japan "in order to obtain its own independence."[5] Simultaneously Chang pursued negotiations with the Kuomintang government of Chiang Kai-shek, who had occupied Peking on June 6, for the accession of Manchuria to Nationalist China. But on highly attenuated terms. The three provinces would be virtually autonomous, there would be no Kuomintang branches of propaganda organs set up, and Jehol would be added to Manchuria as a fourth province. Even this agreement was for a time blocked by Tanaka, who took alarm at the unilateral denunciation of China's treaty of commerce with Japan. For some months Tanaka attempted to strengthen Japanese ties with Chang Hsueh-liang and to consolidate an independent Manchuria, but the pulls of Chinese nationalism—and of bargaining power against Japanese imperialism—proved too strong for him. Ineluctably, Manchurian politics were intertwined with those of Kuomintang China once more.

Improvement came only with improvement in relations with Nationalist China. Tanaka's tortuous negotiations over the Chinan Incident were long and difficult, because of the Kuomintang demand for prior withdrawal of Japanese troops and the Japanese military's refusal to lose face in this matter. During the negotiations even Tanaka's "positive" policy came under attack from Minseitō politicians as "weak." A settlement was finally reached in the spring of 1929, in return for Japanese recognition of the Kuomintang government of China. Recognition became effective exactly a year after the Shantung Incident had delayed that unification, on June 3, 1929. And shortly afterward a group of Japanese that included Minister Yoshizawa, Inukai Tsuyoshi, Tōyama Mitsuru, and Miyazaki Torazō was sent to Nanking as Japanese representatives to the ceremonies for the final interment of Sun Yat-sen on Purple Mountain. During all of this period Tanaka was under strong and increasing pressure from court conservatives to do something about military discipline. Shortly after he tried to close the issue by telling the emperor that investigation showed that no Japanese had been involved in the murder of Chang Tso-lin after all, he resigned.

In July 1929 Tanaka's "strong" and "positive" policy had thus achieved none of its purposes. Anti-Japanese feeling was a stronger component of Chinese nationalism than it had ever been before. A partly cooperative militarist had been replaced by his more suspicious and fearful son, who inherited none of his father's reluctance to cooperate with a Kuomintang Nationalist government. The tides of national revolution had swept beyond Peking. Kuomintang branch councils and organizations in Manchuria could not long be delayed. Thus Tanaka left many uncompleted and difficult projects for his successor, Shidehara.

Seki's monograph takes up during this second period of Shidehara's service as foreign minister. There was, he shows, no sweeping change in policy. All further thought of an investigation of the Manchurian murder was put aside. New efforts were made to turn the Kuomintang, and especially Chang Hsueh-liang, against the Russians. When a dispute over the Chinese Eastern Railway brought the Russians to break off relations with Nanking and to open war with Chang Hsueh-liang in the late summer of 1929, Japan was inevitably the beneficiary in Chinese opinion.

But not for long. The mysterious death of Saburi Sadao, minister to China, and the unfortunate selection of a man associated with the Twenty-one Demands as his successor brought new controversies. A customs agreement was worked out in March of 1930. Japan changed its style of reference to China from "Shina" to the "Republic of China." But in most respects the tide of Chinese nationalism focused on Japan. Chang Hsueh-liang challenged the Japanese by a program of railway building that would, they feared, transfer goods from the South Manchurian network to a new Chinese system designed to carry freight to the port of Yingk'ou. Industrial developments began to sprout in areas long dominated by the South Manchuria Railway, giving rise to alarmed comment about the maintenance of Japan's "lifeline" in Manchuria.

The world depression struck the profits of the South Manchuria Railway as it did Japanese well-being at home. The Kuomintang flag having been accepted in Manchuria, pressures of Chinese competition and Chinese nationalism seemed to imperil the gains of a quarter century of Japanese effort in an area purchased, as the Japanese nationalists had it, by their forebears' blood. New anti-Japanese and anti-Korean movements sprang up in the Chientao area of Manchuria. In the fall of 1930 in Tokyo, debate raged over the London Conference agreements for naval reductions in Tokyo, Hashimoto Kingorō formed his Sakurakai, and Prime Minister Hamaguchi Osachi was fatally wounded. By early 1931 Chang Hsueh-liang was asking the Nanking government for financial assistance for building railroads in Manchuria. By March there were Kuomintang bureaus in all principal Manchurian cities. And in April 1931 C. T. Wang, Nanking's foreign minister, announced that China intended to reclaim all rights and all concessions; tariff autonomy, extraterritorial rights, and all settlements, all leased territories, and all railroad and other communication rights would have to be given back.

Thus Chinese nationalism and Japanese right-wing nationalism resonated with each other, and the vibrations of that resonance gave confidence and intensity to the military planners who saw it their mission to lay the plans for the first step in what was to be the long-range transformation of East Asia into a single economic and political sphere under Japanese domination. Itagaki and Ishiwara, as Seki begins his account, succeeded Kōmoto in the Kwantung Army staff in 1928. By 1931 they felt they had little time to lose. The Soviet Union was well along in its Five-Year Plan, Chinese nationalism was taking deep root in Manchuria, and by then both of them were due for reassignment.

TWO

The Manchurian Incident, 1931

SEKI HIROHARU

Translated by
MARIUS B. JANSEN

The fuse for the military action at Mukden on September 18, 1931, was lit by the Kwantung Army. But the overall vision and organization of that event came from the brain of Lieutenant-Colonel Ishiwara Kanji of the Kwantung Army General Staff. Ishiwara's plans had in turn been nursed along by Colonel Itagaki Seishirō, a senior staff officer of the Kwantung Army, who had the political ability and influence to shield them from the numerous domestic factors that could have prevented their realization. It is, therefore, reasonable to describe the Manchurian Incident as the joint product of Ishiwara's conception and Itagaki's implementation, or perhaps of Ishiwara's ingenuity and Itagaki's influence.[1]

Ishiwara's views concerning the need to employ military force took form under his consciousness that Japanese rights in Manchuria and Mongolia were in immediate danger of infringement. Consequently, a discussion of the formation and development of Ishiwara's vision must be prefaced by an account of the circumstances prevailing at the time in Manchuria and Mongolia.

In his memoirs Matsuoka Yōsuke, who was vice president of the South Manchuria Railway and who supported the army completely, declared that "most informed people" believed that the cries of alarm about the seriousness of the situation in Manchuria and Mongolia were raised primarily by "an obstinate and bigoted minority," but within the Kwantung Army and among the leaders of the Japanese community in Manchuria, Manchuria-Mongolia was seen as a holy land, "consecrated by the sac-

---

This is a translation by Marius Jansen of Seki Hiroharu, "Manshū jihen zenshi (1927–1931)," in *Taiheiyō sensō e no michi*, vol. 1, part III, sec. 2 and 3, pp. 359–440, together with footnotes.

rifice of one hundred thousand brothers who shed their blood in the war led by the great Meiji emperor."[2] It was because Manchuria and Mongolia were significant in terms of both present and past that Ishiwara's plans and the tactical schemes to which they led sprang to life within the Kwantung Army and grew until, without having attracted much attention, they suddenly came to dominate Japanese politics.

Within Japan the universal manhood suffrage act of 1925 ushered in a modern parliamentary system, however imperfect, and the first elections under its provisions were carried out on February 20, 1928. But there was no mechanism for representation of the Japanese in Manchuria, who were dependent on the disposition of administrators appointed from the home country. Many of the journalists in Manchuria attributed to this the sense of helplessness felt by their fellow nationals who, as they put it, felt cooped up in a small area "under the pressure of Chinese economic activities."[3] These journalists deplored the fact that leftists and liberals alike had begun to advocate the abandonment of Manchuria and Mongolia, and they did their best to offset this by encouraging the establishment of organs of public opinion among Japanese young people in Manchuria. Their most important achievement to this end was the establishment of the Manchurian Youth Congress, which was designed to bring about the transformation of a "Manchuria and Mongolia entrusted to administrators" into a "Manchuria and Mongolia bought by the blood of the entire nation." The Dairen Newspaper Company, which sponsored the public election of ninety delegates to the Youth Congress, stressed the need to build a "last ditch defense" of Manchuria and Mongolia "on the basis of the high resolve and patriotism of the young."[4]

The significance of this was that in Manchuria, which was Japan's frontier, demands for political participation were inseparable from the hypersensitive, antiforeign nationalism typical of a colony. The manifesto issued at the opening of the Manchurian Youth Congress emphasized that the congress was being established "to mark the enthronement of the present emperor" and stressed that Manchuria and Mongolia formed a "historical, geographical, economic, and security zone inseparable from our empire."[5] But in the first model Diet, which met from May 4 to 6, 1928, the deliberations went so far as to take up a "Proposal for an Autonomous State of Manchuria."[6] In this parliament there were, all told, ninety delegates representing twenty districts and organized into parties, including a Young Men's Liberal Party with Hirajima Toshio as president, a Young Men's Dōshikai, a Young Men's Independence Party, a Liberal League, a Democratic Party, and various "neutral" groups. All this, designed to hold up the torch for the creation of an ideal state in Manchuria, must be seen as the product of nationalism suffused with romanticism. Prime Minister Tanaka Giichi sent the gathering a message of congratulation for having inaugurated a parliamentary system, in response to which the parliament approved unanimously the resolution of thanks offered by its chairman Hirajima.[7] The delegates then went on to consider Japanese policy toward the mainland, including a heated discussion of the proposal that "we should send troops into Shantung and hold the entire zone as guarantee."[8] After this a model cabinet was set up under Kohiyama Naotaka. The new cabinet, more chauvinistic than the Tanaka cabinet in Japan, represented a distinctively colonial phenomenon.

During 1928 relations between Japan and China gradually worsened. There was a second Japanese intervention in Shantung, the outbreak of hostilities at Chinan (Tsinan) on May 3, the murder of Chang Tso-lin on June 3, and on July 18 the announcement by the Nationalist government that it would no longer recognize the unequal treaties. The movement against Japanese goods reached mass proportions, particularly after the Chinan incident. In Manchuria Chang Hsueh-liang's government delayed public display of the Nationalist flag for a time after the death of Chang Tso-lin, but that delay was to end in mid-November. On November 5 the Manchuria committee of the Chinese Communist Party made its first assertion of Manchurian freedom from foreign domination with an announcement that "the unequal treaties are all null and void." The communists thus seized the opportunity provided by the wave of anti-Japanese sentiment to inaugurate action in Manchuria. Their declaration called on "all Manchurian workers, peasants, soldiers, merchants, and student leagues to join in a struggle to contest [the South Manchuria Railway's] transport rights" and demanded the return of Port Arthur, Dairen, the South Manchuria Railway, mines, and forests and the expulsion of "Japanese militarists" from the territory, as well as the overthrow of the Mukden warlords and the Nationalist Party (Kuomintang).[9] This marked the first response to the anti-imperialist and anti-Japanese campaigns of the Nationalists, which had hitherto met with little support in Manchuria and Mongolia.

Six days later, on November 11, the second Manchurian Youth Congress was convened in the Dairen YMCA. This time the number of delegates had risen to several hundred. They adopted a "Plan for the Formation of a Youth League,"[10] drafted on October 3, that called for an "ideological struggle in Manchuria."[11] The basic nature of the image held by the delegates was shown in the pronouncement made by Chairman Kohiyama and endorsed by the congress. "Manchuria and Mongolia are at the brink of peril," Kohiyama declared, and he warned that if the youth of Manchuria did not emulate the young activists of the Meiji Restoration by addressing themselves to the dangers of the Shōwa era, "the ancestral country will be overwhelmed by disastrous misfortune." Leadership of a "movement to establish a fundamental policy for Manchuria and Mongolia," he urged, should be taken out of the hands of "old-fashioned administrators" preoccupied with political in-fighting, and Manchuria and Mongolia "rescued" by a true "people's diplomacy."[12] The new Youth League that was established set its policy line in January 1929 with the declaration that "the territories of Manchuria and Mongolia must truly become our ideal home."[13] Tours to stir up public feeling and support were carried out in the areas of Japanese settlement along the South Manchuria Railway line, and branches of the league were established. The young firebrands took as a slogan the "Great Challenge of a Shōwa Restoration," for, they declared, "although our object is the construction of a new state in Manchuria and Mongolia, we must never forget the strains of our country's national anthem."[14]

On June 1–3 the first congress of the Manchurian Youth League was held in the South Manchuria Railway's Concord Hall in Dairen. The delegates began by singing the national anthem *Kimi ga yo* and heard a message of greeting from the head of the local reservists organization. They went on to adopt a "Plan for Self-Government for Manchuria and Mongolia" and proclaimed that the league was "a young people's movement for national development in Manchuria and Mongolia."[15] Because of uncertainty that the 30 million people of Manchuria would accept the idea of building "an autonomous state with the help of an outside country," formal adoption of the plan was put over to the next congress. But this was the voice of a small minority; the general insistence was that something had to be done in Manchuria and Mongolia in the face of the strong anti-Japanese movements that were arising.

Ishiwara's Plans for Manchuria

When he appeared as a witness at the International Military Tribunal for the Far East in Tokyo, Ishiwara Kanji attacked the American prosecuting attorney in these terms:

> Haven't you ever heard of Perry? Don't you know anything about your country's history? . . . Tokugawa Japan believed in isolation; it didn't want to have anything to do with other countries and had its doors locked tightly. Then along came Perry from your country in his black ships to open those doors; he aimed his big guns at Japan and warned, "If you don't deal with us, look out for these; open your doors, and negotiate with other countries too." And then when Japan did open its doors and tried dealing with other countries, it learned that all those countries were a fearfully aggressive lot. And so for its own defense it took your country as its teacher and set about learning how to be aggressive. You might say we became your disciples. Why don't you subpoena Perry from the other world and try *him* as a war criminal?[16]

Ishiwara Kanji was born in Yamagata prefecture in January 1889. He attended the military preparatory school (Yōnen Gakkō) in Sendai and graduated from the Military Academy with its twenty-first class. When he graduated from the Army War College he was considered "the most brilliant student in the history of the college," but at the same time his character was described as "rough and carefree." From 1920 to 1921 he was in Hankow attached to the command of the Central China Expeditionary Forces, and during that time he renewed close connections with Itagaki Seishirō, then on the staff of the Expeditionary Forces, whom he had known at the Yōnen Gakkō and with whom he would team up in the future. In 1922, when he was an instructor at the War College, Ishiwara was sent to Germany for study; he returned in 1925 to resume his post at the college. In the meantime he had become a disciple of Tanaka Chigaku in Nichiren Buddhism.

On August 10, 1928, Ishiwara was promoted to lieutenant-colonel. Two months later, on October 10, he reached Port Arthur. There he was assigned to Kwantung Army staff headquarters and attached to the Operations Section. This was four months after Colonel Kōmoto Daisaku had engineered the murder of Chang Tso-lin and about a month before the formation of the Manchurian Youth Congress. When Ishiwara arrived, the anti-Japanese movement in Manchuria was at flood tide, and

Kwantung Army opinion had begun to be phrased in terms of "necessity to prepare war plans against China in anticipation of security contingencies."[17] This was also immediately after Prime Minister Tanaka had sent the commander of the military police (Kempeitai), General Mine Yukimatsu, to Manchuria to investigate the circumstances of the explosion that took the life of Chang Tso-lin. At the time of Ishiwara's arrival there, Kōmoto was averring to all who would listen the need of a military solution for Manchuria and Mongolia, and Ishiwara is said to have agreed with this as a matter of course. Thoroughly familiar with the debate that was taking place everywhere in connection with the murder of Marshal Chang, Ishiwara prepared analyses of war plans for the staff of the Kwantung Army. At that time the Mukden (Fengt'ien) authorities had at their disposal about 20,000 picked men in and around Mukden, and in addition planes and tanks, as well as military industries such as arsenals and mortar workshops; in the province as a whole there were close to 250,000 Manchurian troops.

To deal with these the Kwantung Army had six battalions guarding the railway lines on the basis of 15 men per kilometer, plus one integrated division as a nucleus, for a total strength of slightly more than 10,000 men. It had no planes and no tanks, and it was weak in artillery and engineering, as well as in transport. That being so, it is interesting to see how Ishiwara worked out a military strategy whereby the Kwantung Army, despite its position as underdog, could seize control of the Mukden fortifications.

The plan the Kwantung Army staff adopted called for "a lightning strike against the forces in the vicinity of Mukden and seizure of political control" when "the time comes to strike."[18] Inevitably, this plan, while pretending to be a defense plan, greatly increased the possibility of a full-scale clash. In fact, it is not far wrong to say that it built in the necessity of a preventive attack. The details of the plan were worked out on the basis of this assumption. When the first meeting of branch chairmen of the Manchurian Youth League was held on February 28, 1929, those who attended had of course no knowledge of the Kwantung Army's plan for direct action, but Ishiwara's thinking received curiously appropriate support from Chairman Kohiyama's statement that Japan must never be permitted to "suffer the fate of lowering its flag" and retreating from Manchuria and Mongolia.[19]

On May 14 it was announced that Colonel Itagaki Seishirō was being transferred from command of the 33rd Regiment (at Tsu) to be senior staff officer of the Kwantung Army, replacing Colonel Kōmoto Daisaku, who had been one class ahead of him at the Military Academy. In actuality he had already arrived in Mukden in April to take up his duties. As has been noted, Itagaki had come to know and trust Ishiwara in earlier periods of service in Sendai and Hankow. Between 1924 and 1926 Itagaki had served in Peking as aide and as staff officer to Honjō Shigeru with the rank of lieutenant-colonel.[20] Itagaki's assignment to the Kwantung Army thus meant a return to familiar haunts on the continent, as well as the resumption of a close relationship with Ishiwara. At the same time he had close ties with men like Nagata Tetsuzan in Japan. The development of the Ishiwara-Itagaki team at a time of rapid change thus meant the emergence within the Kwantung Army of a new advocacy of a military solution to the Manchurian and Mongolian questions, a view that was able to command support within the central headquarters of the Japanese army.

Another dynamic that came into play with these Manchurian discontents was that of factionalism within the imperial army. To bring this into the picture the story must move back briefly. On October 27, 1921, three men met quietly at Baden-Baden in Germany: Major Nagata Tetsuzan, then military attaché in Switzerland; Major Obata Toshishirō, who had just been posted to the Soviet Union and had decided to spend a few days at Baden-Baden on his way there; and Major Okamura Yasuji of the Army Ministry, who had been sent to Europe and the United States to study propaganda methods.[21] All three had graduated together in the sixteenth class of the Military Academy, and Nagata and Obata had graduated with honors from the same class at the War College; Okamura had been two years later at the War College. They were all "outsiders" with respect to the Satsuma-Chōshū factions that dominated the army: Nagata was from Nagano in Shinshū, Obata from Kōchi in Tosa, and Okamura belonged to a *hatamoto* (Tokugawa) family from Tokyo.

Army leadership at the time was still in the hands of the Sat-Chō clique. The Chōshū genrō Yamagata Aritomo was alive, and the Army Ministry was headed by Tanaka Giichi's protégé Yamanashi Hanzō and Vice Minister Ono Sanenobu, with its Military Affairs Bureau under Kanno Shōichi; Uehara Yūshaku was chief of staff and Kikuchi Shinnosuke vice chief of staff; Akiyama Yosifuru was inspector-general of military education, and Kojima Sōjirō chief of the Central Office of Military Education.

Personnel matters were decided on the basis of *han* origin, and anyone outside the chosen group was sure to run into a stone wall. Already Utsunomiya Tarō, as a major and a senior among the "outsiders," had organized some of his fellow prefectural malcontents into a sort of secret society, and these "Saga outsiders," as they were known, had penetrated the army's Tokyo headquarters. The society included many who were not from Saga, men such as Mutō Nobuyoshi, Muraoka Chōtarō, Mazaki Jinzaburō, Hata Shinji, Araki Sadao, Ishimitsu Maomi, Fukuda Masatarō, Yamaoka Shigeatsu, Yamashita Tomoyuki, and Tsuchihashi Yūichi; Obata, the leading figure in the secret meeting at Baden-Baden, was also a member. As factions opposed to the Chōshū clique gradually made their way into the army organization, Chōshū power began to decline.

In February 1922 Utsunomiya realized he would not rise again from his bed. He summoned the members of his group who were in Tokyo and gave them as his benediction a glorious vision of expansion, a dream of destiny for men who were disadvantaged by clique favoritism. He pointed to a world map that hung in his sickroom and ordered Captain Tsuchihashi, then at the War College, to "draw a line with red pencil at the 60 and 170 degree lines." "That must all become Japan's!" he said.[22] The area he claimed in his final testament included all of Siberia, China, India, and Southeast Asia as far as Australia and New Zealand. This powerful and aggressive image bequeathed by a dying man made a profound impression on men of Obata's generation, and it is significant that it found its origin in the anti-Chōshū group.

From the secret understandings reached at Baden-Baden came an organization called the Dōjinkai (Universal Benevolence Association), composed of Nagata, Obata, Okamura, and their classmates of the sixteenth class at the Military Academy. After they returned to Japan they often met at a restaurant in Shibuya, from which they took an alternative name, the Futabakai,[23] and the group was soon enlarged to include graduates from the fifteenth class (like Kōmoto) to the eighteenth, all of them now middle-rank field officers. At its peak the association had 18 to 20 members, all opposed to the inflexible conservatism of the army leadership and all anxious to adopt the modern military techniques that World War I had shown to be necessary.

Others were likewise stimulated to organize. A National Policy Study Association (Kokusaku Kenkyūkai) was established by about ten graduates of the twenty-first to twenty-fifth classes,[24] and on November 3, 1928, with Lieutenant-Colonel Suzuki Teiichi as chairman, its first meeting was held at the Kaikōsha (Army Officers Club) in Tokyo. Ishiwara, who had just taken up his duties on the Kwantung Army staff, took the trouble to attend and discussed his pet subject, "The Nature of War." A second meeting, held on December 3, was attended by Nagata Tetsuzan of the Futabakai, Tōjō Hideki, and others, and the resulting debate about Manchuria and Mongolia was heated. The National Policy Study Association eventually merged informally with the Futabakai, although it continued to meet separately on Thursdays and was therefore also known as the Thursday Club. In joint meetings important discussions were led by men like Nagata, Okamura, Itagaki, Doihara (sixteenth class), Tōjō (seventeenth class), and Ishiwara (twenty-first class).[25] All of them did their best to get their comrades into important posts in the Army Ministry, the General Staff, and the Inspectorate of Military Education, and from these positions they tried to influence higher authorities, leaving no effort undone to bring their superiors to see their point of view about policy.

The Futabakai worked with all the influence at its disposal against the idea of punishing Kōmoto Daisaku, of the fifteenth class, for the murder of Chang Tso-lin. Its members enlisted officers of the General Staff in his support, as well as the politically ineffectual Field Marshal Uehara Yūsaku, the Satsuma veteran who was chief of the anti-Chōshū faction, and in the end Uehara's protégé, Mutō Nobuyoshi of the Saga clique, managed to squelch the idea of punishment or trial.

On May 19, 1929, the Futabakai and the Thursday Club met together at the Fujimiken restaurant in Kudan formally to join ranks. About 40 officers of field rank (colonel to major), graduates of the fifteenth to twenty-fifth classes at the Military Academy, were present and agreed to name the new organization the Issekikai (Evening Society). Inaugurated just after the fall of the Tanaka cabinet, the Issekikai was indicative of the strong development of horizontal, middle-rank organizations in the army that had helped bring about Tanaka's fall. At this first meeting the new society affirmed strongly the need for new personnel policies for the army, finding a solution of the Manchuria-Mongolia issue, and support for Generals Araki, Mazaki, and Hayashi Senjūrō in building a new army.[26] In this way they set themselves on the road to a military solution in Manchuria and Mongolia.

Itagaki had returned to the continent before the meeting at the Fujimiken and on May 1 scheduled an intelligence conference for the Kwantung Army staff.[27] In addition to army staff members, it was attended by Major-General Hata Shinji, chief of the Mukden Special Service Agency, and Colonel Hayashi Daihachi, adviser to the Chinese Kirin army. It was decided that, in view of the danger of a "full-scale outbreak of hostilities" with the Chinese Manchurian armies, a thorough study and careful preparations must be made, and to this end the Kwantung Army staff should carry out a reconnaissance trip to study "plans for conflict with the Soviet Union." Army Commander Muraoka Chōtarō apparently wished to cancel the decision, but Itagaki prevailed upon him to allow it to be carried out.

The reconnaissance mission was carried out according to plan from July 3 to 12. Its objectives included studying how to attack Harbin and how to defend Hailar. It was symbolic that while the mission was being undertaken, the Kirin military authorities began the reoccupation of the Chinese Eastern Railway. On July 4 in Ch'angch'un Ishiwara lectured to Kwantung Army specialists, including Itagaki, on "Views of War Today" and on "The Role of War in Modern History,"[28] after which he proposed a research project on the administration of occupied areas, to be conducted by Captain Sakuma Ryōzō. Ishiwara was later reported to have spoken with emotion about this occasion, saying, "That night in Ch'angch'un marked the first step on the road leading to the Manchurian Incident."[29]

Ishiwara's lecture on "The Role of War in Modern History," which gave expression to his view of "the final war," was based on conclusions he had reached from reading the writings on war of Frederick the Great, Napoleon, and von Moltke that he had studied during his three years in Germany. He had delineated his ideas as early as 1927, in lectures at the War College on "Japan's Security Today and Tomorrow." His basic theme was that the study of history led to the conclusion that the next war would be the "final war of mankind," one which, because of advances in military technology, would be a "war of destruction from the air." The old dimensions of line, zone, and front, he predicted, would be transformed, and for the first time in history there would be all-out, total war between peoples. To be sure, Ishiwara did not go beyond a description of the changes in warfare that would follow from technological developments with which he was familiar, but he concluded with an

apocalyptic element when he declared that "Saint Nichiren had proph-
esied a final great war for the unification of the world." Thus Ishiwara
was preparing for this inevitable end.

Ishiwara saw three conditions as preliminary to the outbreak of the
final war: first, Japan must become the center of civilization in East Asia;
second, the United States must become the center of Western civilization; and third, airplanes must be able to circle the world without having
to land. But while these conditions were derived by working backward
from his conviction of a final apocalypse, they were also to some extent
brought closer to reality by his actions. What gave his forecast its self-
fulfilling character was that his solutions to the problems in Manchuria
and Mongolia were premised on their serving as preparation for the
coming war with the United States.

On the third day of the mission Ishiwara produced a discussion document entitled "A plan for the solution of the Manchurian and Mongolian problems as a basic national policy to revolutionize our country's
destiny." [30] Its purport was that "if we are to prepare for war with the
United States, we should not hesitate to seize political control in Manchuria and Mongolia at once." Such control was necessary to preparations for the inevitable war with America, but it would also bring added
benefits in that "the rational development of Manchuria and Mongolia"
would "automatically restore Japan's prosperity and solve unemploy-
ment"; moreover, solution of the Manchuria-Mongolia problem "should
enable us to extinguish anti-Japanese agitation in China at the same time."
While it may be that this aspect of his argument had no necessary relation to his basic premise, it helps to explain his illogical insistence on
the use of force in settling the problem of Manchuria and Mongolia. He
may also have been influenced by the romantic historical school of Inaba
Kunzan, who in 1915 had declared that "Manchuria and Mongolia should
not be conceded to the Chinese people" but should be seized by the
Japanese. [31] Once the seizure was accomplished, Ishiwara believed that
Japan had to be prepared, "if war should be inescapable," to "have the
principal areas of China come under our control" as well; but then, "the
obstacles removed," it would be possible to develop a new relationship
between Japan and China. The key to any solution, in Ishiwara's view,
"is in the hands of the Imperial army." His was a doctrine of force, based
on developments in military technology. But it grew out of his convic-

tion that ultimately a "protracted war with America" was inevitable and must be prepared for. Thus, his views on China policy were fundamentally bound up with his views on policy toward the United States.

During the mission Ishiwara drafted concrete plans in a document entitled "Plans for the Occupation of Manchuria and Mongolia by the Kwantung Army."[32] "Section I: Conquest" stipulated that local military and bureaucratic cliques would have to be destroyed and their property confiscated, that the Chinese system of government must come under the control of the Kwantung Army, and that the former ruling groups should have no future in the areas controlled by the Japanese. "Section II: Government" stated that in areas under army control the "three races—Japanese, Korean, and Chinese" would be allowed to compete freely. On further reading, however, it develops that Japanese were to provide "model large-scale industries and enterprises requiring special abilities," the Koreans to "develop paddy agriculture," and the Chinese "small businesses and labor," a division of classes reminiscent of the old samurai-scholar, peasant, artisan, and merchant distinctions. Ishiwara also spelled out the administration in great detail, but on the whole his policy avoided rapid change and attempted to harmonize with the existing structure. "Section III: Defense" made direct mention only of the Soviet Union, when it specified "four divisions in preparedness for a Soviet invasion"; it said nothing of a war with the United States. Additional study was to be carried out on the following topics:

1. Organization of administration (Captain Sakuma)
2. Organization of finance (Paymaster Itō)
3. The effect on the Manchurian economy of a war with the United States and how it should be planned for (Itō)
4. Organization of the governor-general's administration (Itō)

Was Ishiwara influenced by the Marxist theories that had such a profound impact on intellectuals of the 1920s? That he recognized the challenge posed by Marxism is evident, for he lectured on Marx at the Army War College, a fact of which he was later ashamed. Certainly there were points of agreement, in particular in the emphasis both Ishiwara and Marxist writers at the time placed on Manchuria as the locale of the ultimate political struggle between feudalism and capitalism. The Soviet academician Vladimir IA. Avarin, for example, in his *Imperializm v Manchzhurii*, published before the Manchurian Incident, concluded that "in this unprecedented economic crisis historical development is moving forward rapidly. The so-called 'brakes' or 'safety factors' of capitalist development have become completely inoperative." And he predicted that the real crisis would be precipitated by the tendency of "the ruling class of China, whether in Nanking [the Kuomintang] or in Manchuria [Chang Hsueh-liang], to come increasingly under American influence." Similarly, the Marxist Terajima Kazuo, in his "Lectures on the China Problem" published in July 1930, argued that the United States, in supporting tariff and tax autonomy for China, was motivated by concern for profits and sought the establishment of a single, national government to assure the security of its investments in China. He therefore concluded that American support for Chiang Kai-shek was inevitable. In Terajima's view Britain, which during World War I had lost to Japan its leadership in the export to China of consumer goods, including cotton textiles, had been pursuing a very clever but restrained policy to make Japan the target of the anti-imperialist movement. "The advance of American imperialism" had dealt Japan a double blow when American and British recognition of the Kuomintang regime had forced upon Japan an awkward reversal of policy. Nonetheless, the contradictions in international relations that swirled around the mixtures of feudal militarists and national bourgeoisie in China were, in Terajima's view, "bringing a final clash nearer" minute by minute, and in particular Manchuria and Mongolia seemed on the edge of the abyss. This Marxist endeavor to explain international developments in terms of the requirements of investment and capital security in the postwar era, with Manchuria the focus of the political struggle, contrasted sharply with the visions of Foreign Minister Shidehara Kijūrō for cooperation between Japan and the United States in the development of Manchuria and Mongolia.

The Marxist model does seem to have influenced Ishiwara's eclectic philosophy to some degree, giving it a deceptively logical structure in strange combination with his military science and apocalyptic vision. For the communist movement itself he had only condescension, but as a would-be theorist he must have felt his inferiority in the face of the logical structure of Marxist thought. His own image of the logical inevitability of war with the United States and, ultimately, a world conflagration, in preparation for which Manchuria and Mongolia must be controlled by military force, reversed the traditional Marxist view of the causal relationship between war and economic crisis.

His attitude was further complicated by the purity of his faith in the emperor. Soviet staff officers, visiting his sick room after he was named a witness for the International Military Tribunal, laughed at his faith in the emperor. In response, Ishiwara compared their attitude toward Stalin with his own toward the emperor and ordered them out of his room. Is it not possible that Ishiwara, whose concepts of the inevitable war and final world conflagration were strongly reminiscent of the enemy ideology of Marxism, actually harbored a subconscious dread of the Soviet Union? Maruyama Masao has stated that Ishiwara's advocacy of seizing Manchuria and Mongolia by force without the help of revolutionary movements had a role in Japanese military fascism, which was itself the "most radical and militant expression of counterrevolution in the twentieth century."[33] For Ishiwara and those he influenced, his faith in the emperor, within his inverted framework of Marxism, imbued his ideas of Manchuria and ultimate world war with the character of a divine myth of national defense.

On July 18, four days after Ishiwara's party returned to Port Arthur, Chinese-Soviet relations were broken off because of the forced retrocession of the Chinese Eastern Railway to the Kirin authorities. Chinese relations with other powers were also delicate. The executive committee of the Manchuria branch of the Chinese Communist Party issued a declaration to the people of Manchuria on August 1, "this day of opposition to war throughout the world," beginning with the warning that "a second world war is being planned." It called for the destruction of Kuomintang authority, which it considered responsible for and a "running dog" of imperialism.

As a result of the break in diplomatic relations between the Soviet Union and China, anti-Japanese agitation in China subsided for a time. Toward the end of August the Chinese communists launched a drive aimed at workers, peasants, students, and women in Manchuria in order to strike at imperialism and the Kuomintang. As a result of the Kuomintang's anti-Soviet propaganda, the movement met with little success at the time, but thereafter the anti-Japanese movement in the countryside had close ties with the Korean communist movement. The riots that began in 1930 in the Chientao region among Korean emigrés were in part a result of this. At the end of August 1929 the Mukden authorities arrested Wang Chen-hsiang and fourteen other communists who had been trying to build up a base among the coal miners at Fushun. Although anti-Japanese feelings had apparently subsided, the ability of the Communist Party to assume leadership was growing. In July Kasaki Yoshiaki, the principal figure in the rightist organization Tōkō Remmei, was shifted from his post as personnel director of the South Manchuria Railway's East Asian Economic Research Bureau in Tokyo to the head office of the South Manchuria Railway at Dairen. There he organized the Daiyūhōkai (later the Yūhōkai), which was to play an important role in the Manchurian Incident.[34]

The Kwantung Army, however, did not pay as much attention to all this as might have been expected. What it did do was assign Ishiwara the task of drafting proposals for the administration of occupied Manchuria.[35] Captain Sakuma, to whom Itagaki and Ishiwara delegated the actual work, finished a draft in September 1930 and it was printed in December, just after the second series of riots in Chientao. When it was given to Chief of Staff Miyake Mitsuharu, he is reported to have said, "It would be fine if we could use this later, wouldn't it?" and put his seal on it without having looked at so much as a page of it. Ishiwara said with great satisfaction, "This is fine. Two more years."[36]

Meanwhile, following the completion of the reconnaissance mission, Itagaki, Ishiwara, and others undertook a similar trip to the Liaohsi region in southwestern Manchuria, their aims including geographic reconnaissance for the development of plans for an attack in the Chinchou area. It is said that the information gathered on this trip was the basis for Ishiwara's advocacy of the bombing of Chinchou in 1932. Oddly, relations between the Kwantung Army and the Chinese Manchurian Army apparently improved greatly after these missions.

At the same time attitudes among Japanese civilians in Manchuria were hardening. The second congress of the Manchurian Youth League was held at Mukden on November 23–24. The resulting "Declaration Concerning Manchurian Policy"[37] was so intemperate in its denunciation of anti-Japanese movements and boycotts that some feared it might spark off a new, more serious period of anti-Japanese activity. A further statement that it was "premature to give up extraterritoriality"[38] prompted suggestions that, since this touched on foreign relations and might embarrass the government, it ought to be withheld, but the hard-line advocates won out, and the League issued both statements.

At the end of the year an anti-imperialist periodical called *Hsientsai hsunk'an* (Today) appeared, published three times a month, which grad-

ually aroused to activity students in the Harbin area. By March it had
also begun to influence the People's Council on Foreign Relations, a
Chinese patriotic organization.

In 1930 the Kwantung Army began drawing up serious tactical plans
for action. Ishiwara, Sakuma, and others drafted an "Outline for the Seizure of the Mukden Fortifications," together with detailed topographical
reports for night attacks. Beginning in January the entire staff of the
Kwantung Army met each Saturday in a seminar called "Project To Study
the Occupation and Administration of Manchuria and Mongolia." On
March 1 Ishiwara was invited to address members of the Research Section of the South Manchuria Railway in Dairen, and he demanded full
cooperation from them. He detailed to them his theories, beginning with
the "inevitable war between Japan and the United States." What must
be noted particularly is his stress on the necessity for Japan to be prepared for the ultimate war with the United States before it made any
attempt to seize Manchuria and Mongolia. He called on his fellow nationals to realize the value of Manchuria and Mongolia and the justice of
occupying them, urged his listeners to set aside their misgivings about
a protracted war with the United States, and stressed the importance of
bringing about the proper moment to resort to military force.[39]

In order to prepare for the war with the United States, study groups
to examine specific topics relating to Manchuria and Mongolia were set
up within the Kwantung Army and the Research Section; responsibility
for China proper was designated the province of the Army General Staff
and the South Manchuria Railway's East Asian Economic Research Section. Ishiwara got full cooperation from the railway's research staff: Sada
Kōjirō, chief of the Research Section in Dairen, Matsuki Tamotsu, head
of the legal division, and Miyazaki Masayoshi, head of the Russia Section, all took on assignments related to his plans and needs. In this manner Ishiwara was able to further his research preparations while at the
same time he turned his attention to preparing public opinion within Japan.

In May the chief of the Operations Divison of the General Staff in
Tokyo, Major Hata Shunroku, whose older brother Lieutenant-General
Hata Eitarō was commander of the Kwantung Army, came to Manchuria
to review the work. From Ch'angch'un he traveled through Manchuria
with members of the Kwantung Army staff. On May 20 Ishiwara spoke
at Ch'angch'un on the topic "A Japanese-American War from the Military Standpoint."[40]

In this lecture Ishiwara divided the war between Japan and the United

States into a war of endurance and one of decision. The latter would come "in a few decades." The war of endurance would begin over the issue of China. As Ishiwara put it, "Helping a China that knows no peace is Japan's mission; at the same time it is the only way for Japan to help itself. Therefore we shall have to prevent the United States from interfering with our efforts." He concluded: "First we must unify the nation through the war of endurance and establish the foundations of the nation; thereafter, in the war of decision, we can devote ourselves to the great task of unifying the world." There is no doubt here about his debt to Nichiren's teachings on "the universal return to the sacred law."

Ishiwara's argument for a military unification of the country was in opposition to Kita Ikki's position that "the country has to be united first." Ishiwara put it as follows: "This, like the Meiji Restoration, is a time of rapid change of direction. At such a time the successful application of military force is essential." It was in this setting that Ishiwara foresaw his war of endurance and the final, total war.

On May 31 Hata Eitarō died, to be succeeded as Kwantung Army commander by General Hishikari Takashi. Under his command, Ishiwara's designate Sakuma continued with his plans for the occupation of Manchuria.

Military Coup or Manchurian Takeover?

In August 1930 new appointments were made within the Army Ministry in keeping with the practice of periodic rotation of posts. Lieutenant-General Sugiyama Gen was named army vice minister, Major-General Koiso Kuniaki took over as chief of the Military Affairs Bureau and Colonel Nagata Tetsuzan as chief of the Military Section, while Colonel Okamura Yasuji remained as chief of the Appointments Section. The Military Affairs Bureau had long had the responsibility of coordinating the various sections within the ministry; it was directly responsible to the vice minister and assisted in negotiations with the Foreign Ministry. Nagata's Military Affairs Section, which was organizationally closest to the Military Affairs Bureau, was responsible for general planning, study, and lower-level liaison with other ministries. The positions held by Koiso and Nagata could therefore be described as the most important offices within the Army Ministry.[41]

Army Minister Ugaki Kazushige had served under Tanaka Giichi as chief of the Army General Staff's General Affairs Division when Tanaka was vice chief of staff fifteen years earlier. Although he was from Okayama, as army minister he had resisted the anti-Chōshū line set by Generals Uehara Yūsaku and Fukuda Masatarō in the period since the Kiyoura Keigo cabinet. He was regarded by Tanaka as the last representative of the Chōshū faction. In fact, Ugaki was conscious of the general anti-Chōshū mood and did not assemble a regional faction but rather tried to build up a broader and more personal following. Together with his Military Academy classmate Suzuki Sōroku, he recruited Kanaya Hanzō, Minami Jirō, and Tatekawa Yoshitsugu; another classmate, Shirakawa Yoshinori, helped him recruit men like Kawashima Yoshiyuki. He appreciated the importance of Hata Eitarō and did his best to enlist Hata Shunroku, as well as Abe Nobuyuki and Matsui Iwane.[42] Ugaki had been army minister in the Katō Takaaki and Wakatsuki Reijirō cabinets in the mid-1920s, but during the Tanaka cabinet he had deferred to Shirakawa and was himself appointed to the Supreme War Council (Gunji Sangikan Kaigi). In July 1929 he again became army minister in the cabinet of Hamaguchi Osachi. Now, in 1930, he used the rotation regulations in the interest of strengthening his faction. Sugiyama, Koiso, and Major-General Ninomiya Harushige, who in December 1930 was promoted from head of the General Affairs Division in the General Staff to vice chief of staff, were all classmates of Hata Shunroku in the twelfth class at the Military Academy. Tatekawa, who had been involved in the assassination of Chang Tso-lin, had already been reassigned in August 1929 and was now head of the General Staff Intelligence Division; he retained his ties with Ugaki.

After the death of Tanaka Giichi in 1929, numerous ties between the Ugaki faction and middle-rank field officers were established. Now the Ugaki faction was waiting for the opportunity offered by the general antimilitarist mood of the times to get more nearly complete control over the military establishment. In the process of cutting the army by four divisions in 1925—in the "Ugaki cutbacks," as they were known—he had already combined this goal with modernization of the army. To that end he had used Nagata Tetsuzan who, as chief of the Mobilization Section in the Army Ministry's Equipment and Supplies Bureau, believed it a matter of critical urgency to update the army technologically.

Unfortunately for Ugaki's plans, in the period after the London Naval Treaty the imperial army became extremely apprehensive in the face of the Soviet Union's five-year plan and opposed further military reductions on the grounds that Japan could not be allowed to be unprepared to face the Russians in five or six years because of financial restrictions.[43] As chief of staff Kanaya went so far as to oppose the 70-percent naval ratio vis-a-vis the United States at the London Naval Conference on grounds of preparedness for war against the Soviet Union, because of his fear that naval restrictions would directly affect army manpower. If Ugaki failed to get the cooperation of middle-ranking officers who exercised the real power in the army bureaucracy for his program of personnel reduction and military modernization, it was likely that the opposition to decreases in the armed forces would become increasingly strong and vocal. The confusion stimulated by the deep economic crisis and the Hamaguchi cabinet's policies of retrenchment were beginning to exercise great influence within the military.

On May 5, 1930, the Central Committee of the Chinese Communist Party convened a congress of representatives of Manchurian soviets and thereafter issued directives for the establishment of regional soviets throughout Manchuria. The Harbin Committee of the party and the Harbin Committee of the Chinese Communist Youth League called for a Struggle Day against War and Imperialism; the Struggle Day took place on August 1 but had little impact. At the end of July, however, disorders broke out in eastern Manchuria along the Kirin (Chilin)-Tunhua railway line in response to the Chientao disturbances in May. On September 15 the first issue of the *Red Flag of Manchuria* was published. At this point the Manchurian Committee of the Chinese Communist Party was renamed the Committee for General Mobilization of Manchuria, and a Military Affairs Committee was established. Under the influence of Li Li-san, plans were drawn up for direct action by all groups and units, including members of the Korean Communist Party, and the communists prepared for a second wave of violence in Chientao. Elections were also set in motion with the aim of sending five Manchurian delegates to the forthcoming national congress of the Chinese Communist Party.[44]

In the meantime the third congress of the Manchurian Youth League was convened at Ch'angch'un on September 21–22. Its "Proposal for Advancing a Positive Policy for Manchuria and Mongolia"[45] was opposed by a minority of the delegates, who feared the effect on the Chinese of flaunting such an extreme policy, but the chairman refused to recognize their interjections and gaveled the proposal through.

About this time, in Japan, a new grouping of young officers coalesced around Lieutenant-Colonel Hashimoto Kingorō. On the last day of September 1930 the first formal meeting of what came to be known as the Sakurakai (Cherry Blossom Society) was held at the Kaikōsha in Tokyo. Most of those who attended were young officers from line units, command schools, and staff offices. Lieutenant-Colonel Sakata Yoshirō, of the twenty-first class at the Military Academy, was in the chair, and Hashimoto addressed the meeting. The resolution that was adopted declared, "The renovation of our country must be our aim, and we should not rule out the use of military force to bring this about."[46] Thereafter a smaller committee met at the Fujimiken, including Sakata and Hashimoto, Lieutenant-Colonel Nemoto Hiroshi, Major Tsuchihashi Yūichi, Captain Chō Isamu, Captain Tanaka Kiyoshi, and Captain Tanaka Wataru. They divided along three lines of opinion. The first, represented by Hashimoto and Chō, amounted to a simple-minded affirmation of individual heroics; it held that the demolition of the existing governmental structure was the main order of business and that, after the destruction, reconstruction would take care of itself. The second group felt reconstruction would not be accomplished so easily and argued that a specific plan ought to be worked out first, with destruction held to a minimum; this view was held by Tanaka Kiyoshi, who was auditing a course at Tokyo Imperial University, and others who were more aware of economic complications. Nemoto and some others stood somewhere between these two positions.

A second general meeting was held at the end of November. Tsuchihashi, who was opposed to talk of a coup d'état, did not take part, but most of those who attended the first meeting were present, with some additions that brought their numbers to about 60, among them Colonel Shigetō Chiaki, chief of the China Section of the General Staff, Major Wachi Takaji of the same section, and Lieutenant Tsuji Masanobu of the War College. All but one or two, like Obama Ujiyoshi, were products of the War College. Attendance at subsequent meetings ran from a handful to ten or more. They agreed to adopt the pleasant name *sakura* (cherry blossom) that Hashimoto had proposed for their organization.[47] As far as finances were concerned, Ninomiya, who was in touch with Tatekawa, helped, and it is said that Major Kawabe Torashirō and Lieutenant-Colonel Mudaguchi Renya of the General Staff also cooperated. In later years Tatekawa acknowledged his own contributions to the society.[48]

After the outbreak of violence between Chinese and Japanese guards at the city of Lungching in Chientao on the night of October 6, the militancy of communist organizations in Manchuria increased sharply. On November 5 Foreign Minister Shidehara, overruling the objections of the Korean Government-General, forced the guard reinforcements to withdraw across the Korean border. Chang Tso-hsiang, the governor of Kirin province, promised to control the "communist bandits," but the Manchurian Communist Action Committee pushed a vigorous program of direct action and staged numerous uprisings, with the aid of 24 leaders trained in the Soviet Union. At the end of October leaflets were distributed in the name of the "Communist Action Committees of Yenchi and Holung," calling on their readers to "blow out the brains of the swine Miura of the Japanese Foreign Ministry's Asia Bureau."[49] In fact, Miura Takemi opposed the Kwantung Army line supported by the Korean Government-General and had come from Japan precisely to secure the withdrawal of the guard troops from Korea.

In December 1930 Sakuma's "Study of the Administration of Occupied Areas in Manchuria" was printed by the Kwantung Army.[50] Sakuma divided the period of occupation into three stages. The first, lasting from six months to one year, would be a period of military operations during which only part of Manchuria would be administered by the military. During the second stage, lasting one to two years, the entire area would be occupied, but because it would not be completely under control, military action would still be required. In the third stage he foresaw the area completely pacified under a military government. During the second stage he expected 40–50 percent of the revenues collected by the three Manchurian provinces (120–130 million yuan) to be available, the balance coming from the funds of the imperial army; in the third stage he anticipated 160–170 million of a total Manchurian revenue of 200 million yen to be available. Industrialization was to be based on agricultural development, and industries using Manchurian raw materials were to be developed to the degree that they did not constitute threats to industry in Japan itself. Seen as a whole, the aim was to "prepare for war by making war." It was clear that the occupation period would have to be a long one to enable Japan to prepare for the protracted war that was the reason for Japan's occupation of Manchuria and Mongolia. Ishiwara's ideas were being pushed to their logical conclusion.

About this time Kōmoto Daisaku, Nagata Tetsuzan, and Shigetō Chiaki one after the other visited Port Arthur. Kōmoto's purpose was to begin preparations for making the former Hsuan-t'ung emperor P'u Yi head of state once the Manchuria problem was solved. Kōmoto had returned to Japan after investigating the Wushe incident in Taiwan* and exchanged views with Military Affairs Bureau Chief Koiso, then went to Port Arthur to consult with Itagaki and Ishiwara. Thereafter he headed for Tientsin, where he reached general agreement with the former Ch'ing officials Lo Chen-yü and Cheng Hsiao-hsu. After further talks with Ishiwara and Itagaki at Port Arthur, he returned to Tokyo to report to Koiso.[51] Kōmoto was enthusiastic about the plans being developed by Ishiwara and Itagaki for Manchuria and accepted the assignment of seeking support from military and political leaders in Tokyo. He had learned from the assassination of Chang Tso-lin that their aims were unlikely to succeed unless opinion in Japan backed them. He therefore concluded that they must first ensure support from the Kwantung Army, second, make certain that the Kwantung Army bureaucracy was united, and third, secure the necessary funds.[52] He believed with Itagaki and Ishiwara that the first two goals had been achieved but nonetheless felt it a wise precaution to send a well-known person like Reserve Captain Amakasu Masahiko around the area to make sure that things would go off properly. Amakasu had been arrested for the murder of the anarchist Ōsugi Sakae in 1923 but through the intervention of Tatekawa, then head of the Europe-America Section of the General Staff, had been assigned to study in Paris from the fall of 1927 until the spring of 1929.[53] Now, in the fall of 1929, again thanks to Tatekawa, he had come to Manchuria, where he enjoyed special and irregular lines of communication with both Tatekawa and Nagata.

The problem of funds was handled as follows: Kōmoto's original sponsor had been the retired army officer Kuroki Shinkei, reputedly the private backer of Araki Sadao as well. In addition, through his contacts with the ultranationalist Ōkawa Shūmei, Kōmoto had access to the East Asian Economic Research Bureau of the South Manchuria Railway. Following his investigations in Taiwan, the Chung Kung She, a China trading firm, became a further source of funds through the influence of Mori Kaku. It is probable that before the Manchurian Incident support also came from

---

*Anti-Japanese risings by Taiwanese aborigines near T'aichung, October-November 1930.

Fujita Isamu, president of the Tokyo *Mainichi* newspaper, who was related to Shigetō Chiaki (see below).[54] This rather allayed Kōmoto's worries about money, for he knew that in 1929 the secret funds available to the Mukden organization of the Kwantung Army had not amounted to much more than ¥2,000.

On October 30 Nagata was ordered to go to China,[55] and in mid-November he began a month-long reconnaissance tour of Korea, Manchuria, and north China, in the course of which he had long talks with Ishiwara and Itagaki in Mukden about military solutions to the problems of Manchuria and Mongolia.

Before his departure the General Staff's Intelligence Division had drawn up preparatory arguments in its annual "Situation Estimate," which was directed toward 1931. This evaluation concluded that a narrow military solution would not suffice and asserted the need for a total national reconstruction in Japan.[56] This was a result of the arguments advanced by Hashimoto, Sakata, and Tanaka that internal renovation should be given priority over action abroad. Both Hashimoto, as chief of the Intelligence Division's Russia desk, and Nemoto Hiroshi, who headed the China desk, had taken an active part in the preparation of the document. The "Estimate" outlined three possible ways of solving the Manchuria-Mongolia problem. The first called for efforts to make the Manchurian authorities take a position more favorable to Japan, whereupon outstanding issues could be negotiated with them. The second proposed installing a pro-Japanese leadership and negotiating with them. The third declared that since, "from the standpoint of national defense, it is essential to seek an immediate solution to the problem of Manchuria and Mongolia," and that if such a solution should prove impossible, "we should resort to military measures to bring it about."[57] Concerning the circumstances under which Nagata transmitted these proposals to the Kwantung Army, his biographer has written:

> At that time our cabinet was weak, and Japanese officials and officers in the field were blindly following government policy. The consulates-general, the Government-General of the Kwantung Leased Territory, and the South Manchuria Railway were all meekly following the north China authorities. What was needed in these three plans, therefore, was to reverse the situation and return the nation to its true course. But the discussion did not resolve the issue easily, for it was very complex. Even after the participants had argued right through the night, the solution was

not clear. Nagata saw problems in each of the three schemes and adjourned the meeting with the feeling that further study would be necessary.[58]

After a lengthy debate on these alternatives, Ishiwara hinted to Nagata that the real reason behind Nagata's inability to endorse the use of force might be his acceptance of the weak diplomacy that had caused the trouble in the first place. Ishiwara's solution to the problem was, of course, the third alternative, which called for the Japanese army to take over Manchuria. Nagata tried to make Ishiwara understand his reasoning, asserting that while he was well aware of the need for a military solution, if he had at the time expressed approval of a military solution, implementation of the plan would have become impossible. As much as a decade earlier, in 1920, Nagata himself had written a "Memorandum on Total National Mobilization."[59] He saw then the main problem as one of creating a favorable climate for a military solution, not just among the military but among the general public as well, and during the 1930 talks his concern seems to have been to keep alive the idea of such a solution, first among the central military authorities, and secondly within the Kwantung Army. But Ishiwara was intent on action and took the opportunity to seek Nagata's counsel on obtaining heavy artillery from Japan.[60] He also revealed the fact that military action would begin at Liut'iaokou, just north of Mukden.

In December Shigetō Chiaki arrived in Manchuria. There were discussions about a plot involving Captain Imada Shintarō, and secret strategies were drawn up to give full backing to separate plans for war with the Soviet Union that after 1929 were part of the General Staff's intelligence estimates. This phase of the planning was entrusted to a separate intelligence organization set up independent of the Kwantung Army.[61]

Late in November, after returning from Manchuria, Kōmoto got together with Ōkawa Shūmei, who had been reorganizing the South Manchuria Railway's East Asian Economic Research Bureau, to discuss means by which parliamentary government in Japan might be replaced by a renovationist political order. It seemed to them that the communist activities in Chientao and the Wushe incidents in Taiwan posed a grave threat to the Japanese empire and that, given the agrarian crisis in Japan, politics must be kept free of corruption in order to prevent the spread of communism. Prime Minister Hamaguchi had recently been assaulted and severely wounded by Sagōya Tomeo, a member of the Aikokusha

(Patriotic Society), and it was known that in the background were right wing groups allied with Hiranuma Kiichirō, vice president of the Privy Council.

Army Minister Ugaki too had ties with right wing nationalist groups. In April 1928, when he was a member of the Supreme War Council, he had met with right wing leaders like Ōkawa Shūmei, Takabatake Moto-yuki, and Yasuoka Masaatsu; thereafter he had maintained personal contact with Ōkawa. Meanwhile, plans for "renovation" were being worked on by Captain Tanaka Kiyoshi (twenty-ninth class at the Military Academy), who had formed a study society for national renovation, Captain Watanabe Hideto (twenty-ninth class), Captain Yamaoka Michitake (thirtieth class), and Captain Iwakuro Hideo (thirtieth class).

Following the attack on Hamaguchi in October, Prince Saionji Kimmochi's private secretary Harada Kumao decided it would be prudent to guard against further intimacy between Ugaki and Hiranuma's right wing protégés by appointing Ugaki prime minister, and for a time Saionji and Lord Privy Seal Makino Nobuaki showed some signs of favoring the plan. In the end they rejected the proposal because of the violent attacks of Seiyūkai extremists in the 59th Diet, urged on by Mori Kaku, against the Minseitō cabinet and its "weak" Shidehara diplomacy. To army bureaucrats such as Vice Minister Sugiyama, Military Affairs Bureau Chief Koiso, Vice Chief of Staff Ninomiya, and Intelligence Division Chief Tatekawa, prospects for Ugaki's appointment still appeared favorable, and in January 1931 they assigned Hashimoto the task of preparing a plan for a political coup. Ugaki felt that public opinion was developing in his favor and seems to have expected Hashimoto to cooperate with Ōkawa and with Shimizu Kōnosuke of the Yūzonsha, as well as with Nemoto of the China desk, Shigetō of the China Section, and Captain Chō Isamu, in working out the details of the coup.

Those who favored assigning a higher priority to action in Manchuria, however, were convinced that any attempt to stage a coup at this time would damage the organization and potential of the army in the future. Okamura Yasuji, head of the Appointments Section, opposed the involvement of Sugiyama, Koiso, Ninomiya, and Tatekawa in Ōkawa's plans. He consulted with Nagata, who had just returned from his talks with Ishiwara and Itagaki in Manchuria and who agreed on priority for Manchuria, then set about dissuading the supporters of a coup. Tanaka Kiyoshi and Suzuki Teiichi, who disapproved of the way Shigetō and

Hashimoto had gone about their plans, likewise did all they could to stop the coup.

Late in February 1931, through the help of Hashimoto, Ōkawa and Shimizu obtained a supply of 300 blank cartridges. By now the climate of opinion had changed and become unfavorable to their plans. They had made contact with the proletarian parties, which had agreed to mount demonstrations in their support, but these were not likely to amount to much. After Sugiyama, Koiso, Ninomiya, and Tatekawa also changed their minds about an uprising, Ugaki himself decided to have nothing to do with Ōkawa's scheme. By March 6, when Ōkawa sent Ugaki a final exhortation to rise, Ugaki had already changed his mind and decided that matters in Manchuria and Mongolia were the first order of business. Now even Hashimoto, Nemoto, and Shigetō took a passive attitude toward the crude plans Ōkawa and Shimizu had worked out. Something might come of them, but they would merely be spectators, watching to see how events turned out.

On March 11 Shimizu went up to Tokyo from Fukuoka with about thirty young ruffians. The plans called for them to start some kind of disorder in the center of Tokyo on the 20th. Okamura, Nagata, and Koiso feared their activities would bring the army into disrepute and therefore urged Kōmoto and Itagaki, who had just arrived from Manchuria, to dissuade Prince Tokugawa Yoshichika, the source of funds. Together they managed to make Ōkawa and Shimizu call the whole thing off.

So the putsch was aborted. The real importance of the March Incident, with respect to the internal balance of power in Japan, is that it led to a reaffirmation among influential middle-ranking officers that military action in Manchuria and Mongolia now had to be given top priority.

The Kwantung Army Prepares Its Plans

On January 24, 1931, while plans for the March Incident were still under way in Japan, Sada Kōjirō, head of the South Manchuria Railway's Research Section in Dairen, addressed the staff of the Kwantung Army in Port Arthur. His lecture, "A Scientific Look at Policies for Manchuria and Mongolia,"[62] was divided into four sections: (1) Premises for a Manchurian and Mongolian policy. (2) How can we assure ourselves economic freedom and personal security? (3) Steps to implement our purposes. (4) Conclusions.

The steps Sada proposed for implementing his self-styled "scientific" program were, first, for the Kwantung Army to use anti-Japanese incidents and insults along its railway right-of-way as justification for seizing the South Manchuria Railway "even if its means flouting the mother country"; then, with railway revenues in hand, it could carry out the military occupation of important areas like Kirin and Mukden to maintain order and stability. His conclusion was that further study was needed and should be carried out by the Kwantung Army. Although Sada's ideas were different from Ishiwara's, he provided additional support for an Ishiwara-style military occupation of Manchuria.

Sada's talk illustrates the areas of agreement that existed between the South Manchuria Railway and the Kwantung Army and the informal collaboration that from this time existed between organizations like Kasaki Yoshiaki's Daiyūhōkai and the Buddhist Youth League, which came to provide links between the South Manchuria Railway and the Manchurian Youth League. Between trips to Japan to rally support, Kōmoto was in contact with these groups, and, together with other plotters like Amakasu and the lawyer Nakano Toraitsu, he also kept in touch with Tatekawa in Japan.

The Kwantung Army now established a study group to take up the details of Sakuma's draft "Study of the Administration of Occupied Areas in Manchuria." Itagaki returned to Manchuria in March and lectured on "A Military View of Manchuria and Mongolia" to a group of instructors at army midcareer schools, who were there on an inspection tour of Manchuria and Korea.[63] His topics were: (1) The destiny of the Japanese empire in Manchuria and Mongolia, (2) Strategy in Manchuria and Mongolia, (3) The history of the development of Manchuria and Mongolia and their raw materials, (4) The United States and the Manchuria-Mongolia problem, and (5) China and the Japanese in Manchuria-Mongolia. His conclusion was that since a peaceful diplomatic settlement of the problem did not seem to be in sight, a military solution would be necessary. Manchuria and Mongolia were treated as essential bases for war with the United States and the Soviet Union, and his thinking, characterized by narrow military speculation and blithe unconcern with international politics, became even coarser and less sophisticated than that of Ishiwara.

In March Sakuma was rotated back to Japan. A Kwantung Army Re-

search Office was now set up under Lieutenant-Colonel Takeshita Yoshiharu and soon came under the influence of Ishiwara and Itagaki. Two
works by Ishiwara, "Japan's National Defense Today and Tomorrow" and
"A History of War," were reprinted.[64] These two works provided the
Research Office with the fundamentals of Ishiwara's views, which were
brought into sharper focus by the revised version of his "History of War."
He left no doubt about his expectation that it would require war with
the United States, the Soviet Union, China, and Great Britain to achieve
a final solution of the problems of Manchuria and Mongolia.

In these works Ishiwara argued that "the reason we don't need to
fear making enemies of the rest of the world" was that Japan would enter a war of decision and not a long-drawn-out war of attrition. He argued that if Japan relied on the territory it was to occupy in Manchuria
and Mongolia for the provision of raw materials essential to the war effort, the country's "position will to some degree resemble that of Napoleon in his war with Britain, except that Japan's position will be far more
advantageous than his."

A more concrete exposition of his ideas may be found in the draft
conclusion of a lecture he gave in April to the Research Office on the
history of war in Europe, together with items entitled "Outline for War
with the United States" and "Outline of War Plans for Solution of the
Manchurian and Mongolian Problems."[65] Here the problems involved
in his plans were repeated with precision and detail and the dangers im-
plicit in these one-sided military speculations made very clear.

For instance, in a section discussing war with the United States entitled "Principles in waging war," Ishiwara said Japan should first "try to
make America fight alone" and at the same time, "in order to avoid involvement of our manpower in China, we must use intimidation to prevent Chinese anti-Japanese activities and participation in the war." If this
should prove impossible, however, Japan should "occupy the principal
areas of north China." Every effort should be made to secure British understanding, but in the final analysis Japan should not hesitate to fight
Britain. Moreover, attempts should be made to reach an understanding
with the Soviet Union, but "should it become unavoidable, we shall not
hesitate to engage in all-out war with the Soviet Union." Radical changes
in internal politics in Japan were to be avoided, but he strongly advocated resolute steps for internal reform "under martial law."

Ishiwara's self-fulfilling prophecies went so far as to propose the establishment of a fascist state, suggesting that "if the course of the war goes badly and we are boycotted by the rest of the world," in order to continue fighting Japan might have to implement a planned economy in Japan and in its occupied territories, bringing about "a great expansion of our industry and a great reform in China." Moreover, it would be necessary for the Japanese people to realize that they might be called upon to "make severe sacrifices," for if conditions should become impossible because Japanese territory was subjected to enemy bombardment, economic and political establishments would have to be "moved to the continent." The cycle that Japanese history was to follow from the Meiji period to its defeat in 1945 was foreshadowed in this blueprint of Ishiwara's fateful reasoning. Section 3 of his plan for war with the United States, "the army's task," was divided into an occupation of Manchuria and Mongolia, war with China, and war with the Soviet Union; he then went on to discuss the navy's role. Section 4, "the government's task," was divided into home and foreign affairs. His plan for a military fascist regime was based on the premise that "the Chinese are unable to maintain stability by themselves," from which he concluded that the Japanese army was justified in occupying Manchuria and Mongolia and providing political leadership for China itself. In the end, he was convinced, "We will be able to win eternal praise in world history for our military strength, for the Chinese will ultimately welcome our political control of their country."

In mid-April the 2nd (Sendai) Division under Lieutenant-General Tamon Jirō replaced the 16th (Kyoto) Division as the main striking force of the Kwantung Army. Late in May, after the officers had been briefed, maneuvers for an attack on Chinchou were carried out. When the officers met on May 29 they were instructed by Army Commander Hishikari that because outside influence was permeating "our struggle with China," a fundamental solution of the problem of Manchuria and Mongolia would require the resolve of a nation united as one; the army was "ready and waiting" to do its duty.[66]

This was followed by a series of lectures by Itagaki "On the Manchurian and Mongolian Problem," based on a "Plan for a Solution of the Manchurian and Mongolian Problem" that had been completed, probably by Itagaki, in May.[67] In these talks he took up the nature of the problem, the relationship of Manchuria and Mongolia to national defense and national survival, their relationship to China, and the international dimension of the problem. In these he advocated absorption of Manchuria and Mongolia. Whether one looked at the situation from a capitalist or proletarian viewpoint, he stated, Japan could not extricate itself from the world depression and deepening crisis without "solving the Manchurian and Mongolian problem." With regard to the Soviet Union, he argued that Japan must force that nation to cease its expansion eastward, and by extending its control over the Maritime Province of Siberia, Japan would be able to "complete our preparations for the coming world war." Japan must either plan for the long-term development of the Japanese race or be prepared to accept existence as a tiny state without a sense of independence. As for China, at the moment the lives of the common people were completely separated from political and military affairs; their only contact with the ruling groups was in matters related to taxation and the police. The populace was largely indifferent to whoever held political or military power. Except in the unlikely event that "a hero should arise and sweep away all the professional militarists and all the professional politicians by resolute use of military force, there was no prospect of happiness and order for the Chinese people unless the job was entrusted to an outside country."

Itagaki was evidently influenced by many Japanese China specialists who were convinced of the static nature of "unchanging China." Thus he was able to see only what was wrong, only the contradictions and perversions of the relationship between Chinese leaders and the nationalist feeling that was becoming widespread in the country. To Itagaki the anti-Japanese movement in Manchuria and Mongolia was a trend toward "sinification." It was, he felt, "implemented directly or instigated by Chinese officialdom." Nor could he see anything in Chang Hsueh-liang's rule except oppression of the people for the warlord's personal advantage. Added to this was a fear that unless the problem of Manchuria and Mongolia were solved, it would be difficult to maintain Japanese control in Korea. Manchuria and mainland China would also be important sources of war matériel in a future naval conflict with the United States. But the problem must be solved, he believed, before 1936, when the naval ratio established at the 1930 London Naval Conference would go against Japan. Itagaki was even more optimistic than Ishiwara about Japan's ability to hold out in a prolonged war, and he called on the military to accept its total responsibility and act promptly.

These lectures might be seen as a somewhat popularized version of

Ishiwara's ideas. In the lectures relating to China and to the international dimension, which he did not publish, Itagaki took up in detail the tasks that would await the Kwantung Army in executing its plans for bringing about the independence of Mongolia and of the Chientao area and for instigating riots in northern Manchuria. The time, he said, was not yet ripe, but he was preparing plans for setting up large-scale anti-Japanese outbreaks that would provide the occasion for military action.

At the core of Itagaki's thinking was the conviction that the Kwantung Army should determine to overthrow the government of Chang Hsueh-liang and occupy his territory. To this end he sought to maintain contacts with key people in the Kwantung Government-General and in the South Manchuria Railway administration, and he did all he could to arouse the public in Japan itself.

Meanwhile, a "Plan for the Independence of Mongolia"[68] was set forth by Kawashima Naniwa and Reserve Colonel Mugita Hirao. A Mongolian banner prince began military training with an independent reserve force in Kungchuling in northern Jehol, where he gathered about fifty students who in April had completed training with Chang Hsueh-liang's army. Through Kawashima's influence a Mongol known to the Japanese as Kanzurchiap became the central figure in this group, which was funded by Dairen Mayor Ishimoto Kantarō, who had close connections with Kawashima since the latter had formed the Loyalist Party after the fall of the Manchus.* Ishimoto's younger brother Matsui Seisuke, a former colonel, was given overall responsibility for working out details of the plot.

On another front, Amakasu himself took charge of planning for new outbreaks in Chientao.[69] After consulting with Lieutenant-Colonel Kanda Masatane of the staff of the Korea Army, he returned to Japan and showed his plans to Nagata. These called for getting weapons into the hands of reserve soldiers living on land held by Ishimoto Kantarō in a bend of the T'umen river, then issuing a declaration of independence from the government of Chang Tso-hsiang. Nakano Toraitsu, the lawyer, was also involved. Nagata looked at Amakasu's plans, made some notations, and suggested fitting them into the larger scheme. However, these plans were given up when Ishiwara opposed them after the murder of Captain Nakamura Shintarō in early June. Amakasu then drafted a third scheme for

---

*Kawashima twice tried, with army support, to organize loyalist independence movements, which he called Tsung She Tang, for Manchuria and Mongolia.

fomenting disorders in northern Manchuria, which he was working on at the time of the explosion at Liut'iaokou.

In contrast to Itagaki, who was all for using former soldiers and rōnin in the plots, Ishiwara thought in terms of a purely military attack. He made this very clear in a "Personal Opinion on the Manchurian and Mongolian Problem" in May.[70] Of its five sections, the third, entitled "Moment for the Solution," shows the difference between his thinking and Itagaki's.

In this document Ishiwara, like Itagaki, took 1936 as the target date for achieving a solution, and he fully accepted that priority should be given to action overseas, as determined after the abortive March Incident. As he put it: "We must lose no time in forcing our country to undertake expansion abroad. In the course of this we can determine on internal reconstruction when conditions are ripe." In section four, "Timing the Solution," he wrote: "When military preparations are complete, we need not go to great lengths to find a motive or occasion. All we need to do is pick our time and then proclaim to the world our absorption of Manchuria and Mongolia as we proclaimed the annexation of Korea." He conceded, however, that if the situation seemed unpropitious, it would be possible for the military to "create the occasion with a plot and force the nation to go along." He also agreed that it was not out of the question to "hope for the achievement of great things by having the Kwantung Army take the lead" if the opportunity should present itself. In section five, "The Present Duty of the Army," he proclaimed his faith in the emperor, emphasizing that success would be difficult unless the army maintained its "faith in the august power of the imperial line" as the "center of its strength."

In mid-June inspections of the (Mongol) Independent Reserve were carried out, and in July Itagaki and Ishiwara made their third inspection trip to northern Manchuria. During the ten days of this trip they made a thorough "Study for an Attack on the Soviet Union."[71] Their preparations for the events of September 18 were nearing completion.

As the Kwantung Army was making preparations for military action, the Manchurian Youth League was taking action of its own to unite opinion among the Japanese residents of Manchuria and to work up public opinion within Japan.

During interpellations in the 59th Diet in March, Foreign Minister Shidehara stated that the "root cause of the difficulty in Manchuria and

Mongolia" lay with the antiforeignism of the Japanese there, who "on the one hand cause trouble by adopting an attitude of superiority to the Chinese and on the other turn around and demand protection from their government." This infuriated the leaders of the Youth League. That same month they organized an "All-Manchuria Japanese League for Autonomy" and proclaimed: "We do not rely on the government. We organize this league of our countrymen throughout Manchuria to demand an independent, autonomous Manchuria and Mongolia and to protect our national sovereignty."[72]

The Youth League also issued 10,000 copies of a pamphlet entitled "The Truth About the Manchurian and Mongolian Problems," which they distributed to government offices, Diet members, newspapers and periodicals, prefectural offices, youth groups, and many other organizations in Japan, as well as in Korea and Manchuria.[73] This pamphlet was a historical exposition of the issue as they saw it. "Manchuria and Mongolia," it asserted, "are our first line of defense. Not only are they invaluable to our military because of their stores of raw materials, but they play a central role in our national existence because of their industrial raw materials and food surpluses." From this premise, the pamphlet declared that it was essential "from political considerations, indeed from considerations that transcend politics," to insist on Japan's special rights in dealing with "China in the first instance, but also with the powers." Furthermore, in this time of "danger, when dearly won rights are being snatched away, . . . we rise to urge our 90 million compatriots to consider." The imagery and rhetoric were inspired by "the era of colonization that began in the 18th century," when there might have been something left for Japan; but in the contemporary world, when Africa, the East Indies, the South Pacific, Australia, the American continents, and "every reef in the boundless oceans is occupied," where was there any spot to be found to substitute for Manchuria and Mongolia?"

The movement to popularize this sort of thinking entered a second stage with the convening of a "Congress To Find a Way Out of Our Perilous Problems" at Dairen on June 13.[74] Trumpeting their slogans— "Protect Treaty Rights!" "Ensure Survival!" and "Find a Way Out of Our Peril!"—the delegates adopted a five-point program calling for an end to divided responsibility in Manchuria, the establishment of representation for Japanese in Manchuria, an end to the railway negotiations, abolition of anti-Japanese materials in education, and the establishment of cooperation between the races in Manchuria and Mongolia. Thus demands for representation were coupled with calls for a stronger foreign policy.

A second round of speechmaking began at Shahok'ou on June 20. A branch chairman by the name of Yūki declaimed: "The time has come for us to stand up and be counted. Our countrymen in Manchuria demand total mobilization in response to their determination." He was followed to the rostrum by 22 members of the Youth League whose speeches were in the same bellicose vein.[75]

Campaigns and speaking tours carried this mood of insistence on a military solution to Port Arthur, Anshan, Mukden, and all parts of Manchuria. Thanks to the activities of the Manchurian Youth League, the plans of Itagaki and Ishiwara to unite and organize public opinion among Japanese residents of Manchuria were almost effortlessly taking the form of a colonial fascist movement and may indeed have had the potential of serving as a bridgehead for the development of a fascist structure in Japan itself.

Within Japan the political situation continued to be unstable. When Wakatsuki was asked to form a cabinet on April 14, Prince Saionji made known his strong opposition to a general resignation.[76] Since the attack on Hamaguchi, the genrō had been of the opinion that a general resignation would merely encourage similar political assassinations, and he therefore supported continuation of the Minseitō cabinet in office. Saionji of course knew nothing about the plans of Itagaki and Ishiwara for a military solution in Manchuria or of the fevered activities of the Manchurian Youth League, nor is there evidence that he had been informed about the March Incident at that time. All that can be said is that the Wakatsuki cabinet was established in accordance with Saionji's wish.

On April 2, shortly before the establishment of the Wakatsuki cabinet, General Ugaki, the retiring army minister, addressed his last meeting of divisional commanders. "It is essential that we work out a solution to the Manchurian and Mongolian problem," he said, "because Japan cannot survive alone as a self-sufficient economic unit." While Ugaki revealed at this meeting his intention to hand his duties over to a successor, he was also reported to have pledged, "Quite apart from my duty as a soldier, as an individual I stand prepared to serve my country in any way that may prove necessary in the future. At this juncture there seems to be no one other than myself who has contacts with both of the political parties and who would be able to control the Diet."[77] Ugaki left his successor a very difficult situation. Since the March Incident the main current of army opinion had called for a solution of the Manchurian and Mongolian problem and had put first priority on action overseas. To this was now added a new fear of budget cuts.

It was in this setting that General Minami Jirō, appointed army minister on April 14, 1931, called a meeting of representatives of the Army Ministry and General Staff to consider military reforms necessary as a result of a ¥1 million retrenchment in Finance Minister Inoue Junnosuke's budget for the following financial year. The meeting decided to reduce the strength of the wartime army from 32 to 28 divisions.

From this time extremists like Hashimoto and his Sakurakai associates, whose expectations of the army high command had been betrayed in the abortive March Incident, shifted their focus of activity to company grade officers of line units, whom they endeavored to agitate and inflame. The All-Japan Patriots Joint Struggle Council (Zen Nihon Aikokusha Kyōdōtōsō Kyōgikai), formed in April, normally took a line indistinguishable from that of organizations such as the Sakurakai, and under the smokescreen they provided, Kōmoto was able to carry on unobserved his contacts with people like Itagaki, Amakasu, and Nakano Toraitsu. But he had little influence with Army Minister Minami, who showed little agreement with a document Kōmoto drafted on "The Advisability of a Military Solution for Manchuria and Mongolia." On the contrary, he regarded Kōmoto as a madman and denied him entry to the Army Ministry. Kōmoto therefore intensified his efforts toward members of the Sakurakai and traveled throughout the country speaking to young company-grade officers, men among whom Hashimoto's influence was in the ascendance. Among higher ranking officers, only Araki Sadao, who commanded the 6th Division, agreed with Kōmoto; even Captain Katakura Tadashi of the Kwantung Army had doubts about giving Kōmoto access to that organization.[78] Araki visited Ugaki at his home, shortly after the latter had given up his duties as army minister, and harangued him about the "pressing problems of communist subversion and danger within Japan." Araki urged that "it is necessary to take resolute action in advance of public opinion," and went on to advocate the completion of military preparations by the time of the 1936 deadline. But Ugaki did not take him seriously. "We can take care of the young officers by discharging them," he said, "and we can use force against the rōnin."[79]

Under the new army minister, those in central headquarters adopted a moderate line in public but continued to lay their secret plans. At this time the General Staff's "Situation Estimate, 1931" was formally completed.[80] It had been prepared under Tatekawa's direction by Europe-America Section Chief Watari Hisao, China Section Chief Shigetō, Nemoto of the China desk, and Hashimoto of the Russia desk. Its main emphasis was the need for a fundamental solution of the Manchurian and Mongolian questions, toward which end it set out a three-alternative solution of the question that proposed a new pro-Japanese political structure on the continent, a Manchurian regime independent of Nanking, or the outright seizure of Manchuria and Mongolia.

Before the plan was finalized, Hashimoto had urged upon Tatekawa and the others that, in view of the outcome of the plans for the March Incident, "We've got to add a statement emphasizing the necessity of making a decision and a commitment, or else this will remain a piece of paper and nothing will come of it."[81] Tatekawa hesitated but finally went along, and the following sentence was added: "In the event the government does not take action on the basis of this 'Situation Estimate,' the army should devise its own means for dealing resolutely with the situation." Perhaps as a result of this, on March 24, at a meeting of bureau and division chiefs, Army Minister Minami asked Operations Division Chief Hata Shunroku for his opinion on whether the USSR was likely to make war on Japan. "The USSR has a five-year plan," Hata replied, "and may well seize the opportunity offered when it begins negotiations with China on Manchurian problems. Although the Russians probably won't start anything for two or three years, to say flatly that they won't would be a mistake." It was his view that the Soviet Union had to be the target of Japan's military preparations. Minami asked what was meant by the phrase Hashimoto had added about "dealing resolutely with the situation," to which Tatekawa responded vaguely that the phrase merely "showed great intensity."[82]

As far as Itagaki and Ishiwara were concerned, the third alternative set forth in the "Situation Estimate"—the seizure of Manchuria and Mongolia—had now been fully decided on. The same was true of Nagata, who knew that the imposition of military control over Manchuria was planned to follow the Liut'iaokou Incident, and it seems reasonable to assume that Tatekawa was also aware of this. On April 25 Army Minister Minami had a private meeting with Chief of Staff Kanaya, who opposed the military cutbacks of the Wakatsuki cabinet and refused to accept Minami's judgment that "Russia will not start anything."[83] The General Staff kept up its pressure on the Army Ministry through Hata's opposition to retrenchment and Tatekawa's demands for a military solution in Manchuria and Mongolia. At the same time, it is clear that Tatekawa and other division chiefs in the General Staff were under increasing pressure from their subordinates.

After the "Situation Estimate" was reported to the Throne, Hashimoto began declaring openly that it had been decided to "deal resolutely with the situation."[84] Under the influence of Hashimoto and his hard-line Sakurakai associates, the confidence of company-grade officers in the high command declined. The Sakurakai was itself divided between an extremist and a moderate faction. On May 24 the extremists held a lecture meeting at the Japan Young Men's Hall (Nihon Seinenkan) at which Ōkawa Shūmei discussed the current situation; 97 are said to have attended.[85] A meeting in mid-June of the Sakurakai, at which Captain Tanaka Kiyoshi (who opposed the philosophy of destruction) invited Professor Yoshida Seichi of Tokyo Imperial University to give a scholarly talk on the preconditions for national renovation, was blocked by Hashimoto on the ground that academics were congenitally incapable of reaching conclusions and decisions. He and his friends remained determined to establish a military dictatorship through a coup d'état. About the same time Major Hanaya Tadashi of the Mukden Special Service Agency returned to Japan for talks with Hashimoto and Nemoto. The three agreed that, "Once military action begins in Manchuria, it ought to be easy to capitalize on it to implement reconstruction in Japan,"[86] and it is thought that they supported Ishiwara's Manchuria-first plans on this assumption. Nonetheless, Hashimoto and his supporters had by no means abandoned their "coup first" hope, and they pressed on Hanaya the desirability of doing both simultaneously, in October. The three reached agreement on this basis.

While all this was going on, the Kwantung Army formally pressed upon the General Staff the necessity for making a decision about a military settlement in northern and southern Manchuria. It contended that the time was favorable for military action and that "stabilization of the buffer zone between Japan, China, and the Soviet Union is the cornerstone of East Asian security."[87] On June 11 Army Minister Minami agreed to arrange a top secret meeting of army representatives to discuss urgent Manchurian and Mongolian problems.

Thus, a military solution in Manchuria and Mongolia came to be formally discussed at the highest levels, just as Nagata had confidently expected. The conferees, who were sworn to strict secrecy, included, from the Army Ministry, Nagata and Appointments Section Chief Okamura; and from the General Staff, Organization Section Chief Yamawaki Masataka, Europe-America Section Chief Watari, and China Section Chief Shigetō; the committee was headed by Tatekawa.[88] Its first meeting was held at the Kaikōsha, subsequent ones at places like the Kinoshita Inn and Kokuhonsha headquarters. By the 19th it had adopted a "General Outline of a Solution for the Manchurian Problem,"[89] which proposed the following:

> 1. The Foreign Ministry should undertake negotiations to stop anti-Japanese activities in areas controlled by Chang Hsueh-liang.
> 2. If anti-Japanese activities should get out of hand, military action will probably be necessary.
> 3. The army minister through the cabinet, and the Military Affairs Bureau and the General Staff Intelligence Division through close cooperation with various divisions of the Foreign Ministry should acquaint the Japanese people and foreign powers with the true facts of anti-Japanese activity; in the event military action proves necessary, attention is to be given first to mobilizing national opinion and to measures to prevent outside countries from exerting preventive pressure.
> 4. The General Staff should draw up plans for the size, operations, and leadership of forces to take the field in the event military action becomes necessary.
> 5. A period of about a year, that is until the spring of 1932, is to be spent on working for domestic and foreign understanding of these aims.

In late June Kwantung Army Chief of Staff Miyake returned to Tokyo and was given a copy of the Outline by General Minami, who repeated several times the advice to exercise patience and self-control.[90] In contrast, at a Transport Liaison Conference convened in Tokyo that month for representatives of the railways in Korea and Manchuria and appropriate members of the Army General Staff, South Manchuria Railway Director Sogō Shinji urged the necessity of preparing plans for communications and transport in case of emergency and suggested that the time for military action was at hand. Sogō had been appointed in the spring of 1930 by South Manchuria Railway President Sengoku Mitsugu, who had succeeded Yamamoto Jōtarō. Since taking office he had been strongly influenced by Itagaki and Ishiwara through frequent contacts with them.

In midsummer Prince Saionji and Lord Privy Seal Makino first learned about the army's plans for Manchuria, but they did not seem to attach any great significance to them. On June 25 Kido Kōichi, chief secretary to the Lord Privy Seal, heard from Harada Kumao about "rather considerable plans for Manchuria being prepared by the military,"[91] and he reported this to Makino the next day. It can be assumed that Saionji would also have been informed by his secretary, but the fact that Harada's diary makes no mention of it suggests that Saionji did not yet attach importance to the report.

On June 24 the army "Big Three" (Minami, Kanaya, and Inspector-General of Military Education Mutō Nobuyoshi) considered the attitude the army should adopt toward the financial retrenchments undertaken by the Wakatsuki cabinet, which were so severe as to require structural reforms.[92] On the 27th the trio met again to discuss problems of army organization. Arguing that implementation of the finance directives would affect naval as well as military strength, they determined to oppose them. However, when the Supreme War Council met on June 30 and received the plan of the Big Three to transfer one division to Korea, the council, in turn, opposed this, and no action was taken.

The Supreme War Council met again on July 1, and now it retreated by deciding to consult the Big Three and leave it to them to decide whether a division should be moved to Korea or not. This time Generals Shirakawa Yoshinori and Suzuki Takao advocated postponing the transfer, while General Inoue Ikutarō went so far as to propose reducing the army by two divisions. But in the end they endorsed the proposal of the Big Three. Now Chief of Staff Kanaya was able to assert that, since the proposal to transfer a division to Korea rather than eliminate two divisions had been approved by the Supreme War Council, the army minister must support it as well. General Ugaki, who had in the meantime become governor-general of Korea, vacillated. To Saionji he supported Kanaya's requests, but to Minami he equivocated, saying, "Don't be in too much of a hurry."[93]

Army spokesmen were less successful with cabinet leaders. On July 3 Wakatsuki asked Military Affairs Bureau Chief Koiso to come to his official residence after a cabinet meeting to explain to the other ministers how the Soviet five-year plan affected Manchuria. Koiso noted that the total Soviet budget for the five-year period was 90 billion rubles, of which 20 billion were for military expenditures, and he argued that this demonstrated a forward posture in East Asia. But when Finance Minister Inoue asked him about Soviet financial resources, he was unable to answer; nor could he tell Foreign Minister Shidehara what conversion rate between yen and rubles should be used for the charts he displayed. Finance Minister Inoue got him to go along with the suggestion that Soviet preparations, "as of the present, do not seem to be pointed outward or intent on so-called imperialism, even though the army seems to think so."[94] Koiso, who was not able even to raise the Manchuria-Mongolia problems that were most important to him, was crestfallen.

When on July 4 Minami, responsive to the urgings of the General Staff, placed before Wakatsuki a request for the funds needed to transfer a division to Korea, the prime minister tried to put him off and suggested that he talk to Finance Minister Inoue about the matter.

Vice Chief of Staff Ninomiya and Tatekawa now took a position of leadership in bringing political pressure to bear on the government. They began by urging the government to transfer a division to Korea, then proceeded to propose measures they claimed would resolve the Manchuria-Mongolia problem.[95]

At the same time army authorities solicited the concurrence of the navy. Late in June they invited naval section and division chiefs, as well as the chief of the Navy General Staff, to the Kaikōsha, where Tatekawa explained the "Situation Estimate" to them. This effort was not successful. The navy was not so concerned with the Manchuria-Mongolia problem, and Sakano Tsuneyoshi, head of the Naval Intelligence Office, anticipated difficulties in carrying out the plan because in any action in "Manchuria and Mongolia, Japan cannot ignore the American attitude."[96] It is also probable that the navy was misled and reassured by the phrase "one year of preparation" in the "Situation Estimate," and hence Itagaki and Ishiwara met with little naval opposition to their preparations.

The opposition party, the Seiyūkai, had meantime undertaken a vociferous campaign against the "weak-kneed diplomacy" of Shidehara, which it called a threat to the national polity. It set up a special study committee on the Manchuria-Mongolia problem. On June 20 an Emergency Alliance Executive Meeting was convened, with Yamamoto Teijirō, a former minister in the Tanaka cabinet, in the chair. In a progress report, under "China Policy," Yamamoto stressed that Japan, because of the Manchuria-Mongolia problem, could not simply hand over its rights of extraterritoriality and its concessions as the Western powers seemed prepared to do.[97] The Executive Meeting determined to do everything it could to rouse public opinion on these points and reverse the official attitude on them.

In answer to a Seiyūkai document of June 27, the Minseitō issued on June 30 a declaration defending Shidehara's foreign policy.[98] It stated that the Tanaka (Seiyūkai) foreign policy had "aroused anti-Japanese feelings in China and throughout Southeast Asia and that Japanese exports to China and Southeast Asia had fallen to a critical point" as a result. Indeed, it went on, because of Tanaka's ignorance of foreign policy, "our country's China policy had fallen into an almost hopeless predicament." But with the establishment of a Minseitō government, "anti-Japanese boycotts had been stilled, a Sino-Japanese customs agreement had been reached, negotiations about the Manchurian and Mongolian railways that had been bogged down under the Seiyūkai had been resumed, bandit activities in Chientao had been stopped and the communist apparatus there totally destroyed, and talks for a revision of the commercial agreement between Japan and China centered on the problem of extraterritoriality were about to begin." In these terms the Minseitō sought support for Shidehara diplomacy.

Meanwhile, Colonel Hashimoto and Major Chō were turning their attentions to forming a new political grouping of young officers. The abortive March Incident had reduced to fourteen or fifteen the number of War College graduates in the Sakurakai, and on July 17 more than fifty officers of the rank of major and below, representing the twenty-eighth to forty-second classes at the Military Academy, met with them at the Kaikōsha to organize the Kozakurakai (Little Cherry Blossom Society). The group sent to Saionji a manifesto containing more than 140 signatures, which was also sent to all officers of company grade beginning with the twenty-eighth class.[99] The thirty-fifth class, however, sent Saionji a document of its own, which affirmed that "the Shōwa Restoration means the overthrow of political party government" and urged that captains and lieutenants all over the country become the "standard bearers of the Shōwa Restoration."[100] To carry out their policy of "destruction of internal as well as external enemies," the thirty-fifth class declared its determination to band together to forge a unity of blood and spirit. Hashimoto's and Chō's instigations again aroused to activity extremists bent on internal reform, like those of the thirty-fifth Military Academy class. However, Hashimoto now directed their efforts overseas, saying, "This time we start abroad first."[101] Kōmoto reported all this to Itagaki and Ishiwara.

The Manchurian Youth League Carries Its Campaign to Japan

The Manchurian Youth League moved its activities into a second phase with the issuing of 5,000 copies of "Three Topics on Manchuria and Mongolia," which it distributed in both Japan and Manchuria on July 23. The pamphlet was divided into three sections: "The Importance of Manchuria and Mongolia," "The Seizure of the Rights and Interests of Japanese in Manchuria," and "Cooperation of the Races in Manchuria and Mongolia."[102]

The first section took a pseudo-Marxist approach in explaining the danger to the Japanese race inherent in "the present stage of Japanese capitalism and the Chinese revolution." Because of the rise of Chinese industry, it said, Japanese light industries were gradually facing ruin. There was no way out for Japan short of seeking new markets elsewhere for the products of its light industry or developing a new heavy industry. However, it went on, Japan had inadequate supplies of raw materials within its customs area, and because its production was tied to old-fashioned machinery, it stood little chance in open competition with more highly developed capitalist economies. For that reason there could be no hope for Japan if it once lost the China market. With the future crisis of Japanese capitalism in mind, "our former leaders" had established special rights in Manchuria and Mongolia. It was therefore natural for Japan to want to protect those rights as part of its right to survival.

The second section began with an exposition of the position of Japanese in Manchuria, where some 200,000 colonists were totally unrepresented in the Diet and thus lacked any representation in parliamentary government. As a result, they were discriminated against relative to residents within Japan with regard to industry and government. Capitalism was succeeding in bringing about the modernization of Manchuria, but the position of Japanese settlers there was no better than that of Koreans and Mongols. Despite the frequent affirmation of their situation in parliamentary debate, the Minseitō and the Seiyūkai merely used their predicament to attack or support government policy. Japanese settlers were treated as enemies by the authorities in Manchuria and Mongolia and as orphans by authorities in Japan. Section two concluded that the burden of oppression and exploitation must be lifted and there must be created in Manchuria and Mongolia a paradise of interracial cooperation and harmony based on Japanese culture.

Section three reverted to a bogus Marxism with a discussion of injustice and misery under "the despotism of the semi-feudal ruling structure in the four northeastern provinces." It charged that through this feudal political structure the authorities of Manchuria had done their best to suppress the revolutionary consciousness of the people by issuing propaganda calling for the overthrow of Japanese imperialism. Not only had the Japanese government yielded to the pressures of European and American diplomacy "in disregard of the existence of millions of Japanese subjects and the rights which were the basis of Japan's economy," but in addition the powers had acquiesced in the violence of that semi-feudal Manchurian government in hopes of gaining a foothold in the China market. So long as the political structure of Manchuria and Mongolia remained unchanged, occupation of the area by Japanese troops was necessary. Rather than asserting that Japanese rights in the area were a hindrance to the establishment of a unified and revolutionary China, the Chinese government should realize that its first task must be to overthrow the semifeudal Manchurian regime whose existence necessitated Japanese military intervention. This logic, which called on Japan to bring about a military revolution to rescue other equally defenseless minority groups there, rephrased Ishiwara's scheme in Marxist language and may thus have made it possible for many on the left to justify their conversion to the nationalist cause at a later date.

With the help of the Dairen *News*, the Manchurian Youth League decided in mid-June to send a delegation to Japan with the aim of stirring up public and governmental opinion. The continued bland indifference to their problems, they felt, was akin to "dancing on a volcano."[103] The delegation was composed of Okada Takema, director of the league headquarters, Ozawa Kaisaku, head of the Ch'angch'un branch, and Nagae Ryōji, director of the Antung branch; chosen by election were Takatsuka Gen'ichi, director of the Manchuria-Mongolia Study Association, and Satake Reishin, a league councillor. When they left Dairen on July 13, 1931, the delegates carried declarations that existing treaties were the lifeline of the empire and must be defended to the death.

On July 16 a meeting to welcome them was set up in Akasaka by the Dai Nihon Seisantō, a pseudosocialist organization that had been established in June. It was advertised as a "meeting of promoters of the People's Alliance on the Manchurian and Korean Problems." More than a hundred leaders of the right wing movement—men like Uchida Ryōhei, Tsukuda Nobuo, and Kuzū Yoshihisa—attended. The gathering resolved to "punish unruly China and overthrow the weak diplomacy of Shidehara."[104] On the 18th the delegation's efforts in Tokyo began when they met with Prime Minister Wakatsuki. Thereafter they attended a "People's Meeting on the Korean and Manchurian Problems" in Ueno Park, which included prominent figures such as Baron Inoue Kiyosumi, Reserve Major-General Satō Yasunosuke, Dr. Miyake Yūjirō, and Major Endō Saburō of the Army General Staff.

On the 20th the delegates accompanied Major Endō to a meeting with Inukai Tsuyoshi, the head of the Seiyūkai. Inukai assured them of his personal concern over "Mr. Shidehara's weak diplomacy" and recommended that the group have a talk with Matsuoka Yōsuke, who headed the party's Political Study Group. The same day the delegates saw Army Minister Minami, Minister of Overseas Affairs Hara Shūjirō, and Foreign Minister Shidehara. Minami assured them that, "as a Japanese, it is natural for me to give strong support to the government; I would like to lead public opinion in working to carry out the policies that have been set." Hara, however, parried them by saying, "We will think about this after making an on-the-spot survey of Manchuria and Korea." Shidehara was stronger still in his disapproval. Although "many Chinese seem to know all about President Wilson's Fourteen Points," he wondered whether "any Japanese have heard of them" and went on to argue that they should not "be misled by newspaper sensationalism or the slanted propaganda of a small number of people." He further asked them what they thought about the abrogation of extraterritorial rights and, when they announced undying opposition to such a move, countered with, "If Britain and the United States renounce them and Japan does not, the ill will we would reap in China would do much more harm than giving up those rights would." The delegates retorted that if Japan should give up extraterritorial rights in Mexico, there was no reason to be surprised if the United

States refused to do so; similarly, it was natural for Japan to take a different line because of its proximity to Manchuria and Mongolia.

Feeling they had scored a great victory over Shidehara, the delegates then headed for a "Tokyo Residents Volunteers Mass Meeting" in Aoyama, accompanied by Reserve Lieutenant-General Ishimitsu Maomi. Ozawa, Nagae, Satake, and Okada told the crowd about the Wanpaoshan Incident, the customs and tax problems, and the background of the Manchurian problem; they also gave an account of their talks with the prime minister and the foreign minister. The following day the delegates conferred with Koiso of the Military Affairs Bureau and with people at Minseitō headquarters, as well as making an appearance at a "Meeting on the Manchurian and Korean Problems" that was held at the Seiyōken restaurant in Ueno and chaired by Reserve Lieutenant-General Kikuchi Takeo. At the latter the customary strong resolutions about the Manchurian and Mongolian problems were adopted.

On the 23rd, after a conference with Tani Masayuki, chief of the Foreign Ministry's Asia Bureau, the delegates attended a reception at the Japan-China Club where some sixty individuals influential in political and economic affairs heard them talk about the Wanpaoshan Incident. They then went to the home of Yamamoto Jōtarō to meet with Yamamoto and Matsuoka, with whom they discussed Shidehara diplomacy, "the product of a law school student's brain," and went on to talk of the inevitability of liberation for Manchuria and Mongolia. That evening there were more speeches at a mass meeting, this time the "Japanese People's League for the Manchurian and Korean Problems," attended by some 2,000 people. Once again strong sentiments dominated the rostrum.

On the 25th the delegates called on Tatekawa Yoshitsugu at Army General Staff headquarters. When they asked about the determination of the military, Tatekawa, who had just shifted from the Intelligence Division to a post as chief of the Operations Division, assured them that "the military have already prepared for a final decision" and strongly encouraged the Youth League to continue its work of building up agitation and demand. On the 26th the delegation visited the headquarters of the Kunibashirakai of Tanaka Chigaku, who was Ishiwara's mentor in Nichiren Buddhism. He too urged them on. On the 27th they visited Lord Privy Seal Makino at his villa and urged him to transmit to the Throne an account of the urgency of the situation in Manchuria and Mongolia. From then until the 30th there were visits to the Tokyo Chamber of

Commerce, the Seiyūkai, the House of Peers Study Group, as well as a lecture meeting put on by the *Tōkyō Nichi-nichi shimbun* and a public reception at which leading figures from the business world greeted them.

On July 31 the group shifted its focus to the Kansai area and carried their message to business and financial leaders in Osaka who had been advocating abandonment of Manchuria and Mongolia. The delegates visited the offices of the *Ōsaka Mainichi* and *Asahi* newspapers, the Osaka Chamber of Commerce, the Kobe Chamber of Commerce, and the Shimonoseki Chamber of Commerce, as well as the public hall of the *Fukuoka Nichi-nichi shimbun*, everywhere carrying their message of the need for a stronger line. On August 10 they sailed for Dairen.[105]

The pressure exerted by the Youth League had a strong influence on business and financial circles in Osaka. It is also claimed that in Tokyo a total of 71 organizations went on record with demands for a stronger line. Powerful groups and figures behind the scenes, such as the House of Peers Study Group, the Kōseikai, and Fukuda Masatarō and Itō Miyōji in the Privy Council, veered toward approval of a strong line. On August 5 "people's meetings" were called in Ueno and Hibiya parks amid signs that a national movement was beginning.

The High Command and Party Politics

In mid-July Imamura Hitoshi, who had been chief of the Recruitment Section in the Army Ministry's Military Affairs Bureau, was recommended for appointment as chief of the Army General Staff Operations Section by Military Affairs Bureau Chief Koiso Kuniaki. According to Koiso, Tatekawa, in his new post as Operations Division chief, had asked for Imamura as his section chief. Nagata Tetsuzan in the Military Affairs Section also thought Imamura would be a good partner in the preparation of detailed plans for military action in response to anti-Japanese activities in Manchuria.

Imamura at first declined the post on the ground that he knew too little about Manchuria, but he accepted it after personal encouragement from Nagata. On August 1, when Imamura first reported at the Operations Division, Tatekawa immediately showed him a copy of the "General Outline of a Solution for the Manchurian Problem" and told him to study the document. "In the course of implementing this," Tatekawa told him, "Nagata is taking charge of policy aspects, and I want you to plan the operational aspects, so that it can be submitted to a conference of division and bureau chiefs for their examination. I know you're new in this post, but I'd like you to finish this up during August so we can plan to have it taken up by the conference early in September."[106]

If it is assumed that Tatekawa and Nagata knew that Ishiwara's thinking pointed toward a military solution in the latter part of September, then it is easy to understand why they wanted a detailed plan ready for examination at an early September meeting. But the "General Outline of a Solution for the Manchurian Problem" handed to Imamura specified that the resort to forceful measures would come only after understanding had been built among the Japanese people and with foreign powers. The fact that the outline anticipated a year of preparation reassured Imamura, who was new to the whole thing, in his confidence in the prudence of the central military authorities.

Well before this, the July 17 meeting of the five section chiefs that had produced the outline had also prepared the substance of the instructions the army minister delivered to a special emergency meeting of army regional and division commanders that was called for August 3 and 4. It was decided that precedent should be broken and that the army minister's instructions, normally restricted to those present, should be issued publicly.[107] At a General Staff meeting on August 3 Chief of Staff Kanaya gave an exposition of the military reorganization, and the commanders of the three armies—General Honjō Shigeru, newly appointed to the Kwantung Army, General Mazaki Jinzaburō of the Taiwan Army, and General Hayashi Senjūrō of the Korea Army—were instructed to read the "Situation Estimate" with particular care. At the Army Ministry on August 4 General Minami issued his charge. He called attention to 'irresponsible outsiders and those indifferent to national defense" who accused the military of putting forth unreasonable demands in disregard of the country's difficult situation. Such people championed arms reduction with propaganda that was hurting the nation and the army, he warned, and he urged those present to do everything within their power to counter such "proposals for a sell-out." In regard to the problem of Manchuria and Mongolia, he went on, it was the antiforeign sentiment behind the rights recovery campaign in China and China's rising economic strength that made the new focus on the development of Manchuria and Mongolia so important. In connection with the disarmament conferences, he deplored the tendency in Japan to encourage premature reduction of armament spending, and he urged each division commander to speak out on the issue of defense cutbacks.[108]

Minami's instructions were, contrary to normal practice, published in the newspapers. In the same issue of August 5 the *Tōkyō Asahi shimbun* published an editorial criticizing his stand. "Was it not a revelation of the rash intentions of one group within the military to drag diplomacy toward Manchuria and Mongolia along in line with their thinking?" the paper asked, and it suggested that "the army minister, who as a soldier enjoys extraterritorial rights in a political party cabinet," had overstepped his powers in delivering a frankly political speech. The paper held that if the government wanted to put forth a demand for a stronger policy, it should have proposed such a policy along lines provided for in the constitutional structure, and it deplored the government's apparent lack of spirit in making no response to Minami's speech.

The Minseitō also seized on this issue to attack the army minister. Prime Minister Wakatsuki, however, refrained from criticizing Minami in the cabinet. Just before a meeting on August 5 he commented to Shidehara: "I don't imagine that as foreign minister you're much in favor of speeches against your policies. Still, I hope you won't say anything against the army minister just now." Shidehara agreed, for "If I say anything, it will only create an impasse; it's probably better to let it go for now in view of the political situation."[109] At the time Shidehara was involved in negotiations for a settlement of the Nakamura incident and knew a solution would require the concurrence of army authorities. For his part, Wakatsuki was anxious not to provoke Minami to resign just as he was in the process of drafting his budget.

It should have been obvious by this time that the army was following a policy opposed to that of the government. Shidehara and Wakatsuki, of course, had no knowledge of the plans worked out by Ishiwara, Itagaki, and Nagata for a military solution in Manchuria, nor were they aware of the attitudes toward Manchuria of the army high command. Thus, there was no cabinet-level response of any sort to the Minami speech. The army, however, encouraged the newspapers to report as if a fight had been going on in cabinet meetings and attempted to provoke a confrontation with the Minseitō.

On August 6 the *Tōkyō Asahi shimbun* published an article entitled "The Army Minister's Beliefs"; that same day the Army Ministry's Press

Office issued a statement on "The Army's View on the Interference of Soldiers in Politics."[110] The former article, quoting a declaration by Wakatsuki at a Minseitō convention in Akita prefecture to the effect that "We must stop at no sacrifice to safeguard the nation's existence, and we must take a courageous stance," concluded that army policy did not run contrary to government policy. The article went on to deplore "critics of the army minister [who] wrongly charge him with impropriety in discussing policy toward Manchuria and Mongolia" and stated, "If there is any attack to be made, it should be directed against the China policy of the present cabinet."

Minami declared to an army gathering at the Seiyōken restaurant on the 6th: "In these critical days we have to be of firm resolve, and we must work to realize our ideals."[111] Ogata Katsuichi, chief of the Army Technology Division, applauded this "very profound statement" and on behalf of those present vowed to march forward by the side of the army minister.

On August 6 Harada Kumao, meeting with Saionji at Gotemba, told him what he had just learned of the details of the March Incident from Inoue Saburō, head of the Mobilization Section of the Equipment and Supplies Bureau. Saionji's immediate reaction was that Vice Chief of Staff Ninomiya, Koiso, and Tatekawa would have to be dismissed and that Ugaki would also as a matter of course have to leave his post as governor-general of Korea.[112] But in the five months since the incident, the political situation had changed greatly. The political parties had already lost much of their power to resist the army, and thus the restraining influence of Saionji, a rather archaic remnant of the earlier genrō power structure, was consequently weakened.

Itagaki was in Tokyo before the meeting of army regional and division commanders and had met with both Shigetō Chiaki and Hashimoto Kingorō at the Kaikōsha. When Hashimoto asked, "Is the Kwantung Army going ahead with it?" Itagaki answered, "Yes." Hashimoto then took upon himself the responsibility for organizing a coup d'etat in Japan and arranging financial backing. An argument ensued over whether Manchuria and Mongolia were to be independent or declared to be under Japanese domination.

That evening Hashimoto and Kanda Masatane of the Korea Army, who had accompanied General Hayashi to Tokyo, held a party attended by the three overseas army commanders and others such as Koiso, Sugiyama, Nagata, and Okamura, the occasion being paid for out of secret funds Kanda had brought with him from Korea. Nagata seemed to show some misgivings about Hashimoto when he warned him, "I hope you know what you are getting into." Okamura too evidenced some reservations. Both were doubtful about Hashimoto's plans for a coup in Japan and thought it more important that Ishiwara's and Itagaki's plans for a military solution in Manchuria and Mongolia succeeded. Both men mistrusted Hashimoto and feared his plans for a coup would arouse the cabinet and strengthen Shidehara's hand in foreign policy, with the result that their plans for Manchuria and Mongolia would end in failure. Hashimoto and Kanda spent the next two days and nights at the Masudaya restaurant at Karasumori, consoling themselves with the pretty geisha while they discussed the problems involved in having the Korea Army cross the border into Manchuria.[113] Hashimoto had already discussed with Amakasu Masahiko the latter's plans for a coup in Harbin. Ōkawa Shūmei was evidently aware of these plans, for about the same time he commented to his associate Shimizu Kōnosuke that while the March Incident had been a failure, he expected "a man named Amakasu to work out something better at Harbin with the help of people like Colonel Itagaki of the Kwantung Army."[114]

Saionji meanwhile had become involved in a controversy with Hiranuma over the latter's proposed reform of the Privy Council, ostensibly in order to strengthen that body but in fact to ensure Hiranuma's control over it. Lord Privy Seal Makino supported Hiranuma's proposal to strengthen the council by the addition of five members and was unable to understand Saionji's opposition to this step. But Saionji continued to distrust Hiranuma. "What do you suppose Hiranuma is up to?" he asked Harada on August 10.[115] Hiranuma wrote in his memoirs:

> The last time I saw Saionji before the Manchurian Incident was in Gotemba. I told him he ought to reexamine his position, for the present unsatisfactory policy would cause a serious reaction that would not be easily controlled. He passed it off with some compliment, but at heart he wouldn't listen to me. That was it. You can't say he caused the Manchurian Incident, but do-nothing-ism ends up by provoking action.[116]

Hiranuma, like Yamagata Aritomo, believed that "the white race will never admit colored peoples to full standing"[117] and that "only the Japanese race" was in a position to resist. And he insisted on the need for a "de-

cisive Russo-Japanese showdown in order to achieve a complete settlement of the Manchuria-Mongolia problem."[118] It is true that Hiranuma's
Kokuhonsha (National Foundation Society) had close links with the military, and it has been said that he adopted a stronger stance than many
in the army did. But he was certainly opposed to any program that would
have used the outbreak of war in Manchuria and Mongolia as the occasion for restructuring the Japanese social hierarchy.[119]

On August 8 Harada met with Admiral Okada Keisuke of the Supreme War Council to ask for the navy's cooperation in the issues that
had been raised between the government and the army.[120] On August
12, in reply to Saionji's urging that Ninomiya, Koiso, and Tatekawa be
dismissed, Inoue Saburō declared that to do so would only incite the
army and make the situation worse, and he suggested that Saionji settle
for the dissolution of the Sakurakai. This would be acceptable, according
to Inoue, because Ninomiya, Koiso, and Tatekawa were finding that organization somewhat difficult to control. It would appear, however, that
Tatekawa had reached some sort of understanding with the Sakurakai
through Hashimoto. Moreover, Inoue himself had already talked to Koiso and had sounded out the General Staff about its dissolution. Feeling
that they were under some suspicion, the members of the Sakurakai met
shortly after August 10 at the Kaikōsha and resolved that, given the view
of the central miltary authorities, they would completely change the society's purpose to that of moral uplift. But this was nothing more than a
camouflage agreed upon by Hashimoto and his friends in the Russia and
China sections of the General Staff.[121]

On August 18 Harada met with Saionji. It was the day after the army
had publicly announced the disappearance of Captain Nakamura, and
Saionji had just seen Wakatsuki and Makino. Now he said to Harada:
"There is a very dangerous state of affairs in the army. The Kwantung
Army has let Yen Hsi-shan, who was in Kwantung, get away by plane. I
can't help but think the imperial army is cooking something up in Manchuria, Mongolia, and China. Admiral Okada and the Foreign Ministry
are extremely worried about this too. We've just got to be more careful."[122] On the 20th Saionji once more saw Makino and discussed the
young officers movement and the proposed enlargement of the Privy
Council. On the 19th Harada met with the prime minister and told him
what Saionji had said the day before.[123] Two days later he again met with
Wakatsuki, who told him in strict confidence that "I am thinking of call-

ing in the army minister and asking him to warn army circles against the tendency about which we have been concerned for some time."[124] With Saionji's encouragement, Wakatsuki arranged to talk with Minami that same day.

At their meeting, the prime minister first discussed other matters with Minami for a time. Finally he said: "Actually, I want to speak in confidence with you. I am very worried about the situation in our country. I think we ought to work together and devote ourselves to our country." He went on to talk about the escape of Yen Hsi-shan, the help that had been given to Shih Yu-san in his revolt against Nanking in Hopei, the March Incident, and opinion among the young officers, and he quietly asked Minami for his full cooperation in restoring discipline in the army.

Characteristically, Minami did not give the prime minister a clear answer. Instead he glossed things over by pointing out that political parties were criticizing the army and soldiers were indignant because there was a good deal of talk about the army's uselessness.[125]

On the same day Harada heard from a branch manager of the Sumitomo bank that "on the 20th a rumor that troops would soon be dispatched to Manchuria spread in Osaka and resulted in a sudden drop in the stock of the South Manchuria Railway."[126] That night he met with Inoue Saburō, who told him that Home Affairs Minister Adachi Kenzō had ordered the military to refrain from making speeches concerning political and diplomatic issues. Inoue thought Adachi's action was dangerous and might invite serious consequences.[127]

That evening, in a meeting with Wakatsuki, Harada heard about the prime minister's conversation with Minami. Harada relayed this to Prince Saionji on the 22nd. At the genrō's request, Harada sought out Wakatsuki, Superintendent-General of the Metropolitan Police Takahashi Morio, Asia Bureau Chief Tani Masayuki, and Railways Minister Egi Tasuku, told them of the talks between Saionji and Makino, and asked each for his cooperation in handling the army.[128]

Unknown to the leadership in Tokyo, events in Manchuria were developing rapidly. Toward the middle of August Itagaki had returned to Port Arthur in advance of General Honjō, who was to take command of the Kwantung Army. There he discovered that Ishiwara, without waiting for him, had reached agreement with South Manchuria Railway Vice President Eguchi Teijō concerning the demands to be presented to the Mukden command of the Fengt'ien army to facilitate a Japanese investigation of the disappearance of Captain Nakamura Shintarō. Ishiwara had requested that the South Manchuria Railway provide men and materials for the investigation.[129] An armored train and a mixed regiment of infantry and artillery were already at Ssup'ingkai, but instructions from central headquarters had so far kept them from being dispatched.

On the 13th, presumably still before Itagaki's return to Port Arthur, Ishiwara sent Nagata a very strong recommendation on procedure in the Nakamura case. Ishiwara did not fully understand that Nagata and Okamura were endeavoring to reconcile the use of force in Manchuria and Mongolia with Japan's standing and honor among the powers, nor did he care about their concern for political harmony between the Kwantung Army and central headquarters in Tokyo. When on August 7 he had seen a telegram to the Kwantung Army stipulating that the Nakamura incident was "not to be considered an appropriate occasion for settlement of the Manchurian and Mongolian problems,"[130] he wondered whether central headquarters was losing its nerve.

In his message to Nagata, Ishiwara argued that "a soldier who travels in the Chinese interior is in violation of no international usage of any sort. For instance, U.S. military officers are free to inspect our military establishment so long as they abide by security regulations. In the same way even military inspection trips in China, provided they do not violate Chinese domestic law, should arouse no resistance whatever."[131] He did not necessarily think that the Kwantung Army, "like the Germans in Shantung, should seize on the Nakamura incident as the occasion for establishing direct control over Manchuria and Mongolia," but he warned that "today people with understanding are coming to the realization that there is no solution possible short of one worked out through armed strength." It was necessary to ensure that Minami's timely instructions would not turn out to be mere empty words. "Solution of the Manchuria-Mongolia question is the first step in deepening the people's faith in the army's leadership." In short, the letter showed Ishiwara's indignation at the orders the Kwantung Army was suddenly forced to issue to withdraw the train and men from Ssup'ing just as tension had reached its peak, and he demanded that the central army authorities take greater account of the opinion of local army leaders.

What Nagata's reaction was to Ishiwara's letter is not clear, but the committee formed to plan action on the basis of the "Situation Estimate" had begun to meet on August 9, and Nagata had explained the way things had developed to men like Tōjō Hideki, who had replaced Yamawaki as chief of the Organization Section, Operations Section Chief Imamura, and Isogai Rensuke, chief of the Second Section of the Inspectorate-General of Military Education. On August 17 newspaper censorship with respect to the Nakamura incident was lifted. And in the latter part of August Hanaya Tadashi returned to Tokyo to ascertain what measures Tokyo was considering in the Nakamura affair.

Hanaya's memoir states that he asked Ninomiya and Tatekawa not to "interfere too closely" when "the Japanese and Chinese armies clash." While "we don't know how far we can check the government," they replied, "we'll do our best to back you up."[132] Remembering that Tatekawa had already reached agreement with Itagaki on the much more serious problem, such a promise could be expected to follow as a matter of course. Hanaya's notes show that he also exchanged opinions with Koiso and Nagata, but there are good reasons to suppose that he did not obtain much information from Nagata, who probably would not have revealed the larger scheme he had in mind. As for Koiso, who did not know of the Ishiwara-Itagaki plans, he strongly supported the policy of central headquarters laid out in the "General Outline of a Solution for the Manchurian Problem," saying that since "there is danger of a clash with the Soviets if we get into an incident in Manchuria," it was "important to avoid war, whatever the situation, until all preparations are fully completed."[133] "And what happens if the army finds itself forced to move by the exigencies of the situation?" Hanaya asked. Koiso avoided a direct answer by rejoining, "I cannot answer such a hypothetical question. It assumes that war is impossible to avoid, and since that means calm thinking and policymaking will have been bypassed, it poses a completely different problem. It's our policy to avoid such a contingency."

Hanaya also had discussions with Hashimoto and Nemoto, and he was a good deal more frank with them. "We're all set and ready to go ahead as planned," he told them. Nemoto urged delay, warning that "the Wakatsuki cabinet is hard to handle. I wonder if you shouldn't wait for it to fall. If you move too fast, you may simply force General Honjō to commit hara-kiri." Hanaya countered, "The arrow has left the bow," and paid no attention. A startled Nemoto told this to Shigetō, who upon meeting Fujita Isamu, a businessman with political connections and Shigetō's brother-in-law's nephew, promptly asked him for a financial contribution.[134] As a start Fujita at once gave Hashimoto and Nemoto ¥2,000, of which half was taken to the Kwantung Army's Special Service Agency by Major Wachi Takaji of the China Section, who pleaded ill to get sick leave.[135] A week later when Wachi returned to Tokyo, he went to see Fujita, again with Hashimoto, and told him of the plans for an explosion at Liut'iaokou.[136] This time Fujita provided ¥100,000; on September 7 Kōmoto Daisaku left for Mukden with ¥30,000 of it. In mid-September Ōkawa Shūmei's protégé Nakajima Shin'ichi was entrusted by Tatekawa with a mission to Itagaki. He left for Dairen with ¥30,000. Last of all Mukden Special Service Agency Chief Doihara Kenji returned to Manchuria with ¥20,000.[137] According to Kōmoto the Kwantung Army's cache of secret funds was down to ¥10,000 at the time. All this activity can be regarded as a rather ominous shadow on the fringes of the Ishiwara and Itagaki plan, but in the larger sense it should probably be seen as a necessary element in the implementation of Ishiwara's promises.

Within the army many feared that the activities of middle and lower ranking officers in collaboration with others outside the military would lead to a dangerous and "disadvantageous situation for the military." Kempeitai commander Toyama Bunzō, in instructions to his officers concerning "policies toward the situation among young officers," explained that if the tendency to organize by rank and with outsiders should spread beyond the young officers, it would reach a "point where it threatened the foundations of the entire army," and he asked them to maintain contact with commanders of posts to which they were attached and do their best to contain the young officers movement.[138]

Despite this, on August 25 a group of about forty army and navy officers and civilians met at the Takaratei restaurant in Shinjuku in disregard of Toyama's adjurations. The following day, at the Japan Young Men's Hall in Gaien, agreement was reached among several groups on cooperation to bring about a military solution to the Manchuria-Mongolia problem and on plans for a parallel coup d'état (the October Incident).[139] The civilian participants included Nishida Mitsugu and the Nichiren monk Inoue Nisshō; from the army there were Suganami Saburō, Ōgishi Yoriyoshi, and Noda Matao; and from the navy Fujii Hitoshi, Mikami Takashi, Yamagishi Hiroshi, and Hama Yūji, all of them senior lieutenants in rank. Nishida was a disciple of the radical national-socialist Kita Ikki, and behind Suganami was the Kozakurakai with its links to the Sakurakai and Ōkawa Shūmei. The proposed coup was to center around Hashimoto and Ōkawa; the Manchurian problem was to be dealt with thereafter. A faction led by Inoue, however, considered that Hashimoto and his followers were plotting in contravention of the "emperor's august mind" and decided to murder Tatekawa, Koiso, and others they thought were central to Hashimoto's scheme. Hashimoto, who had originated the idea for a coup, had concluded on the basis of the failure of the March Incident that he would keep the details of his plans from moderates, not only in army headquarters but also within the Sakurakai itself, and rely only on a very small number of trusted associates. This had had the contrary effect of stirring antagonism against Hashimoto and his friends even among the more extreme elements. It was an illustration of the cancerous progress that was to lead Japan to final ruin.

The campaigns of the Manchurian Youth League and the army's activities against the political parties quickly resulted in demands for a strong line by every faction in the House of Peers once details of the Nakamura case were published in the press, and this was used by Mori Kaku of the Seiyūkai to forge a broad movement against the Minseitō cabinet. All the factions in the Peers—the Kenkyūkai, the Kōyūkurabu, the Dōwakai, and even the Minseitō-affiliated Dōseikai—considered the Nakamura incident a failure of Shidehara diplomacy, and they called for a government investigation and kept a close watch on the negotiations conducted by Consul-General Hayashi Kyūjirō at Mukden. The situation was ripe for an antigovernment campaign, and it all depended on Hayashi's results. Even the voices that had previously criticized the army's hard line were silenced.[140] The army meanwhile held lectures throughout the country, talking of the need to strengthen the national defense. The political parties were at the same time holding election rallies in support of candidates for the prefectural assemblies. But while the army's lectures were well attended, the political parties had difficulty finding meeting places.

Cognizant of the parties' difficulties, Mori Kaku asked Koiso Kuniaki what he thought about the situation. Koiso answered that if the parties were "sensitive to the direction of the people's thinking and would pledge themselves to devote their full efforts to the realization of national defense, their audiences would undoubtedly increase very quickly," and he suggested that the army would be very pleased if its lecture series were coordinated with and followed by a political party lecture series.[141] Mori quickly decided that it would benefit the Seiyūkai to cooperate with the army as Koiso had suggested.

In the middle of July Mori had gone to Manchuria and Mongolia for a four-week investigation that centered on the Chientao district, where he wanted to study the conditions of Koreans who had clashed with Chinese in the Wanpaoshan area. He took with him the experienced newsmen Yamazaki Takeshi and Tōjō Tei and returned on August 13. Their trip was undertaken on behalf of the Seiyūkai to aid in developing a concrete party policy toward the region. Everywhere he went Mori found the Japanese residents full of indignation against Shidehara diplomacy and becoming "worshippers of the military" because of the weak-kneed tactics of officials of the consular service and the Kwantung leased territory. He concluded that the demands for a strong policy had hitherto fallen far short of what was needed.[142] Especially with regard to the Chientao problem, he came to believe strongly that "Japanese diplomacy, with its back stiffened, should eradicate the Chinese military police, attack communist banditry, and restore order." Mori also deplored the fact that local Foreign Ministry officials, "true to the do-nothing-ism of the ministry in Tokyo," seemed to suppress information about the murder of Koreans and Japanese because they feared it would provide fuel for advocates of stronger policies. They could do this, he complained, because they were able, "in disregard of the indignation of their fellow nationals, to lead a civilized life within their consulates, surrounded by high brick walls, and safe behind their batteries."[143] Mori also thought that the South Manchuria Railway, "once it realizes that it cannot give up its imperialist position, will have to take a positive stand."[144]

Yamaura Kan'ichi, who also accompanied Mori, wrote: "Chientao is the setting for a Sino-Japanese war between communism and imperialism. It is the wellspring of Korean nationalism. The communist bandits summon nationalism to do battle with imperialism. Imperialism is actually on the defensive."[145] This was probably the way Mori himself saw it. As soon as he returned home, Mori headed for the army minister's residence to talk with Minami and give him this encouragement: "Your speech of instructions was not a bit extreme and by no means beyond your authority. This was immediately obvious to me when I visited the area. I belong to the party of the opposition, but I am in complete agreement with your view of the Manchuria-Mongolia problem. I beg of you to continue your endeavors."[146]

On August 18 officers of the Seiyūkai held their regular meeting. First, Board of Directors Chairman Kuhara Fusanosuke reported on several

matters, then Secretary Mori, just back from Manchuria, delivered a report condemning the weak foreign policy of Shidehara and calling for the
overthrow of the cabinet.[147] It was decided that Mori's report on Manchuria and Mongolia was to be formally adopted later in the month. In
the meantime Mori went to Nasu with Secretary-General Inukai to inquire after the emperor's health. But Grand Chamberlain Suzuki Kantarō, who mistrusted Mori, did not allow him to have a private audience
with the emperor; Mori was so angry that he complained to Prince Konoe
Fumimaro.[148] Mori's above-mentioned visit to Koiso probably took place
about this time.

On August 31, at the San'entei in Shiba, the Seiyūkai officers met
with the members of their special committee on policy toward the Soviet Union and China.[149] Mori, Yamazaki, and Tōjō Tei delivered the
report on their investigations in Manchuria and Mongolia. Tōjō began
with an "Overall View of Manchuria," Yamazaki followed with "Incidents of Clashes Between Koreans and Chinese," and Mori ended with
"The Conclusions We Have Reached." These were that, "however much
Japan may try by compromise and concessions to establish Sino-Japanese relations on a basis of reasonableness, it is a fact that the situation
is already beyond settlement by such means"; one therefore had to conclude that only "the exercise of national power" could resolve the matter
and that it was "beyond doubt that the situation in Manchuria and Mongolia has reached the brink of war."[150] The report was accepted by those
present, who agreed to make it the basis of a party statement.

On September 1 the Seiyūkai quickly settled upon a "party position
on the China problem," and on the 3rd at a meeting of the Kantō Seiyūkai at Utsunomiya, Inukai personally took the field and launched a fierce
nationwide opposition party campaign for solving the Manchuria-Mongolia
issue and bringing about a general revision of Japanese foreign policy.
This was the outcome of the inspection trip Mori and his companions
had made to Manchuria and Mongolia.

On August 31 General Suzuki Sōroku, head of the Imperial Reservists Association, in a speech to reservists raised the first public voice in
support of Minami.[151] Chief of Staff Kanaya had already made available
to Uchida Ryōhei by way of Hashimoto ¥50,000 for the use of ultranationalist organizations in stirring up public opinion. Hashimoto, in response to Ōkawa's urging that "we have to activate the Reservists Association,"[152] had handed ¥70 to the reservists organizations in Shitaya and

Asakusa with instructions to them to contact units in all parts of the country. Fearing reckless action on the part of Hashimoto and his compatriots, Ōkamura and Nagata contrived the convening of a regular meeting of the Reservists Association to discuss the matter, only to have the audience addressed with impassioned speeches from General Suzuki and Hashimoto too.

On August 30 Harada Kumao questioned Inoue Saburō about Minami's apparent lack of concern over the March Incident and discussed with him the activities of the advocates of force in Manchuria and Mongolia.[153] The next day Harada first got word of a campaign for the establishment of a "national unity" cabinet headed by Hiranuma. He was also informed that, although the prosecuting attorney's office of the Justice Ministry had knowledge that Ugaki's supporters were implicated in the March Incident, it was not taking any action lest Hiranuma be involved.[154]

The advocates of a strong policy toward Manchuria and Mongolia were meanwhile stepping up their campaign to win public support for their demands. On September 4 Shidehara told Harada he had heard from newspapermen that at a recent periodic callup of reservists, the regimental commander had lined up the young men and read to them from a printed sheet an exhortation concerning the army's position on and the spirit it should display toward the Manchuria-Mongolia problem. "From the way he howled at them, you would have thought war was about to break out. One of the reservists, apparently a fishmonger, is said to have whispered that the commander must have lost his mind."[155] Newspaper reporters also passed on to Prime Minister Wakatsuki their readers' queries about when the troops would leave for Manchuria, but Wakatsuki refused to reply to such questions. On September 7 airplanes of the 3rd Air Regiment, attached to the 16th (Kyoto) Division, scattered over cities such as Fukui, Kanazawa, Toyama, and Matsumoto 100,000 leaflets entitled "Wake Up to National Defense!" and containing maps illustrating Japan's rights in Manchuria.[156]

That same day in the House of Peers the Shōwakai (made up of the Kōseikai, Dōseikai, Kōyūkurabu, and Tuesday Club) invited Koiso to address them on the army's view of the Nakamura incident. Koiso gave a detailed explanation of the geographical, military, economic, and political importance of Manchuria and Mongolia and told them it was the army's intention to use the Nakamura incident to urge the development of a firm and immovable continental policy.[157] Also on the 7th Major Kagesa Sadaaki of the Army General Staff addressed a meeting in Tokyo called by a "mass unity society" to consider the China problem. In his speech he went much further than Koiso in espousing a forceful solution. Kagesa pointed out that although Wakatsuki, in a speech at the *tōhoku* (northeastern) convention of the Minseitō, had affirmed his party's determination "to take strong action in the event our rights in Manchuria and Mongolia are violated," in fact those rights had already been violated, and yet the government was doing nothing about it. Kagesa deplored the government's diplomacy of retreat and argued, "It is natural for Japan, the leader of East Asia, to attack China in order to chastise its unrighteousness; it is totally unnecessary for Japan to defer to any other country."[158] Since war was no longer avoidable, he urged his audience, they should support the army and give it their encouragement.

On the same day the General Council of the Minseitō was convened. Aware of the growing demands on all sides for a strong policy toward Manchuria and Mongolia, it decided to establish a special China committee to carry out a study of the situation with a view to safeguarding Japanese rights in Manchuria and Mongolia.[159] Two days later this committee agreed that while Japan should take bold defensive measures in response to violations of its rights, it was necessary to await the outcome of the negotiations concerning the Nakamura incident. Meanwhile, the committee would continue to assess the situation.[160]

On September 8 the *Tōkyō Asahi shimbun* declared editorially that while "the people are not able to give unconditional support either to Shidehara's low-key diplomacy or to the army's advocacy of a strong line, a consensus on national policy is acutely needed." The *Asahi* had hitherto expressed strong support for Shidehara's policies; therefore this apparent shift gratified the army's hard liners immensely.

At the Aoyama Assembly Hall on September 10 an "All Groups United Meeting on Manchuria-Mongolia Problems" was held. Among the organizations supporting the assembly were the Society of Those Agreed on Foreign Policy, People's Alliance on the Manchurian Problem, People's Alliance for Solution of the Manchurian Problem, East Asian Economic Council, Manchurian Youth League, Manchuria-Mongolia Problems Research Association, Manchurian Japanese Autonomy Alliance, and the North Manchuria Japanese Residents Association. At the meeting a resolution was presented stating: "As the key to solving the problem, we have no choice but to harden our resolve and use force to put an end to lawlessness, holding to our objective without fear." And an intransigent twelve-point platform was adopted.[161]

On the 11th a radio broadcast on "The Situation Between China and Japan" by Colonel Hayashi Daihachi, commander of the 7th (Kanazawa) Infantry Regiment, who had just been transferred from Manchuria in August, was canceled by central headquarters. Three days earlier a talk concerning the Manchuria-Mongolia problem had been scheduled on a Kanazawa station, but the broadcast by Leiutenant-Colonel Kijima of the same regiment, entitled "On Army Flag Day," had been so inflammatory that he had been cut off in the middle of the broadcast.[162]

The Army General Staff and the Army Ministry had already, on September 7, agreed to insist on a strong line in the Nakamura incident negotiations.[163] The Asia Bureau of the Foreign Ministry had also discussed the matter with the Military Affairs Bureau of the Army Ministry and had reached agreement on the 9th that in the event the Mukden authorities failed to give evidence of sincerity, Japan would have to adopt "measures of retaliation agreed upon by international law and practice."[164] It was approved at a meeting of high officials of the Foreign Ministry on September 11. Two days earlier, on the 9th, at the League of Nations in Geneva, Ambassador Yoshizawa Kenkichi gave a speech that attempted to reconcile Japan's policy in China with the League Covenant and the Kellogg-Briand Pact by asserting Japan's residual right of self-defense. On the 11th in the Assembly the Chinese delegate, Saoke Alfred Sze, charged that Japan was planning for military action in Manchuria and Mongolia; "if sanctions against Japan are not adopted," he warned, "the Kellogg-Briand Pact will become empty words."[165]

In a conversation with Tani Masayuki at the residence of Prince Konoe on the 10th Kido Kōichi was told of the proposal to appeal to the right of self-defense. Kido expressed his support for this course of action.[166]

Nonetheless, men like Nagata were extremely dissatisfied with the existing state of affairs and sought ways of aggravating the situation further. To this end they used the visit of Colonel Doihara Kenji, head of the Mukden Special Service Agency, who arrived in Tokyo on September 10 for talks at central headquarters. He had been involved as chief of the Special Service Agency at Tientsin in the plans for Yen Hsi-shan's return to Shansi at the end of July, when the Kwantung Army had hoped to enlist Yen and others against Chang Hsueh-liang at the time of Shih

Yu-san's revolt as a preliminary to the use of force by Japan. In fact, this plan had failed, and Doihara had been assigned to the same post in Mukden, where he had taken command on August 18. Ishiwara felt a strong dislike for Doihara, who was always cooking up small schemes, and he was said to have been delighted to have Doihara leave for Japan just before the explosion at Liut'iaokou was to occur. Still, Doihara was extremely useful in Japan. On the morning of his arrival he held a news conference at which he stated that if the Nakamura incident could not be solved by the Foreign Ministry, it would probably have to be settled by force. The Kwantung Army, he added, had intended to take direct action right after the incident became known but had not done so, because of government objections.

Doihara now made his way to the Army General Staff, where he presented a report, prepared by Major Hanaya Tadashi of his agency, denying that the Mukden regime was becoming conciliatory. In the afternoon a meeting of senior officials of the ministry and General Staff, including Kanaya, Ninomiya, Minami, Sugiyama, and Nagata, agreed that the Kwantung Army should be told to go ahead according to policies that had been worked out previously.

On the 11th Doihara saw Shidehara and Tani. Shidehara was still seeking a diplomatic solution to the Nakamura incident and expressed the hope that the army would remain prudent.[167] Doihara went on to a meeting with Ninomiya, Sugiyama, and Nagata in the vice minister's office at the Army Ministry, where for two hours they discussed means of using direct action in retaliation against the Chinese.[168]

That evening the Tenth Day Group, consisting of the heads of sections concerned with Manchuria and Mongolia in the Foreign, Army, and Navy ministries and the Army and Navy General Staffs, met at 7 o'clock at the Chikuyō restaurant. From the Foreign Ministry came Kurihara Tadashi of the Documents Section, Mitani Takanobu of Personnel, and Sakuma Shin of Cables, each a section chief; from the Army Ministry came Nagata and some other section chiefs; from the Navy Ministry, Senior Adjutant Takahashi Ibō and Naval Affairs Bureau First Section Chief Sawamoto Yorio; from the Army General Staff, Tōjō Hideki and Watari Hisao; and from the Navy General Staff, Kondō Nobutake of the First Section, Noda Kiyoshi of the Second Section, and some other section chiefs. In all twenty men were there. After Nagata had set out the army's policy, the group agreed that "We must take the Nakamura incident as the occasion for seeking an overall solution of railway and other pending problems."[169]

At 7:30 P.M. the Seiyūkai's Committee To Resolve the China Problem met at party headquarters.[170] Mori Kaku proposed a campaign to arouse the public and unify public opinion, and the committee agreed to instruct all prefectural and city branches to refer to the Manchuria-Mongolia problem in election speeches and to organize special speaking tours to arouse public opinion.

The political situation was now moving in the direction that Nagata had hoped and planned it would, and under the circumstances it is not surprising that he decided there was no real hindrance to the use of military force in Manchuria and Mongolia. Given the success of the Kwantung Army's plan to "avoid becoming isolated from Japan," there was every reason for Nagata and others working behind the scenes to anticipate their activities would continue to bear fruit.

Warnings of the Kwantung Army's plans did reach government leaders in Tokyo. Sometime before September 5, probably about the 4th, a telegram arrived at the Foreign Ministry. It was not from the Mukden consulate, more likely from the Kwantung Leased Territory Police Bureau. It warned that "a plot is afoot among young officers in the Kwantung Army to thrash the Chinese army."[171] Some have said that the plot had been leaked by Yoshimura Gō, who was employed by the Kwantung Army's Special Service Agency, others that Hanaya had let it slip while drunk.[172] It is also true that ultranationalist activists in Japan, such as Ōkawa, spread rumors about military action. Tani asked Koiso about it immediately, while Shidehara telegraphed the following instructions to Consul-General Hayashi in Mukden: "Word has reached us that of late Colonel Itagaki of the Kwantung Army and others have a lot of money and have had active dealings with the National Essence Society and other China adventurers, and that they have decided, in view of the fact that negotiations over the Nakamura incident have not reached a satisfactory result, that they must start direct action in the middle of this month. Please make further arrangements to control these adventurers."[173]

Harada Kumao, meanwhile, was increasingly concerned about the situation he saw developing in the army. On September 8 he talked with Wakatsuki. He then went to see Makino and proposed that Kido Kōichi be sent to discuss the matter with Prince Kan'in Kotohito. Makino, however, mistrusted Kido and thought it would be better if he talked to Prince

Kan'in himself. That same day Harada asked Grand Chamberlain Suzuki to urge his younger brother, General Suzuki Takao, to oppose infractions of military discipline.[174] Harada also sought the support of Railways Minister Egi. When he met with Admiral Okada on the 9th, he asked Okada what he thought of a request by Wakatsuki and Makino for Harada to ask Saionji to send his own warning to Army Minister Minami. Okada replied that he was afraid it would lower Saionji's position to that of the army and in his view it would be better for Wakatsuki to speak to Minami himself. Harada immediately passed Okada's opinion on to Wakatsuki, who finally made up his mind and on the 10th spoke rather sharply to Minami.[175] On the 11th Harada informed Saionji of Okada's position. The genrō agreed that it was better to wait "until the chips are down." He went on: "I may tell Minami to keep a sharp eye on military discipline, but it would be unwise to criticize him on every little issue."[176]

Around September 9 Makino discussed with Saionji a proposal to have the emperor ask Minami and Kanaya some searching questions about military discipline at the fall maneuvers at Kumamoto. Saionji, for once, gave a direct answer: "We can't wait until fall. It can't wait; we have to do it right away. And if the emperor summons the army minister, he will have to summon the navy minister also, even though they may meet on a different day."[177]

As a result, on September 9 Navy Minister Abo Kiyokazu had an audience with the emperor. "There is a good deal of public criticism of military discipline, is there anything to it?" he was asked.[178] Abo was as startled as if he had been awakened by having water poured into his ear, and he returned to the ministry in amazement to recount the audience to Vice Minister Kobayashi Seizō. On the 11th the emperor summoned Minami to warn him about military discipline.

Minami, of course, knew nothing about Ishiwara's and Itagaki's plans for the Liut'iaokou Incident. Taking the initiative, he declared that the army regarded associations of young officers as being "very undesirable from the point of view of military discipline"; therefore, he assured the emperor, "we are controlling them very carefully." Moreover, "it is our policy by the use of military regulations to control speeches on political matters by the military and those attached to the military." He acknowledged that foreign policy lay "within the jurisdiction of the Foreign Ministry" and that "we have to be careful to keep the military from meddling in this, for it would create a contentious situation."[179] Thus, it has been charged, did Minami put up a defensive smokescreen to forestall the emperor's queries.

A day later Minami was in Gotemba to see Saionji. The newspapers then were speculating that because Imperial Household Minister Ichiki Kitokurō had been to Gotemba shortly before this, he and Home Affairs Minister Adachi Kenzō were resigning,[180] but Harada surmised that elements in the army were trying to make changes in the group that was close to the emperor. Minami offered Saionji numerous reassurances, "as though he had memorized them," whereupon Saionji delivered the following admonition:

> To begin with, it has been extremely unpleasant to have ne'er-do-wells, so-called toughs or floaters, or members of strong-arm organizations of the right sent to Manchurian territory. It would be especially unfortunate to have the military make use of fellows of this sort; it hurts the country's dignity and the army's prestige. . . . We may call that territory Manchuria and Mongolia, but the fact remains that it belongs to China. Diplomacy should be left to the foreign minister, and it won't do at all for the army to go barging in on its own. It is my opinion that you, with your responsibilities as an adviser to the Throne and as head of the army, ought to be particularly careful about controlling the military.

"I will exercise my responsibility and be extremely careful," Minami answered coolly. Saionji had the feeling that he was pushing against a swinging gate, and he expected little from this exchange.[181]

Harada also spoke with Army Vice Chief of Staff Ninomiya on the 12th. Ninomiya complained about the Foreign Ministry and asked Harada to come to General Staff headquarters the next morning to pick up documents the army had used in its exposition of the Manchurian problem to the emperor, which he wished Saionji to see. On the 13th Wakatsuki visited Saionji, who told him about his talk with Minami the day before and discussed with him the activities of groups close to the emperor.

According to Harada, it was at this point that the army and the Seiyūkai joined together against the Minseitō by replacing the emperor's closest advisers with fanatics such as Hiranuma.[182] Wakatsuki held a press conference on his way back to the capital and said his discussions with Saionji had included vacancies in the Privy Council and the Manchurian problem. Saionji, he added pointedly, had felt that because it "concerns the welfare of the nation," it would be unfortunate if there should be any rash action to solve the Manchuria and Mongolia problem, and the genrō had asked him to take it very seriously and work for a proper settlement.[183]

Harada collected the materials on Manchuria and Mongolia from Ninomiya at General Staff headquarters on the morning of the 14th and showed them to Wakatsuki and Shidehara. However, they served only to anger Shidehara, who regarded them as excessively critical of his diplomatic policy.[184]

On September 14 Tatekawa received a telegram from Kwantung Army Chief of Staff Miyake Mitsuharu, telling him that, while the army was doing its best to abide by the instructions it had received in July to maintain the peace, "the Chang [Hsueh-liang] regime is growing more and more contemptuous, and of late the offenses and insults have become extremely difficult to bear."[185] He urged that Tatekawa and Koiso come to Manchuria to see the situation for themselves. That morning Major Shibayama Kaneshirō, a military adviser to Chang Hsueh-liang, arrived in Tokyo, his mission being to transmit to the top army authorities Chang's regrets over the Nakamura incident. After conferring with Intelligence Division Chief Hashimoto Toranosuke and China Section Chief Shigetō, he relayed Chang's message to Kanaya and Ninomiya in the chief of staff's office.[186]

Senior officials of the Army Ministry and General Staff now met[187] to consider Miyake's telegram, Shibayama's report, the telegram to the Foreign Ministry from Manchuria warning of the young officers' plot, which Tani had brought to Koiso's attention, and Doihara's views on the present situation in Manchuria.

At first the opinion was expressed that the Kwantung Army would have to take action, but when Minami indicated the attitude of the emperor, it was agreed that for the present the Kwantung Army would have to be restrained. Since Koiso could not be spared from Tokyo in view of the military reforms and budget problems, it was decided to send only Tatekawa to Mukden by way of Korea.[188] According to Harada, Koiso told Minami that "Tatekawa is the only one who can control those young fellows."[189] Koiso's influence on the younger officers had declined since the failure of the March Incident, but it was thought that Tatekawa, who was a close friend of Itagaki, had not lost the trust of Hashimoto and the others to the same degree.

The plot for which Nagata and the others had worked appeared now to be suddenly reversed. The emperor's attitude seems to have made it possible for the Saionji-Shidehara line to prevail, at least temporarily, at central military headquarters, which now adopted a more cautious stance. When Tatekawa returned from the meeting, Hashimoto visited him at his office.[190] There Hashimoto copied the special codes for transmitting messages between Tatekawa and Itagaki. He then composed telegrams for Itagaki; their exact wording is not known, but there seem to have been three:

Plot discovered.
Tatekawa coming; strike first to avoid implicating him.
If Tatekawa arrives, take action before receiving his message.[191]

On September 15 Shidehara received a secret telegram from Consul-General Hayashi in Mukden: "Kwantung Army assembling troops bringing out munitions seems likely start action near future."[192] As will be shown later, this telegram was based on information relayed to Hayashi by Godō Takuo, managing director of the South Manchuria Railway, who had learned of instructions issued by Company Commander Kawakami Seiichi of the Independent Garrison's 2nd Company at Fushun. When Shidehara brought up the matter in cabinet, Minami asserted, "We can't put any confidence in this without checking it out."[193] Nonetheless, Minami assembled Kanaya and other leading ministry and General Staff personnel and thereafter is said to have written Honjō to give up any plans for military action just then. This letter was allegedly entrusted to Tatekawa.[194]

Tatekawa was asked also to look into Hayashi's charges. Just before leaving he said to Imamura, in what was his public posture: "The Kwantung Army seems pretty worked up, but it's going to have to be patient a little longer. Except for Home Minister Adachi, most of the cabinet members are unaware of the seriousness of the situation. The army minister and chief of staff think so too and have asked me to impress upon the army the importance of patience."[195] But Tatekawa also secretly contacted Ōkawa Shūmei and asked him how to ascertain Ishiwara's and Itagaki's attitude before he himself talked with General Honjō. Ōkawa obliged by sending Nakajima Shin'ichi, who was living in a house belonging to Okamura Yasuji, to Dairen by plane. Thus Tatekawa was able, all innocence, to board a train in civilian clothes at Tokyo station that night at 9:45.[196] Twenty minutes earlier Doihara, in full uniform, had departed on a westbound train.[197] Doihara, however, disembarked enroute to Mukden and arrived only after the Liut'iaokou explosions had occurred. The telegram to Miyake officially informing him of Tatekawa's mission was somewhat late in being sent and said only that Tatekawa was on his way.[198]

Among the younger section chiefs of the Foreign Ministry who had met with Nagata and other army representatives were a number of hardline advocates who, like the soldiers, favored using the Nakamura issue to force an overall settlement of questions in Manchuria and Mongolia. Once the Mukden regime admitted on September 11 what had happened, however, these men fully supported Shidehara's separate approach to a settlement. They agreed that to try to link other issues in Manchuria with the Nakamura incident and attempt to achieve a total settlement would be like trying to catch a fish in a tree.[199] Shidehara also had strong supporters in Minister to China Shigemitsu Mamoru in Shanghai and Consul-General Hayashi on the scene in Mukden, and on the 16th Shidehara met with Wakatsuki and got his support for his policy.[200]

At the army minister's residence on the 16th a meeting centering around Chang Hsueh-liang's adviser Shibayama was held, with Minami, Sugiyama, and Koiso present. This was followed by an emergency meeting of the Supreme War Council. Minami opened the latter with a report on the policy the army had adopted on the Nakamura incident, on military reforms, and on administrative and financial retrenchment; Vice Minister Sugiyama supplemented his report. Kanaya then spoke on the present state of affairs in Manchuria and Mongolia and army policy on the numerous issues at stake there, his report being in turn supplemented by Vice Chief of Staff Ninomiya. Each councillor now expressed his opinion. The strongest line was taken by former Kwantung Army Commanders Shirakawa Yoshinori and Hishikari Takashi. "What we ought to do," they said, "is put all our efforts into solving the Nakamura incident in such a way as to obtain a resolution of all other outstanding issues at the same time. We have to guard our rights."[201] The Kwantung Army command should "use force," they argued. But the council, it would seem, was induced to adopt a softer attitude by Minami's report of the message brought earlier that day by Shibayama calling for a peaceful settlement and by his recounting of the desire for a peaceful settlement the emperor had expressed during his audience on the 11th. It was therefore agreed that the army should refrain from using military force, and Tatekawa's mission was endorsed.

About this time various groups in the House of Peers were meeting to discuss Manchuria-Mongolia problems. For instance, on the 14th the Political Study Committee of the Kenkyūkai invited Doihara to speak to them on the subject, including the Nakamura incident. Doihara argued that Chiang Kai-shek, disregarding the fact that the Chinese people's primary need was food, was bleeding them with heavy taxes. As a result, they had virtually abandoned any hope for the Three People's Principles and "communist power is spreading rapidly throughout central China," a development that was also directly related to the Soviet Union's ambitious five year plan. This would become the root of future trouble in East Asia; therefore it was incumbent upon Japan, "for the future peace of the East," resolutely to "establish and protect its existing rights," a determination that the Japanese people would have to share.[202]

On the 15th the Kōseikai called a general meeting to discuss the policies to be adopted toward Manchuria-Mongolia problems, and that afternoon a China Discussion Group of interested individuals from all factions—including the Tuesday Club, the Kenkyūkai, the Kōseikai, the Kōyūkurabu, and the Dōwakai—heard statements by Vice Foreign Minister Nagai Matsuzō and Asia Bureau Chief Tani. After the two officials had left, the group criticized the Foreign Ministry's handling of the Nakamura incident as an isolated case, characterizing its efforts as halfhearted, and, in order to bring about a more positive policy, agreed to work together to "move the Foreign Ministry authorities" off dead center. The Nakamura incident itself was only an isolated outrage. The roots of the Manchuria-Mongolia question lay in the larger complex of South Manchuria Railway problems, commercial taxes, oppression of Korean farmers, unfair taxation, and problems of law and security; a satisfactory situation could be achieved only to the degree that these questions were collectively solved.[203]

On the 16th the Dōseikai, which was affiliated with the governing Minseitō, also decided on its stand. A consensus was growing in the House of Peers that an overall settlement should be sought, and agreements to this effect were reached binding all factions. Shidehara's policies now no longer found support within the House of Peers.

The Seiyūkai also called a meeting of party officials to discuss Manchuria and Mongolia, and Secretary-General Kuhara Fusanosuke was given the responsibility of working out a party position. Kuhara and Yamamoto Teijirō, chairman of the party's special committee on the Manchuria-Mongolia problem, quickly agreed that the aim should be the adoption of a strong line in place of Shidehara's weak diplomacy, and the overthrow of the cabinet. The campaign would be launched in Tokyo about October 5, once the local prefectural elections were over.[204] Given the domestic political situation on the eve of September 18, once military action broke out in Manchuria Shidehara's efforts to localize the outbreak were doomed to failure. Already among the Peers and the Seiyū-kai, even more than among the military, the question was more the timing than the desirability of military action, and the efforts for moderation of Saionji and other representatives of the old political structure were to little effect. What was left in Japanese political life of the rational thinking of the Meiji years was on the point of coming to an end.

The Kwantung Army on the Eve of the Liut'iaokou Incident

Itagaki's and Ishiwara's trip to north Manchuria to study "problems that would be involved in a war with the Soviet Union" began at Port Arthur about July 10 and lasted ten days.[205] They first heard of the disappearance of Captain Nakamura Shintarō of the Kwantung Army staff when they reached Harbin on their way back to Port Arthur from Manchouli. Together with Isugi Nobutarō, a sergeant-major in the reserves, Nakamura had set out from Iliehk'ate in southeastern Hailar on June 6 to inspect the topography of the Hsingan mountain range. The Itagaki-Ishiwara party had already boarded their train at Angangch'i when Isugi's wife, the landlady of a Japanese inn there, the Kōeikan, told them she had had no word of her husband for nearly a month and asked them to initiate army inquiries when they returned to Port Arthur. Upon their return to Port Arthur on July 20, they heard an account (traced to Uematsu Kikuko, the mistress of an officer in the Chinese garrison army) that had been passed along to the Special Service Agency of the Kwantung Army by one Satō, an employee of the South Manchuria Railway at Tsitsihar. About July 17 Uematsu had told Satō's wife that two Japanese, a Russian, and a Mongol had been killed on the night of June 27 by members of the 3rd Regiment, commanded by Kuan Yü-heng at Suokungfu.[206]

Several members of Itagaki's party felt a personal involvement in the men's disappearance. Katakura Tadashi, who had been added to the group, was a Military Academy classmate of Nakamura. Sakuma Ryōzō (who had drawn up the "Study of the Administration of Occupied Areas in Manchuria" for the Kwantung Army) had earlier traveled with Isugi from T'aonan to Wangyehmiao and on his way back had met Nakamura at T'aonan and told him he had sent Isugi on. A good deal of topographical research was being conducted in the area at the time. Captain Chō Isamu had been involved in topographic studies in Holon Pailu and Outer Mongolia since early May, and after Nakamura's departure in the latter part of June, Captain Mori Takeshi of the General Staff had come to Tsitsihar to carry out similar studies in the western and northern regions.

Before Mori returned to Japan, Ishiwara told him: "The Nakamura incident adds just one more issue to the others. The army should now refuse help from the Foreign Ministry, take matters into its own hands, and solve them."[207] Amakasu Masahiko had hitherto been working on a scheme to spark off disturbances similar to those at Chientao and had been reporting to Ishiwara in accordance with directives from Nagata, who was coordinating Amakasu's schemes with the overall plan. Now Ishiwara told Amakasu there would have to be a change of policy. Ishiwara had evidently decided the Nakamura incident could serve as an excuse to dispatch troops outside the leased areas and thus as sufficient reason for the use of military force at Liut'iaokou. The Mukden Special Service Agency, however, had decided on a somewhat different plan, according to which Yen Hsi-shan would be spirited back to Shansi from Port Arthur to act in concert with Shih Yu-san's army in attacking Chang Hsueh-liang and penning the latter's forces within the Shanhaikuan barrier. Only then, they believed, could the Nakamura incident safely serve as a prelude to military action. Chief of Staff Miyake was in agreement with this, and Staff Officer Arai Masao therefore asked Reserve Colonel Mugita Hirao, then serving as head of the Dairen office of Japan Airlines, to take over planning on this matter. Early in August Mugita, himself at the controls, flew to Japan and reported on the plan to Koiso, who said, "If you take full responsibility for it, it's all right with me."[208]

Koiso feared the Foreign Ministry might protest. However, he does not seem to have thought this was a plan to start an incident and concluded that if Chang Hsueh-liang could be restrained by an alliance of Yen Hsi-shan, Shih Yu-san, and Shantung Governor Han Fu-chü, it would be all to the good. Agreement on details was also worked out with Doihara, still chief of the Tientsin Special Service Agency, who is said to have gone personally to persuade Shih Yu-san.

On August 5 Yen Hsi-shan flew to Tat'ung in Shansi in a plane piloted by Mugita. Yen had procured the understanding of Tsou Lu, who had gone to Mukden as the representative of the Canton government and who went from Dairen to Tientsin on July 30.[209] It looked as though a Canton-Shansi alliance had been formed in opposition to that between Chiang Kai-shek and Chang Hsueh-liang, one that could be useful in overcoming the anti-Japanese movement in Manchuria. Ishiwara is thought not to have approved of plans that risked close involvement in Chinese internal politics, whereas Itagaki, with an eye to developing conditions for the direct action that was to come, considered such schemes necessary. In the end, Ishiwara seems to have agreed with Itagaki on the need for some scheme to prepare the way for military action.[210]

In any event, by the time Yen Hsi-shan appeared in Tat'ung on August 5, Shih Yu-san's army found itself threatened from the rear by the army of Yen's subordinate, Shansi Governor Shang Chen, who supported Nanking. Shih's army was thus already routed. Shidehara was worried that Nanking would claim the Kwantung Army was meddling in internal Chinese politics because of its involvement with Yen Hsi-shan. He had intended to ask the help of Tsukamoto Seiji, governor-general of the Kwantung Leased Territory, in keeping Yen out of trouble in Port Arthur, and he now complained bitterly that the army had stabbed him in the back.[211]

We have seen that word of the Kwantung Army's involvement in the Yen affair reached Saionji by way of Admiral Okada and the Foreign Ministry before August 18. Ishiwara felt that schemes of this kind increased the Foreign Ministry's distrust of the army to no purpose whatever, and because he feared the plan to use the Nakamura incident as the occasion for military force might have been put in jeopardy, he was very put out with Doihara, as his August 13 letter to Nagata showed (see above).

At the end of 1930, when Nagata visited Manchuria, the Kwantung

Army had requested him to supply it with a cannon and to have a division transferred to Manchuria. In July the 2nd Company of the Mukden Independent Garrison managed to have a 24-cm. heavy-siege gun sent out from Tokyo, which it set up in its barracks. Beside it were set gauges aiming at enemy targets in the vicinity of Mukden, and preparations were thus completed for firing it. The army hid the cannon by building a zinc roof over it and claimed that it was a well drill, but the consulate suspected the truth.[212]

Ishiwara was still dissatisfied with the "General Outline of a Solution for the Manchurian Problem." In particular he opposed the assumption that military activity would be deferred for a year and that any action would be taken only in accordance with General Staff planning. Ishiwara was convinced that the international situation just then was uniquely favorable for the exercise of force. The Soviet Union's five year plan, launched in 1928, was in midcourse, while the United States, Britain, and France were still in economic crisis and competing in the Far East. Consequently no country would be in a position to intervene against military action by Japan. The League of Nations was likewise powerless. Moreover, he reasoned that Japan had to decide whether it would lose Manchuria completely or take the whole of it. If Japan were to wait a year, the Soviet Union would be stronger, the distrust of the powers would have increased, and the situation might no longer be favorable for the use of force. Ishiwara therefore decided there was no alternative to pursuing his course resolutely, whether or not he ultimately was reviled as a result. His final problem was how they were to avoid damaging "the emperor's august virtue."[213] Here his Nichiren Buddhist faith came to his support: "I will be the pillar of Japan; I will be the essence of Japan." As he testified to the International Military Tribunal after the war:

> In practical terms, if Japan had withdrawn completely from Manchuria, it would have meant not the loss of our rights alone, not merely that Japanese residents in Manchuria would have been in great danger. As we could already see from the fighting between the Soviet Union and China, it would have meant the return into Manchuria of the Soviet Union, which was staging a comeback in East Asia. And in view of traditional Russian policies in that area, once the Soviet Union had advanced into Manchuria, it would have become a source of communist influence. Not only would it have been impossible to maintain order in Manchuria; Japan would have been unable to ensure its own national security, and China too would have been in great peril with respect to its own defense.[214]

Late in June during their preparations for the inspection trip with the Kwantung Army staff, Itagaki and Ishiwara told a few people in the Kwantung Army that they thought hostilities would begin at Liut'iaokou in early September and asked for their cooperation. Their first choices as confidants were Hanaya and Captain Imada Shintarō, who was adjutant to Chang Hsueh-liang's adviser Major Shibayama; to these they added Major Mitani Kiyoshi, commander of the military police at Mukden.[215] Captain Ono Masao, commander of the 1st Company of Lieutenant-Colonel Takagi Yoshito's 2nd Battalion, Mukden Independent Garrison, asked Captain Kawashima Tadashi, who had served under Kōmoto Daisaku in the 14th (Kokura) Regiment and now commanded the 3rd Company stationed at Hushihtai, "If the army acts, are you going to be with us?" Kawashima and Ono then went to Hanaya, who declared that anyone who didn't support them would be reassigned to Japan and proceeded to explain the plan to seize the Chinese barracks at Peitaying. Their discussions concluded on the second floor of the Mukden Special Service Agency with Imada added to their number. Two or three further meetings were held to work out their plans for an explosion on the railway line at Liut'iaokou. They were particularly concerned about the individuals to be involved. They thought Commander Takagi (who was subsequently replaced by Leiutenant-Colonel Shimamoto Masaichi) might not give the plot his full support; therefore they confided their plans to Major Kojima Masanori of the battalion and made him responsible for ensuring the battalion's participation. They were likewise dubious about Captain Kawakami Seiichi, commander of the garrison's 2nd Company at Fushun, but decided that they would include the 4th Company at Mukden, led by Captain Takahashi Kin'ichi. At Imada's suggestion a pledge was drawn up, to which they subscribed their seals in blood. Apparently they rejected an initial plan whereby Nakano Toraitsu and one Kataoka Shun would have tipped over railway cars at a crossing near Peitaying, because they thought it would be difficult to carry out without being discovered by the railway guards; instead they decided that Kawakami's company should set off the explosions at Liut'iaokou. Imada secretly called in Captain Kōmoto Suemori, who had training in the use of explosives. Meanwhile, Amakasu continued with his plans for disturbances in north Manchuria, as laid out in the "Plan for a Solution of the Manchurian and Mongolian Problem."[216]

When Itagaki returned from Japan in August, he and Ishiwara immediately organized a briefing session at the Yamato Hotel in Dairen, attended by influential men from the city. Itagaki explained to them that if Japan lost Manchuria, its heavy industrial base would be ruined. To underline the strategic importance of Manchuria, he asserted: "If the problem of Manchuria and Mongolia is completely solved, the Soviet Union will have to give up all thought of a war with Japan."[217] What Itagaki was promising was that his proposals would ensure Japan's national security. "Even if there should be a protracted war between Japan and the United States," he said reassuringly, "we will not need to worry because we will be able to lead China."

Interestingly enough, it was Itagaki's view that whereas Manchuria might not then have possessed any great economic value, "from the standpoint of building a future national defense structure, it is an absolutely essential base for Japan." In this manner he prepared the leaders of Dairen for military action and asked for their support. Some expressed doubts about Itagaki's facile judgments, basing their criticism on the lessons of World War I and worrying whether Japan might not become a "second Germany" if it put all its reliance on military force. Ishiwara answered for Itagaki: "There is nothing to worry about. Japan is truly a divine nation. As a maritime nation, it is a natural fort strategically." Ishiwara went on to argue the contrast in the geography of Japan and Germany and concluded rhetorically, "What will a Japan that has taken care of Manchuria have left to worry about?"

An indigenous movement for Manchurian independence had begun under the leadership of an individual surnamed Chang. The only way to change the situation in Manchuria and Mongolia, Chang felt, was to ask for Japanese help, but unilateral intervention by Japan would provoke international recrimination. He proposed, therefore, that an independent country be established, tied to Japan by mutual security and customs union arrangements, which could develop the institutions needed for an independent Manchuria and Mongolia. He also anticipated that in time the strength of this independent country could be used to bring about the unification of China. This, he thought, would stop the Soviet Union from advancing southward, aid in solving Japan's population and food problems, and attract public support in Japan for the unification of China. Chang was in contact with the Manchurian Youth League, one of whose directors visited him in Tientsin on July 25.[218]

On August 11 the Manchurian Youth League convened a public

meeting in Dairen to hear the report of the delegation that had just returned from Japan. Before the meeting the group called on Tsukamoto Seiji, who expressed the fear that they were manufacturing a crisis out of what was only a small problem and might thereby be running the risk of inciting the army to action. His words were subsequently attacked by Okada Takema, who protested at the meeting that "we representatives have the support of 1,300,000 of our countrymen," a figure in which he included Koreans.[219] Satake Reishin told the crowd that now that "the cabinet ministers have come around to supporting a strong line," he hoped Japanese rights in Manchuria and Mongolia might be realized "by the force of public opinion before Foreign Minister Shidehara has another chance to argue his position."[220] And Takatsuka Gen'ichi, urging that the discussion be based on acceptance of Japan as a "divine country," said that if China should try to "nullify the Sino-Japanese treaties by threat, we must recover the Liaotung peninsula," which Japan had once been forced by Germany, France, and Russia to return to China, "and thus obtain the final say in deciding the fate of Manchuria." "If anyone thinks it's all right to give up Manchuria," he shouted, "we will draw on our three thousand year old national character, breathe our national spirit, swallow our tears, and issue a declaration of independence for Manchuria regardless of what our motherland may do."[221]

The league now arranged lectures at various places in Manchuria. After the Nakamura incident was made public on the 17th, they strengthened their demands and called for the "occupation of the Ssup'ing-T'aonan railway" as government policy; telegrams to this effect were sent, among others, to the prime minister, the foreign and army ministers, the chief of the Army General Staff, the speakers of both houses in the Diet, and all the newspapers.[222] On August 27 the league's Mukden branch, in cooperation with the Independence Alliance, held a memorial service for Captain Nakamura.[223]

Immediately after the public announcement on the 17th, the staff officers of the Kwantung Army invited the officers of the league to a meeting; Kanai Shōji, Okada Takema, Yamaguchi Jūji, and two others went to the Army Officers Club.[224] Chief of Staff Miyake, who presided, asked about the views of the Youth League, which both Kanai and Okada explained. Yamaguchi, addressing Ishiwara, then put forward his plan for an independent Japanese-Manchurian state and requested that the army show "only determination, bring it about by force." Okada complained about the Kwantung Army, wondering whether its swords weren't really just shiny bamboo sticks. "It doesn't matter whether we're impressive or not or whether our weapons are bamboo," Ishiwara replied. "It's enough to get rid of Chang Hsueh-liang. . . . As the man responsible for military operations, I can assure you that when it comes to blows, Mukden won't hold out for two days. It will be settled in one lightning stroke." He responded sympathetically to Yamaguchi and others who criticized both "the imperialism of the Japanese government and the spinelessness of the Manchurian warlords," and he came away from the meeting with respect for the ideas of the Youth League. In this way the Youth League came to exert a good deal of influence, not only through arousing public opinion in Manchuria but also through turning Ishiwara's thoughts from a purely military occupation of Manchuria to the idea of a Manchurian state.

Ideas of "Manchukuo" had also been upheld by another youth group, the Yūhōkai, whose membership included high South Manchuria Railway officials like Kasaki Yoshiaki.[225] Sometime around August 18 the head of the South Manchuria Railway's Mukden area office and the head of the Japanese Residents Association called on Hirata Yukihiro, commander of the 29th Regiment (part of Tamon Jirō's 2nd Division), to ask whether the army could put on a small demonstration to "bring an end to rock-throwing by Manchurian people at Japanese children when they go to their school in the leased area. Many of them can't get to school at all." Hirata declined because he was "afraid of inviting misunderstanding."[226] The situation had, however, become bad enough for the Japanese to regard the stealing of railroad ties by Chinese soldiers as a premeditated attempt to harm a Japanese passenger train.

Captain Mori Takeshi of the Army General Staff, who in July had been sent to Manchuria for talks with Ishiwara about the Nakamura problem, returned to Mukden on August 18 attached to the consulate-general as military observer of the diplomatic negotiations concerning Captain Nakamura.[227] To apply pressure from a different direction, Mori visited Tsang Shih-yi, chairman of the Liaoning provincial government, at his residence and warned him strongly that if the Manchurian authorities did not show "sincerity," the Japanese military would be forced to seek a solution through direct action. On the 19th the press broke the news of the incident, publishing the full details released to them by the special service organizations. Consul-General Hayashi, who felt that

Hanaya had stolen a march on him, telegraphed Shidehara to complain.[228]

On August 20 Honjō Shigeru, the new commander of the Kwantung Army, arrived at Dairen, after meeting his predecessor in Tokyo five days earlier to discuss matters pertaining to the transfer of command.[229] Honjō, who had been commander of the 10th (Himeji) Division, had learned of his new command on July 20 and, after being transferred on August 1, had attended the meeting of regional and division commanders on August 3–4 accompanied by Itagaki as his staff officer. Beginning on the 9th he met with top officials at the Army General Staff, the Army Ministry, and the Foreign Ministry. He also had separate talks with men like Nagata, Okamura, Shigetō, and Obata; on the 9th he is said to have talked with Itagaki, who then preceded him to Manchuria.[230] Even so, it is hard to suppose that Honjō had knowledge of the plans to start military action at Liut'iaokou late in September.

Following his arrival at Dairen, Honjō met with Chief of Staff Miyake and other staff officers on the 21st, then called on Governor-General Tsukamoto. From the 22nd to the 25th he inspected every unit at Port Arthur, visited the headquarters of the South Manchuria Railway, and met with officials and leading citizens of Port Arthur and Dairen. On the 26th he received reports from Shibayama and Doihara.[231] On the 29th he instructed Itagaki and Miyake on policies to be followed in the Manchurian situation; these instructions are believed to have followed the lines of central headquarters' "General Outline of a Solution for the Manchurian Problem."

On September 1 Honjō spent the morning being briefed by Ishiwara on operations plans; he asked Ishiwara to return that evening to present his views on solving Manchurian and Mongolian problems. It is unlikely that Ishiwara revealed the entire plan for the military action at Liut'iaokou, but one can assume that he argued for a much stronger line than that of central headquarters and that he urged the necessity of military action and the case for using the Nakamura incident as the occasion for such action.

At any rate, Ishiwara and Itagaki seem to have believed that they would be able to implement their plans under the new commander. In his general instructions to the Kwantung Army on September 1 Honjō declared, "I shall act resolutely," and he asserted that "the Kwantung

Army faced truly heavy responsibilities" in the situation in Manchuria and Mongolia.[232]

On August 31 the communications committee of the Three Eastern Provinces sent a telegram to the Railways Bureau of the Kuomintang government asking it to order railways throughout the country to refuse to carry Japanese goods.[233] Already, on August 15, a Chinese military agent sent to Dairen had dispatched the following telegram to the commander of the Northeast Area Defense Command:

> The Japanese government is utilizing the incidents at Wanpaoshan and Chientao as an excuse to dispatch Japanese troops to Manchuria and to take military measures under the pretext of protecting Japanese immigrants. Since officials and people in the northeast remain prudent and calm and give no opening, however, the Japanese are plotting conspiracies. First they tried to use Chang Tsung-ch'ang, and when this ended in failure, they cultivated Yen Hsi-shan. As a first step they protected him and helped him to return safely to Shansi. . . . At every center in Manchuria there is a league of Japanese settlers which petitions the South Manchuria Railway Company and the Kwantung Army command to transfer their headquarters to Mukden. Their reasons for requesting the move to Mukden are as follows: (1) They want the Japanese to threaten with force the recent cooperation between officials and populace in the northeast that has been manifested in the anti-Japanese movement. (2) When, as we think inevitable, war erupts again in the northeast between Feng Yü-hsiang and Yen Hsi-shan, they think it is inevitable that the Communist Party will seize the opportunity and start a rising. Although Japan could move in troops on the excuse of defending its settlers, they would expect opposition from China and all the powers. The alternative is to increase in advance their garrison in Mukden.[234]

Accordingly, the Mukden Public Security Bureau deepened its warnings of Japan and on August 25 issued the following instruction: "Since the Japanese are preparing all manner of excuses for sending troops to the northeast, we must be patient, keep our self-control, and leave them alone no matter what they do" in order to avoid a disturbance. Should an incident break out, the instructions went on, "send people who can speak Japanese, work for a peaceful settlement, and on no account exchange fire; if the Japanese fire, retreat to the branch post and avoid violence."[235]

On September 1, Chairman Tsang Shih-yi presided over a meeting of Mukden government leaders called to discuss the investigation into the Nakamura incident. Although the investigators had been unable to carry out an adequate study, they had decided to take the position that the Japanese claim that Captain Nakamura had been assassinated had no basis in fact and that the incident should be allowed to end in obscurity.[236] That same day Hanaya Tadashi visited Consul-General Hayashi and urged him to maintain a firm posture whatever the attitude of the Chinese.[237] As Doihara's assistant, so long as he remained sober, Hanaya could talk with Consul-General Hayashi.[238]

Meanwhile, Chang Hsueh-liang, disturbed by stories of a Japanese plot to murder him, canceled his plan to return to Mukden from Peking on September 10, and Chang Tso-hsiang likewise remained in Chinchou; they wanted to avoid direct negotiations with the Japanese.[239] Shibayama had returned to Peking on September 2, following his consultations with Honjō on August 26 and had told Chang Hsueh-liang of the strong attitude being taken by the Kwantung Army. Thereafter Shibayama, as noted earlier, returned to Japan with the details of Chang Hsuehliang's intentions for a peaceful settlement. On September 3 Doihara met with Tsang Shih-yi to urge that an early settlement of the Nakamura incident be reached and at the same time relayed to him the demands for a strong policy that the military were pressing.[240]

Also on the 3rd Honjō met with 2nd Division Commander Tamon Jirō and Mori Ren, commander of the Independent Garrison, both strong supporters of the Kwantung Army.[241] In their talk they discussed the fact that the "anti-Japanese activities of Chinese officials and people" were gradually becoming organized and that the time for a final solution was approaching. They took note of the fact that "low-ranking Chinese officers" were now "contemptuous of the Japanese army and instilling anti-Japanese feelings into their men." Since this was the case, in areas where the two sides were in confrontation and where the Chinese soldiers were "foolishly and blindly following their superiors, it is likely that they will provoke the Japanese into fighting." Should a frontal clash occur, clearly "the army, for its part, must act resolutely." They further agreed that any "inviting opportunity" for a settlement of the Manchuria-Mongolia problem should be seized, noting that, since the government in Tokyo did not realize the need for "firm and resolute disposal" of the problem, the army had covertly supported the idea of sending propagandists from organizations of Japanese settlers in Manchuria to Japan. It was necessary "to get the people to call for a settlement of the Manchuria-Mongolia problem rather than have the army do it itself" (i.e., liberation of the territory by political action rather than war). Military men, they agreed, should not take part in "political activities or secret dealings with China adventurers."

On the 3rd C. T. Wang, the Nationalist foreign minister, announced that on the basis of the investigation into the Nakamura incident it was clear that the incident had been "fabricated by the Japanese" and had no basis in fact.[242] The Manchurian authorities had reached the same conclusion two days earlier, but the young Kuomintang officials who surrounded Wang took a much stronger line.

On the 4th the Japanese Foreign Ministry retorted that the matter was being discussed by the authorities in Mukden and their investigations were still incomplete.[243] Wang was dismayed by the Japanese response and the next day, after conferring for several hours with Chiang Kai-shek, corrected himself in a news conference with a group of Japanese reporters. He said that the report he had received from his subordinates, whom he had personally dispatched to the scene, had concluded that Japan's allegations had "not been true to the facts," and in an effort to patch things up, he again amended his earlier statement by alleging that the incident had been cooked up by "Japanese hoodlums" and not by responsible Japanese officials.[244]

Minami was unmollified. "Are they still saying such things?" he asked. "Our army has positive evidence that can't be passed off with that sort of abuse. We have asked the Foreign Ministry to take diplomatic responsibility in the matter . . . but we're not going to yield an inch on this."

On September 6 Consul-General Hayashi met with Tsang Shih-yi at Mukden. Hayashi asked whether the investigation might not have been inadequate because the inspectors feared for their own safety, and he asked Tsang to send out another inspection team that would conduct an inquiry worthy of respect. Immediately after their meeting, Tsang declared to a correspondent for the *Tōkyō Asahi shimbun* that it was "not clear whether Nakamura had been murdered or not," that he had no idea what the second inspection team would report, and that he had just had a telegram from Chang Hsueh-liang telling him to find out exactly what had happened.[245]

On September 7 in a speech at Nanking, Chiang Kai-shek referred to the visit to Japan in July of Eugene Chen, foreign minister in the opposition government at Canton, and charged that Japan had lost its right to international trust by helping and encouraging internal political rebellion in China through supplying arms and munitions to the Canton rebels.[246] Japan's relations with China, already sufficiently harmed by the controversies that swirled around Manchuria and Nanking, seemed again at the brink.

Chang Hsueh-liang now told his chief of staff Jung Chen that the Nakamura incident should be investigated impartially and ordered him to ensure that it was not permitted to harm relations between the two countries.[247] On the 9th Jung told this to Consul Morioka Shōhei, who was conducting the Nakamura negotiations for the Japanese side, and the next day Morioka passed it on to Consul-General Hayashi. Not to be upstaged by the Young Marshal, the Kuomintang government considered having the newly appointed minister to Japan Chiang Tso-pin stop at Mukden on his way to Tokyo, to organize a joint Sino-Japanese committee of investigation.[248] In the end it was decided a settlement with Japan should be sought through the Nanking government rather than through the Mukden authorities.

On September 9 Major Wu Ken-hsiang, the head of the second investigating committee, announced at the headquarters of the Northeast Area Defense Command that "there is reason to believe that Kuan Yü-heng had ordered his subordinates to kill Nakamura and steal his valuables."[249] Alarmed, Tsang Shih-yi and Jung Chen got together to work out a joint response. The Nanking government was also aware of the grave implications of the announcement, and on the 10th a meeting of the National Military Council was convened at Peking and adopted a "Plan for an Early and Peaceful Settlement" drawn up by Chang Hsueh-liang. The same day Chang met with Japanese Counselor Yano Makoto at the Peking legation and told him that he had ordered Tsang to "deal with utmost sincerity and make concessions so as to minimize differences in the negotiations with Japan."[250] On the 11th Jung Chen said to an *Asahi* reporter that there seemed to be a factual basis for the Nakamura incident after all. He did his best to soothe the situation by saying, "I wouldn't like to see a problem like this cause a break in good relations with Japan. A paper like the *Asahi* has a great deal of influence, and I wish you would work with us to keep the feelings of our two peoples from reaching extremes."[251] The facts of the Nakamura incident having been acknowledged, the Manchurian authorities that same day initiated negotiations between Consul-General Hayashi and T'ang Erh-ho at Mukden. At Nanking a day earlier T. V. Soong met with Minister Shigemitsu Mamoru in a final effort to achieve a peaceful settlement of the issues between China and Japan.

On September 7 General Honjō began an inspection of the 2nd Division, which had been assigned garrison duties in the middle of April. One by one he visited the main units at Tashihch'iao, Antung, Lienshankuan, Mukden, T'iehling, Kungchuling, Ch'angch'un, again at Mukden, and Liaoyang.[252] On the 8th, accompanied by Ishiwara, he called on Hayashi at the Mukden consulate-general. Hayashi asked to "discuss the situation" with him, but Ishiwara intervened, declaring to Honjō, "You have to continue your inspection trip as scheduled." "My talk with General Honjō isn't a private matter," Hayashi assured him, only to have Ishiwara turn him down with, "This is no time for a chat, when the commanding general is reviewing maneuvers." Hayashi gave up, expecting that he would be able to talk with Honjō when the commander returned to Mukden on the 15th. Ishiwara, however, had no intention of giving Hayashi such an opportunity, for in August the consul-general had tried to restrain his activities.[253]

Aware that Hayashi was watching him, Ishiwara told Imada, Mitani, and Hanaya that he had given up plans for the incident that was to take place in late September. But when Kōmoto, who had come to Manchuria with the money Fujita had provided the plotters, expressed his dismay at this, Ishiwara reassured him, "I wanted the rumor to spread so that it would appear that we'd given it up." Itagaki too assured Kōmoto that "I haven't changed my mind for a minute."[254]

On the 12th Honjō inspected the command post of the Independent Garrison at Kungchuling. The officer in charge, Mori Ren, warned him that "the anti-Japanese movement, both official and unofficial, is becoming very organized. At the same time incidents of banditry are increasing at an extraordinary rate. Recently they've begun to be contemptuous of our army, and now they appear to be taking things into their own hands along the South Manchuria Railway and within the leased territories as well." Before his departure the next day Honjō made an unusually strong speech to the Kungchuling garrison, stating, "You must take positive and forceful action against bad elements in order to secure the defense of the railways and eradicate any cause for anxiety among the Japanese settlers."[255]

At this juncture the provincial authorities in Mukden, in conformity with directives from Chang Hsueh-liang, issued to military police and all local government heads secret orders that, in view of apparent Japanese preparations for war, they were to "adopt a pacific attitude no matter what the provocation and under no condition take measures that could lead to open conflict."[256]

On September 14 Captain Kawakami Seiichi of the 2nd Company at Fushun called a meeting of the chief of police, the station master, and the president of the reservists association to coordinate their activities in the event of an emergency. "If it comes to action," he told them, "the Fushun company has the job of attacking Mukden airport."[257] When word of this reached Godō Takuo, he went straight to Consul-General Hayashi accompanied by the head of the railway's Fushun division, who reported that he had been told "the Fushun Garrison may not be around for long."[258] Then on the 17th Fushun Police Chief Terada came to the consulate-general to report that "we have been told by the garrison that the police are to prepare a plan to protect resident Japanese and keep order, because the Fushun garrison unit is to engage in maneuvers in expectation of attacking and occupying the Mukden fortifications at dawn on the 18th."[259] Maneuvers in preparation for an attack on Mukden were in fact carried out on the nights of the 14th, 15th, 16th, and 17th.[260]

The three telegrams Hashimoto had sent on the night of the 14th (see above) reached Itagaki the following day. After sundown that evening a final conference was held in the headquarters of the Mukden Special Service Agency, attended by Ishiwara, Itagaki, Imada, Hanaya, Kojima, Majors Mitani Kiyoshi and Nagura Kan, and Captains Kawashima Tadashi and Ono Masao.[261] Hashimoto's telegrams were discussed. Ishiwara is said to have started out with, "Well, what are you fellows going to do?" Itagaki, who had previous and private understandings with Nagata and Tatekawa, merely laughed and did not join the discussion. Imada urged that they should go ahead with their plan. Hanaya, however, argued that if the General Staff were opposed, it was useless to light the match, and he urged that they should "decide after talking with Tatekawa" and wait for another occasion. "If we're all agreed on action," Kawashima suggested, "we can always go ahead with it. If we hold off, we just wait for another occasion."[262] About 2:00 in the morning the group was balloted and a majority voted to hold off. Mitani, Imada, Kawashima, and Ono were distraught as they left the meeting. Later that morning Ishiwara telephoned Mitani from the Hanyōkan, where he was staying. Mitani rushed over to see him and, according to the story, was told that if the garrison unit was inclined to go ahead, Ishiwara was ready to change his mind and go through with it. The two men agreed to entrust implementation to Imada and Kawashima. "Well, let's do it!" Itagaki exclaimed, and so the final decision was made. Imada, who had earlier asserted that he would "prefer to act before Tatekawa gets here and the situation changes," acted as soon as Ishiwara told him the plot was to be carried out as planned. Kawashima was ordered to prepare to act as soon as possible, preferably by the 17th, but that was too soon and it was finally decided to begin action on the 18th. The one fear that remained concerned the Chinese response. The Mukden defenses would have to be occupied even if the Chinese did not respond strongly, but the plotters were uncertain whether 29th Regiment Commander Hirata Yukihiro would back them up.[263]

Itagaki and Ishiwara were also worried about Nagata's ability to deliver at central headquarters in Tokyo. They had no way of knowing from Hashimoto's telegrams exactly what kind of political change had taken place; therefore it seemed necessary to wait for Tatekawa. On the other hand, if his official mission were to transmit Minami's instructions to Honjō, they might have to cancel the whole project even though their preparations were complete. At the same time they were inclined to think that if Tatekawa had no real intention of preventing their plot, they would be able to work secretly with him and therefore should continue their preparations meanwhile. Eventually they agreed that the situation might make it necessary for Itagaki to issue the military orders on his own authority. With this in mind, they made preparations for Itagaki to return to Mukden before September 18.[264]

Katakura Tadashi, who had gone to make an on-the-spot investigation of the Nakamura incident, returned to Mukden on the night of the 15th bringing with him a suspect, as well as some evidence he had picked up. This could not give the Kwantung Army an excuse on which to act, however, since the Manchurian authorities had already admitted that Nakamura had been murdered. When Katakura met with Ishiwara, the latter told him, in a half-joking, half-despairing manner, "I'm giving up my post in Operations. You take over." Katakura was baffled.[265] Hanaya, no longer quite trusted by Ishiwara and therefore uninformed about the September 18 date, was despondent. "It's no good, no good," he told Katakura. "It's been postponed." But Katakura was sure that something had happened. On the 16th he returned to Port Arthur, where he met Nakajima Shin'ichi, who had flown there at Tatekawa's express request to meet with Itagaki. Nakajima apparently told Katakura, "Tatekawa is coming as a spoiler." Meanwhile, also on the 16th, Itagaki and Ishiwara, together with General Honjō, left Mukden for Liaoyang by train at 1:30 P.M.

On September 17 Hayashi and Morioka called on Tsang Shih-yi and told him that it was essential to work out a speedy settlement of the Nakamura incident "to deprive the Kwantung Army of an excuse for going into action."[266] For the first time Tsang and Jung Chen began seriously to expedite the negotiations. The day before Tsang had ordered a clampdown on the anti-Japanese movement in Manchuria, and Kuan Yü-heng, the man responsible for the Nakamura incident, who had been brought to Mukden, was placed under arrest by the Northeast Military Police Command and held for court martial.[267] The Kuomintang government too was endeavoring to work out a peaceful settlement, and on the 16th Chiang Tso-pin conferred with Hayashi.[268] The desperate activities of Nanking and Chang Hsueh-liang's subordinates in Mukden, while uncoordinated and sometimes at variance, were an eleventh-hour effort to head off the pressures for a hard line being exerted by the Japanese military. In Peking on the 16th T'ang Erh-ho assured officials of the Japanese legation that the Young Marshal wished to achieve a political settlement both of the issue of Koreans residing in Manchuria and of the many incidents that had arisen between Japanese and Chinese in Manchuria. To this end, he went on, the Nanking government wished to establish a committee to study these matters, and it was "in overall agreement with the plans of Marshal Chang Hsueh-liang."[269] In Nanking that same day Foreign Minister Wang explained to Japanese reporters at a news conference that Chiang Kai-shek's speech of the 7th meant "only that one could say the Canton government had ties with imperialism. There are imperialists within the Republic too," he pointed out, "and it's a misinterpretation to say that this was aimed at Japan." Taking a conciliatory tone, he declared that, although he had said on the 5th that because Nakamura had been a private traveler the case did not raise issues of international law, "if he should have met his death at the hands of the military, then stern punishment according to military law has to be carried out."[270]

These efforts at reconciliation on the part of the Chinese met with a placatory response from Minister Shigemitsu at a news conference on the 17th. "In the fact of all these eventualities," he said, "the Japanese government will weigh its actions very carefully, refrain from damaging the relations between the two countries, and do its best to bring about a friendly settlement as soon as possible." Talk of "some sort of mobilization plan by members of the Japanese armed forces," he reassured them, was empty propaganda without basis in fact.[271]

The Fuse Is Lit

As Shigemitsu was expressing his hopes for a peaceful settlement through negotiations, Imada received orders from Ishiwara to inform Hanaya that "we'd better go ahead before Tatekawa gets here after all."[272] Hanaya immediately began to make final preparations. At Mitani's office Amakasu received ¥30,000 from Kōmoto, and some money was also handed to Hanaya.[273] Hanaya got in touch with Wada Tsuyoshi and others who were to act as a guerrilla band at the scene, and Amakasu went off to prepare his Harbin mischief. Hanaya had been for postponement and was a bit out of spirits, but Amakasu, who had been living on money from the ¥200 Ōkawa Shūmei had been sending Nakano Toraitsu every month and who saw in the scheme an opportunity to restore himself to good standing after being dishonored for his murder of Ōsugi Sakae, was in high spirits and full of enthusiasm. That same day Chief of Staff Miyake had telephoned Honjō at Liaoyang from Port Arthur to ask officially that either Itagaki or Ishiwara be left in Mukden to receive Tatekawa on his arrival from Tokyo.[274] Meanwhile Ōkawa Shūmei's emissary Nakajima Shin'ichi had arrived at Liaoyang and presumably told Itagaki, among other things, that Tatekawa would like to detrain at Pench'i to talk with him. That night Itagaki and Ishiwara talked secretly in Itagaki's room at the Hakutō Hotel in Liaoyang and agreed that Itagaki would take responsibility for events in Mukden and Ishiwara for those at Port Arthur.[275]

At 9:00 A.M. on the 18th Honjō delivered his final comments on his

inspection of the troops in Manchuria to 2nd Division Commander Tamon at the Liaoyang division headquarters. He took a strong, albeit
somewhat abstract, line. "With the present uneasiness in Manchuria and
Mongolia growing daily more pronounced, we cannot be complacent,"
he said. "If violence should break out, I trust each unit will take resolute
action and adhere to its purpose with unwavering resolution."[276] His party
then boarded a 2:00 P.M. express for Port Arthur. There Honjō left his
entourage, went to the house of the painter Noda, and after seeing a
portrait of himself that had just been completed, returned to his official
residence at 10:00 P.M.[277] This was minutes before the explosion on the
railway tracks at Liut'iaokou.

On the morning of the 18th Itagaki left Liaoyang alone for Mukden
to meet Tatekawa. The latter was supposed to reach Mukden on the
1:00 P.M. train, but instead he got off at Pench'i at 11:29 A.M., while
Itagaki was taking care of the final arrangements for the explosion at
Liut'iaokou. Once Itagaki knew the arrangements were completed, he
headed for Pench'i to meet Tatekawa.[278] That afternoon the Antung police telephoned the consulate-general that a civilian identified as Tatekawa had left for Mukden by train. Although the man in question had
denied the identification, there apparently was no question that he was
in fact Tatekawa.[279] Consul Morishima Morito and South Manchuria
Railway Director Kimura Eiichi feared that Tatekawa's visit foreboded
something serious. They had received word of the practice maneuvers
for the seizure of the Mukden defenses the day before and felt that the
Kwantung Army was about to provoke an incident. On the morning of
the 18th they went together to Hayashi and urged the need to take preventive action. Hayashi, however, was not convinced tnat the situation
was critical and simply wrote Honjō a personal request for vigilance, which
he sent off by special delivery.[280] This entreaty fell into Katakura's hands
at Port Arthur and did not reach Honjō immediately, even after the explosion at Liut'iaokou.[281] Hayashi sent no report to Shidehara of his personal request to Honjō until the next morning.

On the afternoon of the 18th in confidential talks at the Mukden consulate-general, Japan's four-point demands for a settlement of the Nakamura incident were agreed upon: a formal apology, restitution for
damages, punishment of those guilty, and future guarantees. On the last
point reference was also made to the "impossibility of avoiding the use
of military action," but Consul Fujimura Toshifusa's proposition that Ja-

pan seize the Mukden defenses as security was rejected on grounds that it would "only play into the hands of the Kwantung Army." Instead it was agreed to put forward a proposal, as old as the Tanaka cabinet, for the establishment of a Japanese consulate at T'aonan. The conferees realized, however, that if the Kwantung Army did not participate in the talks, they would get nowhere, so after the meeting ended at 8 o'clock, Morishima went to look for Doihara and Hanaya.[282]

Tatekawa and Itagaki had boarded the 5:18 P.M. train at Pench'i and reached Mukden at 7:05 P.M. It is reasonable to assume that they talked things over together. Hanaya came from the Special Service Agency to meet them at the Mukden station and saw them to the Kikubun restaurant. There Tatekawa and Itagaki put on a little act for Hanaya's benefit: "Aren't the young officers tremendously stirred up because of the Nakamura incident?" "Oh, no, not at all." "I'm certainly glad to hear that. I'm worn out now, so let's go on tomorrow."[283]

Itagaki did not join in the drinking but hurried to the Special Service Agency while Hanaya stayed on to drink and talk with Tatekawa. According to Hanaya after the war, he tried to ascertain Tatekawa's opinion but gained only the clear impression, never stated explicitly, that he was of no mind to call things off.[284] No doubt Hanaya had been assigned to entertain Tatekawa because Ishiwara had lost confidence in him.

Meanwhile, Morishima had been unable to locate Doihara, for the simple reason that Doihara had not yet returned to Mukden. Since Hanaya had gone to the Kikubun, and Morishima later asserted that he had checked the restaurants and inns, it is possible that when he stopped at the Kikubun he was told his man was not there.[285] At any rate, Morishima gave up and went back to his house, which was near the consulate-general. Hayashi had gone to a wake for a friend and consequently was out. It was now probably just before 10 o'clock.

Itagaki, back at the Special Service Agency, waited for the hour when, taking full charge, he would set in motion the plot to use military force. Imada, responsible for its implementation, had already completed preparation of 42 square, yellow-wrapped packages of blasting powder. Imada, Hanaya, Kawashima, Tadashi, and Kōmoto Suemori had previously agreed that they would time their explosion to go off just before an express train was due. Finally, on the morning of the 18th, Imada told the first lieutenants attached to his company—Kōmoto, Noda Sukuo, and Tamura Tadashi—that the day for execution had arrived. Kōmoto alone knew the details in advance. Immediately they carried out an inspection of the equipment of Kawashima's company, made arrangements for moving out, and, as evening fell, drilled with full equipment. Kawashima took 105 men to the south of Wenkuantun, about three kilometers from Liut'iaokou, and set up a command outpost. The rest of the force was deployed along a front facing Wenkuantun.[286] The one who actually set the charge was thus Kōmoto, who had been dispatched to Liut'iaokou to command a railway patrol. It was he who took seven or eight men under Sergeant Matsuoka to the scene, put the yellow packages of blasting powder that Imada had prepared on both sides of a joint in the east rail, and lit the fuse.[287] It was now 10:20 P.M., just before the 10:40 Mukden express was due to pass. The plans called for the train to be overturned, but in fact it miraculously passed over the spot, for although one track had indeed been moved about 1.5 meters, it was on a perfectly straight, downhill grade, with the result that the train bumped along past it.[288] Kōmoto was flat on the ground nearby with his hands over his ears. When the train had passed, he gave a sigh of relief. While planning, it had been easy to imagine using the probable casualties of the train wreck as an excuse for military action; but if the train had overturned, their first duty would have been to go to the aid of the injured, and what would have become of military activity in that event? He decided he was now free to attack the Chinese relief force that should, according to the plan, be coming from Peitaying and thus provoke the military action. He headed for Peitaying and began the attack, sending Private First Class Konno to Kawashima with the message, "Engaged in action with Peitaying Chinese forces which set off explosion along railroad." Kawashima acted very surprised and set out on the run at the head of his troops for the railroad sector. He also issued orders for bullets to be distributed to the rest of his command.

The report from the Liut'iaokou detachment that the tracks of the South Manchuria Railway had been the scene of an explosion reached the Special Service Agency and the headquarters of the Shimamoto battalion by portable field telephones as planned. Near to the area were the adventurers Nakano Toraitsu and Kataoka Shun who, quite independently of the Kwantung Army's plot, had tried and failed to bomb the Liaoyang railway bridge the day before; now they busied themselves with patrol and liaison under the direction of Reserve First Lieutenant Wada Tsuyoshi.[289] According to the Kwantung Army's "Basic Plan of Operations," once the opposing forces came into contact, "the army will press toward Mukden with all its strength, deliver a united attack against the center of the Mukden army, settle that garrison's fate, and resolve the matter with the utmost expedition."[290] All that had to be done was to wait for things to happen. Battalion Commander Shimamoto had just gone to bed when he was awakened by the telephone call. He immediately ordered the 1st (Ono) and 4th (Takahashi) companies from Mukden into action and called for the 2nd (Kawakami) Company at Fushun to advance to Liut'iaokou. About 10:40 P.M. 29th Regiment Commander Hirata received a telephone call from Shimamoto. He ordered his regiment into emergency formation and ran to the barracks, where he met Shimamoto thundering in on horseback and shouting, "I am going to attack the enemy at Peitaying!" To which Hirata replied, "I am to attack the enemy in the Mukden installations."[291]

Morishima, deputizing for the consul-general, got the news from the Special Service Agency and rushed to Itagaki's residence to propose that efforts be made to reach a peaceful settlement. Itagaki shouted that he had no business interfering with the army's right of command, and Hanaya, who had just returned from the Kikubun, went so far as to unsheath his sword with the threat, "I'll kill anybody that interferes."[292] Hayashi got Itagaki on the telephone and tried to persuade him to stop the fighting, but Itagaki announced, "The army will deal with this in the way it has planned."

The 24-cm. siege gun had already opened fire on the Peitaying barracks. As he had planned, Itagaki approved an attack by the Independent Garrison unit on Peitaying and by the 29th Infantry Regiment on the inner Mukden defense works. He reported these actions to Honjō.

At Port Arthur Ishiwara carried out their plan for bringing Honjō around. When Itagaki's first report came in, Chief of Staff Miyake called together Staff Officers Arai Masao, Takeda Hisashi, Nakano Ryōji, Katakura Tadashi, and Takeshita Yoshiharu. Katakura and Arai pleaded with the others not to "let Itagaki and Ishiwara down the way we did Kōmoto Daisaku," with good effect, for the group determined to support Ishiwara.[293] About twenty minutes past midnight, just after Itagaki's second report arrived informing them that the Hushihtai company had occupied a section of Peitaying shortly after 11 o'clock, Honjō went to his office.[294] He had just rejected Ishiwara's plans for a full-scale occupation of Manchuria and agreed only that the forces in Mukden should combine to seize the city. Even so, after contemplating for five minutes Ishiwara's opinion, supported by his staff, that "we must resolutely make ourselves the masters of the enemy garrison," Honjō decided to order a general assault. "Yes," he said, "let it be done on my responsibility."[295] Thus, in the name of national defense, that sacred slogan of the twentieth century, Japan entered the long road that would ultimately end at the outbreak of the Pacific War.

THREE

The Extension of Hostilities, 1931–1932

Introduction

AKIRA IRIYE

The Manchurian Incident became a subject of intensive study almost as soon as it broke out. Journalists, public officials, historians, and political scientists have been fascinated by the event for several reasons. Coupled with the world economic crisis, the Manchurian Incident served to mark a turning point in modern history. It was after 1931, it is often asserted, that the League of Nations' peace-maintaining mechanism began to crumble, Japanese militarism put an end to a brief era of party government, and China started on its road to crisis and upheaval. Subsequent events have tended to reinforce the historical significance of the Manchurian crisis. Because Japan eventually turned against the United States and fought a Sino-American coalition, it has seemed that there was a direct link between the events of 1931 and those of 1941. Since Japanese militarism triumphed and a totalitarian regime came to be organized, their roots have been traced to the domestic and external affairs of 1931. The place of the military in Japanese decision making, the role of junior officers in the military hierarchy, the independence of the field army, army-navy rivalry, civilian ultranationalists—all these concepts have been examined with reference to the Mukden Incident, which offers a convenient starting point. It is no exaggeration to say that much generalization on prewar Japanese history has been based on the study of the Manchurian crisis.

The study of the episode has been helped tremendously by the abundance of source material. Ever since the Lytton Commission issued its report, there has been no dearth of primary documents, whether of Japanese, Chinese, or Western origin. Many new data were uncovered during the Tokyo war crimes trials, and no writer of memoirs has failed to mention several "confidential" accounts of the Mukden episode. A number of these memoirs and other biographical works have contributed greatly to the clarification of details. A bulk of Foreign Ministry manuscripts has survived war and destruction. Most valuable military records have recently been unearthed, and those dealing witht the Manchurian Incident have been almost exhaustively printed in *Gendai shi shiryō* (Source Materials on Contemporary History) and in the documentary supplement to the seven-volume *Taiheiyō sensō e no michi* (The Road to the Pacific War), of which the following work is a partial translation. There has thus accumulated a tremendous amount of fresh and exciting raw material waiting to be used and interpreted.

This task has been undertaken by a number of writers. Although no comprehensive single volume has yet appeared embracing the varied aspects of the Manchurian Incident, several monographs have tried to tackle the event from different angles. To take only those that have appeared since 1960, Robert H. Ferrell, Elting E. Morison, and Armin Rappaport have focused on Secretary of State Stimson's attitude during 1931–32; Ueda Toshio and Ichimata Masao, among others, have once again looked at legal ramifications; Takehiko Yoshihashi has located the political and economic factors behind the "rise of the military"; Usami Seijirō has applied a Marxist analysis to the documents; and Sadako Ogata has vividly described the thought and behavior of Kwantung Army officers.[1]

The present work is a valuable addition to this growing volume of scholarship on the Manchurian crisis. The author has long been a leading authority on prewar militarism and has published a number of articles and edited documentary collections on the 1930s, among them a book on the Kwantung Army.[2] His concern with military history has led him to focus on the role of the military in decision making and to view the history of prewar Japan consistently from the military perspective. He has relied almost exclusively on Japanese military sources. When the present study was published in 1962, it was the first serious monograph to have used valuable unpublished documents of the Kwantung Army and the Army General Staff. He made particular use of the General Staff-compiled documentary history of the Manchurian Incident, as well as of the war diary kept by Katakura Tadashi, a junior staff officer of the Kwantung Army. The result has been to enable the author to see the event through the eyes of some of its most direct participants, in fact of those who had personally brought it about.

The author cites liberally from military documents to illustrate military thinking and behavior. The purpose has not been to present a case for the military, as has sometimes been alleged by critics. Rather, the author has tried to look at one aspect, perhaps the most important aspect, of the whole incident by letting its participants speak for themselves. Nor has he neglected the task of evaluating and correlating some of these documents. Obviously they contain factual errors and distortions, written as they were in the middle of a drama by its actors. As Colonel Ishiwara Kanji said of the Katakura diary, "It is generally quite to the point, although there are a few dogmatic and prejudiced passages." Writers of diaries and documentary histories must have had hidden motives and even ambitions that they hoped to have reflected in their writings. Their accuracy can be judged and their significance evaluated only by applying to them a rigorous and objective analysis and a degree of restraint lest one be too easily impressed with the appearance rather than the substance of what the documents tell. Actually, the author is often critical of the military and does not always take what they say at its face value. Still, he is fascinated by the diverse currents and crosscurrents of military thought and behavior; he is never prone to give facile generalizations about them as a group. In this sense, then, this work may be taken as a reliable documentary history, on the basis of which further generalization can be attempted. In this sense it is in contrast to Ogata's excellent *Defiance in Manchuria*, which clearly focuses on the Kwantung Army and takes as its consistent theme the impact of Kwantung Army actions on Japanese politics and governmental processes. Problems and the author's analytical framework in dealing with them are less explicit in the present work, and it becomes the reader's task to draw conclusions.

The work here translated deals with events between the fall of 1931 and the spring of 1932. So much more happened during this half year than perhaps in any other period in recent Japanese history that one is prone to look at the whole period in one color, as a constant and spontaneous flow of events. The author's account of six different episodes shows that such was never the case. If one takes only the first and the last of these, what stands out is the Kwantung Army's victory, not only over the Chinese army but also over the hesitant national leadership. But the road had not been smooth. There were instances of retreat, frustration, and anger, and they must all be examined in their place. While the incidents overlap chronologically, the author narrates each one separately. The effect of this method of writing is to dramatize the complexity of the whole Manchurian affair while retaining textual clarity.

In translating this work, I have shortened long telegrams and memoranda, which abound in the original version. Those who wish to examine the complete texts of these documents may consult the documentary collections mentioned above. Footnote citations are here exceedingly simple, referring only to the sources from which documents are taken. When there are no footnotes to quotations, it is assumed that the texts themselves clearly indicate their sources. I have, however, indicated whenever possible where the documents quoted may be found in their entirety. I have in the translation reduced the space devoted to strictly military operational data and rearranged a few passages to make their transitions smoother.

Certain points would seem to emerge from the following study of the Manchurian crisis. First, there did exist what may be termed an "army policy" toward Manchuria and more basically toward China. Men such as Ishiwara Kanji and Itagaki Seishirō at Mukden and Nagata Tetsuzan, Tatekawa Yoshitsugu, and Imamura Hitoshi in Tokyo, as well as their superiors, were basically agreed on the need to carry out "positive action" in Manchuria. All of them were determined that Manchuria should somehow be placed under Japanese control and treated distinctly from China proper. One basis of this positive policy was an optimistic estimate of Japanese strength vis-a-vis the Soviet Union. The army on the whole believed Japanese designs in Manchuria could be promoted with impunity, without incurring Soviet retaliation.

Within this broad framework, however, there were points of difference, most notably between the Kwantung Army and central headquarters, but also between the General Staff and the Army Ministry. Basically, the dispute between Mukden and Tokyo was over the execution of policy, not over the policy itself. The army central authorities wished to retain control over the Kwantung Army, even while approving of the latter's actions. The supreme command was unwilling to tolerate openly a breach of discipline by the army in the field. Its veto of the Kwantung Army's proposed expedition to Harbin and occupation of Tsitsihar, in September and November respectively, exemplified the determination to safeguard the formal line of command. In the latter instance Tokyo army headquarters was so strongly intent on asserting its leadership that it obtained authority from the emperor for issuing operational orders to the Kwantung Army. In the end, however, the occupation of Tsitsihar by a small force was sanctioned, as was an expedition to Harbin. But this was not because the Kwantung Army defied Tokyo's command; rather, it was because the latter had in time come around to accepting the field army's recommendations. There never was an instance of the Kwantung Army's openly challenging Tokyo's authority and defying its orders. Staff officers frequently fabricated crises, accumulated *faits accomplis* without obtaining prior endorsement from Tokyo, and privately complained of the supreme command's attitude; some of them even "shed tears" on occasion, disgusted with Tokyo's "softening." This situation is often referred to as one of "field army defiance," a theme so often stressed in historical writings. But it must be recalled that the field army's initiative and influence are a phenomenon in all periods of history; it is only when it disregards orders from the center or revolts against political authority that its "independence" becomes a fact. The Kwantung Army, on the other hand, did not plot revolt, and it honored specific orders from Tokyo, no matter how much the staff officers grumbled about them and how confident they were of eventually overcoming Tokyo's opposition to their plans.

Thus it becomes obvious that the supreme command's attitude was an essential variable in determining Kwantung Army behavior. The former might or might not sanction the latter's action and tactics, and as time passed it came more and more to approve of Mukden's plans. One determinant here was the supreme command's relations with the civilian leadership in Japan. Evidence indicates that the supreme command was unwilling to openly defy the cabinet and the emperor. Despite many instances where the military leaders maneuvered behind the scenes, at least outwardly they sought cabinet approval of their policy while in their turn honoring the emperor's and the government's wishes. Since the latter had to consider domestic and international implications of army action, it followed that the supreme command, too, was sensitive to the nonmilitary aspects of strategy and tactics. Responses by the League of Nations, for instance, were always watched closely by the military in Tokyo, while such was never the case with those at Mukden. Thus no study of the supreme command's attitude can be complete without a detailed analysis of the civilian government's policy, as well as the policies of foreign governments. This is beyond the scope of the present study, but the present work shows the way to such an inquiry.

A specific question in this connection arises: Why did the Tokyo military become more and more compliant with the Kwantung Army's policies? One could agree with the author that the phenomenon was brought about by the army terrorism of October 1931. The silent pressure produced by the prospect of an armed uprising was such that the civilian government became less and less determined in opposing army action. This in turn meant greater freedom for the supreme command to sanction Kwantung Army plans and machinations. Such pressure also brought down the Minseitō cabinet and substituted for it a Seiyūkai cabinet, whose army minister, Araki Sadao, was well liked by military positivists. It is noteworthy that after mid-December when the Inukai Tsuyoshi cabinet was formed, the supreme command became more and more willing to respond to Kwantung Army promptings. On the other hand, this may have been because the deed had been done already. After all, Araki was one of the Big Three even before December, when the change is alleged to have taken place. It would be difficult to say whether the Kwantung Army would have accomplished more if the cabinet in September had been headed by Inukai and the Army Ministry by Araki. It is just as plausible to argue that Inukai would have been more determined than Wakatsuki Reijirō in opposing army extremism as it is to argue otherwise. It should also be pointed out that even if one grants the change after December, one will still have to say that there was basic agreement between the now-weakened civilian government and the emboldened Kwantung Army. In other words, there was no clear dichotomy between civilian and military policy; therefore, there was no complete civilian capitulation. The military may, directly or indirectly, have brought about the atrophy of civilian government, but the latter was much more than a passive mouthpiece for the military.

Finally, the lack of ideology strikes one as characteristic of the Japanese military. It has become customary to talk of Ishiwara's Nichiren Buddhism, the Kwantung Army's anti-capitalist "socialism," young officers' ultranationalism, and other manifestations of "Japanese fascism." Yet what emerges from the present account is an almost total absence of ideology as a driving force behind military action. The Kwantung Army and the Tokyo military seem to have believed that their acts were logical expressions of a rational strategy, designed to carry out what to them was a legitimate goal of national policy. There was little room for moralizing, sentimentalizing, or emotionalism. Even the often alleged strain of anti-Western pan-Asianism was never more than an afterthought, or at most a result, not a cause, of military action. Force and the use of force as a necessary means of obtaining a coldly calculated goal, rather than adherence to a vaguely defined doctrine, characterized the military's behavior.

Even if the focus of inquiry is confined to military thinking and behavior, certain questions immediately present themselves. How unique were the Japanese military in the 1930s? Why did they emerge so prominently just at that particular moment? How should one evaluate their achievements and their role in Japan's road to war? These questions concern fundamental problems of modern Japanese history. Here it may be suggested, first, that Japanese military policy was a response to a specific situation existing at home and abroad in the 1920s. More specifically, it was a response to a foreign policy that was characterized by an emphasis on economic factors and an assumption of a more or less indefinite period of peace among nations. The military postulated an alternative view of national policy, in which security considerations were uppermost and the need to create a "national defense state" was emphasized. It was a historical accident that in the 1920s civil-military relations in Japan took the form of competition between these two views of foreign policy. But the military represented change and promised greater success when the civilian approach seemed to have resulted only in continued economic stagnation and bellicose Chinese nationalism. It was another significant accident that Japan in 1931 had strikingly few alternatives to these two views. Given the world economic crisis and the powers' conservative foreign policies in the Far East, and excluding such extreme alternatives as an internal revolution in Japan or a return to free trade, there would seem to have been only four choices open to Japan: continuation of the existing unsatisfactory situation; Sino-Japanese cooperation based on maximum concessions on the part of either China or Japan; cooperation with a strong third power such as the United States, Britain, or the Soviet Union; and positive recourse to force to bring about a new situation. The first three alternatives had been tried by the exponents of the economic foreign policy but with no visible success. The only other alternative was the one pushed by advocates of military policy. Here was an instance in which the military and military policy asserted their supremacy as a response to the failure, whether real or apparent, of all other alternatives pursued by the nonmilitary. This explains the initial support given to the military by those who had been alienated from the civilian government.

The emergent military policy certainly underestimated Chinese nationalism, and there is no doubt that the Kwantung Army's actions signaled the beginning of the Sino-Japanese conflict, which could have been ended only by a decisive victory by one side. It would be wrong, however, to jump from here and say that all subsequent acts by the Japanese military were foreshadowed by the events of 1931–32. It is true that here was a beginning of what later developed into a grandiose "bloc policy," the idea of organizing an economically self-sufficient and militarily impregnable empire in Asia. Such an idea, against the background of a European war, would ultimately result in an open clash with the colonial powers in Asia, including the United States. As of 1931, however, all this was but dimly anticipated. For it was not only the Japanese military who made crucial decisions. There were armies and navies and foreign offices in other countries, and in the end these would play even more important roles than those in Japan in bringing about the Pacific War.

Finally, it may be hoped that this study will be useful as a case study of a military group in a modern state. Only comparative study will enable us to delineate what was "Japanese" in the Japanese army, what was common to societies at a similar stage of economic development and modernization, and what was typical of all human responses. Only after we have succeeded in tracing the course of military thinking since the time of Machiavelli and even before, examining the political structure of the army in all authoritarian states, and studying the role of the military in modernization, will we be truly able to look at the Kwantung Army or the Tokyo General Staff in perspective.

THREE

The Extension of Hostilities, 1931–1932

SHIMADA TOSHIHIKO

Translated by
AKIRA IRIYE

The Manchurian Incident

It was shortly past one o'clock in Tokyo on the morning of September 19, 1931. Officers on night duty at the Army General Staff were alerted by the arrival of an urgent telegram from Mukden. Reporting a clash between Japanese and Chinese soldiers north of Mukden, the telegram marked the beginning of an agonizing page in Japanese history. There followed two more telegrams, attributing the clash to a Chinese attack on the South Manchuria Railway and reporting retaliatory measures being taken by the Kwantung Army. The seriousness of the situation was hinted at, as was the possibility of a request for reinforcements.

Thus dawned a hectic day for the Army General Staff. Tatekawa Yoshitsugu, chief of the First (Operations) Division, was away in Manchuria, and in his absence Colonel Imamura Hitoshi had temporarily taken over his functions. Imamura was chief of the Operations Section, with eleven members under him, including Lieutenant-Colonel Kawabe Torashirō and Major Endō Saburō. They were engaged from morning till night in making studies and drafting operational plans. Major Shibayama Kaneshirō, an adviser to Chang Hsueh-liang, who happened to be in Tokyo, was also invited to join them. Not only these men but many others in the General Staff were excited and affected by "a peculiar psychology," according to the official confidential history of the incident. These were men who had long waited for the moment when they would once again find a "place in the sun." For over twenty-five years since the Russo-

This is a translation by Akira Iriye of Shimada Toshihiko, "Manshū jihen no tenkai," in *Taiheiyō sensō e no michi*, vol. 2, part I, pp. 1–188, together with footnotes.

Japanese War, professional soldiers had not fought a real war. They had not fared well in an age of disarmament. In recent years, however, they had felt that perhaps times were changing, as they saw fascistic movements springing up around them. They had been outraged by the anti-Japanese outbursts in China, as revealed most recently in the Captain Nakamura incident;* and they were convinced of the need to strengthen national defense by occupying Manchuria and even part of China. For these men the incident of September 18 was what they had been looking for. They were naturally excited and inevitably drawn to the office of the Operations Section to find out more about what had occurred.

Meanwhile, the earliest top-level conference in the General Staff had been held at seven in the morning. Participants included, from the Army Ministry, Vice Minister Sugiyama Gen and Military Affairs Bureau chief Koiso Kuniaki, and from the General Staff, Vice Chief Ninomiya Harushige, General Affairs Division Chief Umezu Yoshijirō, Intelligence Division chief Hashimoto Toranosuke, and Imamura. No one contradicted Koiso when he declared, "The Kwantung Army's action is entirely just."[1] He did concede that public opinion might suspect a plot, but everyone agreed on the need to send reinforcements. On the basis of this decision by the top military leaders, the Operations Section proceeded to study the possibility of diverting part of the army in Korea to the scene of fighting, as well as of dispatching the 10th Division (stationed at Himeji) to Manchuria. In the Army Ministry the Military Section prepared a draft proposal for reinforcements, to be submitted for cabinet consideration. It is obvious that immediately after the outbreak of the incident, the army supreme command was entirely disposed to cooperate with the Kwantung Army.

Even before the General Staff completed its planning for reinforcements, Commander Hayashi Senjūrō of the Korea Army had decided on his own initiative to send reinforcements to Manchuria. Shortly after seven in the morning he telegraphed Tokyo, "In view of the situation in the Mukden area, I have dispatched two companies (one combat and one scout) from the 6th Air Regiment [stationed at Heijō (P'yŏngyang)].

---

*This incident in June 1931 involved the execution by Chang Hsueh-liang's army of Captain Nakamura Shintarō, a staff officer of the Kwantung Army, and three companions for spying activities. The killings were kept secret for a time and aroused the public in Japan when revealed by the government in August 1931.

Preparations are also being made for sending one mixed brigade from the 20th Division [at Ryūzan (Yongsan)] to Mukden. I have in addition ordered the 19th Division [at Ranan (Nanam)] to make plans for sending as many troops as possible." Hayashi had even arranged for the departure of part of the mixed brigade at about 9:30 A.M.[2] Receiving the telegram, but not knowing that Hayashi had already ordered troop mobilization, the supreme command determined that an imperial order would have to be obtained for sending troops across the border.

One element of confusion had thus already entered the picture. Since 1900, when Japanese troops were sent to China to suppress the Boxers, the tradition had been established that the dispatch of troops abroad required cabinet approval and an imperial order. However, there was another tradition, that of *dokudan senkō*, arbitrary decision and execution, meaning the ability to act flexibly on one's own initiative. Japanese soldiers were taught and trained to respond calmly to all situations and take advantage of every good opportunity, instead of waiting for orders. There had been no complete resolution of the contradictions between these two traditions. Hence the confusion and chaos as soon as the Korea Army's action became known in Tokyo. At first the Operations Section of the General Staff was inclined to the view that an imperial decree should be immediately obtained to give *ex post facto* approval to the sending of the air regiment and that customary procedures should be followed before dispatching further forces. In other words, the Operations Section was intent on maintaining a clear line of command and protecting the military in Korea from censure for overstepping their authority.

Such an attitude was reaffirmed when the next telegram was received from Korea, stating definitely that a mixed brigade would be sent to Mukden in response to a request from the Kwantung Army. The brigade was to leave about 10 o'clock A.M. and would be placed under the Kwantung Army's command upon its arrival. Receiving this information, Operations Section Chief Imamura and a few others felt that General Hayashi's behavior was "lacking in propriety." They countered the suggestion of other staff members that the Korea Army's action be ratified. Chief of Staff Kanaya Hanzō and Vice Chief Ninomiya agreed with Imamura, and a telegram was sent to Hayashi at 12:30, enjoining him to wait for an imperial order before sending reinforcements. Similar orders were telegraphed to the commander of the 39th Infantry Brigade at Heijō and to the commander of the garrison army at Shingishū (Sinŭiju), who was told not to authorize the crossing of the Manchurian border by Korea Army troops except those of the air regiment.

The hectic events of September 19 revealed that the army supreme command faced two serious problems. One was the question of how to deal with the Korea Army, which had decided to cross the Manchurian border. The other was the question of how to relate the Mukden Incident to the overall policy toward Manchuria and Mongolia that the army had been developing. More specifically, Tokyo had to decide whether to give *ex post facto* approval to General Hayashi's action and whether or not to expand the war.

At 3:50 in the afternoon the General Staff received General Hayashi's reply to its order to postpone troop movement. The telegram said: "First, the bulk of the expeditionary force has already departed and will cross the border by tonight. Second, due to the situation in which the Kwantung Army is placed, I feel it is imperative to assist it immediately." The order to halt the expedition had been completely ignored.

The supreme command persisted in its stand. Junior officers of the General Staff, such as the Operations Section's Lieutenant-Colonel Shibata Shin'ichi (in charge of aviation matters), Major Mutō Akira (supplies), and Major Endō Saburō (drafting orders), were inclined to endorse the Korea Army's decision, but the senior officers remained adamant. After 6 o'clock, Kanaya telegraphed Hayashi to hold the troops, except the air regiment, at Shingishū until further notice. Two hours later, the chief of staff of the Korea Army was instructed to report immediately whether the troops were in fact so held and not proceeding to Manchuria.

The Korea Army, however, was equally adamant. It telegraphed Tokyo: "We still think it is necessary to dispatch a mixed brigade in view of the Kwantung Army's request for reinforcements and other general conditions, especially the need to guard the Antung-Mukden Railway. We would like to know, for our future reference, what special consideration has caused you to order us to postpone sending the brigade." This communication was regarded by some members of the Operations Section as impertinent, "daring to ask for explanations for our orders and directives." But it was felt "there was some justification for patiently explaining our stand so as to dispel misunderstanding on the part of the military in the field." Accordingly, shortly after midnight the following telegram was sent to Hayashi in the chief of staff's name.

> Your unilateral action this morning is not necessarily objectionable, in view of then-existing conditions. However, as the situation around Mukden has somewhat improved, I have given my consent to the cabinet decision not to extend hostilities for the time being, unless unexpected conditions should develop. Your army's movement out of Korea must wait upon imperial approval. It is necessary to gather and hold the mobilized troops at Shingishū until further notice. Please telegraph immediately the present whereabouts of the mixed brigade.

This message is said to have been drafted by the Operations Division. Its effort is evident in the way three factors—improvement in the Mukden situation, the cabinet decision (see below), and the need for imperial approval—were arranged so as to impress the Korea Army with the reasonableness of the supreme command's position. The original draft of this telegram had even stated, "I do not object to your unilateral action this morning." Chief of Staff Kanaya, however, wanted to omit reference to himself, and the wording was changed so as not to refer to any individual as "not necessarily objecting." This was an alteration calculated to obscure where the ultimate responsibility lay in the matter.[3] At any rate, the 39th Mixed Brigade, scheduled to arrive at Mukden between dawn and early afternoon on September 20, was temporarily halted at Shingishū. The General Staff's authority had at last been reasserted.[4]

Why did the supreme command persist in such a strong stand? One reason was the cabinet decision not to expand hostilities. Before the cabinet met on the morning of September 19, Prime Minister Wakatsuki Reijirō had asked Army Minister Minami Jirō if the Kwantung Army's action was a purely defensive move, taken in retaliation against Chinese soldiers' "violence and provocation." The army minister had answered in the affirmative, probably because he had been kept entirely in the dark about the Kwantung Army's intentions, although any army minister would have answered such a direct question in the same way.[5] At the cabinet meeting, opened at 10 o'clock, Foreign Minister Shidehara Kijūrō read from various reports his office had gathered. They all depicted the army in an unfavorable light. One report said that the Kwantung Army was making preparations for action on the night of September 18. Another said that the garrison army at Wushun had planned maneuvers on

the 17th, in order to prepare for emergencies, but changed the date to
the 18th at the last moment. The garrison army had requested the use
of South Manchuria Railway trains on the 17th; when the date was changed
to the 18th, railway officials relayed the information to Consul-General
Hayashi Kyūjirō, who immediately telegraphed Shidehara.[6] Hearing these
reports, Army Minister Minami "felt dispirited," according to the confidential history, "and lost courage to propose reinforcements from the
Korea Army." Thus the cabinet decided on the policy of nonexpansion.
Some in army headquarters must have felt Minami's indecisiveness was
responsible for obstructing the Korea Army's action.

The second factor behind the supreme command's strong stand vis-
a-vis the Korea Army was Chief of Staff Kanaya's imperial audience, which
took place at 3 o'clock the same day. He had heard that the emperor was
displeased with General Hayashi's unilateral action; as a result, Kanaya
took the initiative to express to the Throne his intention to investigate
Hayashi's action, which he said he extremely regretted.[7] Thus, while the
army minister bound the army's operational freedom of action at the
cabinet meeting, the chief of staff did likewise at the palace. The problem was that neither of them was really convinced of the rightness of his
act; they were actually in agreement with their staffs' stand, but they
lacked courage to speak out for them either at the cabinet meeting or in
front of the emperor. It was only with reluctance that they ordered the
Korea Army to stop at the border.

The best evidence for this is that the supreme command failed to telegraph further instructions to the Korea Army until September 21. It in
effect was hoping that the Korea Army would disobey its orders and unilaterally cross the Manchurian border. In this way a *fait accompli* would
be created, which the supreme command really wanted but could not
openly bring about, now that it had bound itself to the cabinet and to
the emperor. Such seems to have been the army's hidden policy at this
time.

During the afternoon of September 19 the Operations Section had
already discussed the steps to be taken if the Korea Army should disregard Tokyo's command and proceed to Manchuria. If that should happen, the section staff concluded that General Hayashi should be given,
not a reprimand, but an *ex post facto* imperial approval. This was to be
obtained through a direct appeal to the Throne by the chief of staff. Next
day Section Chief Imamura sent a personal message to Major Hirata Sei-

han, whom the General Staff had dispatched to Manchuria, asking him to convey the supreme command's gratitude to the chief of staff of the Korea Army for having sent the air regiment to Manchuria. Since this telegram was sent in care of the Korea Army, Imamura must have expected that the message would be read immediately by Korea Army headquarters and prod it to undertake unilateral movement across the border. That same afternoon the army's Big Three (the army minister, the chief of the General Staff, and the inspector-general of military education) conferred and decided to circumvent the cabinet for the time being on matters dealing with troop reinforcement, since the cabinet had already decided on nonexpansion of the conflict. It was agreed that the army minister should first intimate to the prime minister that necessary steps might have to be taken to cope with the rapidly changing situation. The cabinet was to be consulted "at an opportune moment."[8]

At 8:35 P.M., September 20 the supreme command received what must have been a welcome message from Korea. It said: "We understand your instruction to wait for an imperial order before dispatching forces to Manchuria. However, an imperial order would imply war between Japan and China, and the situation could become serious. In order to treat the issue as a local problem, it would be more expedient to take the form of unilateral troop mobilization. We hope you will give us enough leeway to dispatch part of our forces unilaterally if occasion should arise." Apparently such an occasion arose in less than twenty-four hours. At 2:40 P.M. September 21 a telegram was received from the commander of the 39th Infantry Brigade, which said, "The brigade plans to leave by train at 1:00 P.M. today." Even before the excited General Staff had time to draft and send an inquiring message asking how the decision had been made, a telegram from General Hayashi arrived, stating that the sending of the brigade, held at Shingishū, to Manchuria had been decided on in view of repeated pleas for assistance from the Kwantung Army, which had expanded the sphere of operation to the Kirin (Chilin) area. The decision, Hayashi said, had been made "as the sense of justice impelled it." He expressed his regret at having violated the supreme command's orders and said he alone was responsible for the crossing by the brigade of the Manchurian frontier. By 4:30 the same afternoon the expeditionary force had crossed the Yalu, passed Antung, and entered under the Kwantung Army's command.

The crucial factor behind Hayashi's decision seems to have been the

Kwantung Army's Kirin campaign, as revealed in the telegram above. The Kwantung Army had in fact decided on this course of action precisely because such action was thought to justify participation of the Korea Army in the conflict. It was judged by Itagaki Seishirō, Ishiwara Kanji, and other staff officers at Mukden that once hostilities expanded to Kirin, the Kwantung Army would be spread so thin that it could legitimately appeal for outside assistance. The Korea Army then would not remain immobile. Only by thus joining Japan's Manchurian and Korean forces could the supreme command be impressed with the seriousness of the Kwantung Army's intentions and the need for bold action to solve fundamental questions. Commander-in-Chief Honjō Shigeru was at first cautious, and only after long solitary deliberation, lasting until 3:00 A.M. September 21, and under strong pressure from his staff, did he make up his mind.[9]

The General Staff, as expected, welcomed the news from Korea. It had already worked out the general tactic: to obtain *ex post facto* imperial sanction by means of a direct appeal by the chief of staff, and to request cabinet ratification of the *fait accompli*. To make doubly sure that the Korea Army's action was "not a violation of the imperial prerogative," four junior officers of the General Staff were instructed to draft a paper justifying General Hayashi's decision.

The paper as written cited four reasons why Hayashi had not encroached upon the imperial authority. First, "The emperor has long given the commander of the Korea Army the duty to dispatch part of his troops (about the size of the troops being mobilized this time) to Manchuria in case strategic and tactical needs required it, in order to assist the Kwantung Army. Various plans have been made for this eventuality, and approval has been given them. When the incident broke out at this time, the commander of the Kwantung Army informed the Korea Army commander of the developments and requested reinforcements. He . . . thus made preparations for action, sent reports to the chief of staff, and under the latter's order gathered forces at Shingishū, restraining them from proceeding to Manchuria. He then waited for an imperial order." Subsequently, the paper continued, unilateral action was taken in view of the Kwantung Army's repeated requests for help and as a result of the Korea Army's own judgment of the developing situation. Even then, it argued, this could not be taken as a violation of the imperial prerogative, since the chief of staff was duly informed of the decision. This account is obviously inaccurate, for the brigade had started for Mukden long before the General Staff was notified.

The second reason given by this memorandum in defense of General Hayashi was a more reliable fact: "As the chief of staff . . . instructed the Korea Army to hold the brigade at Shingishū and wait for further orders, the army obeyed the instruction and waited for an imperial order, while observing the development of the situation." However, as the Kwantung Army was compelled to send troops to Kirin and in doing so desperately needed assistance from Korea, the Korea Army judged that there was not enough time to wait for orders and began moving across the Yalu. "These steps were taken in response to changing situations and cannot be said to have ignored the imperial right of supreme command. The Korea Army acted unilaterally only because it believed imperial approval would be duly given." This reasoning is factually sound, but it does not really prove the Korea Army's submission to the command of the General Staff.

Third, the paper noted that independent initiative and the ability to respond flexibly to all possible situations were characteristic of the imperial army. Therefore, "to call the Korea commander's unilateral action a violation of the imperial prerogative is to invite the army to give up these characteristics and revert to the old practices of the Tsarist Russian army." Here the ambiguity already noted remains; it was never clear at which point flexibility ceased to count and imperial approval became necessary.

Finally, some legal explanations were given. The memorandum pointed out, without giving specific reasons, that the increase of forces in Manchuria did not violate the existing treaty arrangement by which the number of troops guarding the South Manchuria Railway was restricted. Also, it was stated that since the two countries were actually fighting each other, there had been no violation of the rule that an army should not cross the border in time of peace. Such unconvincing argument cannot be said to have constituted a good case for Hayashi, but it may be even more correct to say that something was the matter with General Staff officers' mentality if they managed to convince themselves with this type of reasoning.

Actually, not all was smooth sailing for the General Staff. The strongest obstacle to its scheme came from the Army Ministry. Imamura had felt sure of Army Ministry compliance, since the Big Three had already decided to resort to a direct appeal to the Throne to obtain imperial approval of the Korea Army's action. Convinced that the vice army minister and his subordinate officials concurred in the decision, Imamura urged the chief of staff to have an audience with the emperor while he himself went to the Army Ministry's Military Section to obtain its formal consent. There, however, Section Chief Nagata Tetsuzan and his staff adamantly opposed the General Staff's scheme. They pointed out that "It is improper to resort to the expediency of appealing to the emperor directly, without going through the cabinet, since troop increases involve expenditures and thus require cabinet approval. Should the cabinet fail to sanction the dispatch of troops, the ultimate decision would have to be carried to the emperor. This is not the way to conduct ourselves as his subjects." Nagata declared that the General Staff's action was tantamount to expressing its lack of confidence in the chiefs of the Army Ministry's Military Affairs Bureau and Military Section, for they had been entirely bypassed and only the army minister's views had been consulted. This may have been Nagata's way of expressing his dissatisfaction with his chief, Army Minister Minami. Imamura admitted that there had been insufficient consultation between junior officers of the General Staff and Army Ministry, and he expressed willingness to reconsider steps that had been taken. Nagata then relented somewhat and said he would take back the strong statement he had just made. His basic reason for opposing Imamura was that he felt cabinet approval and a subsequent imperial order were the only correct way to authorize troop reinforcement; he would avoid the irregular and extraordinary tactic of a direct appeal to the Throne. At any rate, Imamura was persuaded to postpone putting into effect the General Staff's strategy. He telephoned the palace and was able to stop Kanaya, who was just on the point of seeing the emperor. Kanaya, as a result, merely reported to the Throne that a brigade had been dispatched by a unilateral order of the Korea Army's commander and that the merits of this action needed to be carefully examined.[10]

A direct appeal to the Throne was thus given up. Since the cabinet was scheduled to meet on September 22, bureau and section chiefs of the Army Ministry and General Staff met late in the evening of September 21 to devise an alternative strategy. It was considered likely that the cabinet would declare the Korea Army commander's action a violation of the imperial prerogative. There were reports that the government was displeased with him and that the Minseitō was highly agitated. If the cabinet should in reality condemn General Hayashi's decision, the army had to clarify its own attitude. As seen above, there was virtual unanimity among the military about the justice of Hayashi's action. It was natural, therefore, that the conferees should have decided virtually to declare war on the government and the Minseitō. They concluded that both the army minister and the chief of staff should resign in protest against cabinet disapproval of the Korea Army. At first Imamura insisted that at least as a matter of form the two—the army minister and the chief of staff—should behave separately, and this idea was supported by Umezu and Hashimoto. But Nagata held out strongly for a simultaneous resignation, and a majority of the conferees supported him, saying this was a grave moment and the army had to act realistically and boldly to combat the government, rather than worry about the procedural and prestige-involving problem of who should resign first. Deep into the night, letters of resignation for both the army minister and the chief of staff were drawn up, the actual writing being done by the chief of the General Affairs Section of the Army Ministry. As for the resignation of other military officials, Imamura felt there was no need for Vice Chief of Staff Ninomiya to resign. Fearing that he might insist on acting with his chief, Imamura saw Ninomiya early on the morning of September 22 and succeeded in persuading him that he need not do so.

All these precautionary steps and plots proved utterly unnecessary, for the government ended by endorsing the Korea Army's action. Before the cabinet meeting on the morning of Septmeber 22, Prime Minister Wakatsuki had told Koiso "there is nothing that can be done now" about the Korea Army's crossing of the Manchurian border. The cabinet itself decided to approve that action and to defray its expenses. The basic reasoning was similar to Wakatsuki's: since the troops had already crossed the border, all the government could do was to ratify the deed. Few cabinet members actively supported the move, but none was opposed to it. Foreign Minister Shidehara and some others may have felt that here was a clear violation of the imperial right of supreme command, but no one had the courage to speak out against the Korea Army. Accordingly, the prime minister hastened to the palace and reported the cabinet decision to the emperor.[11] Feeling relieved, Chief of Staff Kanaya and Army Minister Minami proceeded to obtain formal imperial approval for the dispatch of troops to Manchuria. The expedition, its organization, and execution thus won the needed authorization. The commanders in Manchuria and Korea were immediately informed of this victory. General Hayashi won fame and glory as the "border-crossing general." His unilateral decision had ended in the government's capitulation.

The second problem facing the supreme command was how to relate the Mukden Incident to the army's overall policy toward Manchuria.* Already in April 1931 the General Staff had devised a three-alternative plan for solution of the Manchurian question. The first alternative (Plan One) was "to break the deadlock in the existing situation in which Japan's justifiable treaty and contractual rights are undermined by China's treacherous acts, and to affirm and expand Japan's rights realistically and efficiently." Japan would replace the Chang Hsueh-liang regime with a pro-Japanese government in order to carry out this plan, but this new government would still recognize the national government's titular sovereignty. The second alternative (Plan Two) cannot be stated with accuracy, for all crucial documents have been lost. It seems likely that this envisaged the setting up of an independent government in Manchuria as a separate entity from Nanking, thereby going a step farther than under Plan One in planting Japan's rights and interests in Manchuria. The third alternative (Plan Three) was obviously military occupation of Manchuria.[12] This flexible program had established a framework for military thinking. When the Mukden Incident occurred, therefore, the supreme command had the choice either of treating it as a minor incident to be settled immediately or of comprehending it within the larger framework.

To put it simply, the supreme command, with the exception of Chief of Staff Kanaya and Army Minister Minami, early decided to adopt Plan One in dealing with the incident. Already on the morning of September 19 Vice Chief of Staff Ninomiya, Vice Army Minster Sugiyama, and Inspector-General of Military Education Araki Sadao conferred and, "discussing whether to use the incident to solve the Manchurian question, decided in the affirmative."[13] The "solution" here was to consist of "completely upholding the existing treaty rights, and was not to imply

---

*The term "Manchuria and Mongolia" was frequently used in Japanese military circles at this time. Here "Manchuria" will be sufficient, since the term usually referred only to Jehol Special District and eastern Inner Mongolia plus the three northeastern provinces, and not to Manchuria and Mongolia as such.

military occupation of the whole of Manchuria." This was a clear adoption of Plan One and rejection of Plan Three. But this decision was opposed by Chief of Staff Kanaya. At a meeting of the General Staff's division chiefs that afternoon, he said it was necessary to abide by the cabinet decision on nonexpansion of the conflict. It was most important to settle the matter as quickly as possible on the basis of the military status quo. "While circumstances beyond control have brought about the incident," he said, "we should quickly settle it and return to the old state of affairs." Imamura, acting for the absent chief of the Operations Division, countered, "The die is cast. To halt it now and restore the old state of affairs will not only have an unfortunate effect on the morale of the Kwantung Army but will also be a serious blow to the nation's army as a whole. It is necessary now to overcome all obstacles, uphold the prestige of the nation and the army, and endeavor to achieve our great goal." Kanaya replied, "A man in my position must be aware of his obligation to be calm and not to be dragged on by younger bloods, especially if he is to achieve great matters. My feeling now is exactly that of Ōishi Yoshio toward the forty-seven *rōnin*. I want to take all responsibility for the incident." This cryptic statement could be taken to mean that Kanaya, like Ōishi, was secretly in agreement with the "younger bloods." Whether this was in fact the case, or whether he had to make such a statement to please his subordinates, cannot be determined. The Operations Section, at any rate, decided to interpret the Ōishi statement in the way it saw fit.

Determined to drive Kanaya to acceptance of its position, the section staff drafted a telegram to the commander-in-chief of the Kwantung Army. It said:

> 1. Your determination in handling the matter after the night of September 18 is most appropriate and has enhanced the prestige of the imperial army.
> 2. In view of the Chinese attitude since then, and in deference to the cabinet decision not to complicate the matter unnecessarily, please keep this principle in mind when planning further action by the army.

This telegram, it is obvious, rejected Kanaya's insistence on restoring the status quo and in fact implied adoption of Plan One. Kanaya nevertheless gave his approval to the telegram, which was sent at 6:00 P.M. Imamura, who showed the draft message to the chief of staff, found Kanaya "apparently deeply resolved" to support the more radical approach. This is very doubtful; rather, the Operations Section's strong pressure seems to have forced Kanaya's compliance.[14]

The Operations Section then proceeded to draft a memorandum on "the settlement of the current crisis in Manchuria." It rejected the restoration of the military status quo and called instead for speedy execution of Plan One. The Foreign Ministry was to be urged to demand solution of the Captain Nakamura and Mukden incidents from the Chinese; the construction of the militarily crucial Kirin-Kainei (Hoeryŏng) and Ch'angch'un-Talai railways was to be speeded through negotiation with China; necessary military measures were to be taken if these negotiations proved fruitless; and the government in Tokyo was to be pressed to accept this plan—the army minister might even threaten to resign if the government remained unmoved. This draft program was discussed at a meeting of the Big Three on the morning of September 20. Araki insisted that the Manchurian question was a political one; it was therefore inappropriate for the army to be talking about its solution. To avoid misunderstanding and distortion by outsiders, it would be better to take a purely military viewpoint and talk mainly about the prestige of the nation and the army. The phraseology of the memorandum was accordingly somewhat changed. But the basic principle, that "the Kwantung Army is not to return to the status quo ante," was never touched. The Big Three further agreed on a basic tactic: "If the government does not accept this draft plan, the army will not bestir itself even if the cabinet falls as a result." Thus the Operations Section's ideas had been accepted not only by the General Staff as a whole but also by the Big Three.

What was the attitude of the Kwantung Army at this time? The first indication of how it regarded the situation was contained in a telegram sent by Commander-in-Chief Honjō at 5:40 P.M. on September 19. It reported that the Kwantung Army had cleared the Mukden area of Chinese troops, had disarmed enemy forces at Yingk'ou and Feng-huangch'eng, and was attacking the Chinese army near Ch'angch'un. The army was "doing its utmost to protect the South Manchuria Railway." The telegram concluded: "Now that the situation has thus developed, this seems the best opportunity for the Kwantung Army to assume responsibility for the maintenance of public order in the whole of Manchuria. To carry out this task it will be necessary to have three additional divisions. I am sure that Manchuria can bear the cost of maintaining them." After sending this telegram, the Kwantung Army received information from Tokyo that the cabinet intended not to expand the conflict. Accordingly, around seven in the evening, another telegram was dispatched to Tokyo, declaring:

> This is the best moment to solve the Manchurian question. Should our army fail to grasp it and adopt a conservative attitude, it will forever become impossible to solve the question. Moreover, the current crisis has been brought about entirely by the reckless Chinese attack on the railway and the railway guards army. . . . All of this is a result of Chinese' slighting the power of our nation and our army. We hope you will make a grave resolution so that the entire army will march toward achieving the nation's fundamental and long-lasting goals.

These telegrams clearly show that the initial objective of the Kwantung Army was to execute Plan Three, namely, military occupation of Manchuria. This was perhaps to be expected, for Lieutenant-Colonel Ishiwara, who had brought about the September 18 plot, had long advocated such a plan.

Late on the night of September 19, Ishiwara joined Colonel Itagaki, Major Hanaya Tadashi, and Captain Katakura Tadashi to confer in secret with Major-General Tatekawa Yoshitsugu, the Operations Division chief who had been dispatched from Tokyo just before the outbreak of the incident. Ishiwara was disappointed to find that Tatekawa did not agree with his view that Plan Three should be pushed with vigor. Though Tatekawa had been a fellow conspirator for positive action in Manchuria, he now insisted that at the present moment Plan One should be adopted. After a heated debate, Tatekawa said that while he still thought he was right, he would not obstruct the Kwantung Army's positive measures. But he added that military action should be confined to Kirin, Ch'angch'un, and the T'aonan-Angangch'i Railway. The result of this meeting was telegraphed to Tokyo on September 20 over Tatekawa's signature and with Commander-in-Chief Honjō's approval. The telegram expressed the view that while "territorial solution" should probably not be pushed, a passive policy such as the cabinet was expected to adopt must be resisted with utmost vigor. It was no time to indulge in a conservative policy, said the telegram, now that hostilities had actually commenced and the Japanese army had crushed the Chinese. Therefore, Tatekawa would recommend that Japan proceed according to Plan One,

looking toward the establishment of a pro-Japanese government in Manchuria, over which Japan would exercise supervision. He mentioned Pu
Yi, the last Ch'ing emperor, as a possible head of the new government.
Adding that Commander-in-Chief Honjō was in agreement with these
views, the telegram declared: "At a time when the Manchurian regime
has crumbled, Manchuria's key areas have all fallen to the Kwantung
Army, and the world recognizes our ability to execute these plans and
bring happiness to the people of Manchuria, the cabinet must immediately make up its mind, declare its decision to the world, and proceed
steadily to the realization of the decision."

Receiving these telegrams, the Operations Section believed the time
had come to convey to the Kwantung Army the supreme command's basic attitude. Drafts of the message were prepared separately by the Army
Ministry and the General Staff throughout the night of September 20,
and the two drafts were compared the next day. There was some discussion over the last sentence in the Army Ministry's draft, which said, "Your
military action should be confined within limits prescribed by the need
to maintain public order." Imamura and Tōjō Hideki, chief of the Organization and Mobilization Section, objected to this phraseology and insisted that it be eliminated. Among Army Ministry officials, Nagata agreed
with Imamura, but Vice Minister Sugiyama said the sentence accurately
reflected Minami's thinking. As a compromise, it was decided to add the
phrase "with respect to local administration" to the sentence in question. As a result of these deliberations, the army minister and the chief
of staff separately sent telegrams to the Kwantung Army. The former said:

> The army supreme command is endeavoring to convince the govern-
> ment of the need to solve once and for all the problems that have arisen
> as a result of Chinese officials' and people's slighting our nation and army.
> But we do not want to occupy Manchuria and Mongolia immediately, as
> suggested in your telegram. Rather, we hope to normalize conditions of
> life in this region and make it a haven for both Japanese and Chinese,
> while retaining Chinese administration. . . . Regarding military admin-
> istration in the occupied territory, strictly refrain from imposing taxes on
> Chinese or seizing customs revenues. With respect to local administra-
> tion, your military action should be confined within limits prescribed by
> the need to maintain public order.

The chief of staff's telegram expressed his appreciation of the Kwantung Army's effort to uphold national prestige and exhorted it to observe
events with an impartial attitude, keeping in mind the army's primary

functions. This message was elaborated by a third telegram, sent by the vice chief of staff, which explained that public opinion at home and abroad had generally approved of the Kwantung Army's action thus far. However, where to go from there was a matter of national policy. The telegram warned: "If the Kwantung Army departs from its primary functions, goes beyond the objective of self-defense, expands its occupied territory, seizes railways, and otherwise extends the conflict, the present favorable tone of public opinion will steadily change. Therefore, unless conditions alter drastically, it will be best to preserve the status quo and calmly watch the situation. I believe this is the best way to achieve the initial goal set by the Kwantung Army and to solve the Manchurian question to our advantage." The message concluded by instructing the Kwantung Army to seek the supreme command's approval before undertaking fresh action, such as an expedition to Harbin. These telegrams revealed the supreme command's adoption of Plan One, instead of Plan Three as the Kwantung Army insisted. At the same time, it is obvious that Plan One had been forced upon the reluctant army minister and chief of staff by their subordinates.

The gap between the central army authorities and the Kwantung Army had somehow to be filled. On the morning of September 22, staff officers of the Kwantung Army met and discussed what to do next. The conferees included Itagaki, Ishiwara, Katakura, and Colonel Doihara Kenji, in addition to the army's chief of staff Miyake Mitsuharu. According to Katakura's diary, Doihara insisted that there should be established in Manchuria and Mongolia a "republic of five races" under Japanese leadership. Others felt that existing circumstances called for a more practical solution. In the end they drew up a memorandum "On the Settlement of the Manchurian Question." Its preamble stated: "A Chinese government headed by the Hsuan-t'ung emperor and with Japanese support is to be established over the four northeastern provinces and Mongolia, which is to become a paradise for every race in the region." The new government was to undertake internal administration, but Japan was to retain control over defense and foreign policies. The main transportation and communications networks were also to be administered by Japan. Five Chinese—Hsi Hsia in Kirin, Chang Hai-p'eng in the T'aonan-Solun area, T'ang Yü-lin in Jehol, Yü Chih-shan in the Tungpien region, and Chang Ching-hui in Harbin—were to be charged with maintaining public order in their respective regions.

Here was a blueprint for establishing a pro-Japanese regime whose

defense and foreign affairs were to be controlled by Japan. It was assumed that the new regime would be detached from China proper and
would eventually form a new state. In other words, Plan Two was here
being accepted. This was a step backward from Ishiwara's favorite scheme,
envisaging the execution of Plan Three. Actually, at the conference of
September 22 Ishiwara himself opposed military occupation of Manchuria when the idea was brought forward by Doihara. It would seem that
Ishiwara decided to back down for the time being in view of the strong
opposition from Tatekawa, whom he had regarded as a mentor among
his comrades.

While these plans were being developed at Mukden, in Tokyo the
cabinet was also debating the next steps to be taken. All cabinet members agreed to take advantage of the situation to settle, once and for all,
the outstanding issues in Manchuria and Mongolia. But they could not
agree on the role of the Kwantung Army. Army Minister Minami argued
for maintaining the existing military positions in Manchuria to give weight
to the settlement of these issues, but Foreign Minister Shidehara objected, recalling the failure of such a tactic during the Chinan (Tsinan)
crisis of 1928. He insisted that eventually troops would have to be withdrawn to their original positions. Minami countered, denying that the
Tsinan and Mukden incidents had anything in common. The gap between the two views was not narrowed, and the cabinet did nothing to
formulate an explicit policy toward the question. Its indecision and hesitation were in sharp contrast to the Kwantung Army's determination to
create one *fait accompli* after another.

Chientao and Harbin: The Kwantung Army Retreats

Chientao* and Harbin were two centers that the Kwantung Army and
the Korea Army hoped to capture in addition to Mukden, Ch'angch'un,
and Kirin. The Korea Army concentrated on Chientao and the Kwantung Army on Harbin.

Chientao is situated on the eastern border of Manchuria. To the south,
beyond the Tumen river, is Korea, and to the east lies Russia's Mari-

*This district has now been absorbed into Kirin Province as the Yen-Pien Korean Auton-
omous District.

time Province. Historically, a majority of the inhabitants of Chientao were Koreans; as a result the area had become a base for the Korean independence movement, in addition to being a point of contact between Japanese and Russian influences. The Korea Army decided to send an expedition to Chientao almost immediately after the outbreak of the Mukden Incident. Commander Hayashi telegraphed Chief of Staff Kanaya on September 19: "The situation is serious in the Chientao-Hunch'un region. It seems necessary to send about one mixed brigade to the area to establish a base for future action, in response to the moves undertaken by the Kwantung Army." The first sentence was totally inaccurate; a serious situation existed only in the military's imagination. Their real intention was disclosed in the second sentence. The Korea Army, while attempting to cross the Yalu to move to Mukden, was also planning to cross the T'umen river to establish a foothold at Chientao and establish control over Koreans there.

Upon receiving Hayashi's message, the General Staff was initially inclined to accept his suggestions. Preparations were made by the Operations Section to obtain an imperial order for a Chientao expedition. But when the cabinet on September 19 decided on nonexpansion of the conflict, the supreme command changed its stand and instructed the Korea Army not to carry out the expedition for the time being. This did not mean that central army authorities were opposed to the idea itself. In fact, they seem to have tried to so interpret the cabinet decision as to justify a Chientao expedition. An Army Ministry memorandum of September 20 proves such a line of thought. Entitled "On the Need To Send Troops to the Chientao-Hunch'un Region," it stated: "In accordance with the spirit of the cabinet decision, it seems necessary to send a minimum security force to the Chientao-Hunch'un area in order to prevent the further worsening of Japanese-Chinese relations." Four reasons were given for the recommendation. First, Chinese authorities in the region had treated Korean inhabitants with brutality and violence, and it was feared that the latter might retaliate, just as they had done during the Wanpaoshan farm incident* of the preceding summer. Second, according to newspaper reports the situation in the area was critical; Chinese had at-

---

*In June 1931 Chinese peasants attempted to eject a community of Koreans, encouraged by Japanese policy to migrate across the border, from the Wanpaoshan area. Although Japanese police prevented any fatalities, the incident led to anti-Chinese feelings in Korea and Chinese boycotts of Japanese goods.

tacked a Japanese post office and arrested newsboys. Third, the Japanese consular police were not likely to be of much help since their prestige had declined as a consequence of Japan's indecisive policy. Fourth, even a small force would on its own be capable of preventing an untoward incident and containing the existing crisis. The army supreme command maintained this position at least until the evening of September 21. When the Korea Army telegraphed that the 19th Division had been ordered to be in readiness for proceeding to Chientao, the General Staff replied: "We are making plans to obtain an imperial order, even resorting to a direct appeal to the Throne by the chief of staff if necessary, as soon as circumstances call for the dispatch of specific units to the South Manchuria Railway zone and to the Chientao-Hunch'un area." This telegram obviously encouraged the Korea Army to go ahead without waiting for an order.

The General Staff nevertheless decided on September 22 to desist from explicitly approving an expedition to Chientao. The chief of staff had received many telegrams from Korea and Chientao, from both Japanese and Korean residents, urging an expedition. Most of the residents of Hunch'un were preparing to return to Korea, and some of them had to be accommodated at the consular building. The situation was also growing tense at Chützuchieh in Yenchi hsien. The supreme command, however, realized that much of the commotion in Chientao had been manufactured by the military and that even Foreign Ministry officials knew of it.[15] Under the circumstances it would be difficult to obtain cabinet approval for a Chientao expedition. The General Staff wanted to minimize trouble; it had its hands full following the Korea Army's crossing of the Yalu. Accordingly, Vice Chief of Staff Ninomiya telegraphed the Korea Army chief of staff, instructing him never to authorize the 19th Division to cross the border and enter Chientao.

Once it had made up its mind, the supreme command remained unmoved by further pleas from Korea. One such plea, received on September 24, said: "To leave Chientao in a state of uncertainty will cause the 400,000 Koreans in Chientao and 20 million of them in Korea to feel that only Japanese are given protection. They will resent us and render difficult our control over Korea." But the General Staff could not be reckless. It had first to deal with the Korea Army's crossing of the Yalu, and the Chientao project had to be postponed for the time being, no matter how much the supreme command was attracted to it in theory.

Meanwhile, in Harbin a relative quiet had prevailed following the outbreak of the Mukden Incident, owing primarily to the precaution and vigilance of the Chinese authorities. On the night of September 24, however, violent anti-Japanese handbills began to be disseminated, and the following day bombs were thrown into the Japanese consulate, the office of the Bank of Korea, and the headquarters of the Japanese-managed *Harbin Daily.* Suddenly an atmosphere of insecurity and tension covered the city.

In fact, all of these hostile acts were the work of the Japanese military, including Lieutenant-Colonel Hyakutake Haruyoshi, chief of the army's special service agency (*tokumu kikan*) at Harbin, and Amakasu Masahiko, who had been involved in the famous murder of Ōsugi Sakae.* They had resorted to the familiar tactic of creating an incident that would serve as a pretext for a military operation. The Kwantung Army, fully cognizant of the game being played, judged the time had come to undertake the Harbin operation. It justified its decision in this way: "Harbin is our only economic base in northern Manchuria and feeds our South Manchuria Railway. If we lose it, all our rights and interests will be gone and the efforts of 4,000 Japanese will have been wasted. The outcome may be different under a stronger cabinet, but such a result is inevitable as long as we have the present weak-kneed cabinet."

Not only the military but the consul-general at Harbin, Ōhashi Chūichi, entirely went along with the plot. In contrast to Mukden, Kirin, and Tsitsihar, where military and diplomatic personnel clashed on almost anything, at Harbin there was complete agreement. On September 21 Ōhashi telegraphed Consul-General Hayashi at Mukden, "If an incident occurs here, I will have to ask for troops to be dispatched, since our residents have no military force and will be entirely wiped out without such help."

Harbin had, of course, been an important base of operations for Tsarist Russia. Though the situation was somewhat different under the revolutionary regime, the Kwantung Army could not ignore the Soviet Union if it were to send an expedition to Harbin. On this matter, the Kwantung Army had bits of information at its disposal, such as that the Soviet representative at Harbin had warned against a Japanese expedition, that

---

*Ōsugi Sakae was an anarchist who, with his wife and young nephew, was strangled following the arrest of radical leaders in the atmosphere of unrest that followed the Tokyo earthquake of September 1923.

a portion of the Red Army had left Manchouli, and that the Soviet consul at Manchouli had offered the Chinese garrison commander the use of 3,000 Red troops. On the basis of these reports and rumors, the military in Mukden judged:

> While the Soviet Union might exhibit its readiness to use force, depending on how we proceed, and while the Chinese would undoubtedly try to solicit Soviet help, internal conditions in Russia would seem to be such that it could not do much more than engage in propaganda work. By means of propaganda it will try to prevent our influence from extending to northern Manchuria, while using Chinese to gain its own advantage. Russia might possibly take advantage of the present opportunity to occupy the Chinese Eastern Railway by force. . . . But it will not do so at the risk of war with Japan. In conclusion, while there is always the danger of war with the Soviet Union if we move to Harbin, we should be able to avoid it by careful planning and instantaneous execution of our plans, giving the Russians no opportunity to respond except with passive tactics.[16]

The Kwantung Army's view of the situation vis-a-vis the Soviet Union was optimistic. There is no reason to believe that such a view was based on accurate information and careful analysis, but it nevertheless proved to be correct; we now know that Soviet policy at that time was one of maintaining the status quo and avoiding interference in other countries' affairs. At any rate, the Kwantung Army judged that here was a good opportunity to extend its influence to northern Manchuria. On September 22 Commander-in-Chief Honjō ordered his troops to be ready for an expedition to Harbin. It was necessary to set the target date after the 22nd, when the Korea Army's 39th Brigade was to arrive and free Kwantung Army troops from the duty of protecting Mukden. Honjō telegraphed Tokyo, "As the situation grows more and more serious in the Harbin area, we are planning to gather the 2nd Division in Ch'angch'un as soon as practicable."

It was at this juncture that the Kwantung Army received the instructions from Tokyo, already cited, enjoining it to maintain existing military positions and refrain from sending troops to Harbin for the time being. Army Minister Minami specifically advised that the government's fundamental policy was not to advance troops north of Ch'angch'un or to police railways other than the South Manchuria Railway. Minami had already dispatched Colonel Andō Rikichi, chief of the Military Service Section, to Mukden to convey personally the army minister's intent.

Obviously, the supreme command was determined to apply the policy of nonexpansion to Harbin.

There were two reasons for this. First, the central army authorities were becoming sensitive to the growing uneasiness among leading circles in Japan—the emperor, elder statesmen, the cabinet, political parties (especially the Minseitō), and the navy. The army feared these groups might turn entirely against it and that public opinion too might become antagonized. Second, the supreme command feared an open clash with the Soviet Union. Not that it disagreed with the Kwantung Army's optimistic assumptions regarding the Soviet Union, but it felt Japan's leadership was unwilling to sanction a strong policy toward Russia. Unless the prevailing fear of Soviet power could somehow be eradicated, it was judged unwise to precipitate a crisis by carrying out an expedition to Harbin.

Undaunted by the decision in Tokyo, the Kwantung Army continued to urge military action in Harbin. Itagaki telegraphed Nagata: "We should never be satisfied with passive propaganda warfare but should take advantage of this great opportunity to solve the Manchurian question. If we at least manage to create a new state here, we will never have to worry about hostile propaganda." Honjō followed up by telegraphing his view that a grave decision was called for to save Harbin and Kirin, especially as the Japanese consul-general at Harbin was requesting an expedition. On the afternoon of September 22 a final telegram was received in Tokyo, reporting that the Kwantung Army recognized the time for action had come.

The supreme command, already dismayed by these communications, was shocked when it heard a radio report in the late afternoon that Japanese troops had entered Harbin. This proved false, but Vice Chief of Staff Ninomiya was so alarmed that he ordered Imamura to telegraph Mukden to ascertain the truth. The inquiry, sent at 9:10 P.M., reminded the Kwantung Army commander that dispatching troops to Harbin without prior approval of Tokyo was "strictly forbidden." This small episode reveals how fearful the supreme command was of possible unilateral action by the Kwantung Army.

When on September 21 the Kwantung Army unilaterally sent troops to and occupied Kirin, a new situation had arisen, confronting the supreme command with the need for fresh thinking. Now that the principle of maintaining existing military positions had been violated, central headquarters had to decide how far such violation should be tolerated. There was a need to clearly define the limits of the Kwantung Army's military action. Here again Tokyo's thinking was guided by the framework of Plan One.

On the morning of September 23 Sugiyama, Ninomiya, Koiso, and Araki met and agreed on the following "Principles on the Limits of Military Occupation."

> 1. The Four Eastern Provinces are virtually in a state of anarchy. Under the circumstances, if the army is to perform its primary functions and maintain its own security, it will be necessary to place railway guard units along the external limits of the South Manchuria Railway. At the least it will be necessary to control (a) in the west, the Liao River line, embracing Chengchiat'un, [Shuangliao], Hsinmin, and Yingk'ou, and (b) in the east, the Kirin-Hailung area.
>
> 2. Depending on China's military response and the intensity of anti-Japanese activities, it may become necessary to extend these spheres of defense and militarily occupy (a) in the west, the T'aonan-T'ungliao-Tahushan zone, and (b) in the east, Tunhua and the Chientao-Hunch'un area.

This memorandum indicates that military leaders in Tokyo were at this time prepared to endorse occupation of an extensive area, along both sides of the South Manchuria Railway and including Chientao, now that the policy of the military status quo had been violated. At the same time, they were not willing to extend the sphere of action either to northern Manchuria, including Harbin, where Soviet influence was considerable, or to the area west of the Liao River and beyond to Jehol, where Chang Hsueh-liang's power remained.

The memorandum needed to be presented to and approved by Chief of Staff Kanaya and Army Minister Minami. The former at first readily consented to the principles therein shown, but Minami objected vehemently and even persuaded Kanaya to take a common stand against the memorandum. Minami insisted that the sphere of operation should be confined to the South Manchuria Railway zone, except that the forces already diverted to Kirin should be kept there. He visited Kanaya's residence and after two hours of talk succeeded in obtaining the chief of staff's concurrence.[17] As a result, late on the night of the 23rd members of the Army Ministry and General Staff conferred again. Imamura and Koiso strongly opposed Minami's view, and it was decided that the vice chief of staff, the vice army minister, and the chief of the Military Affairs Bureau of the Army Ministry should visit Minami and explain their position. Minami received them, expressed appreciation of their effort, but still held to his view, saying the army should concede minor matters and concentrate on solving the Manchurian question. This task could be facilitated, he asserted, by stationing all the troops, except those that had been dispatched to Kirin, in the South Manchuria Railway zone and giving them freedom of action.

Minami's strong stand seems to have been due to peculiar circumstances at the time. His freedom of action had been restricted, first, by Prime Minister Wakatsuki's report to the Throne on September 22. The report confirmed that no expedition would be undertaken to protect nationals in Harbin and Chientao; in case of emergency, residents would be evacuated. The memorial had not been preceded by a cabinet decision on the matter, as was usually the case. Wakatsuki had simply based his report on the cabinet decision on nonexpansion of the conflict, and thereby tried to forestall extensive action by the military. Secondly, Minami had bound his own hands. On the afternoon of September 23 the prime minister summoned the army, foreign, and finance ministers to discuss the Kirin expedition. As the latter two insisted on a withdrawal of forces from Kirin, Minami resorted to a bargain; to win his colleagues' consent to the expedition, he declared there would be no further expedition by the Kwantung Army outside of Kirin.[18] Thus, through different routes the army minister and the cabinet had come to the same conclusion: it was necessary to confine military action within the South Manchuria Railway zone, with the sole exception of Kirin, which the 2nd Division had already occupied. This position was in direct contrast to the stand taken by all other military leaders in Tokyo, with the possible exception of Kanaya, that spheres of military action be extended beyond the railway zone.

The conflict between the two opposing policies was solved in the army minister's favor. On September 24 General Staff officials, including Tatekawa, who had just returned from Mukden, tried once again to persuade Minami to change his mind. All to no avail. Minami stood his ground and secured anew Chief of Staff Kanaya's agreement.[19] Under the circumstances, nothing could be done except to revise the draft "Principles on the Limits of Military Occupation." This was done, and a modified instruction, drafted by Imamura, was sent to the Kwantung Army:

The chief of staff, appreciative of the efforts being made by the army minister in the cabinet, has accepted his view that it will be best to endorse and conform to the government's policy, so long as it does not interfere with the fundamental objective of settling the Manchurian question. Accordingly . . . now that the first stage of military action has been completed, we consider it advantageous for the Kwantung Army to recombine small units outside the railway zone, avoid permanent occupation of Chengchiat'un, Hsinmin, and Tunhua, withdraw from Kirin if the situation permits it, and preserve intact the main force of the army in the South Manchuria Railway zone. These steps will help reveal the army's fair attitude, enable the army minister to act efficiently in the cabinet, and be of advantage from a general point of view as we try to achieve the ultimate objective. We are sending Major-General Hashimoto [Toranosuke] to you to convey our intent in detail.

The telegram was sent in the late afternoon of September 24. Simultaneously, the chief of staff instructed Commander-in-Chief Honjō never to undertake the Harbin expedition. In an accompanying telegram from the vice chief of staff it was explained that the army had decided to honor the government's policy of withdrawing nationals from Chientao and Harbin in case of emergency. This decision was unalterable, for the policy had already been reported to the emperor and the cabinet had determined to deal with an emergency without recourse to force. Similar instructions were sent to the Korea Army. Army Minister Minami's personal effort had resulted in the cancellation of premeditated expeditions to Chientao and Harbin.

Tsitsihar: The Kwantung Army's Offensive

The Kwantung Army's northward thrust had been stalled. But the idea was never given up, and Tokyo was not likely to be able to impose its will forever. Actually, although the Harbin expedition had been called off, the army central authorities expected that the Kwantung Army would seize another opportunity to go north. The anticipated occurred in November, when a sudden thrust to Tsitsihar was made.

Already on September 22 and 24 part of an army corps was sent to Chengchiat'un and T'aonan, respectively. The Kwantung Army had also approached Chang Hai-p'eng to draw him over to its side. The attempt was successful, and on October 1 Chang, hitherto nominally tied to Chang

Hsueh-liang's regime as its T'ao-Liao regional commander, broke with the latter and set himself up as "commander of peace preservation at the frontier." He then prepared to move north toward Heilungchiang province under the Kwantung Army's support.

Standing against Chang Hai-p'eng was Wan Fu-lin, military governor of Heilungchiang and concurrently deputy commander of the Northeast Border Defense Army, who was at that time in Peiping. On October 7 Wan ordered the main force of the provincial army to assemble in Tsitsihar, and the next day he appointed as its commander Ma Chan-shan, commander of the Heilungchiang garrison army and the 3rd Infantry Brigade. To halt Chang Hai-p'eng's northward push, which began on October 15, the Heilungchiang army burnt bridges in the Nonni river region at T'ailai and Chiangchiao. This gave the Kwantung Army just the sort of excuse it had been waiting for. The T'aonan-Angangch'i Railway that ran over the bridges had been constructed with Japanese capital. Moreover, this was just the time when farm products from north Manchuria were being shipped by the railway; the destruction of the bridges was estimated to have cost the South Manchuria Railway ¥5 million as a result of the loss of this lucrative shipping.

Furthermore, just at this time a Japanese military plane flying over the area was fired upon by the Heilungchiang army; it dropped several bombs in retaliation. These incidents gave the Kwantung Army a good case for advocating punitive measures. It called for speedy reconstruction of the bridges by the South Manchuria Railway before freezing weather arrived. Although the Heilungchiang authorities promised to repair the bridges themselves, the Japanese had their own plans. As they telegraphed Tokyo on October 24:

> Concerning the destruction by the Heilungchiang army of the Nonni river bridges belonging to the T'aonan-Angangchi Railway, we have urged the South Manchuria Railway and the consulate-general to start repair work immediately. They are in general agreement with such a policy but seem worried about the League of Nations' response. . . . We hope you will exert pressure where needed to carry out this plan. If repair work is to be carried out, the Kwantung Army will assist it and upon completion forbid the use of the bridges to the Chinese armies.

This was not all. On October 24 the Kwantung Army decided to dispatch units of the 2nd Division to railway stations south of T'aonan, on the pretext that more than a thousand bandits had attacked the T'aonan-Ssup'ingchieh Railway, causing it to stop operations.

The supreme command judged from these moves that the Kwantung Army intended eventually to move to Tsitsihar. Some felt it should be warned against such action, at least until the central authorities' "fundamental attitude" toward the north Manchuria question changed. But in the end no warning was issued, as Imamura and Tatekawa were both absent from Tokyo at the time and Shigetō Chiaki, chief of the China Section of the General Staff, did not feel an expedition to T'aonan was inappropriate.[20] Unmindful of the debate in Tokyo, the Kwantung Army made plans, on October 26, to send even larger forces to Chengchiat'un and T'aonan.

Meanwhile, in Tsitsihar the Japanese army had created a special service agency. Its chief, Major Hayashi Yoshihide, arrived on October 26 and the next day presented a demand to Ma Chan-shan, the acting head of the provincial government, for speedy repair of the damaged bridges. If the repair work should not be completed by November 3, he threatened, the task would be carried out by Japanese. Hayashi knew full well that the repair would take at least two weeks, even if carried out by the South Manchuria Railway. He made the impossible demand in the knowledge that the Kwantung Army was looking for a convenient pretext to move into Heilungchiang province and that, if the Chinese should fail to repair the bridges, the Japanese had to have sufficient time to do it themselves before the river was closed by ice.

The supreme command feared that these steps by the Kwantung Army indicated its intention not only to penetrate north Manchuria by all possible methods but also to destroy the incipient Soviet power that was seen standing behind Heilungchiang province. Here again Japan's policy toward the Soviet Union became crucial. The army central authorities resolved still to adhere to the existing policy toward Russia. Accordingly, following deliberations between Army Ministry and General Staff officials, a telegraphic instruction was sent to Mukden on October 30. It said: "It is not proper to compete with Russia's forceful invasion of northern Manchuria by also resorting to force. It is believed much better to let the Russians penetrate to some degree and then crush them with determined effort and strategy. Consequently, until the chief of staff adopts appropriate measures, please refrain from carrying out positive strategic action in north Manchuria." The Army Ministry followed up this message with one of its own, suggesting that the Kwantung Army resort to nonmilitary tactics such as strengthening Chang Hai-p'eng's forces or bribing Ma Chan-shan's army.

By the time these messages reached Mukden, the Kwantung Army had already been in receipt of information, sent by the Harbin special service agency, that the Soviet Union had no intention of interfering with Japanese action in Heilungchiang province so long as Japan did not interfere with the Russian position in the Chinese Eastern Railway. At least this was what the Soviet consul at Harbin had told Consul-General Ōhashi. The Kwantung Army concluded that its judgment regarding Soviet passivity had thereby been proven. Accordingly, it sent the following reply to the supreme command's telegrams:

> It will be a long time, if we allow Russian penetration of northern Manchuria, before it is necessary to resort to resolute action in retaliation; nor does it seem likely that the Soviet Union will in fact move forces into northern Manchuria, to engage in scheming there. . . . It is also impractical now to bribe Ma Chan-shan. But it may be possible to bribe his men and in other ways to undermine his influence. We are trying to do this, although on a very small scale. We agree on the need to strengthen Chang Hai-p'eng's force. We have decided to distribute to them the arms we have seized. Please send at least about ¥3 million for use in secret maneuvers and bribery. . . . Lastly, please understand that it will be most essential for the settlement of the incident to occupy Chinchou and Tsitsihar. This we believe is the best time to do so.[21]

The Kwantung Army seems to have felt the supreme command was generally, though hesitantly, supporting its stand on northern Manchuria. At any rate, the intent of this telegram was clear: the Kwantung Army was determined to push to the north.

As expected, Ma Chan-shan not only did not comply with Major Hayashi's demand for speedy repair of the bridges but also refused to recognize the South Manchuria Railway's right to do the work. His reasoning was that while the railway had been financed with Japanese capital, its creditors had no right to assume the debtor's task to repair the bridges. Instead he promised to have the work carried out by the T'aonan-Angangch'i Railway Administration. Nothing had been done to this end when, on October 30, the Kwantung Army adopted basic directives for the repair of the bridges and for military cover during the repair work. At the same time the 16th Infantry Regiment was ordered to be ready for action. On November 1 a detachment of troops under the commander of the regiment left Ch'angch'un and Kirin and assembled at T'ailai the following night. Ma Chan-shan and Chang Hai-p'eng were notified of these developments and told to withdraw their forces beyond 10 kilometers from the bridges and to refrain from using the railway for military purposes. It was only on the morning of the 2nd, after the Nonni detachment had begun its movement, that the Kwantung Army reported these measures to Tokyo. Obviously it wanted to prevent the supreme command's interfering with its scheme.

Central army authorities were genuinely worried. In view of Ma Chan-shan's reportedly firm attitude, they feared a clash between Japanese and Chinese troops. Such a clash might necessitate a shift in Tokyo's policy of passivity in northern Manchuria.[22] On November 2 the chief of staff telegraphed the commander-in-chief of the Kwantung Army that while military cover could be given to accomplish the repair work, the troops must be withdrawn immediately after the mission was accomplished. "Under no circumstances move the troops farther north than the Nonni River," the telegram added in strong language. This strict command is said to have been added by Tatekawa after he talked with Imamura, who had just returned from Manchuria. Imamura was an exceptional individual, who, unlike so many of his colleagues, was not easily influenced by what he saw and heard in Manchuria.[23] Another telegram sent simultaneously from the Army Ministry explained that speedy repair work and troop withdrawal were necessary, for the Council of the League of Nations was scheduled to open on November 16. It was desirable to give the Foreign Ministry a chance to explain to foreign countries Japan's position on the Manchurian question. In addition to the League, the supreme command must also have been concerned about the reaction of the emperor, the cabinet, and the elder statesmen.

The Kwantung Army, however, was not to be deterred. Its attitude at this time is clearly revealed in an entry in Katakura's diary:

> We intend to use the repair of the Nonni River bridges as a means of strengthening Chang Hai-p'eng's influence and, if things develop in our favor, as an excuse for sending troops in the name of protecting our rights and nationals in the Tsitsihar area along the T'aonan-Angangch'i Railway. The idea was first brought up by Katakura, taken up by Itagaki, and approved by Ishiwara. How to obtain a good excuse for sending troops to northern Manchuria has been a serious problem, and we have all worked

at it. If we cannot carry out the expedition, we will have to give up our strategy in northern Manchuria. Nor can we expect to solve the Manchurian question. Our determination since September 18 has been very strong. We have successfully induced the South Manchuria Railway to cooperate with us, and we have skillfully utilized the Foreign Ministry.

It would appear that Commander-in-Chief Honjō was in an extremely difficult position, caught between his staff on one side and the more passive supreme command on the other. All he could do was telegraph Tokyo that he would do his utmost to carry out the supreme command's policy. He intended to relay Tokyo's instructions to the detachment commander at the Nonni river, but Katakura was opposed and nothing was done.[24]

Honjō's difficulties multiplied after November 4, when Japanese troops at the Nonni river finally clashed with a battalion of the Heilungchiang army. In the morning of the 4th a provincial emissary had arrived to express the Heilungchiang army's peaceful intentions. But when, at noon, the Japanese repair corps advanced toward the Tahsing railway station, it was suddenly attacked by Chinese infantry and artillery forces and forced to retreat. The main force of the Nonni detachment decided to retaliate. Ishiwara, who had been sent to the area, immediately asked Kwantung Army headquarters for additional troops. Accordingly, on the morning of November 5 two infantry battalions and three artillery companies were ordered dispatched to the Nonni.

Honjō now realized the seriousness of the situation. When Katakura, Itagaki, and others again opposed his sending a telegram instructing the Nonni detachment to abide by Tokyo's policy of caution, he decided to act on his own initiative. He personally telephoned the commander of the 2nd Division, reminding him that the reinforcements being sent to the Nonni detachment were solely for the purpose of repairing the bridges and had not been given a mandate to destroy the Heilungchiang forces. Honjō also relayed the supreme command's instruction not to move troops northward and asked the division commander to enjoin his subordinates to contain the incident.[25]

The supreme command in Tokyo took even more drastic steps. It was aware that the Soviet Union had supplied arms to Ma Chan-shan's army and, consequently, considered it unwise to invite trouble with Russia by driving Ma's army farther north. Although, as noted earlier, Tokyo was generally sanguine regarding the possibility of Soviet intervention, it did not want war at that specific moment. Since the Kwantung Army was obviously ignoring such a policy and seemed intent on advancing northward, the supreme command felt it imperative to resort to drastic measures to curb Mukden's extremism. The method employed in this connection was the invocation of the "entrusted right of command," precedent for which had been established during the Russo-Japanese War: the emperor would be asked to entrust the chief of staff with command over operational matters in Manchuria. In other words, the right of supreme command, which belonged to the emperor, would be temporarily and partially delegated to the chief of staff. This meant in effect that Kwantung Army headquarters would be deprived of part of its command authority. On November 5 Chief of Staff Kanaya had an imperial audience and presented a memorial stating:

> It has become necessary to coordinate military action with political action, in view of the intricate political conditions at home and abroad. The Kwantung Army's action must therefore be regulated and controlled. But to obtain an imperial sanction for each command decision not only would be troublesome for His Majesty but, in case urgent decision is needed, might even fail to be timely.

The chief of staff asked that he be entrusted with decision making and command over that part of Kwantung Army decision making relating to minor operational questions. Major decisions were still to be referred to the Throne, and all decisions were to be reported to the emperor for his subsequent approval. Imperial approval was duly given to this memorial. This was an unusual step that revealed the supreme command's determination to control the actions of the Kwantung Army, as well as its fear of the army's northward advance.[26]

The staff officers at Mukden were shocked when they heard of Kanaya's action. Katakura declared that in reaching such a decision Tokyo was in "extreme violation of the right of supreme command" and thereby raised the question of confidence in the Kwantung Army commander. Katakura, Itagaki, Miyake, and the rest of the staff decided to send telegrams of protest. Commander Honjō, no more desirous than they of having the army's decisions controlled at the center, offered to resign but was persuaded to wait until the situation was further clarified. The telegrams sent to Tokyo asked first to which aspect of strategy and tactics the chief of staff's new authority applied. Did it include questions of troop numbers, their sphere of operation, their aims, their tactical operations, or all of these? Second, the officers protested that they could not carry out their mission effectively if their actions were controlled in detail from Tokyo. "If the army commander who is given the task of maintaining peace and order abroad is to function smoothly and adopt adequate and positive measures, he must be given clearly defined instructions through imperial orders." In other words, imperial orders should be issued to give the Kwantung Army broad directives, but these directives should clearly state what new functions had been added to the original task of protecting the Kwantung leasehold and the South Manchuria Railway. Apart from fundamental and broad principles, the commander-in-chief should be given discretion to deal with each situation as he saw fit.[27]

The General Staff was in turn shocked to receive these defiant messages. Some officials insisted that the telegrams, using such extreme language, need not be answered, but a majority, including Tatekawa, decided to calm the Kwantung Army officers and at the same time admonish them in clear language about their basic obligations. Telegrams to this effect were drafted and sent on November 7. The chief of staff's new authority, they began, referred "not only to troop mobilization, military action itself, or spheres of operation, but to that part of Kwantung Army action that, in the judgment of the chief of staff, needs to be directed from the center." The supreme command was resorting to ambiguity to cover any unforeseeable development. This was in line with the abstract phrase in the memorial to the Throne which had requested that the chief of staff be delegated authority "on minor questions, apart from important issues." Concerning the Kwantung Army's functions, Tatekawa's telegram to Miyake stated:

> No new functions have been added to the Kwantung Army; therefore, all your actions must be confined to the limits set by your primary functions. We recognize that there are circumstances in which you have no choice but to exceed these functions slightly, given the character of the present incident. In such cases it will be essential to give due consideration to intricate political conditions at home and abroad and to be flexible, keeping the whole picture in view. His Majesty is especially concerned about this matter. Therefore, it will only be proper for the chief of staff to report for imperial consideration and approval every instance of action on your part that exceeds your original functions. However, since urgency is required and since we do not wish to trouble His Majesty all the time,

we have requested and been granted a right entitling the chief of staff to make decisions and issue commands with respect to certain actions on the part of your army.[28]

Rinsan imei (temporary entrusted order) was the abbreviation for the orders issued by the chief of staff under the right of command delegated by the emperor for a specific duration of time. The first such order was issued on November 5, the day after the new arrangements were given imperial approval. It ordered the commander-in-chief of the Kwantung Army to confine military action in northern Manchuria to occupation of the line crossing Tahsing station and reiterated that no positive strategic action was authorized in northern Manchuria. As expected, Kwantung Army staff officers were furious. Katakura thought the order was an extreme instance of interference with army action. He and Itagaki talked with Honjō and Miyake, and all agreed that the supreme command was depriving the commander-in-chief of his right of command. It was felt that the action of a corps in combat could not be directed in detail even by the commander of the Kwantung Army, much less by the chief of staff in Tokyo. It was, therefore, imperative to try anew to ascertain just what rights had been granted to the chief of staff; the command hierarchy needed to be reclarified. Accordingly, two telegrams were sent to Tokyo. One, from Honjō to Kanaya, asked to be informed of the precise nature of the imperial decree entrusting him with the right of command. "Since the matter will stay with us long, until settlement of the incident, I am afraid it may raise some serious questions concerning the prerogative of supreme command," declared the telegram. The second was from Miyake to Ninomiya and reminded the latter that only the army in the field could judge whether to occupy an enemy area or to pursue and destroy the enemy. Even Kwantung Army headquarters could not give detailed and specific orders on such questions; that was why staff officers were sent to the scene of fighting to give guidance to the field army. Both these telegrams remained unanswered, the central authorities apparently believing no answer was needed. They must have found nothing new in the Kwantung Army's assertions that warranted specific reply.

Because the fighting in the Nonni river area continued and Japanese troops were in difficulty, the Kwantung Army decided to dispatch additional reinforcements. In reporting this, Commander-in-Chief Honjō telegraphed on November 6:

The Japanese army has demonstrated its power against small units of the Chinese army. When confronted with a Chinese army backed up by the Soviet Union, however, we have tended to give an impression of passivity. This has caused the enemy to despise us, making it extremely difficult to carry out our Manchurian strategy. Under the circumstances we have no choice but to lose no opportunity to use all our available forces to strike a blow against the main enemy force in Heilungchiang province, even if this may cause a shortage of manpower elsewhere. Should we do it now, we could accomplish the task in the briefest possible period. I sincerely hope that you will trust me and other officers of the Kwantung Army and leave operational details against the Heilungchiang army to the discretion of the army.

This was a strongly worded message. The supreme command at first criticized it as contrary to the instructions already given. But following deliberations both within the Operations Section and among division chiefs, the General Staff decided to relent somewhat and move slightly toward accommodating Mukden's views. The second "entrusted order," sent in reply to the above telegram, revealed this shift. It confirmed the supreme command's basic policy as laid down in earlier instructions, but it authorized the corps already in the Nonni river area to crush the enemy near Tahsing. Pursuit of the enemy force, however, was to be restricted to the Hsinmin-T'angch'ih-Taputai line, and the Japanese units were to return to the Nonni region immediately after they accomplished their objective. This was a compromise plan designed to allow some leeway to the Kwantung Army while checking its advance to Angangch'i or the Chinese Eastern Railway. Though the General Staff realized that such an instruction from the chief of staff was excessively specific and improper, it was nevertheless "reluctantly" sent to accomplish that purpose.[29]

The instruction arrived just as the Nonni detachment had expelled the Heilungchiang army from the Tahsing area and begun assisting in the repair of the bridge. While some staff officers would have liked to let the Nonni corps pursue the enemy to the Chinese Eastern Railway region, threatening Tsitsihar, Commander-in-Chief Honjō decided to honor Tokyo's order. He was supported by a minority of staff officers who thought any positive action at that juncture would be wasted, for Tokyo was sure to order withdrawal of troops going farther north. As a result, the Nonni commander was told to limit his sphere of operation to the Hsinmin-T'angch'ih-Taputai line; he was, however, authorized to send out reconnaissance planes. Thus there was little likelihood of a further clash between the Kwantung Army and the Heilungchiang forces. Mukden and Tokyo had achieved a semblance of compromise.

The compromise proved to be short-lived. The Kwantung Army was determined to penetrate north Manchuria. Since Ma Chan-shan was the chief obstacle, various plans were considered, ranging from outright military action to force Ma's retirement to more subtle moves to win him over to cooperation with Japan. The latter alternative would be pursued if Chang Ching-hui and Chang Hai-p'eng, whom the Japanese had decided to set up as puppets, proved not equal to their task. But the possibility of a negotiated settlement was dim. When on November 8 and 9 Major Hayashi, under instruction, demanded that Ma discuss with Chang Hai-p'eng a peaceful transfer of power in Tsitsihar, the Heilungchiang general procrastinated, saying he could not see Chang, for Japanese troops were in the way.[30]

After their defeat at Tahsing, most of Ma Chan-shan's forces had retreated to Tsitsihar and Angangch'i, but some had occupied areas along the south side of the Chinese Eastern Railway. This was fortunate from the Kwantung Army's point of view, for it meant that Ma's troops were still close enough to justify defensive action on the part of the Japanese corps. Ma's alleged belligerence could be used to legitimize drastic military measures. After November 6 Katakura did all he could to spread rumors about the warlike intentions of Ma's army and even to instigate the latter to attack the Japanese. When on November 8 Foreign Minister Shidehara sought to protest the Chinese occupation of the Chinese Eastern Railway zone, the Kwantung Army immediately saw to it that no such protest was made. The special service agency at Harbin was told, "We do not like the idea of [Tsitsihar] Consul Shimizu Yaoichi trying only to seek peace"; Ma's army must rather be "guided" to move farther south. The following day Commander-in-Chief Honjō telegraphed Tokyo requesting the dispatch of an additional division to stave off an expected attack by the Heilungchiang army. The reasoning here was that, since the supreme command forbade an offensive against the Chinese forces to the north, the likelihood of a Chinese counterattack had increased; reinforcements were thus essential if the safety of the Nonni detachment and other Japanese positions were to be guaranteed.

Meanwhile, the repair work on the Nonni bridges was nearing completion, and the Kwantung Army inclined more and more to an aggres-

sive posture. At a staff conference on November 10 it was formally resolved to discard the alternative of negotiations with Ma Chan-shan and
resort to an offensive against the Heilungchiang army. As a prelude to
military action, it was decided to present three impossible demands to
Ma: his retirement, his army's withdrawal from Tsitsihar, and occupation by Japanese troops of Lungchiang station to guarantee the safety of
the T'aonan-Angangch'i Railway. It will be noted that there was no demand for a peaceful transfer of power from Ma to Chang Hai-p'eng. It
was omitted because the Chinese had already appealed to the League of
Nations, protesting that such an arrangement constituted interference by
Japan in Chinese domestic affairs. Honjō and Miyake did not want to stir
up trouble again. For this they were criticized by Katakura as lacking
"penetrating ideas, the ability to control others, courage to act with determination, and especially willingness to bear all responsibility."[31]

The demands were presented to Ma Chan-shan on November 11, with
a proviso that they be replied to by the following day. Ma flatly rejected
the demands, saying:

> 1. Ma Chan-shan's retirement cannot be seriously entertained in view
> of the disorder and distress such action would bring to the people of the
> province.
> 2. Time is needed to evacuate troops, numbering more than 10,000,
> from Tsitsihar. A hasty evacuation will bring about a clash between Chinese
> and Japanese forces, as happened at Chiangchiao.
> 3. Your proposal to send part of the army to Lungchiang station seems
> to contradict Ambassador Yoshizawa [Kenkichi]'s declaration to the League
> of Nations that the Japanese army will not occupy north Manchuria.
> 4. It is hoped that the Japanese commander-in-chief will explicitly state
> whether, in the event that Ma Chan-shan retires and the Heilungchiang
> army is evacuated, governmental authority in the province is to be trans-
> ferred peacefully to Chang Hai-p'eng or exercised by the Japanese army.

The Kwantung Army decided this reply was unsatisfactory and justified military action. Ma was simply told that this was no time to be
discussing the hypothetical question raised in his fourth point. All talks
with Ma were now terminated, and on November 11 an order was issued to the 2nd Division directing it to gather its main force in the Tahsing area.

Since authorization for action was not yet forthcoming from the supreme command, the Kwantung Army turned to the task of convincing

Tokyo of the seriousness of the situation. On the night of November 10 a telegram was sent describing the plight of the army in view of the enemy's superior strength and repeating the plea for an additional division. "If the request is not granted quickly," the telegram concluded, "we may be forced to resort to unilateral action for self-defense in order to preserve the honor of the imperial army." The supreme command was unmoved by such threatening language. The vice chief of staff telegraphed back, saying: "It is feared that military action based solely on local military intelligence and judgment will complicate the overall picture, damage national unity, and even ruin the great achievements of the Kwantung Army since the beginning of the conflict. The chief of staff is absolutely opposed, in particular, to offensive action in the Angangch'i area as contrary to national policy."

In actuality, this strong stand was never consistently maintained. There is evidence that just about this time some important civilian officials were beginning to shift their stand in favor of the Kwantung Army. A notable example was Consul-General Hayashi Kyūjirō at Mukden. He had initially been strongly opposed to the military, but after the eruption of the Heilungchiang phase of the conflict, he seems to have judged that he was powerless to stem the tide and began to show a willingness to reach a compromise with the military. Indicative of the shift was the telegram he sent to Shidehara on November 11. "Viewing the situation in north Manchuria and the attitude of the Heilungchiang army," he said, "one cannot escape the feeling that the prestige of the empire has declined considerably since before the Nonni expedition. I fear not only that in the future our position in north Manchuria will be very unfavorable, but also that there will be obstacles to solving the Manchurian question and settling the Sino-Japanese dispute." Hayashi stated that he had reluctantly come to the same conclusions as the commander-in-chief of the Kwantung Army, that there was no room for a political solution of the north Manchuria question and that a quick expedition to Tsitsihar was imperative. A few days later he saw Uchida Yasuya, president of the South Manchuria Railway, who had just come back from a month's stay in Tokyo. As will be noted, Uchida had become a self-styled spokesman for the Kwantung Army. He expressed his satisfaction that the army was now determined to "punish" the Heilungchiang army. It was a measure of Hayashi's changed attitude that he now agreed with Uchida, and together they concluded that "the matter was one of life and death for the country and required a firm commitment to carry through positive action." They decided to recommend a Tsitsihar expedition to the prime minister and the foreign minister; in addition Hayashi was to return to Tokyo to press these views personally on the central government.

The army central authorities, too, were subtly changing their stand on north Manchuria. It is recorded that on November 11 they decided first to present proposals to Ma Chan-shan in line with the cabinet's policy and then, depending on the outcome, to give fresh instructions to the Kwantung Army. Three days later the terms of these proposals were telegraphed to Mukden. Ma's army was to be requested to evacuate to areas north of (and including) Tsitsihar and to promise not to send troops south of the Chinese Eastern Railway. The T'aonan-Angangch'i Railway, administered by its own railway administration, was not to be tampered with in any way whatsoever by Ma's forces. If that should happen, the Japanese were immediately to take necessary and effective countermeasures. If Ma carried out these demands by November 25, the Japanese detachment in the Nonni river area was to be withdrawn immediately to areas south of T'aonan and east of Chengchiat'un. The General Staff's third "entrusted order," sent simultaneously with the above instruction, authorized the Kwantung Army to take independent military action in self-defense if Ma refused to accept the demands or, having accepted them, failed to carry them out. The supreme command's policy here outlined did not entirely endorse the far-reaching schemes being developed in Manchuria. But it clearly showed a departure from the policy of absolutely vetoing a Kwantung Army advance to Tsitsihar. Here was a significant shift in Tokyo's stand.

Even the cabinet now retreated a step; it accepted the army's new policy on north Manchuria. There is no question that by then Shidehara's resistance to the military was weakening. The most crucial factor behind the change seems to have been the October Incident. Although the conspiracy itself was devoid of serious content, it nevertheless produced decisive political effects, just as Lieutenant-Colonel Hashimoto Kingorō and his fellow plotters had expected. It must be remembered that there were as yet no "objective" conditions favorable to drastic political change in Japan. The League of Nations had on October 24 voted to demand the withdrawal of Japanese troops from areas of conflict by November 16, when the Council was next scheduled to meet. Internally, the emperor and senior statesmen were growing more and more uneasy over the developing situation. The shift in Tokyo's policy on the north Manchurian question must therefore be attributed to the peculiar atmosphere following the October Incident, as well as to the Kwantung Army's powerful initiative. The spectacle of army terrorism was reducing the cabinet, and even the supreme command, to impotence.

The supreme command, especially the Operations Section, was well aware of the serious implications of the policy change. Once the Kwantung Army was sanctioned to move to Tsitsihar, it was felt, it would never be satisfied with merely attacking Ma Chan-shan's army. The Chinese forces might retreat for the time being, but they would inevitably come back as "bandits" to pester the Japanese army. The Kwantung Army, as a result, would find it necessary to hold Tsitsihar and bring about the establishment of a new government. Since the severe winter season was approaching, it would become essential to station a large force in the area. Thus considered, the authorization for offensive action could only be a prelude to larger reinforcements for the Kwantung Army. The supreme command's new policy meant that it would not hesitate to accept this logical necessity. It is recorded that Army Minister Minami agreed with such an inference but that the Intelligence Division of the General Staff and the Military Section of the Army Ministry, which should have been more concerned with the issue, showed little interest.

The Kwantung Army, on its part, was not very pleased even with the central authorities' new policy. It considered that the proposals to Ma Chan-shan as drafted in Tokyo were not far-reaching enough. As a result, they were unilaterally and significantly altered when presented to Ma. A time limit was added, demanding that he reply by November 16, and the request for his troops' withdrawal to areas north of (and including) Tsitsihar was changed to simply "north of Tsitsihar." These terms were communicated to Ma on November 15. Already by then skirmishes had taken place between Japanese and Chinese soldiers in T'angch'ih and elsewhere. The Kwantung Army judged that since Ma Chan-shan was not likely to accept the proposals, there would be extended fighting on the 17th or the 18th. The supreme command, receiving these reports, concluded that fighting near Angangch'i was inevitable. It recognized the need to augment the Japanese forces as much as possible and ordered three air regiments to proceed immediately to the scene of conflict. The 4th Mixed Brigade, on its way to Dairen to relieve the 39th Brigade, was instructed to land at Pusan in Korea. The vice chief of staff telegraphed Mukden that upon arrival of these reinforcements "it would be advantageous to resort to offensive action in order to deal a severe blow to the enemy."

As expected, Ma Chan-shan failed to reply by November 16. This was welcome news to the Kwantung Army, determined as it was to start action on the 17th or 18th. It had feared that Ma might back down, knowing that Japan was sending reinforcements. If that happened, the supreme command might revert to a passive stand. Time was an important factor, and the Kwantung Army did not want to forfeit the opportunity by unnecessary delay. The central authorities seem to have understood such a tactic in Manchuria and wanted on their part to retain control over the Kwantung Army. On November 16 the General Staff ordered, on the basis of the entrusted right of command, that Japanese troops should not permanently occupy Tsitsihar, although they might have to enter the city and even advance farther north to crush the enemy force. The Kwantung Army, moreover, was not to use the Chinese Eastern Railway, and military action along the railway was to be purely defensive. The main part of the Japanese units engaged in action should, after their mission was completed, return to Chengchiat'un and its eastern vicinity.

The telegram was sent out at 9:10 P.M. No formal cabinet approval had been given, but it was assumed that the cabinet at its meeting of November 16 had arrived at a more or less similar decision on the Tsitsihar campaign. The assumption was basically correct. Cabinet ministers may in fact have been opposed to a Tsitsihar expedition, but none spoke out clearly against it at the meeting of November 16. The shock of the October Incident must still have been felt. On one point, however, the cabinet stood adamant. When Army Minister Minami, going beyond the General Staff's policy, suggested the occupation of Tsitsihar, he was confronted with solid opposition from every other member of the cabinet. Foreign Minister Shidehara threatened to call back the Japanese delegates at the League of Nations; Minseitō members of the cabinet insisted they would have no choice but to resign. Perplexed, Minami visited Prime Minister Wakatsuki the following morning and obtained the latter's consent to the principle that military action at Tsitsihar was wholly defensive and that Japanese troops there would be withdrawn as soon as their task was accomplished. Minami was able to obtain similar approval from other members of the cabinet. To this extent alone the cabinet had shown effective resistance. But the episode revealed Mina-mi's clumsy handling of the matter more than cabinet strength as such. Minami had to take the humiliating step of asking the General Staff to alter the date of its telegram from 9:10 P.M. on November 16 to 10:10 A.M. on November 17.

Added light on this episode is shed by the emperor's attitude. He was then at Kumamoto, attending the army's grand maneuvers. A memorial for his consideration requested his approval of the sending of the air regiments; no mention was made of the Tsitsihar expedition. The emperor, however, had heard of Minami's proposal at the cabinet meeting, and he expressed the fear that the chief of staff might take advantage of his entrusted right of command to order troops to Tsitsihar. His military aide-de-camp replied that this was unlikely, although the army in the field might resort to such action in self-defense. In the end the emperor's suspicions proved correct, for the chief of staff did not think it necessary to obtain imperial approval for ordering troops to Tsitsihar; he thought it could be dealt with within his delegated right of supreme command. Thus the emperor was kept in the dark about the real intentions of the military. Even when the emperor's fears were communicated to the General Staff, the latter judged that there had been no violation of the right of supreme command. The reasoning apparently was that Minami had somehow managed to obtain cabinet approval, and thus all formalities had been followed.[32]

Since there had been much confusion concerning the Tsitsihar expedition, the General Staff decided to dispatch some of its officials to Manchuria to supplement telegraphic instructions. Accordingly, Vice Chief of Staff Ninomiya left Tokyo on the night of November 17, accompanied by a few subordinate officers. The emissaries were under instructions to bring about better coordination between the intent of the supreme command and the action of the Kwantung Army. They carried blank sheets of paper bearing the chief of staff's signature, which were to be used if necessary for writing up specific orders on the spot. But before they arrived, the Japanese detachment in the Nonni river area began an offensive on the night of November 18. The main force of the 2nd Division had also started action without waiting for the arrival of the 4th Mixed Brigade. The Heilungchiang army, under attack since early morning, began to retreat and was pursued by the Japanese division. By the 19th the division had entered the city of Tsitsihar without incident. Chinese officials in the city had been approached beforehand through the Japanese special service agency, and they were instrumental in making the Japanese entry smooth and bloodless.

The Kwantung Army had judged, after the battle of Tahsing, that extreme care was needed in dealing with the Soviet question in north Manchuria. It was not considered likely that the Soviet Union would actually send troops to fight the Japanese army in Manchuria. Rather, it was thought possible that Russian assistance, material and moral, would be given the Heilungchiang army to maintain a balance of power in north Manchuria, that propaganda work by the Russians would be intensified to check a Japanese advance, and that White Russians might plot anti-Japanese moves in view of their strong anti-Japanese feelings in that part of Asia. There was even a possibility that while the Kwantung Army pursued the Heilungchiang army beyond the Chinese Eastern Railway, two or three Soviet divisions stationed at the border might suddenly cross the border and attack Japanese troops from behind. If that should happen, the Japanese army would have to withdraw to the right bank of the Nonni river and wait for reinforcements. For this reason extreme caution had to be taken before the Kwantung Army advanced beyond the Chinese Eastern Railway and engaged in action in the Soviet army's sphere of influence.

As of November 19, when Tsitsihar fell, there were no reports of Soviet troop movement at the frontier. Relieved, Kwantung Army headquarters went ahead with devising strategy against the Soviet Union. In a policy memorandum adopted that day it was decided that in the event of Soviet intervention Japanese forces should take either Hsinganlingchan, the Nientzushan region, or Chinghsing, in that order of preference. To achieve the goal of ultimately expelling Soviet influence from north Manchuria, Ting Ch'ao, commander of the Chinese Eastern Railway guards army, was to be induced to make raids on the railway as a prelude to a general offensive against the Soviet army. Hsi Hsia at Kirin was to be ordered to advance a unit to Ningan to cooperate with Ting Ch'ao's army and check any westward advance by Soviet troops. These provocative measures were designed to incite counteraction by the Soviet Union, presumably a crossing of the border. The Japanese army could then take on the Soviet army, give it a quick and decisive blow, and destroy Soviet influence in north Manchuria.

As often happened in Kwantung Army planning, the proposed strategy was never carried out. On November 23 it was suddenly decided to discontinue the offensive strategy against the Soviet Union. The crucial factor in this shift was a telegram from Itagaki, who had been dispatched on a mission to Harbin and Tsitsihar. The telegram relayed the views of Japanese officials at Harbin that there was no need for an expedition to that area since anti-Japanese agitation had disappeared following the fall of Tsitsihar. Rather, the prospects for a peaceful penetration of north Manchuria seemed to have improved. Secondly, Itagaki reported that the Soviet authorities in Harbin had been demoralized by the failure of their attempt to support Ma Chan-shan and were not likely to resort to forceful action in the near future. Under the circumstances, Itagaki suggested that Japan secretly urge the Chinese to stage a coup against the Communist organs in Harbin. This seemed a timely and ingenious scheme that could completely wipe out Russian influence in north Manchuria. Even if it failed, it would not have done Japan any harm; and if it succeeded, Japan's position vis-a-vis the Soviet Union would have been strengthened. This telegram induced the Kwantung Army staff officers to cancel the Soviet strategy of November 19. Commander-in-Chief Honjō was "overjoyed," for he had not been very sanguine about an anti-Soviet strategy at that stage.[33]

Meanwhile, in Tsitsihar the Kwantung Army had turned to a Chinese general, Chang Ching-hui, to organize a new provincial government for Heilungchiang. Chang had consented to do so, and arrangements had been made for his entrance into the city on November 20, soon after the expected evacuation by the Heilungchiang army. When the day arrived, however, Chang suddenly refused to enter the city and insisted first on a coalition with Ma Chan-shan. Itagaki surmised that Chang's change of attitude was due to his fear that the Japanese army might withdraw soon afterward, to his own poor financial state and that of the province, and to the difficulty of inducing Ma to retain control over the remnants of the Heilungchiang army. Accordingly, Itagaki worked to bring about a Chang-Ma coalition, to be preceded by the Kwantung Army's occupation of Tsitsihar and procurement of funds for administering provincial affairs.

It was on November 20 too that Vice Chief of Staff Ninomiya arrived at Mukden. His primary mission was to enforce the supreme command's decision to stop Kwantung Army occupation of Tsitsihar. As soon as he was confronted with the staff officers' unusual determination on this point,

however, he changed his mind. Perhaps to avoid a complete break between Mukden and Tokyo, he began agreeing with the Kwantung Army's position. On November 22 he telegraphed Tokyo: "Owing to some
hesitation on the part of Chang Ching-hui, some delay seems inevitable
in our army's withdrawal from Tsitsihar; it must stay there to maintain
order in Heilungchiang province. The commander-in-chief, however, is
doing his best to hasten withdrawal of the main force, which he hopes
to accomplish in about two weeks. Given present conditions, I also think
a two week delay is unavoidable." But the General Staff felt itself bound
by the cabinet decision on the Tsitsihar question.

Realizing that Ninomiya's message in effect expressed the Kwantung
Army's opposition to quick withdrawal, the Operations Section felt it was
essential for the prestige of the nation and the army to carry out the
promised withdrawal at least once. Consequently, on November 24 the
chief of staff instructed the Kwantung Army commander to withdraw from
Tsitsihar the main expeditionary force, except for one infantry regiment,
"without regard to other considerations and as quickly as possible." The
remaining regiment too was to be evacuated in two weeks. A follow-up
telegram was sent to Ninomiya, explaining the supreme command's decision.

> As you know, we approved the Kwantung Army's offensive only because
> it seemed desirable to let it take unilateral action in self-defense; we never
> intended to link it to the establishment of a new regime. Should evacua-
> tion be delayed because of political considerations regarding the new re-
> gime, it is feared that the army would be betraying its own declared in-
> tentions and will invite complete loss of confidence in itself both at home
> and abroad. . . . Of course, we hope that once withdrawal is accom-
> plished, the new regime might be induced to request the stationing of
> part of our forces, thus enabling us to effect a semipermanent occupation
> of Tsitsihar. Under the present circumstances, however, it seems best first
> to evacuate troops completely, to demonstrate our fairness, as well as to
> facilitate the execution of our later plans.

These two telegrams again irritated Kwantung Army officers. Ishiwara insisted that they should ignore the instructions or explicitly resist
them, since what they had been told to do was hardly practicable. After
a heated debate, Katakura drafted a reply, which was telegraphed to Tokyo on November 25. It opposed any immediate evacuation of troops
from Tsitsihar for two reasons: first, the safety of the T'aonan-Angangch'i

Railway had to be guaranteed; second, such a withdrawal would encourage Ma Chan-shan to rebuild his strength and decide against submitting to Japan. Army headquarters in Tokyo were in turn repelled by this message, which was seen as tantamount to a rejection of troop evacuation and an unwillingness to submit to the authority of the supreme command. Accordingly, once again the ultimate weapon was resorted to, and a fifth "entrusted order" was issued enjoining the Kwantung Army to carry out the evacuation of the forces immediately "in order to preserve the honor of the nation and the army and in consideration of the overall international situation." According to General Staff sources, the telegram "was a result of strong determination on the part of the supreme command and demanded the complete subordination of the Kwantung Army to the intent of the central headquarters." It was believed that if the commander-in-chief at Mukden still hesitated, his removal and that of his staff officers would have to be seriously considered.[34]

The officers at Mukden were shocked by this telegram. Chief of Staff Miyake is said to have "shed tears that all their efforts had come to nothing." Staff officers agreed that they should all resign at once. Honjō felt differently; although he would also resign, having sent his men to death for no purpose, he thought he had no choice but first to carry out the entrusted order. Ishiwara and Katakura insisted, however, that it would be "contradictory" for Honjō to carry out Tokyo's command and then resign. As they saw the situation, there were only three alternatives open to the commander-in-chief: somehow to contrive not to comply with the order, to resign immediately, or to execute the order and appoint new staff officers. Honjō tried to persuade Ishiwara and others to accept the third alternative rather than the second as they were demanding. No conclusion was reached at this time, for the principals at Mukden decided to wait upon Itagaki's return from Tsitsihar.[35]

Fortunately for all concerned, on November 26 the "second Tientsin incident" (see below) occurred. It involved severe fighting between the Japanese protocol force and Chinese soldiers. As the Kwantung Army received reports on the incident, it decided to send reinforcements to north China. Thus, the main part of the 2nd Division that had occupied Tsitsihar was diverted to Chinchou. Only the 3rd Infantry Brigade and the 9th Air Regiment were left in Tsitsihar. The dispute between Mukden and Tokyo on the Tsitsihar occupation was thereby solved quite accidentally. Moreover, a small Japanese force was destined to remain at Tsitsihar. The situation in north Manchuria was in a state of flux, for Ma Chan-shan was in constant communication not only with Chang Ching-hui but also with Chang Hsueh-liang, Wan Fu-lin, and Chang Tso-hsiang. As the Kwantung Army started its campaign in the south at the end of November, it was feared that the Heilungchiang army might try to re-take Tsitsihar. Since there were only some 500 Japanese troops in the area, suffering from cold and exhaustion, a brigade was sent from Muk-den on November 30. This decision was seconded by Ninomiya, who was still in Manchuria, on the grounds that the reinforcement was nec-essary to maintain the Japanese army's prestige. After he returned to Tokyo, Ninomiya was instrumental in bringing about a change in the at-titude of the supreme command. By mid-December it too had accepted the inevitability of stationing a small force at Tsitsihar. A telegram was sent on December 15 authorizing the Kwantung Army to retain a corps in Tsitsihar "as warranted by the situation there."

Chinchou: The Kwantung Army Advances

Chinchou had become the base of the Manchurian army after the fall of Mukden. At the time of the Mukden Incident on September 18, Chang Hsueh-liang, the commander-in-chief of the Northeastern Border De-fense Army, was in Peiping, ostensibly recuperating from an illness caused by typhus. But his primary goal had been elsewhere. Since the end of 1928, when he accepted the Kuomintang flag, he had established close ties with Chiang Kai-shek. The support given Chiang by Chang, with 70,000 troops, had been a crucial factor in causing the defeat of Yen Hsi-shan, Feng Yü-hsiang, and others who had revolted against Nanking in 1930. After the suppression of the revolt, Chang had remained in Pei-ping. As movements against him began to spread in north China, he steadily increased his forces, especially south of the Great Wall, and by September 1931 his troops numbered 115,000.[36] After Mukden fell to the Kwantung Army, he established a military headquarters and a civil government at Chinchou, appointed Chang Tso-hsiang acting com-mander-in-chief, and summoned Jung Chen, Mi Ch'un-lin, and others to the city. Efforts were also made to concentrate in the area the main force of the Fengt'ien army east of the Liao river.

Thus Chinchou had become the base for Chang Hsueh-liang's counterattack. Moreover, the British-built Peiping-Mukden Railway ran through the city. A more cautious army might have hesitated to attack such a center, but not the bullish Kwantung Army. On October 8 it shocked the world by bombing Chinchou. According to an official Kwantung Army account, the bombing was necessary to frustrate a counteroffensive by Chang Hsueh-liang. By early October 200,000 Chinese troops were estimated to have gathered at Chinchou and Tahushan. According to Japanese sources, Chang Hsueh-liang was secretly ordering local governments in Fengt'ien province to obey and pay taxes to the Chinchou government, sending plainclothesmen and spies to Japanese-occupied areas, plotting the assassination of Japanese and of anti-Chang Chinese officials, and employing bandits and ex-soldiers to disturb local peace by means of propaganda. Because of this, continues a Kwantung Army account, "pro-Japanese Chinese and local organs were never at peace, unstable characters appeared everywhere, there were constant rifleshots in the vicinity of Mukden, shops that had resumed business closed again, people began evacuating once more, and there was tremendous insecurity." Under the circumstances, unless steps were taken the Chinchou army could be expected to join forces with bandits and others and resort to action against the Japanese army. Destruction of the Chinchou regime was thus absolutely essential for "securing the peace of the occupied areas, establishing a firm basis for solution of the Manchurian question, and eliminating the base of machinations and plots." Since ground forces could not be used against Chinchou at the time, the Kwantung Army had to resort to aerial attacks. The army was well aware of Tokyo's decision on nonexpansion of hostilities, as well as of the effect the bombing would have on the debate at the forthcoming League Council meeting. However, it was judged that the risk of inaction, with the possible result of augmenting Chang Hsueh-liang's relative strength, outweighed these negative considerations.[37]

This evaluation of Chang Hsueh-liang's policy on the whole seems to have been accurate, although there was undoubtedly much exaggeration. But there seems to have been another important factor behind the decision to bomb Chinchou that is not mentioned in the account above: the political effect of the bombardment. The Kwantung Army wanted to use the shock of the bombing to paralyze Japanese foreign policy and overawe the Nationalist government. One may say that the attack was not so much on Chinchou and Chang Hsueh-liang as on Shidehara's diplomacy and the Nanking government.

To go back to the bombing itself, at 4 o'clock on the afternoon of October 7 Kwantung Army headquarters ordered the 10th Independent Air Squadron to use as many planes as possible to bomb the provincial government buildings in Chinchou and the barracks of the 28th Division. The raid was to accomplish the "destruction of the base of provincial authority," in view of the steady concentration of Chinese troops at Chinchou. If possible, the attacking planes were to photograph enemy defense installations on the right bank of the Taling river. The commander of the 2nd Division, at that time at Ch'angch'un, was also contacted by telephone and ordered to divert part of the 8th Independent Air Squadron, belonging to the division, to cooperate with the 10th Squadron in the raid. Because it was learned that the Chinchou regime usually functioned in the afternoon, the bombing was to take place between noon and 3 o'clock. In accordance with these instructions, thirteen planes left Mukden at noon on October 8, flew over Chinchou at 1:40 P.M., and dropped 75 25-kilogram bombs over the government offices, the barracks of the 28th Division, and Chang Tso-hsiang's residence. Ishiwara accompanied the raid in a passenger plane and studied Chinese troop movements as he observed the attack. At that time the Kwantung Army's planes were not equipped with bomb-release facilities, and it has been said that the bombs were dropped by hand. If true, the raid could not have been very effective. All the same, some innocent civilians were victims of the attack, as U.S. Secretary of State Henry L. Stimson alleged.[38]

The bombing party returned to Mukden at 4:00. The report to Tokyo stated, "The army has sent its aircraft to fly over Chinchou to observe Chinese troop movements and military plans in the area. As the planes were attacked by ground fire, they bombed the Chinese army at around 2 o'clock on the 8th, apparently with some damage to the enemy." This account was obviously contrary to fact. The same story was telegraphed to the Foreign Ministry, the League of Nations, and the Japanese embassy in Washington to legitimize the aerial attack.

The bombing of Chinchou made a profound impression on the Chinese. In Nanking there was fear of a similar attack on the capital itself, and it was reported that field artillery was being installed and prominent officials were being evacuated. Europeans and Americans, remembering the frightening spectacle of city bombings during the last war, became very agitated and criticized the Japanese action. Public opinion abroad denounced Japan. In the League of Nations pressure grew to expedite the convening of the Council. It met on October 13 and eleven days later voted to demand Japanese withdrawal by November 16. The vote was thirteen to one, with Japan alone in opposition.

The army supreme command understood the reasons behind the raid, but it was critical of the Kwantung Army's unilateral decision. If Tokyo had been given prior notice, it might have been able to allay the suspicions of the powers and have presented the raid as a justifiable act. Intelligence Division Chief Hashimoto, who was then in Mukden, was instructed to convey the supreme command's regrets on this score. The Kwantung Army remained adamant. It went so far as to record its opposition to Hashimoto's very presence. There seemed no justification for dispatching an officer from Tokyo to interfere with operational matters in the field. The mutual distrust that existed between Mukden and Tokyo is also illustrated by the fact that whereas the Kwantung Army already intended to overthrow the Chinchou regime, it was only on October 31 that such a possibility was openly suggested to Tokyo.[39]

The protocol force in Tientsin was even more concerned than the Kwantung Army about the Chinchou regime and Chang Hsueh-liang's influence in north China. In mid-October its commander Lieutenant-General Kashii Kōhei telegraphed Honjō at Mukden, saying: "It will not be easy to let Chang Hsueh-liang fall by himself. To facilitate the solution of the Manchurian question, it is necessary not only to wipe out the old Northeastern warlords in Manchuria but also to destroy Hsueh-liang's influence in north China." The protocol force then consisted of only 583 men in Tientsin, 264 at Shanhaikuan, 40 at Ch'inhuangtao, 30 at T'angku, and a company in Peiping. If Chang Hsueh-liang's army should retreat from Chinchou to Shanhaikuan or decide to engage the Japanese force in north China, the protocol force was obviously inadequate to deal with the situation. The first thing necessary was, therefore, to have its strength augmented.

A favorable situation presented itself on November 9, when the "first Tientsin incident" took place. Under the instigation of Colonel Doihara Kenji, some anti-Chang Chinese plainclothesmen attacked the peace preservation corps at Tientsin. Doihara's hope was to use the resulting confusion to abduct the former Manchu emperor P'u Yi, with a view to making him head of a new Manchurian state. The protocol force, on its part, decided to take advantage of the incident to obtain troop increases. Requests were sent immediately to Tokyo.

The General Staff was unsympathetic. On November 12 Chief of Staff Kanaya telegraphed the Tientsin commander: "I am fully aware of your difficulties in having to cope with a grave situation and carry out important tasks with a very small force. I shall give mature consideration to steps to be taken in extreme circumstances. At present, however, overall considerations make it impossible to send you reinforcements. You are instructed to inspire the morale of your men, maintain close contact with related organs, and be prepared to deal with all developments with your existing strength." The General Staff judged that a small increase in the Japanese force would not solve the Chinese question; Chinese provocation and a few Japanese casualties at that stage might even be welcome if they provided a pretext for a large-scale reinforcement.[40]

The protocol force was not to be daunted. Continuing to cooperate with Doihara, it decided to seek help from the Kwantung Army, which was prepared to coordinate action with the force at Tientsin. If a pretext should be provided, the Kwantung Army was willing to send troops to Chinchou and advance toward Shanhaikuan. The Kwantung Army even telegraphed the General Staff on November 29 that such an expedition "would not necessarily be contrary to the supreme command's intentions, if carried out when there was a serious clash between Japanese and Chinese troops." Vice Chief of Staff Ninomiya opposed, reminding Honjō of his responsibility as a senior officer and telling him, "You must act differently from the young staff officers."[41]

Regarding the Chinchou situation, the supreme command's basic policy was to forbear military action unless unusual circumstances developed, such as an offensive action by the Chinese in Chinchou against the Kwantung Army or a serious clash between the two armies in the Peiping-Tientsin area. Otherwise, a less direct method was to be employed; for instance, bandits and their chief might be organized into disciplined bands and encouraged to take over Chinchou. The Kwantung Army felt, however, that the tactic of using Chinese would not suffice. The use of force, coupled with such a device, was considered essential. Accordingly, on November 24 a memorandum was drawn up on "strategy against the Chinese army." In case the Chinese staged an offensive along the Peiping-Mukden Railway, it stated, the Kwantung Army was to meet the challenge at Hsinmin, 60 kilometers northwest of Mukden. If the Chinese fomented trouble behind Japanese lines, the Japanese army was to attack them in the Tahushan-Koupangtzu region. No sooner had the memorandum been drawn up than action began. Japanese and Chinese soldiers clashed near Hsinmin, resulting in a few casualties on both sides.

These active moves on the part of the Kwantung Army angered Secretary of State Stimson. On November 23 he ordered Ambassador W. Cameron Forbes in Tokyo to warn the Japanese government that the continuation of these moves would try American patience and that an advance to Chinchou would certainly frustrate the efforts of the League to obtain a peaceful settlement. Alarmed, Foreign Minister Shidehara pressed the military authorities to give him the truth. According to General Staff sources, Chief of Staff Kanaya told Shidehara that under the circumstances then prevailing there was no likelihood of the Kwantung Army's immediately attacking Chinchou. Kwantung Army moves near Hsinmin, said Kanaya, were for the purpose of exterminating bandits along the South Manchuria Railway and were not intended as a step toward an attack on Chinchou. When Shidehara insisted that he had heard rumors that Ninomiya had informed military and naval attachés abroad of an impending attack on Chinchou, Kanaya assured him there was absolutely no foundation in such reports. He promised to look into the matter and, one hour later, telephoned the foreign minister, reaffirming that the Kwantung Army's action had been directed only against bandits.[42] This exchange provided the background for Shidehara's reply to the United States on November 24 that Japan had no intention of moving into Chinchou. When the Kwantung Army nevertheless moved west of the Liao river on November 26, Stimson's anger was once more aroused, and he made public the earlier exchange between the two governments. Voices were raised in Japan attacking Kanaya for divulging secret military information and Shidehara for violating the right of supreme command. This in turn alarmed Stimson, who was still intent on supporting Shidehara's effort to check military adventurism in Manchuria. Stimson thereupon apologized to Ambassador Debuchi Katsuji and Ambassador Forbes to Shidehara, thus closing an episode in American-Japanese relations.

Meanwhile, on November 26 the "second Tientsin incident" occurred. Since the fall of Tsitsihar on November 19, there had been an air of uncertainty and insecurity in Tientsin as rumors circulated that, emboldened by the Tsitsihar victory, the Japanese army would start a war with China. As if to corroborate these rumors, the Japanese barracks in Tientsin were attacked by Chinese soldiers at 8:20 P.M. on November 26. This again was the result of Colonel Doihara's machinations.

As soon as it received the news, the Kwantung Army decided to "assist the Tientsin Army in its danger." Two infantry battalions were retained at Tsitsihar, but the rest were ordered to move toward Shanhaikuan. On the morning of November 27 the 4th Mixed Brigade and the 2nd Infantry Battalion began moving south along the Peiping-Mukden Railway. The Kwantung Army also asked for help from the Korea Army, which responded by seeking Tokyo's authorization for the dispatch of one mixed brigade to Manchuria. Receiving this information, the Mukden headquarters asked the Korea Army to move its expeditionary force up to Shingishū. Korea Army Commander Hayashi, already famous for his unilateral expedition in September, is said to have been ready once again to send troops to Manchuria without permission from Tokyo.

News of the second Tientsin incident was received in Tokyo just after midnight on November 27. As General Staff officials sat up all night debating the matter, the Kwantung Army's telegram arrived intimating its intention of moving to Shanhaikuan. Some thought the Kwantung Army should be told immediately to cancel the plan, but Operations Division Chief Tatekawa's opinion prevailed. They should wait, he argued, until the situation at Tientsin was somewhat clarified; if an untoward incident should occur in that city, such as a massacre of Japanese residents, Tokyo would be compelled to approve the Kwantung Army's action. When after several hours there seemed no deterioration in the Tientsin situation, the General Staff telegraphed Mukden at 11 o'clock on the morning of November 27 that the Kwantung Army should not send forces west of the Liao river for the purpose of assisting the Tientsin Army. This was followed by another telegram explicitly prohibiting offensive action against Chinchou and ordering that troops be retained east of the Liao. The telegram added that steps were being taken in Tokyo to cope with the Tientsin situation. When after noon the Kwantung Army commander's message was received requesting reinforcements from Korea, he was at once told not to expect any such assistance. These were clear expressions of the supreme command's lack of interest in the Chinchou strategy.

The Kwantung Army, however, completely ignored these orders. Citing clashes at the Taling river and Tahushan, it telegraphed Tokyo that it was impossible to move back the first contingent of the expeditionary force, the 4th Mixed Brigade, east of the Liao. Consequently, the brigade would remain where it was, to be withdrawn as the situation improved. Angered, the supreme command telegraphed back, ordering the complete and instantaneous removal of the troops east of the Liao, "regardless of existing circumstances." The Kwantung Army was instructed to report troop dispositions after the removal was carried out. Simultaneously a longer explanatory telegram was sent to Vice Chief of Staff Ninomiya, who was still in Manchuria. It is obvious that the message was intended for the eyes of the Kwantung Army officers. It said: "We extremely regret that without waiting to receive our instruction or even to ascertain our views regarding Tientsin, the Kwantung Army should unilaterally have decided to assist the Tientsin Army and attacked the enemy around Chinchou. As the chief of staff this morning once again issued orders to stop the Kwantung Army's offensive movement, it is believed that it will obey these orders. We can never approve of the Kwantung Army's disobeying our command or betraying our policies." Ninomiya was also instructed to execute these orders in the name of the chief of staff acting on behalf of the emperor. By the morning of November 28 the Kwantung Army had not replied; therefore another "entrusted order" was dispatched urging it to carry out the previous instructions. Thus, within a single 24-hour period the supreme command had resorted to the delegated right of supreme command as many as four times. Coupled with Ninomiya's personal efforts at persuasion on the spot, the pressure finally bore fruit. The Kwantung Army issued an order to the 4th Mixed Brigade to return to Mukden as quickly as possible, reporting to Tokyo that while there was some delay owing to railway destruction, the brigade was doing all it could to speed up its withdrawal.

Why was the supreme command so persistent on the Chinchou question? It is because the Chinese had proposed to withdraw voluntarily from Chinchou. On November 24 Foreign Minister V. K. Wellington Koo had stated to the British, American, and French ministers that China was prepared to withdraw its troops from Chinchou to Shanhaikuan as a temporary measure until the Manchurian Incident was settled. The offer was made conditional upon Japan's pledge not to violate the territory or interfere with the Chinese administration of the area. The proposal was conveyed to Shidehara by the French ambassador on November 26. The Foreign Ministry consulted the army and navy authorities, and they decided that until the situation changed it would be desirable to refrain from positive military action in the Chinchou area. Given this diplomatic break, the General Staff was persuaded to withdraw Kwantung Army forces from their offensive position.

The Chinese offer of voluntary withdrawal was never made good. On November 25 it was made conditional upon the creation of a neutral zone to be policed by the army of a third power under League Council supervision. A day later, when the Council, without Japanese and Chinese participation, debated the proposal, the plan was found impractical on several technical grounds, and a plan for sending observers to Chinchou was adopted instead. China accepted the proposal, but Japan was opposed, saying the matter should be left to direct negotiations between the two countries. Japan merely stated its readiness to refrain from military action if Chinese forces withdrew completely from Chinchou to Shanhaikuan and beyond and if China maintained only local civilian and police administration in the evacuated areas. The matter was further debated at Council sessions, but there was no agreement on the limits of the neutral zone. Japan insisted on the area between the Hsiaoling river and Shanhaikuan, but Council President Aristide Briand wanted a larger zone, extending the upper limit to the Taling river. Since it appeared that Wellington Koo's initial proposal had been merely a trial balloon, no further League debate took place on this question.

Meanwhile, in China the issue was discussed by officials of both countries, again to no avail. Minister Shigemitsu Mamoru talked with Foreign Minister Koo in Shanghai, while in Peiping Yano Makoto, counselor of the legation, negotiated with Chang Hsueh-liang. Yano's proposal, approved in Tokyo, stipulated the withdrawal of Chinese political and military establishments and personnel to the area west of the Great Wall, in return for retention of Chinese civilian and police administration. No Chinese troops were thereafter to be allowed to move east of the Wall or to engage in destructive action in Manchuria. Japanese troops in Manchuria, on the other hand, were to have the right to pass through the area west of the Hsiaoling river if the security of Japanese lives and property or that of the Japanese army in north China were threatened.[43] The Yano-Chang negotiations got nowhere. This was because neither the army supreme command nor the Kwantung Army was really interested in the idea of a neutral zone. If an accord were to be reached on a neutral zone in the vicinity of Chinchou, the administration of the area would revert to Fengt'ien province, and such a settlement seemed contrary to the policy of destroying the old order in Manchuria. The supreme command actually wanted to see Chinchou administered by the new Mukden regime. Such a demand, however, would only cause China to accuse Japan of violating the Nine-Power Treaty and produce unfavorable repercussions elsewhere; therefore the army was outwardly willing to see Chinese administration remain in Chinchou. There is no question that the army was determined to find a plausible pretext to extend Japan's control over Chinchou. The Kwantung Army, on its part, had the same desire but a different idea for bringing it about. It insisted that the neutral zone, if it had to be created, should cover the area between Shanhaikuan and the Luan river (excluding Ch'inhuangtao). Even then, neutrality should be annulled as soon as there was disorder in the Peiping-Tientsin area. Staff officer Itagaki went farther. Maintaining contact with Major Tanaka Ryūkichi, the assistant army attaché at Shanghai, he decided that Chinese official and public opinion in Peiping, Nanking, and Shanghai should be influenced against the evacuation of the Chinese government and army from Chinchou. The idea was to use the anti-Chang, anti-Chiang sentiment that could result from such a nationalistic movement. On December 10 Itagaki asked his contacts in Peiping, Shanghai, and Tientsin to carry out this scheme. Under such circumstances, Yano's negotiations with Chang Hsueh-liang could not have succeeded. Chang stated on December 7 that he would carry out a voluntary withdrawal, but nothing in fact was done.

It might seem, therefore, that the Chinese proposal had completely caught Japan off balance, and the Japanese had taken seriously what for China was only a time-gaining device. The matter was in reality more complicated, since the Sino-Japanese impasse was precisely what the Kwantung Army wanted. In Japan the view was prevalent that the Kwantung Army's withdrawal from west of the Liao had been due to Stimson's intervention, and on December 1 the army felt obliged to issue a denial. But a similar view was held widely among prominent Chinese. This presented some obstacle to the Kwantung Army's plan of establishing a new regime in Manchuria. At the same time so-called "bandit" activities increased along the Liao, east of the South Manchuria Railway, and in north Manchuria. In Manchuria Japanese from throughout the region held a meeting and demanded the replacement of Shidehara diplomacy by a stronger foreign policy.

Meanwhile, the army intercepted two important Chinese telegrams.

One was from Jung Chen in Chinchou to Chang Hsueh-liang, dated November 30, reassuring him that the defense of the area was in the secure hands of Chang T'ing-shu's 12th Infantry Brigade. Jung suggested that Chang Hsueh-liang withdraw the neutrality proposal. The other, dated December 1, was from Chang Hsueh-liang to Chiang Kai-shek, denying the rumors about voluntary evacuation of Chinchou. Perhaps reflecting this strong stand, the Nationalist government on December 4 instructed the Chinese delegate at the League, Alfred Sze, to oppose the establishment of a neutral zone. Nanking also began making statements to the effect that the proposal had actually originated in Japan and that China would be forced to fight if the League failed to stop Japanese aggression.

These moves by China convinced the Kwantung Army that the Chinese were determined to hold on to Chinchou. Accordingly, on December 10 it requested a reinforcement of one division and increases in heavy guns and mountain guns. This last request was derived from experience: heavy guns and mountain guns, rather than field artillery, had proved effective in the fighting thus far. Three days later Kwantung Army headquarters adopted a "strategy for attacking Chinchou." This specified a north-to-south advance, instead of the previous tactic of attacking the Chinese army's right from the lower reaches of the Taling river. The new tactic was intended to prevent the Chinese army from escaping into Jehol.

This time the supreme command raised no objection to Kwantung Army strategy. For one thing, army central authorities were resentful of what they considered Chinese treachery on the Chinchou question. Also, the supreme command had felt it had acted too drastically toward the Kwantung Army on the matter of withdrawal from west of the Liao. At any rate, in early December, it obtained the Foreign Ministry's consent to the following justification of the new strategy.

> Chinese insincerity has betrayed our wishes, and bandit activities have daily increased in the whole Liao river region. The imperial army has thus found it necessary to carry out their subjugation, in order to assure the security of the army, the safety of Japanese citizens in Manchuria, and the maintenance of order throughout Manchuria. Our action this time has been forced upon us entirely as a result of Chinese insincerity. We do not like to invite fresh fighting, but we will reluctantly have to do so if Chinese troops assist bandits or if undisciplined soldiers provoke the Japanese army as they confront each other in the course of the bandit suppression campaign.

It is obvious from this document that the supreme command sought to justify the expected Chinchou offensive as an "inevitable part" of the bandit suppression campaign. On December 15 the General Staff telegraphed Mukden to instruct the Kwantung Army to synchronize the assault on Chinchou with an attack on bandits. The General Staff was also agreeable to the Kwantung Army's request for reinforcements. The telegram promised the dispatch of one mixed brigade from Korea and offered to consider sympathetically the sending of another mixed brigade from Japan.

Just at this time, on December 10, the League Council adopted a resolution reaffirming the Council resolution of September 30, which had called on the Japanese army to withdraw quickly to the railway zone. The resolution also expressed the hope that Japan and China would refrain from all military action and called for the establishment of a mission to conduct an investigation in Manchuria. Since the Council also accepted Japan's declaration reserving the right to "subjugate bandits," Japanese army authorities in both Tokyo and Mukden decided they had obtained the League's tacit consent to the Chinchou strategy. Moreover, Council President Briand stated there was no time limit for the Japanese army's complete withdrawal. This point was stressed by a Japanese Foreign Ministry announcement of December 11. The Briand statement had actually been a product of strenuous efforts made by Ambassador Yoshizawa Kenkichi at the League. While technically it was Foreign Minister Shidehara who had sent instructions to Yoshizawa that resulted in the reservation declaration, as well as the Briand statement, it is said that certain crucial passages in the instructions had been inserted by Shiratori Toshio, chief of the Foreign Ministry's Public Information Division, under pressure from the military and without prior consultation with Shidehara. If true, here was another instance of the failure of Shidehara diplomacy.[44]

This episode coincided with the fall of the Minseitō cabinet. Despite Home Minister Adachi Kenzō's efforts to organize a coalition government, the Seiyūkai took power and formed its own cabinet on December 13. Prime Minister Inukai Tsuyoshi chose as army minister Lieutenant-General Araki Sadao, who enjoyed widespread popularity among middle-ranking officials of the General Staff and the Army Ministry. Araki's appointment resulted in the removal from positions of influence of the Ugaki faction, which, it was alleged, had maintained an equivocal attitude toward the Manchurian crisis. Chief of Staff Kanaya was replaced by Prince Kan'in Kotohito on December 23, and in January 1932 Vice Chief of Staff Ninomiya was succeeded by Lieutenant-General Mazaki Jinzaburō. Mori Kaku, an exponent of positive continental expansion, was appointed chief cabinet secretary, indicating the cabinet's sympathetic attitude toward the views of the right wing and the military. Inukai acted as his own foreign minister until January 14, when Ambassador Yoshizawa, back from Paris, was appointed to the post. Yoshizawa was not known to have any strong views of his own.

Meanwhile, in Manchuria the Kwantung Army ordered on December 17 an attack on "soldier-bandits" in Fak'u and Ch'angtu *hsien.* This was meant to be a prelude to an assault on Chinchou. The supreme command responded by issuing its ninth "entrusted order," this time for sending reinforcements to Manchuria and Tientsin. On December 18 the Kwantung Army decided on the specific tactics to be used in the Chinchou campaign, and three days later troops began their advance southward. They were now ready to attack Chinchou.

The protocol force in Tientsin was quick to see this as another good moment to act, but its ambitions were once again frustrated by the supreme command. In view of what had happened in November, when the Kwantung Army moved west of the Liao, Tokyo headquarters were determined to forestall rash action by the Tientsin Army. Already on December 12 Vice Chief Ninomiya had telegraphed the protocol force commander, enjoining him to maintain the status quo in Tientsin, even in the event of Kwantung Army action at Chinchou. Ninomiya explained that it would be difficult to send reinforcements to Tientsin with a view to enabling the forces there to cooperate actively with the Kwantung Army and that it would not be proper to find a pretext for hostilities in the Peiping-Tientsin area just because of the attack on Chinchou. The supreme command desired to base military action on more justifiable grounds, such as the right of self-defense or the protection of nationals. Even if the fighting at Chinchou were extended to the Peiping-Tientsin area, the protocol force was not to start fresh action or resort to offensive military tactics. If it should be attacked by Chinese troops, or if the latter should move beyond the Wall to advance to Chinchou, the Tientsin army should continue to maintain the status quo and engage only in defensive action.

The protocol force was unhappy about such a definition of its duties.

It had judged that the fighting at Chinchou would provide the best opportunity for destroying Chang Hsueh-liang's power in north China. It seemed likely that the Manchurian forces would retreat from Chinchou southward into China proper. If they were left unchallenged, their presence would only perpetuate Chang's influence in China. But if the Chinese army at Chinchou could be destroyed, north China would be thrown into confusion, giving Japan a new pretext to resort to action to cause Chang's downfall. Thus reasoning, on December 18 the protocol army suggested to Tokyo that the main body of its troops be sent beyond the Wall to intercept and destroy Chinese soldiers retreating from Chinchou. The protocol army should also attack Chinese soldiers going north beyond the Wall to assist the Chinchou contingent. To carry out these plans, Tokyo was requested to order that all the reinforcements being sent out from Japan be landed at Ch'inhuangtao.

Interestingly enough, the Kwantung Army opposed these tactics being mapped out in Tientsin. Now that an attack on Chinchou had been approved by the supreme command, the value of Tientsin's assistance seems to have declined. It was considered disadvantageous to divide Japanese military resources between Manchuria and north China. If the Chinese army at Chinchou should retire to China proper, their maintenance would raise grave financial problems and their presence might cause political embarrassment to Chang Hsueh-liang and Chiang Kai-shek. For these reasons, Chang was likely to fall without external pressure, and there seemed little to be gained in extending hostilities to the Peiping-Tientsin area.

The Kwantung Army's stand on the question strengthened Tokyo's resolve to suppress rash action on the part of the protocol force. On December 19 Kanaya vetoed the Tientsin Army's suggestion for action and said there would be no diversion of the reinforcements to Ch'inhuangtao. Ninomiya explained that it was desirable to let the Chinese retreat peacefully, so as not to drive them in desperation to attack the Kwantung Army or to retreat out of necessity to Jehol. The telegram pointed out: "Fortunately, the Three Provinces are generally coming under our control and order is being restored. If we solve the Chinchou question, the Manchurian situation will be completely stabilized, and we will be able to begin the constructive phase. Under the circumstances, the situation in China proper is not likely to influence gravely the course of events in Manchuria." The Tientsin Army was therefore enjoined to be extremely cautious and "suffer the unsufferable," in order not to complicate the matter and adversely affect national prestige.

At this time Chang Hsueh-liang seems to have been wavering in his attitude toward foreign policy and domestic politics. Sentiment against him and the Generalissimo had grown tremendously in north China. The anti-Nanking Canton government, established in May, had demanded Chiang's resignation as the price for reunification. Chiang felt it necessary to comply and had resigned on December 15. Chang Hsueh-liang had also been attacked by the Canton faction for negligence and inefficiency in the war effort against Japan. Chang had been barely able to preserve his position by expressing anti-Japanese views. The office of deputy commander of the Chinese army, navy, and air force, which Chang had held, had been abolished, and he had been given the newly created post of peace preservation commander at Peiping. But inwardly he was gravely worried about the situation at Chinchou. He seems at first to have decided to withdraw his men from Chinchou in case of a Japanese attack. On December 22 he telegraphed Chiang Kai-shek to ask for "final instructions" in view of the Japanese advance to Chinchou. At this point the situation changed abruptly, for an alliance between Chiang Kai-shek and Wang Ching-wei appeared imminent. Generals in the Peiping-Tientsin area all clamored for resistance against Japan; it seemed a matter of days before Chiang would resume his military command; strong anti-Chiang factions were silent; and funds were forthcoming to replenish Chang's armies. All these factors led Chang to decide on resistance. On December 26 he cabled his decision to Jung Chen at Chinchou.

Meanwhile, on December 22 the Kwantung Army announced that its military action had been launched solely in self-defense and for the purpose of suppressing bandits. A similar statement was issued by the supreme command. The powers responded quickly. The British and French ambassadors in Tokyo expressed their governments' concern and called Japan's attention to its obligations under League resolutions. The American ambassador expressed hope for a peaceful settlement, declaring that the United States entirely supported the League on the Manchurian question. The Japanese army and government alike replied that the premeditated attack on Chinchou was a necessary part of the bandit subjugation campaign, which had been justified by the Council resolution of December 10. All responsibility lay with China, they said.

Assured of support at home, the Kwantung Army decided on final action. It had considered resort to nonmilitary means, to see if the Chinese forces at Chinchou might not be induced to withdraw peacefully or lay down their arms.[45] But the firm support given by the supreme command encouraged the Kwantung Army to engage in a frontal attack on Chinchou. On December 26, preparations having been completed, an order for an offensive was issued. At the same time, to maintain security behind the lines, Mukden requested that a mixed brigade be sent from Korea as reinforcement. The supreme command, now more than ever compliant, immediately agreed to authorize such reinforcement.

On December 28 the 2nd Division began its advance toward Chinchou. A steady flow of reinforcements began arriving in Mukden. The Kwantung Army feared a difficult fight if the Chinese should decide seriously to engage the Japanese. But actually there was little resistance from the Chinese army, and the attack succeeded beyond expectation. By December 30 reports were flowing into army headquarters that the Chinese were evacuating Chinchou. Believing that Chang Hsueh-liang would not risk his prestige by wholesale retreat, the Kwantung Army remained cautious, lest it fall into a Chinese trap. Instead of advancing to the right bank of the Taling river, therefore, the Japanese army was ordered to gather on the left bank. However, as the Chinese proceeded to withdraw quickly, even resorting to marching on foot, the 20th Division, which had been sent from Korea, was ordered speedily to occupy Chinchou, to forestall Chang's reviving the neutral zone proposal. By January 2, 1932, the Chinese had completely evacuated, and at 10:40 A.M. on January 3 the 20th Division proceeded peacefully to occupy Chinchou. Thus the basis of Chang Hsueh-liang's counterattack collapsed, and his army withdrew to the districts east of the Luan river in Hopeh province.

It is not clear why Chang should have decided at the last moment to abandon Chinchou. He must have realized that his troops were militarily no match for the Kwantung Army and that therefore he should preserve them for a later occasion rather than risk their annihilation. Perhaps an even more pertinent factor was that his position in north China was not really as strong as it appeared. The Chinchou affair occurred during Chiang Kai-shek's period of retirement. Chang could not therefore count on the support of the Nanking government, nor did he have much control over north Chinese generals. There was even a chance that while he poured his force into Chinchou a strong anti-Chang current might develop south of the Wall. Thus, while he called for a counteroffensive against Japan, he could not have carried it through. At any rate, Chinchou had merely been Chang's advance post; his real base was in Peiping, and it was there that he might now be expected to strengthen his retaliatory potential. In other words, the Kwantung Army could not rest peacefully just because Chinchou had fallen; it would now have to worry about Peiping.

On February 5, 1932, the 2nd Division occupied Harbin. The Kwantung Army's long-standing goal had been frustrated the previous September by Army Minister Minami, but this time no obstacle was interposed. A pretext for the expedition had been given by Ting Ch'ao, commander of the railway guards army at Harbin. He had remained hostile to the new regime Hsi Hsia had organized at Kirin under Kwantung Army protection at the end of September. Troops loyal to the former Kirin leader, Chang Tso-hsiang, had established at Pinhsien a government opposed to Hsi and the Japanese. Opinion among the Japanese military and pro-Japanese Chinese in Manchuria was divided over whether the anti-Japanese units should be suppressed by force, but in the end the Kwantung Army decided on military action. On January 5 an army under the command of Yü Ch'en-ch'eng began moving north from Kirin and reached Harbin on the 27th, where it clashed with Ting Ch'ao's army. Within the city riots broke out, resulting in the deaths of one Japanese and three Koreans and imperiling the lives of Japanese residents. On the same day a Japanese plane was shot down by Ting's artillery and its pilot shot as he bailed out of the aircraft.

Commander-in-Chief Honjō decided the time had come for the Kwantung Army to step in directly. The 3rd Infantry Brigade at Ch'angch'un was ordered to Harbin, and a request was sent to the supreme command for reinforcements of about two infantry battalions to protect Japanese nationals. Tokyo, in sharp contrast to its attitude the previous fall, immediately endorsed the Kwantung Army's decision, for obvious reasons. With the supreme command now headed by men popular among middle-grade officers, there was complete rapport between it and the Kwantung Army. Moreover, Japanese and Chinese forces were then engaged at Shanghai, and international and domestic attention was focused on that city. The Harada diary for this period, for instance, is solely concerned with the Shanghai Incident and never mentions Harbin. The Shanghai affair served as a smokescreen for the north Manchurian operation. Finally, Tokyo was now more optimistic about the like-lihood of Soviet Union involvement. The success of the Tsitsihar operation, which had not resulted in any interference by the Soviet Union, was an important source of this optimism. The relative strengths of the two countries' armies in north Manchuria were judged to have been re-versed, and there was no such strong fear of a clash with Soviet forces as there had been the previous fall.[46] It should be noted, however, that the changed attitude did not imply active bellicosity toward the Soviet Union. The supreme command held that serious fighting should still be avoided. It is recorded that when Operations Section Chief Imamura ad-vocated a policy of determined response in the event of Soviet army in-terference with Japanese action, Army Minister Araki opposed him, cau-tioning that Japan was not yet ready to fight the Soviet Union. The Kwantung Army was told that "extreme caution" was needed in devising strategy against the Soviet Union and was admonished to pay most se-rious attention to all reports of Soviet intentions.

As a matter of fact, complications in the Harbin operation developed precisely because of some slight resistance by the Soviet Union. Con-trary to what the Kwantung Army had assumed, the Chinese Eastern Railway, under Soviet pressure, at first refused to transport Japanese troops on the grounds that this would violate its policy of absolute neu-trality. Ting Ch'ao, who had earlier expressed willingness to submit to Japanese control, now changed his mind, apparently encouraged by the Soviet attitude. He was at any rate determined to fight the Kirin army. It was also reported that armed Russians were pouring into Harbin. Worried, Honjō cabled Tokyo, recommending either military occupa-tion of the Chinese Eastern Railway or relaying its rails in the narrower South Manchuria Railway gauge of 4.85 feet so that the latter's cars might be used to transport troops northward. But the supreme command op-posed both these suggestions as too extreme. As a last resort the Kwan-tung Army began extending the width of South Manchuria Railway lo-comotives to enable them to run on Chinese Eastern Railway rails.

Fortunately, at the last moment the Chinese Eastern Railway agreed to provide transport for the Japanese military, probably judging that it could not oppose the Japanese army if the latter decided to use force. On January 30 station masters were told to resume operating the traffic, and cars were sent down from Harbin to accommodate and transport Japanese soldiers. The tension in Soviet-Japanese relations began to subside. The Kwantung Army still entertained the hope that Ting Ch'ao could be induced to submit peacefully to Japan, but when on January 30 his army began an offensive, the Kwantung Army finally resolved on military action. The 2nd Division began its attack three days later, and by February 4 it had reached Harbin. The Chinese barracks were attacked, and on the afternoon of the 5th the city was captured. The anti-Kirin forces, totaling about 12,000, fled to Pinhsien. The supreme command again cautioned the occupying forces to exercise restraint and care in view of the city's international significance. They were ordered immediately to restore general services on the Chinese Eastern Railway, thereby to exhibit the Japanese army's fair attitude and enhance its prestige. The Soviet Union, however, remained passive, and there was no immediate crisis.

Shanghai: The Crisis

Even before the Mukden Incident, Shanghai had been a center of anti-Japanese agitation. In July 1931, following the Wanpaoshan incident and the resulting massacre of Chinese in Korea, an anti-Japanese committee had been formed to organize a boycott of Japanese goods. The movement gained momentum after September 18. On September 22 the anti-Japanese committee was renamed the Shanghai Committee to Resist Japan and Save the Nation, and on October 19 the Chamber of Commerce organized a committee to carry out an economic boycott of Japan. The headquarters of the movement were located at T'ienhoukung in the International Settlement. Though the settlement was under the jurisdiction of the Shanghai Municipal Council, the latter had no control over the Chinese in T'ienhoukung, who enjoyed a sort of extraterritoriality of their own. They held anti-Japanese rallies, put up posters, distributed handbills, made denunciatory speeches in the streets, and staged anti-Japanese dramas and movies. Many Chinese were arrested and held in confinement for having dealt in Japanese goods, and more than 610,000 dollars worth of Japanese goods were confiscated.[47]

The impact of the boycott on Japanese trade was tremendous. Whereas 29 percent of Shanghai's total imports came from Japan in 1930, by December 1931 the ratio had dropped to 3 percent. Japanese shipping along the China coast and on the Yangtze was hit, and the Nisshin Steamship

Company was forced to suspend operations altogether. More than 125 Japanese-operated factories in Shanghai had to suspend or stop production. By the end of November 80 percent had closed down, and by the end of the year another 10 percent had done so. Although nine cotton factories doggedly continued to operate, they were finally forced to suspend operations in January 1932, upon the outbreak of the Shanghai Incident. Damages estimated at ¥41,204,000 were inflicted on Japanese merchants in Shanghai between July 1931 and March 1932.[48]

Beyond the economic boycott a general anti-Japanese movement developed. Many anti-Japanese volunteer corps were organized under the guidance of the Kuomintang. In Shanghai a committee to direct their activities was organized, and it promulgated rules for their training. By November 17 it was estimated that more than 17,000 had applied to participate, and on December 1 three volunteer corps camps were established, on the basis of which an independent volunteer army was formed.[49]

The Japanese government responded by issuing a warning to China. On October 10 Shigemitsu warned the Nanking government that it had sole responsibility for controlling the anti-Japanese boycott and protecting the lives and property of Japanese residents. The Chinese government replied that it could not be expected to suppress the people's right to choose commodities and asserted that the whole world was amazed at the restraint shown by the angered Chinese. Ultimate responsibility for the boycott, it charged, lay in the unfriendly acts Japan had committed over the years. The Chinese government was doing its best to protect Japanese lives and property, and it pointed out that there had been no loss of Japanese lives. Similar views were repeated by Shanghai's Mayor Chang Ch'ün when the Japanese consul-general issued his protests.

Japanese residents, on their part, organized a "committee on the current situation" and held several meetings, the first of which was attended by Japanese in Shanghai and later ones by representatives from all over China. At every meeting a strongly worded resolution and a declaration were adopted, urging the home government to "take resolute steps to punish China's intransigence." Following the first meeting on October 10, 6,000 Japanese returning home clashed with Chinese, and a company of Japanese marines had to be called out to restore order.

The new year saw the worsening of Sino-Japanese relations in Shanghai. On January 9 Japanese residents were angered by an article in the

Min-kuo jih-pao concerning an attempt on the emperor's life by a Korean nationalist that had taken place the previous day. The writer commented, "Unfortunately the bullet hit only an accompanying carriage." The new mayor of Shanghai, Wu T'ieh-ch'eng, had to issue several apologies, order the article withdrawn, and punish the individual responsible before the Japanese were satisfied.[50]

An even more serious incident occurred on January 18. Five Japanese priests of the Nichiren sect, while chanting sutras on Mayushan Road, were attacked by a Chinese mob. One died and two were seriously injured. Actually, the attack had been instigated by Major Tanaka Ryūkichi, who had decided to create an incident to divert foreign attention from Manchuria, where a new state was being established. The site of the attack had been deliberately chosen, being the location of the San-yu Company, a towel factory noted for its anti-Japanese military corps. Japanese could be persuaded therefore that those who had attacked the priests had come from this factory. On the night of the 19th, during a heavy rain, several members of a Japanese youth group, also controlled by Tanaka, invaded the San-yu Company and set fire to its storeroom. On their way back, around 2:30 A.M., they were met by Chinese police of the International Settlement, and casualties occurred on both sides.[51]

Consul-General Murai Kuramatsu issued a strong protest on the killing of the priests. In reply, the Chinese expressed their sincere willingness to solve the incident and accepted all the Japanese demands, including the arrest of the culprits, reparations, and an apology. Unfortunately, the Japanese residents were not to be satisfied by this. They held a general meeting on the afternoon of January 20 and adopted a resolution calling on Japan to send reinforcements immediately and asserting the right of self-defense to destroy completely the anti-Japanese movement. An excited mob of more than a thousand then rushed out of the assembly hall and marched to the consulate-general and the army and marine headquarters. On their way they clashed with the settlement police, and injuries resulted on both sides. The marchers' hysterical outburst reached its peak when they arrived at the marine headquarters. Captain Samejima Tomoshige, the marine commander, declared that he was ready to resort to "resolute action" to protect the residents' lives and property. He assured them that reinforcements could be obtained whenever needed.[52] The marines soon had an opportunity to show their prowess. When the *Min-kuo jih-pao* printed another inflammatory article, alleging that the attack on the San-yu Company had been made under Japanese marine protection, the marines threatened to use force to obtain satisfaction. The settlement police thereupon ordered the closing of the *Min-kuo*. The order was carried out on January 28.[53]

Meanwhile, the Japanese forces at Shanghai had been augmented. On January 23 the cruiser *Ōi* and the 15th Destroyer Squadron were added to the existing naval force under the command of Rear Admiral Shiozawa Kōichi. On the 24th the aircraft carrier *Notoro* was added, and four days later the 1st Torpedo Squadron and the 2nd Special Marine Regiment were sent to Shanghai, increasing the marine force to 1,833. The fluttering of the flags on the ships made Japanese residents all the more belligerent and exerted silent pressure on the Chinese.

At this time the Chinese forces at Shanghai were commanded by Chiang Kuang-nai and Ts'ai T'ing-k'ai. These consisted of some 33,500 men comprising the famous 19th Route Army, which was composed mostly of men from Kwangtung and Kwangsi and was one of the most distinguished components of the Chinese Revolutionary Army. From June 1931 it had been engaged in the anticommunist campaign in Kiangsi, but in December it had been ordered to replace Hsiung Shih-hui's army, which was stationed along the Nanking-Shanghai railway and under the direct command of Chiang Kai-shek.[54] Given the 19th Route Army's strong anti-Japanese inclination, its new duties, coupled with the hysterical fears of Japanese residents in Shanghai, meant that an open clash between China and Japan was only a matter of time.

The military commanders of the various powers in Shanghai had since 1850 organized a defense committee to maintain law and order in the International Settlement in times of civil strife. At a committee meeting on December 18, 1931, revision of the existing defense plans was discussed, particularly in regard to zoning arrangements. The section assigned to the Japanese force was extended from the "Hungk'ou" area (the northeastern part of the settlement) to the embankment of the Shanghai-Wusung Railway. The previous assignment, which had been adopted in March 1927, had included a "trans-settlement road area" which was not strictly included in the International Settlement but whose defenses had been assumed by the foreign powers with China's tacit consent.[55] There was no question, however, that the area newly added to the Japanese defense zone, extending about 640 meters west of North Szechwan Road, was Chinese territory. The revised plan was adopted ostensibly because many Japanese resided in this area, but the real reason was strategic: the Japanese army had discovered that the Chinese could use the houses lying just beyond North Szechwan Road as a line of defense. As it turned out, the Japanese residents in the extended zone evacuated to the Hungk'ou area long before the outbreak of the incident on January 29. Such being the case, the settlement authorities, as well as the defense committee, committed a political blunder in agreeing to the change in the defense plan. Even stranger was the failure of the Municipal Council to inform the Chinese of the revised zone assignments. Historians have rightly attributed much of the trouble that followed to this failure.[56]

At any rate, on January 28 Commander Shiozawa notified his British colleague that Japanese marines would start action the following day. As requested by the Japanese, the chairman of the Municipal Council then issued an order placing Shanghai under martial law. This was at 4 o'clock in the afternoon. Although Mayor Wu had just accepted all the Japanese demands for settlement of the incident involving the Nichiren priests, the settlement authorities judged that tension still existed and that the Chinese did not seem able to carry out these terms. Many Chinese had accused the mayor of weakness, and some were reportedly preparing to attack the Japanese forces.[57]

As martial law was declared, the British, American, French, and Italian forces and volunteer corps were immediately mobilized, and by 6 o'clock they had taken up their assigned positions. At 8:30 P.M. Commander Shiozawa issued two declarations, one calling on the Chinese army to evacuate from the Chapei area, the second prohibiting public meetings that might interfere with military plans and expressing the intention of putting into effect many emergency measures. At 9 o'clock 468 marines were landed to join the 1,365 marines who were already on shore. At 11:30 P.M. the marines began moving into their assigned positions.

It is difficult even today to explain why nearly eight hours elapsed from the time the four foreign powers began action until the Japanese marines moved in. One possible reason is that because taking up positions in the assigned areas implied the beginning of hostilities, the Japanese had to be doubly cautious. This was especially so since the Chinese had accepted the Japanese demands on the incident of the priests. Shiozawa's first declaration was comparatively mild and did not contain the customary threat of action if the Chinese army should fail to evacuate. But why were the declarations issued at 8:30 P.M., more than four hours after martial law was declared? Since the marines were mobilized at 11:30 P.M., this allowed the 19th Route Army only three hours to evacuate, a practical impossibility. Thus a second explanation emerges. The Japanese moved in at night to conceal their intentions. Now that the Kwantung Army had demonstrated its prowess in Manchuria, the navy seems to have been determined to do something in Shanghai. Although the marines were vastly outnumbered by the Chinese army, which numbered more than 30,000, the navy was eager for action to gain for itself a reputation equal to that of the Kwantung Army. As Vice Navy Minister Sakonji Seizō told Lieutenant-General Hata Shunroku, inspector of artillery, "It is now the navy's turn to get to work. . . . Our marines are different from what they were. They are in good shape, numbering 2,000 men and equipped with field guns and armored cars."[58]

Fighting began around midnight on the 28th, when Japanese marines were suddenly attacked as they reached the western side of North Szechwan Road. This was the section added to the Japanese defense zone, a change not notified to the Chinese, and thus a clash at this spot was probably inevitable. Fighting immediately spread to the whole of Chapei, and on the 29th planes from the *Notoro* began bombing, at first without much success because of strong resistance by the 19th Route Army. Further reinforcements were sent from Japan, and a new squadron was organized under the command of Vice Admiral Nomura Kichisaburō. A full attack on Chapei began on February 1, and two days later the Wusung and Kaoch'iao fortresses were attacked. But there was no quick victory.

Marines can fight only for a limited period on land. Sooner or later they will need army assistance. At that time reinforcements from Korea were unavailable, and it would take ten days for troops to arrive at Shanghai from Japan; therefore a quick decision was needed. As early as January 31 Navy Minister Ōsumi Mineo had asked for army support, and at a conference of the army, navy, and foreign ministries the army finally agreed to help. The army supreme command, engrossed in the Harbin question, judged it possible to send some forces to Shanghai as well. The 9th Division, stationed at Kanazawa, was picked for the purpose, and a mobilization order was issued on February 2, following cabinet approval. The Army and Navy general staffs drafted a memorandum on "joint strategic planning" and cooperated in mapping out details of troop transportation, shipping, and landing.

Friction soon developed between the armed services. The army and navy could not agree on control over the number and the use of the troops to be sent to Shanghai. Both sides wanted to exercise such control, reflecting the age-old rivalry between the two services. On February 3 the navy issued a written request for the dispatch of a mixed brigade to Shanghai. Because it stated that such a force would be sufficient and failed to mention the 9th Division, which the army had already ordered to be sent, the Army General Staff was angered. It contended that only the army had the right to decide on the number and makeup of forces to be dispatched. Staff officer Endō Saburō was sent to the Navy General Staff to complain personally to naval Operations Section Chief Kondō Nobutake. Endō charged that the navy had interfered with the sending of army units. "The navy should state its views only on the desirability and timing of a reinforcement," he declared; any specific mention of the number of troops was beyond its competence and jurisdiction. Kondō retorted that the dispatch of a division would unnecessarily excite the powers and was contrary to the principle of localizing the conflict. Endō remained unconvinced. He even threatened to cancel army support if the navy persisted in interfering with matters solely within the army's competence and trying to stop the dispatch of the 9th Division. The army took no steps to obtain imperial sanction for an expedition, and the newly organized mixed brigade at Kurume was told to wait for further instructions.

The navy had to back down eventually, for army assistance was essential in Shanghai. On February 4 it withdrew its opposition to the dispatch of the army-determined number of troops. Satisfied, the army went through the customary procedure to obtain imperial approval for an expedition. As a result, a fourteenth entrusted command was issued, ordering the dispatch to Shanghai of the 9th Division and other units and instructing the commander of the division to cooperate with the navy to protect Japanese nationals in the area.[59]

The 9th Division left Ujina on February 9 and 10, landing at Shanghai on the 15th and 16th. Its commander, Lieutenant-General Ueda Kenkichi, issued a declaration of the purpose of the expedition. The supreme command, meanwhile, had adopted a policy paper entitled "Outline of Principles Governing Military Action in Shanghai." The document, drawn up on February 8, was personally taken to Commander Ueda by Operations Section chief Imamura, who had been appointed to liaise both between the army and the navy and between the supreme command and the expeditionary force. The outline specified that the 9th Division should first seek to have the Chinese troops withdraw peacefully to an area beyond the International Settlement to be delimited by the military commanders of the powers. Foreign troops would then move into the area vacated by the Chinese. If the British, American, and French commanders did not approve of the plan, efforts should be made to persuade them to sanction Japan's demand for Chinese evacuation. If the Chinese should refuse to leave, the Japanese forces were to attack and drive them west of a K'unshan-Ch'ingp'u-Sungchiang line. The area east of the line was to be occupied by Japanese troops. Further reinforcements would be sent if necessary.

In accordance with these principles, the expeditionary army tried to persuade the Chinese to leave on their own initiative. On February 18, through the good offices of British Minister Sir Miles Lampson, the 9th Division's chief of staff Major-General Tashiro Kan'ichirō went to see a representative of the 19th Route Army in the French Settlement. The talks lasted for two hours, but the Chinese never yielded. The Japanese then decided to present an ultimatum. At 9:00 P.M. the Chinese army was ordered to withdraw 20 kilometers beyond the settlement limits by 5:00 P.M. on February 20. If they failed to do so, the Japanese army would reserve to itself the right to take action and would hold the Chinese accountable for all consequences. A similar ultimatum was handed to Mayor Wu by Consul-General Murai and made public.

As expected, the Chinese did not yield. Late on the night of February 19 Ts'ai T'ing-k'ai sent an equivocal reply, Mayor Wu refused to accept the Japanese demands, and the National Government issued a statement to the same effect. Accordingly, at 9:30 A.M. on February 20 Ueda ordered his troops to attack, concentrating on the Chiangwanchen area. But Chinese resistance was vigorous, their encampments were well fortified and hidden, and even after two days of intense fighting the Japanese could not take Chiangwanchen. On February 22 they shifted their attack north of the area but were still unsuccessful. The Chinese even made an offensive attack the following day on the northern wing of the Japanese forces, which succeeded in repelling the attack only with the help of reinforcements.

At first the Japanese officers were not unduly alarmed. Late on February 20 Colonel Imamura cabled from Shanghai that while enemy resistance was strong, the campaign was proceeding as planned. The 9th

Division was in high spirits and confident of dealing with the 19th Route Army without reinforcements. The Japanese army could probably advance to the 20-kilometer line beyond the settlement. Imamura felt, however, that the Chinese should be expelled beyond this line and a neutral zone created in the area. For the purpose of thus extending the objective of the war, Imamura requested reinforcements. This would help speed the settlement of the incident and enable Japanese forces to return quickly to Japan. His optimistic estimate was shared by officials in Tokyo. At a meeting of Army General Staff officers on February 22 it was decided that there seemed no need for reinforcements to assist the 9th Division, and Imamura's proposal for a neutral zone was rejected because of its international implications.

Such optimism soon gave way to serious concern over the course of the hostilities. On the afternoon of February 22 an urgent message was received from 3rd Fleet Commander Nomura.

> British and American, no less than Japanese, merchants have suffered from the decline in business in this area and from the insecurity and unpleasantness resulting from the fighting. They all want quick settlement of the conflict, and their resentment is increasing as the fighting continues. It is obvious that their attitude will soon be reflected in the policies of the British and United States governments. Chiang Kai-shek, on the other hand, is sending reinforcements to the 19th Route Army. Unless we give them a decisive blow, Chiang Kai-shek will increase his assistance and his popularity will grow with talk of victory, leading eventually to war between the two countries. Under the circumstances, it is imperative that hostilities be brought to a quick conclusion by employing an army force of sufficient size and strength. A day's delay will further prolong the war and create complications in the overall situation. As enemy resistance outside Shanghai also appears strong, a quick dispatch of large reinforcements is essential.

At a cabinet meeting the following day Army Minister Araki proposed the sending of reinforcements. It was agreed that two more divisions should be dispatched, and imperial approval was given to the sending of the 11th and 14th divisions. A new headquarters was organized in Shanghai, under General Shirakawa Yoshinori, to have command over all the army's expeditionary forces. Shirakawa and his staff left for Shanghai on February 27 and landed on the Wusung Railway pier on March 1. Part of the 11th Division had already been landed and had immediately advanced southward to attack the Chinese encampments in cooperation with the 9th Division. By this time intelligence reports indicated that the Chinese army was secretly preparing for a general retreat.[60] Emboldened, the General Staff directed the expeditionary force to act quickly to give a decisive blow to the enemy. This was deemed necessary, for the League of Nations was expected to propose a truce at any moment. It was imperative that the enemy not be allowed to slip away.

The Chinese army began a general retreat on March 2. The 9th and 11th divisions, in response to the command from Tokyo, tried to encircle, attack, and crush the retreating army. The Chinese, however, managed to escape their pursuers. Since the League of Nations General Assembly was scheduled to meet on March 3 (March 4 in Shanghai), in accordance with a Council resolution of February 19, it was judged best to cease the hostilities before then. Accordingly, the Japanese force gave up the pursuit and declared a unilateral truce at 2:00 P.M. on March 3. It was only after the truce had been announced that the remainder of the 11th Division and the entire 14th Division arrived at Shanghai.

Truce negotiations had been started soon after the fighting broke out in late January.[61] Foreign governments, especially Great Britain and the United States, were concerned with the neutrality and safety of the International Settlement. It is true that foreign consuls at Shanghai had often expressed sympathy with the Japanese stand and even indicated support for a complete routing of the Chinese army, to ensure the safety of foreign rights and interests.[62] But the foreign governments were annoyed that Japan had acted unilaterally, without consulting them, and had used the settlement as its base of operations. A protest to this effect was presented to the Tokyo government by the United States and Britain as early as January 30.[63] Three days later the British, American, and French ambassadors handed Foreign Minister Yoshizawa a joint communication, suggesting that the belligerents stop all preparations for continuing the hostilities, that Japanese and Chinese troops evacuate Shanghai and a neutral zone be created between them to guarantee the safety of the International Settlement under the jurisdiction of the foreign consuls, and that the two governments commence negotiations for a solution of all pending issues in the spirit of the Kellogg-Briand Pact and the League resolution of December 9. The Chinese government accepted the proposal, but the Japanese flatly refused, except for the creation of a neutral zone. Some in Japan, such as Lord Privy Seal Makino Nobuaki and Finance Minister Takahashi Korekiyo, were so worried about the situation that they insisted Japanese residents should be evacuated from Shanghai, rather than that army reinforcements be sent to protect them. However, the diary kept by Prince Saionji Kimmochi's private secretary Harada Kumao makes it clear that the Japanese government did not accept their views. The powers' joint proposal was unacceptable to the government, probably because it assumed that China and Japan were both to blame and, moreover, because the Manchurian question might have been affected by the proposed Sino-Japanese talks on all outstanding issues.[64]

Meanwhile, in Shanghai truce talks were held on January 29 through the good offices of the British and American consuls-general, and the combatants agreed to stop fighting at 8:00 P.M. Fighting was resumed when the Japanese alleged the Chinese army violated the agreement at 2:00 A.M. on the 30th. Another truce conference was held on the 31st, attended by Admiral Shiozawa, Consul-General Murai, Ts'ai T'ing-k'ai, Mayor Wu, and the foreign consuls, but the talks failed when the Japanese refused to evacuate their assigned defense area. The British persevered. On February 7 Commander-in-Chief Howard Kelly of the British China squadron sailed into Shanghai harbor on his flagship *Kent* and conferred with the combatants. He proposed that in return for a Chinese withdrawal from Chapei, Japanese troops be evacuated from part of the area they occupied. When he saw Admiral Nomura on the 9th, the latter expressed willingness to withdraw Japanese forces "to a safe distance" if the Chinese troops also withdrew. But he did not think the time was opportune for negotiating a truce. As he cabled Tokyo the following day, "It would be best not to make any commitment for the present concerning truce negotiations. We should accede to the British and American demand to refrain from flying planes over and marching through the settlement and meanwhile wait on the progress of the army's fighting. . . . If we arrive at a truce through foreign mediation, the Chinese will talk of victory and there will be grave difficulty in the future." This opinion was accepted by the Navy General Staff, which decided to make no formal commitment until the Japanese forces defeated the 19th Route Army.

As the situation developed into general hostilities, Kelly tried once again to bring both sides together for truce negotiations. Through his efforts a private conference of the combatants was held on board the *Kent* on February 28. Japan was represented by Nomura and Matsuoka Yōsuke, who had been sent to Shanghai as the personal representative of

Prime Minister Inukai and Foreign Minister Yoshizawa to promote understanding with foreign officials and residents, as well as to facilitate communications among Japanese army, navy, and diplomatic personnel. China was represented by Huang Ch'iang, chief of staff of the 19th Route Army, and Wellington Koo, now functioning as Foreign Minister Lo Wen-kan's personal representative. They discussed the timing and extent of troop evacuation, but no specific agreement was reached. However, the Japanese at least managed to impress the world with their willingness to talk peace. This was reflected in the attitude of the League Council, which met on February 29. There Japan was no longer singled out for attack, as had been the case ever since the Chinese delegate, on January 29, had demanded a League investigation of Japanese aggression. A resolution was now adopted calling for a conference of interested powers to settle the incident and guarantee the security of the International and French settlements. This resolution followed a proposal submitted by Yoshizawa on February 26, and the *Kent* conference undoubtedly contributed to improving the atmosphere in Geneva and to acceptance of the Yoshizawa memorandum.

Following the *Kent* conference, the Chinese on February 29 submitted a formal truce proposal. It called for the mutual and simultaneous withdrawal of both armies, to be ascertained by neutral observers. The Chinese police were to maintain order in the evacuated areas. Perhaps this was little more than a trial balloon. The Japanese flatly refused to consider it and proposed instead a truce on the basis of prior Chinese withdrawal to a defined line and the convening of an international conference as laid down in the League resolution. After March 1, however, the course of the fighting changed drastically, and neither the Chinese nor the Japanese proposal was ever seriously considered. Instead, once the Chinese forces were expelled 20 kilometers beyond the settlement, Shirakawa called a unilateral truce, intent on acting as the victor at the forthcoming peace conference. The Chinese, on the other hand, sought to thwart Japanese ambitions by inviting League intervention.

Since both China and Japan had accepted the League resolution of March 4 calling for the opening of truce negotiations, an international committee was organized, made up of British, American, French, Italian, Japanese, and Chinese representatives, to work out details of peace arrangements. Preliminary talks were concluded on March 19, and the formal conference opened five days later. The Japanese delegation consisted of Lieutenant-General Ueda, Major-General Tashiro, Rear Admiral Shimada Shigetarō (chief of staff of the 3rd Fleet), and Minister Shigemitsu. China was represented by the 19th Route Army's Chief of Staff Huang Ch'iang, Political Vice Minister of Foreign Affairs Kuo T'ai-ch'i, and Tai Chi, commander of the Shanghai-Wusung Railway guards army. The ministers and military attachés of the United States, Britain, France, and Italy also participated. The crucial issues were, first, the areas to which Japanese troops were to be withdrawn; second, the timing of their withdrawal; and third, the areas from which Chinese troops would be voluntarily excluded. After difficult negotiations the conferees achieved a compromise solution on the first and third questions, China agreeing to include Chapei and Wusung in the zone to which Japanese troops would be evacuated and to restrict the number of its own soldiers stationed in the P'utung area and south of the Suchow river. But there was complete deadlock on the question of timing; China insisted in vain that Japan should state clearly when its troops would be evacuated.

On April 11 China requested the convening of the League's Committee of Nineteen, which had been organized following an Assembly vote on March 11, to help settle the incident and take over what had hitherto been Council functions in regard to the Far Eastern crisis. In this way the armistice talks were shifted from Shanghai to Geneva. The Chinese strategy was to obtain League intervention by emphasizing how much China had already conceded in Shanghai. The strategy proved a success. Whereas Japan had optimistically expected that the League would eventually refer the matter back to Shanghai, on April 19 the Committee of Nineteen adopted a resolution proposing specific terms for an armistice settlement. Japan opposed it fiercely, holding that the committee had no authority to decide on truce terms. Japan was especially disturbed by Article 11 of the proposed settlement, giving a six-power international committee the right to determine, by a majority vote, the date when Japanese troop withdrawal was to be effected. This was tantamount to giving third powers a say in the timing of Japanese withdrawal, the question over which the Shanghai negotiations had already become deadlocked. The Japanese army considered such a proposition a violation of its right of supreme command, and it even insisted that Japan withdraw from the League if the proposed article were not given up. Confronted with this situation, Sir Miles Lampson, Secretary-General Eric Drummond of the League, and others worked out a compromise plan by which the six-power committee was given the right only to call the attention of Japan or China to a violation of specific terms of the truce, troop evacuation, and the areas from which Chinese soldiers were voluntarily excluded. China readily agreed to this plan, as did the Japanese army. The 24th Mixed Brigade and the 11th Division had already returned to Japan, and the 14th Division had had to be diverted to northern Manchuria. Under the circumstances, the army had no choice but to accept the Lampson proposal, which was subsequently adopted by the League Assembly.

There were a few more complications before the armistice terms were signed. On April 29, as the Japanese in Shanghai celebrated the emperor's birthday, a Korean nationalist threw a bomb into their gathering, killing General Shirakawa and injuring almost all the Japanese officials on the scene, including Admiral Nomura, General Ueda, Minister Shigemitsu, and Consul-General Murai. But the incident did not affect the armistice negotiations, which were now shifted back to Shanghai. However, a new deadlock developed when the Chinese retracted their concession on the voluntary restricted areas, fearing that the establishment of these zones would be the prelude to the creation of a neutral zone. The navy supreme command in Tokyo insisted strongly that Chinese troops be excluded from the P'utung area, for it was the navy that would thenceforth be responsible for protecting Japanese lives and property in Shanghai. The British military, however, supported China, and Japanese naval officials in Shanghai succumbed to their pressure, as, ultimately and reluctantly, did the Navy General Staff. Thus all outstanding issues were settled, and the armistice agreement was signed on May 5.

The armistice was clearly a victory for China. A "victorious" Japan watched in amazement as Chinese diplomacy correctly foresaw the limits of Japanese fighting capacity, recognized Japan's bluff in threatening to withdraw from the League, and chose the best possible timing and methods in appealing to the League. Japanese troops were completely withdrawn from Shanghai by the end of May, and the international conference, scheduled to meet after the armistice to settle residual matters, was never convened, owing to Chinese opposition. But China too paid a price, for it agreed to refrain from stationing troops in certain sections of Shanghai. This agreement was formalized in March 1934, when China was obliged to pledge to notify Japan each time its troops passed through those sections.[65] Still the Japanese army was not satisfied. And as soon as another opportunity presented itself, in 1937, it would pour in a much larger contingent of forces to recapture Shanghai.

The Founding of Manchukuo

The Shanghai truce had been preceded by the creation of a new state in Manchuria. But the birth of Manchukuo had not been easy. The Kwantung Army had at first had to consider possible Soviet reaction. Although several important Chinese had been persuaded to take over the government of the Manchurian provinces independently of the Chang Hsueh-liang regime, they were constantly anxious about the Soviet attitude. As early as the end of September 1931 Itagaki, Ishiwara, and others at Mukden had decided that if the Soviet Union threatened to move into north Manchuria following the creation of the new regime, the Kwantung Army should be ready to take the initiative and fight. But on the whole staff officers in Mukden were optimistic. As a memorandum noted at this time, the Soviet Union would not dare to cross the border if Japan declared its determination to permit no interference with its plans. If the Soviet Union did not heed such a declaration, the army should seize the initiative and move into north Manchuria. "The best strategy is to take the initiative, fight, and use all our resources to arrive at fundamental solutions. If the government [in Tokyo] does not accept this view, we should not care if it fell as a result. Only with such determination can the movement for a new regime be realized, present troubles result in blessings, and a land of happiness emerge in which the Chinese will govern themselves."

The General Staff was essentially in agreement with these views. A secret memorandum written on October 8 by Lieutenant-Colonel Kawabe of the Operations Section is a good example. It said, "It is very doubtful that the Soviet Union would respond if China should appeal to it for help in order to improve its position vis-a-vis Japan. Present-day conditions in Russia seem to be such that it would not want a direct confrontation with Japan." However, it was possible that the Soviet Union might try to use some of the independent governments being established in north Manchuria or even resort to positive action to suppress White Russian partisans, who were expected to become active in the absence of effective government in the area. In such an eventuality, the memorandum continued, Japan should convert its Manchurian strategy to a Soviet strategy. This was because:

> . . . first, the expulsion of Soviet influence from north Manchuria will materially help in achieving a fundamental solution of the Manchurian question; second, in case of war the Japanese army at present is not inferior to the Russian; third, there will be little international intervention with our strong policy toward the Soviet Union.

The supreme command was also in agreement with the Kwantung Army that a Soviet advance beyond Tsitsihar would be most detrimental to Japanese strategy and must be resisted by force. Thus there was little difference in the views of the Japanese military in Tokyo and Mukden. As already seen, what differences there were were due primarily to the supreme command's sensitivity to domestic factors and to the personal attitudes of Army Minister Minami and Chief of Staff Kanaya.

The supreme command was not, however, ready to give the Kwantung Army a free hand in political matters. As early as September 29 the Army Ministry warned the Kwantung Army commander against concerning himself with the rumored scheme for founding a new regime under the former Hsuan-t'ung emperor. Two days later the Kwantung Army was instructed not to involve itself in establishing a new government in Ch'angch'un. Minami wrote privately to Honjō, saying that the army's involvement in politics could only invite disaster. To caution Kwantung Army extremists, the chief of the General Staff's Intelligence Division, Major-General Hashimoto Toranosuke, was dispatched to Mukden. He arrived there on September 28, accompanied by two subordinates.

The Kwantung Army was outraged by this evidence of the army minister's "softening" attitude, according to Katakura's diary. It considered the supreme command's attitude "passive and defeatist" and wondered "if the army central authorities really had determination." Hashimoto and his colleagues got nowhere and were more or less placed in informal confinement. To press its views on Tokyo, the Kwantung Army at this time took several steps. The first was to state its ideas explicitly and once and for all for the consideration of the supreme command. On October 2 Miyake, Itagaki, Ishiwara, Katakura, and Doihara (at the time functioning as provisional mayor of Mukden) conferred, then Honjō sent the following message to Tokyo:

Recently the cabinet and army headquarters, fearing intervention by the League of Nations, Britain, and the United States, have been making apologetic statements. They have also been talking about the possibility of negotiations with the Nanking government or of troop withdrawal. These moves have only encouraged determination on the part of China and have seriously affected the morale of our officers and soldiers. It is absolutely impossible to talk about troop withdrawal when there are so many defeated soldiers roaming around. Such talk will also be a blow to the new regimes being established and will dismay Chinese officials and people who have become favorably inclined toward Japan.

The telegram expressed the view that if Russian troops were mobilized across the border, Japan should firmly oppose them in order to "prevent Manchuria from falling to communism and establish the basis for permanent peace in Asia." The chief of staff responded by merely assuring the Kwantung Army that "there is no change in my true intent." He expressed his sympathy with Kwantung Army officers' "troubled thoughts" but exhorted them "to trust the supreme command's zeal and its efforts to devise an overall plan of settlement."

The second tactic was to make a public statement designed to shock Tokyo out of its lethargy. Ishiwara suggested this approach, Katakura drafted the declaration, Honjō and Itagaki somewhat toned down the draft, and the statement was issued on October 4. The aim here was "to declare the Kwantung Army's beliefs openly at home and abroad, confirm its determination, and express willingness if necessary to challenge the cabinet." The declaration said:

As a result of many years of selfishness and oppression by warlords, people [in Manchuria] have become enraged. They have spread the movement to establish a new government, everywhere admire the imperial army's power, and nowhere are willing to be governed by their old rulers. The Kwantung Army has stood above politics and diplomacy, concentrating on the maintenance of order, and is now quietly watching the course of events while tending to the care of its troops. We are naturally opposed to the establishment of a new regime in Mukden, where order is maintained by the army, or to scheming secretly here. However, we sincerely hope for the early establishment of a region of happiness, in which 30 million people in Manchuria and Mongolia will live according to the principles of coexistence and coprosperity. To promote their unification is entirely moral, and it gives us an urgent opportunity to extend friendship and help to our neighbors. This is the best method for establishing permanent peace in Asia; it is the royal way, which we need not hesitate to proclaim. It is obvious that all justice-loving countries of the world will support and cooperate with such a scheme to promote the happiness of 30 million people.

This was an explicit repudiation by the Kwantung Army of Chang Hsueh-liang's government and an expression of its intention to establish a new regime. The impact in Tokyo was tremendous. The Privy Council, the cabinet, and elements of the public condemned the Kwantung Army's interference in foreign affairs and involvement in politics. But support in the country for the declaration was sufficiently great that Commander-in-Chief Honjō was reported to be "overjoyed."[66]

The third tactic employed by the Kwantung Army to put pressure on Tokyo was the sending of Ugaki Kazushige and Uchida Yasuya to Tokyo. Ugaki, then governor-general of Korea, had long advocated a positive policy in Manchuria. Honjō had been commander of the 10th Division when Ugaki was army minister and had been strongly impressed by the latter's exposition of his views on Manchuria. As soon as the Mukden Incident broke out, the Kwantung Army commander thought of asking Ugaki, now in Seoul (Keijō), to communicate Mukden's intentions to Tokyo. On September 22 Honjō telegraphed Ugaki, expressing the Kwantung Army's opposition to Shidehara's policy of immediate troop withdrawal and settlement of the incident through Chang Hsueh-liang. The telegram stated the army's plan to establish a new regime, though there was no specific mention of an independent Manchuria or of the Hsuan-t'ung emperor.

Ugaki was most cooperative. He noted in his diary that Kanaya, Minami, Honjō, and Doihara were all his men and that he had been instrumental in securing their promotions. "If the incident ended in failure," he wrote, "it could be attributed to inadequacies on the part of those involved, for which I would be blamed."[67] Ugaki was thus ready to play a leading role in the settlement of the incident. He sent numerous telegrams to Prime Minister Wakatsuki and Army Minister Minami, expressing views similar to those being developed by the Kwantung Army. On September 24 he replied to Honjō, accepting the mission to Tokyo and completely supporting the Kwantung Army's stand. "The Foreign Ministry will be shocked to hear of our scheme to establish a protectorate and expel Chang Hsueh-liang," he wrote. His diary of October 20 noted, "Both the army minister and Honjō told me that recently there has been good understanding between the military and the diplomats. But this is not really so. The prime minister has written me in response to my letter of the 10th, apologizing that he was not ready to reply in view of the absence of consensus at the center. Those who have seen the army minister and the foreign minister say there is still a great distance between them on the fundamentals of Manchurian policy. This is to be regretted. I should probably return to Tokyo quickly."

Thus he left Seoul for Tokyo on October 29, there to stay until December 6. He seems to have been as much interested in promoting his own political ambitions as in communicating the Kwantung Army's viewpoint. At any rate, his diary indicates his disgust with the Tokyo government's inability and lack of firm policy. He denounced the indecision of the cabinet and the Minseitō and criticized "Shidehara's crazy idealism and illusion" as obstacles to a solution of the incident. He gave himself the task of overcoming them, but it is difficult to determine how successful he was. He felt that Tokyo leaders generally avoided him. Nonetheless, he does seem to have strengthened Army Minister Minami's position within the cabinet. On November 8 he noted:

> It will take time for basic principles to be adopted by the government and communicated to officials abroad, there to bind their actions so as to ensure complete control over every part of the policy-executing organ. . . . A quick settlement is imperative, as this is an international, not a domestic, affair, and the matter should be settled before League members grow impatient. A delay might result in unexpected political catastrophe. I saw the foreign minister and the army minister and advised them along these lines.

If Ugaki's private diary is to be trusted, the Tokyo cabinet was paralyzed by inability, indecisiveness, and lack of a firm policy.

Meanwhile, Uchida had returned to Tokyo. He had been appointed president of the South Manchuria Railway on June 13 as a key member of Shidehara's staff. He had, in other words, been given a mandate to prevent a crisis in Manchuria. But after September 18 he suddenly became a champion of military action and a collaborator with the Kwantung Army. From this time on his new posture was pushed with increasing vigor, until by 1932 he came to symbolize the professional diplomat's submission to the military. This was a reflection not only of the Kwantung Army's determination to influence Uchida's thinking but also of his own lack of principle. At any rate, the Kwantung Army decided to use him, as well as Ugaki, as spokesmen for its policy.

On October 6 Uchida visited Mukden and conferred with the army staff. After several days' deliberation Miyake, Itagaki, Ishiwara, and others drafted a memorandum outlining the Kwantung Army's position as presented to Uchida, and another paper containing the army's requests of the South Manchuria Railway. Three basic principles were articulated in the first memorandum: the severance of Manchuria from China proper, the unification of Manchuria under a single government, and actual control by Japan over the new government, although outwardly Chinese would administer it. At least in military, diplomatic, and transportation matters, the new regime would have to be placed under Japanese protection. The requests presented to the South Manchuria Railway Company covered such items as the railway's management and operation of the Ssup'ingchieh-T'aonan, T'aonan-Angangch'i, Kirin-Ch'angch'un, and Kirin-Tunhua lines; the taking over of the railways hitherto controlled by Chang's government; speedy construction of the Kirin-Kainei (Hoeryŏng) and Ch'angch'un-Talai lines; destruction of certain Chinese railways considered detrimental to the interests of the South Manchuria Railway; monetary reform; agricultural, forestry, and mining development projects; and the establishment of air services. This document expressed the Kwantung Army's basic policy of controlling the transportation system of Manchuria.

Uchida was more than willing to carry out the mission to Tokyo. He expressed complete agreement with the Kwantung Army's positive stand and determination to establish a new regime in Manchuria. He was opposed to dealing with Chang or the Nanking government. Uchida promised the Mukden leaders to do his best to impress these views on Prince Saionji, Count Makino, and others, especially in view of the report that "court influence" was behind the cabinet's weak policy. On October 10, on his way to Tokyo, he visited Ugaki in Seoul and talked of turning to the Hsuan-t'ung emperor as a possible focus of the contemplated new regime in Manchuria. While Ugaki agreed that a new regime must be established, in his view the choice of personnel was a secondary matter; it was more important to establish the institutional basis of the new government, which could then be headed by any person commanding popular support. He thought the former Ch'ing emperor too archaic a figure, while warlords were to be avoided. In his opinion, a "new group" of men should be brought in.

Uchida's mission was not successful. His advocation of a strong policy shocked Japanese leaders. Prince Saionji thought Uchida had been influenced by the military. Uchida explained that he was advocating strong views to control the young military activists "from within." He wanted, he said, to convey the atmosphere in Mukden to Tokyo so as to establish rapport between them. But he met with little response. Finance Minister Inoue Junnosuke felt Uchida was being used by the army to obtain funds for its schemes. Even the Kwantung Army apparently did not entirely trust him. Honjō's mistrust of Uchida was such that he asked army central headquarters to supervise him to ensure that he was not swayed by Prime Minister Wakatsuki and Foreign Minister Shidehara.[68] Consul-General Hayashi at Mukden seems to have been the only person who thought highly of Uchida at this time. To forestall military interference with nonmilitary matters, Hayashi suggested in a telegram of October 25, there should be created a unified command over all nonmilitary affairs in Manchuria. If this was difficult of realization, Uchida should be made "high commissioner" to carry out all diplomatic and civilian functions.

The views of the supreme command concerning Manchuria still lagged far behind those of the Kwantung Army. It continued to adhere to Plan One, namely, the extension of Japanese rights and interests through a pro-Japanese government in Manchuria, as a memorandum "On the Settlement of the Incident," adopted on October 8 by the army's "Big Three" (the army minister, chief of staff, and inspector-general of military education), indicates:

> 1. A fundamental solution of the Manchurian question must be arrived at through negotiations with a new government that will be established in Manchuria, separate from China proper. To carry out this objective, Kwantung Army troops will be kept at their present positions and maintain public order. Until a new government is established, as many treaty rights as possible should be put into effect through negotiations with local Chinese officials and people.
> 2. Concerning the establishment of the new regime, we should continue to adhere to the principle of nonintervention, whether by our officials or by private persons. Even if we anticipate the separation and independence of Manchuria from China proper, such intentions should be kept secret.

3. Negotiations with the Nanking regime should be limited to general issues affecting Sino-Manchurian relations and should never deal with questions relating to Manchuria proper.

The emphasis here was on taking advantage of the incident to extend Japanese rights in Manchuria. A long list of these rights was compiled, including those granted by treaty but not put into effect, those to be recognized as part of a settlement of the incident, and those to be obtained in the future through negotiations. The first category referred to the construction of new railways, the opening of the interior of Manchuria, and the problem of illegal taxes, all of which had vexed the Japanese government during the 1920s. The second group of demands included abolition of anti-Japanese decrees, police reform, freedom of Japanese military action to maintain order, and restriction of the number of troops under the command of the Manchurian government. The last set of items was to be presented to the new regime and referred to vague items such as tariffs, finance, natural resources, and anticommunism. The document also specified that Japan should warn the Chinese government to put a stop to anti-Japanese activities; if nothing was done, Japan should threaten to take "necessary and sufficient measures." In the event that the lives of Japanese residents in China were endangered, they were to be evacuated to Tsingtao, Shanghai, Hankow, and Amoy and there protected by the navy, and to Peiping and Tientsin to be guarded by the army. Finally, Japan was to reject unjustified interference by foreign governments, although it should seek to obtain their understanding.

With the supreme command's position thus clarified, Army Minister Minami's stance in the cabinet began to harden. He pressed for a quick cabinet decision on a solution of the incident, insisting that the Manchurian question must be settled in Manchuria, not in Nanking. This view seems to have been generally accepted by the cabinet by the first week of October. At the cabinet meeting of October 6 Prime Minister Wakatsuki said he would be willing to do anything so long as he was supported by a unified public opinion. Navy Minister Abo Kiyokazu had no opinion on Manchuria, being interested only in central and north China. Finance Minister Inoue insisted that construction of the Kirin-Kainei line should be begun immediately in the least expensive manner. Home Minister Adachi said it would take three or four years to settle the Manchurian question. He emphasized the need for serious preparations and for devising methods to reduce expenses. Foreign Minister Shidehara alone disagreed with these views, saying no effective settlement could be expected unless the Manchurian question were discussed with the Nanking government. He strongly opposed Inoue's suggestion that, since it would be a long time before a new government was established in Manchuria, various outstanding questions should be discussed immediately with de facto local authorities. After the cabinet meeting the prime, foreign, army, navy, finance, home, and agriculture ministers conferred and settled on a compromise plan. Japan was not to interfere with the establishment of a new government in Manchuria or concern itself with the nature of that government. But it would press to secure existing treaty rights, negotiate further details incidental to a solution of the current crisis, and defer other demands until a new government was established.

At this time Japanese leaders were by no means unanimous on the question of establishing a new regime in Manchuria. Many held that Japan should still negotiate with Chang Hsueh-liang. Yamamoto Jōtarō, former president of the South Manchuria Railway, conveyed such a view to the General Staff on October 17. Privy Councillor Itō Miyoji said he was strongly opposed to the army's rejection of Chang, and at the council meeting of October 17 voices were heard insisting that the incident be settled through both Chang and the Nanking government. This by no means implied support of Shidehara. He was attacked at the meeting by former Foreign Minister Ishii Kikujirō, who said the government had committed a grave blunder in allowing League intervention. The fact remains that, despite these attacks on Shidehara and on the army as well, the cabinet managed to hold to its compromise between Shidehara's and the army's views. Prime Minister Wakatsuki seems to have inclined increasingly toward the army's view and pressed its acceptance on the elder statesmen and opposition party leaders. It may be said that through the prime minister the military were steadily overcoming Foreign Ministry opposition and leading the government to the acceptance of a new regime in Manchuria, although the latter was still visualized as being somehow related to the National Government.[69]

Any possibility that Shidehara's moderate approach might have checked extremism was dashed by two events in mid-October. These were the October plot and the rumored independence of the Kwantung Army. On October 17 a group of young army officers were arrested on suspicion of conspiracy. They were led by Lieutenant-Colonel Hashimoto Kingorō and

Major Chō Isamu and had plotted to overthrow the government and establish a military regime under Lieutenant-General Araki Sadao. They had no concrete plans, however, and the October plot itself was merely an empty gesture. But, coming after the March plot and the Mukden Incident, it shocked the Japanese political world. It is no exaggeration to say that Shidehara diplomacy collapsed in the wake of this episode.

The army supreme command had perhaps even greater reason to worry, for just at that moment it received rumors that the Kwantung Army was preparing to declare its independence. Astounded, on October 17 the General Staff dispatched an urgent message enjoining the Kwantung Army to "desist from any new plan of detaching itself from the imperial army and ruling Manchuria and Mongolia." The message added, "Rest assured that the general situation is developing in accordance with the imperial army's intentions." In a second telegram the chief of staff asked the Kwantung Army to trust in his and his staff's "zeal" and refrain from any rash action. These messages were relayed by the vice chief of staff directly to unit commanders of the Kwantung Army. Mukden headquarters replied two days later, expressing annoyance that the supreme command should have believed such unreliable rumors and protesting its violation of the line of command in communicating directly with unit commanders. Tokyo's fear of Kwantung Army independence soon evaporated, but the episode revealed clearly the abnormal fears that were aroused. The sense of crisis was real enough to impel the supreme command to take steps to coordinate thinking between Tokyo and Mukden. To this end General Shirakawa and Colonel Imamura were sent to Manchuria, their mission being not only to communicate to the Kwantung Army the Big Three's policy decision of October 8 but also to restrain the Kwantung Army from taking independent and rash action. In this latter objective the emissaries were notably unsuccessful, as later events were to show.

Plans were being matured in Mukden for the establishment of a new state in Manchuria. As noted earlier, Ishiwara Kanji had long advocated outright Japanese occupation of Manchuria. Although on September 22 he had accepted the plan for an independent Manchuria, he continued to play with his own ideas. On October 1, for instance, he drafted a memorandum "on governing Manchuria" that visualized Japanese rule over the four northeastern provinces, although they would nominally be governed by a Chinese administration. It was only in the winter of 1931–

32 that Ishiwara abandoned his scheme and accepted the independent Manchuria formula.[70] Kwantung Army formulation of the new state of Manchuria was, therefore, worked out quite independently of Ishiwara's personal views.

A basic document expressing Kwantung Army thinking on political matters was a memorandum entitled "Fundamental Policy for a Settlement of the Manchurian Question," adopted on October 24.[71] It began: "Our aim is to establish an independent new state in Manchuria and Inner Mongolia, separated from China proper, which will outwardly be under unified Chinese administration but actually under our control. We will undertake the transfer of power as quickly as possible and meanwhile extend our influence in all directions and found a solid and unshakable base." Specifically, the new state would include Fengt'ien, Heilungchiang, Kirin, and Jehol and would have Mukden as its capital. Political institutions would take the form of a republic, or, as the document put it, a specific form of republic that would bring happiness to all races in Manchuria under the principle of coexistence and coprosperity. No mention of the Hsuang-t'ung emperor was made, but his use had probably been tacitly agreed. Defense and transportation matters were to be under Japanese control, but there would be a system of local self-government at *hsien* and city level. The movement for the new state would be outwardly led by Chinese but internally assisted and promoted by Japanese. In particular they would endeavor to reform the Heilungchiang regime, wipe out the Chinchou government, and overthrow Chang Hsueh-liang's influence. Any military obstruction or interference with the movement for a new state would be met by reprisals.

Specific details of the proposed republican government were worked out by Matsuki Tamotsu, who had just been appointed the Kwantung Army's counsel on international law. His first "Draft Principles for the Government of a Manchurian-Mongolian Republic" was completed on October 21[72] and outlined the following basic structure:

	Legislative Yuan	Upper House
		Lower House
	Judicial Yuan	Supreme court, higher courts, local courts
President		Home Affairs Department
		Finance Department
		Industry Department

Executive Yuan   Education Department
Communications Department
Foreign Affairs Department
Military Affairs Department

Censorate

After further deliberations with Honjō, Itagaki, and Ishiwara, Matsuki drafted on November 7 a document entitled "Basic Principles Concerning the Proposed Establishment of the Free State of Manchuria and Mongolia,"[73] which detailed Kwantung Army thinking on the new state. First, the need to create an independent state, not just an independent government, was stressed. Merely an independent government would still function as part of China and have no authority to conclude international agreements. As a result, it could not be "moved at will" to serve Japanese interests. Moreover, independent regimes tended to degenerate into warlordism. The annexation of Manchuria and Mongolia, though theoretically most desirable, was impractical, the document went on, because of international repercussions and past commitments. Thus, an independent state of Manchuria and Mongolia was the best obtainable solution.

It then listed several high-sounding principles:

1. Warlordism will be eliminated and a civilian-controlled administration will be instituted.
2. Government will be left to the people to the greatest degree possible, reducing bureaucratic control.
3. An open-door policy of equal opportunities will be pursued with vigor, and domestic and foreign capital and technology will be invited to exploit natural resources and promote industry.
4. There will be created a land of happiness and freedom in which taxes will be reduced, public order will be maintained, and the people will have enough to eat and will enjoy peace.

With respect to the political institutions of the new state, the memorandum described them as "democratic" and "constitutional," then immediately qualified these terms by asserting that since the people's "political consciousness" was not very advanced, there would be no representative government; "constitutionalism," it stated, merely referred to the principle of the separation of powers. Administratively, the new state would consist of six regions: Fengt'ien, Kirin, Heilungchiang,

Jehol, the Eastern Province Special District, and the Dominion of Mongolia. Administrative organs at *hsien* and city level would first be instituted, and once they were functioning effectively, autonomous provincial governments would be established. These would be federated to form a central government whose power ultimately would include, in particular, military, constitutional, jurisdictional, and taxation matters. Once these institutions were sufficiently developed, Japan would recognize the independence of the new state and call on other governments to do likewise. Concerning Japan's relations with the free state of Manchuria and Mongolia, the Fundamental Principles stated:

> 1. Japan will undertake the defense of the free state of Manchuria and Mongolia.
> 2. Japan need not interfere in minor affairs of this independent state, but it must exercise complete control over railways, aviation, and other matters absolutely essential to Japanese security, military and economic.
>
> .   .   .
>
> 5. In order to guide and supervise the affairs of the free state of Manchuria and Mongolia, an advisory organ will be created, composed of Japanese citizens, that will reserve to itself the right to pass judgment upon treaties and important laws.

It is obvious that this general blueprint was intended as a counterproposal to the supreme command's plan for an independent government in Manchuria, which the Kwantung Army feared would surely slip away from Japanese control. It is also possible that these ideas were endorsed by Yü Chung-han, a prominent Manchurian official. He is reported to have told Matsuki that a new independent state, relying on Japan for its defense, was essential if the principle of "secure boundary and peaceful life" *(hokyō anmin)* were to be maintained. At any rate, the Kwantung Army pressed its movement with vigor. On November 7 it telegraphed Tokyo that it would never consent to anything less than an independent Manchuria.

All that was now needed was someone to head the new state. As early as September 22 the Kwantung Army had discussed the possibility of turning to P'u Yi, the former Ch'ing emperor, and while Matsuki worked on an institutional blueprint, the army set in motion its grand strategy. On October 10 it decided to send Colonel Doihara to Tientsin, ostensibly to assist the protocol force in working out its response to the Manchurian crisis, but actually through various stratagems to create confusion in the Peiping-Tientsin area, with a view to abducting P'u Yi, then living in the Japanese concession in Tientsin, and taking him to Manchuria. To carry out this plan, Doihara was appointed head of a newly created "North China Special Agency" (Kahoku Kikan), which had the aim of speeding up Chang Hsueh-liang's downfall and to which substantial funds were allocated. Doihara left for Tientsin on October 27.

Foreign Minister Shidehara was adamantly opposed to the P'u Yi scheme. As he telegraphed Consul-General Kuwashima Kazue at Tientsin on November 1, such a device would only give the impression that Japan was trying to create an independent state of Manchuria and would alienate world public opinion, just as the League of Nations was about to convene. To restore the Manchu emperor was an extreme anachronism, not only because he would be portrayed as counterrevolutionary and undemocratic, but also because a majority of the population of Manchuria was no longer Manchu but Han Chinese. Such a move would therefore frustrate all efforts toward Sino-Japanese understanding, as well as Japan's strategy of letting the dust settle before taking constructive steps in Manchuria.[74] Army Minister Minami and almost all in positions of influence in Tokyo at the time seem to have shared his opposition. When Consul-General Kuwashima took precautions to prevent P'u Yi's abduction, the Kwantung Army sent a protest to the Foreign Ministry. Doihara, undisturbed, proceeded to carry out his scheme. The result was the "first Tientsin incident" of November 8, mentioned earlier. P'u Yi, half under pressure but half voluntarily, left Tientsin in the midst of the confusion and on November 13 arrived at Yingk'ou. As provided in the scenario, he appealed for protection to the Japanese authorities, saying he had fled Tientsin to seek security. The Japanese responded by offering him protection "from a humanitarian point of view" and sent him under guard to Lüshun (Port Arthur).

Meanwhile the nation building had been proceeding smoothly. On November 7 the Fengt'ien Peace Preservation Committee declared its independence of the old Northeastern regime and the National Government and began acting as the "provisional government of Fengt'ien province." Four days later Yü Chung-han joined the committee as head of the Local Autonomy Promotion Board (Chihō Jichi Shidōbu). Later in the month he and other Chinese leaders decided to organize an independent federal government, and in December Tsang Shih-yi was appointed chairman of Fengt'ien province. As Chang Hsueh-liang's forces at Chinchou were crushed on January 3, 1932, Ma Chan-shan in north Manchuria also began to soften his anti-Japanese stand.

The Kwantung Army now decided to speed up the organization of the new central government. In a memorandum of early January the army put down its final guidelines for the projected new government, which was to be based on the principle of the centralization of power. It was to be headed by P'u Yi and governed by an Office of Councillors, to consist of one Manchu, one Mongol, three Han Chinese, and three Japanese. P'u Yi would be given the appellation of "president" or other suitable title, and his appointment was not to give the impression that it was a restoration of the old dynasty. The capital was to be located at Ch'angch'un. The new central government was to be established by late February or early March, in other words, before the arrival of the League of Nations commission of inquiry. "While neither the Nine-Power Treaty nor the League Covenant permits Japan to resort to direct action to separate Manchuria from China proper, these treaties do not, and should not be allowed to, interfere with China's partition at the Chinese people's own volition," the memorandum asserted.

Specific procedural details concerning the organization of the new state were spelled out in a Kwantung Army memorandum of January 27. There it was stipulated that Supreme Administrative Council should be organized, made up of the chairmen of Fengt'ien, Kirin, and Heilungchiang provinces, to prepare for the founding of the new state. It was to decide on the name of the new state, its flag, system of government, and personnel. Each province should propose the establishment of a new state under a president, presumably to give the appearance of public support for the movement; the president should then organize the central government, make a declaration, and issue various decrees. On the basis of this procedural framework a Northeastern Administrative Council was organized on February 17 under the chairmanship of Chang Ching-hui. Eight days later the council declared its intention of creating a new state, to embrace the four northeastern provinces and four Inner Mongolian regions. Some, especially old Ch'ing officials such as Cheng Hsiao-hsu, insisted on a monarchical form of government, but in the end a republican government was proclaimed with P'u Yi as "regent." The date was March 1, 1932.

By the end of 1931 the Japanese government and military had come to accept the desirability of creating a new state in Manchuria. Officials of the Army, Navy, and Foreign ministries worked on drawing up a basic program, obviously under pressure from the Kwantung Army and determined to formulate their own approach. As Itagaki was dispatched from Mukden to Tokyo in early January, the officials in Tokyo felt the need to expedite their work. The result was the "Outline of Principles for the Solution of the China Problem" of January 6,[75] drawn up by section chiefs of the three ministries involved, which in a shortened and slightly modified form was adopted by the cabinet. What stands out is the essential similarity between Mukden's and Tokyo's views on what Japan was attempting. The cabinet decision stated, for instance: "Manchuria and Mongolia will be made an essential part of the existence of the empire; the area will be closely related to the political, economic, defense, transport, and communications affairs of the empire, and it will be under Japanese protection." The January 6 draft had used the terms "the eternal existence of the empire" and "under Japanese power and influence." The cabinet version, while it toned down the original draft, still expressed virtually the same aspirations as those of the Kwantung Army. The document went on to add that a new state should eventually be organized in Manchuria; that its police force, under Japanese direction, should be relied upon for the maintenance of public order and the protection of railways other than the South Manchuria Railway; that the new state should not be allowed to have an army; that Manchuria and Mongolia should be made the first line of defense against the Soviet Union; and that negotiations with the new state should be undertaken to revive and expand Japanese treaty rights in the region. In addition to these items the January 6 draft had mentioned the problem of Manchurian-Chinese relations, proposing, first, that the Nanking government should somehow be led to give up Manchuria; second, that Japan should demand strict suppression of anti-Japanese agitation; and, third, that Japan should endeavor to overthrow communism, anti-Japanese warlordism, and anti-Japanese factions in China proper.

The memorandum, with its ominous tone hinting at possible future action toward China, marks a convergence of the views of Japanese military leaders in Tokyo and Mukden. Between the outbreak of the Mukden Incident on September 18 and the founding of Manchukuo on March 1, the Kwantung Army and the supreme command had quarreled over various operational and policy issues, disputes that at times approached crisis proportions. Nevertheless, the areas of basic agreement between them in the end overcame their differences. It was with complete spontaneity and without any sense of agony that the supreme command greeted the emergence of an independent Manchuria.

Tables

TABLE 1
Actual Auxiliary Vessel Strength at Washington Conference and After

| | Strength at Washington Conference | | | Strength Added in Subsequent Five-Year Period | | | | | |
| | | | | Additional Ships Built | | | Ships Under Construction or Planned | | |
	Cruisers	Destroyers	Submarines	Cruisers	Destroyers	Submarines	Cruisers	Destroyers	Submarines
Japan	17	74	42	6	21	14	6	10	17
United States	28	302	108	10	—	40	8	12	8
Great Britain	50	204	63	9	10	8	14	—	9

SOURCE: Yūshūkai, *Kaigun Oyobi Kaiji Yōran* (Handbook of Naval and Maritime Affairs), Appendix, pp. 25–26.

TABLE 2
Actual Auxiliary Vessel Strength at Geneva Conference

| | Cruisers | | Destroyers | | Submarines | |
	Vessels	Tonnage	Vessels	Tonnage	Vessels	Tonnage
Japan	41	267,679	107	118,232	72	64,236
United States	37	304,425	309	368,514	123	92,499
Great Britain	63	383,140	191	227,100	64	55,050

SOURCE: Yasutomi Shōzō, *Kinsei gunshuku shikan* (A Historical View of Arms Limitation in Modern Times), pp. 161–66.

TABLE 3

Plans Presented at the Geneva Conference by the Three Powers

American Plan of June 20, 1929

	Cruisers	Destroyers	Submarines	
Japan	150,000–180,000 tons	120,000–150,000 tons	36,000–54,000 tons	Cruisers = vessels over 3,000 tons but not over 10,000 tons.
United States	250,000–300,000	200,000–250,000	60,000–90,000	
Britain	250,000–300,000	200,000–250,000	60,000–90,000	Destroyers = vessels over 600 tons but not over 3,000 tons.

British Tonnage Requirements as Presented to the Technical Committee

Cruisers		70
10,000-ton, 8-inch-gun vessels	15	
7500-ton, 6-inch-gun vessels	55	
Mine Layers and Small Plane Carriers	5	
Tonnage for above two categories	600,000 tons	Destroyers 221,600 tons

American Plan of July 5, 1929

Cruisers

Japan	10,000-ton vessel tonnage will be in accord with Washington Conference ratio
United States	400,000 tons, among which there will be 25 10,000-ton vessels
Britain	400,000: 10,000-ton vessel tonnage will be in accord with the Washington Conference ratio

Note: Agree that cruisers other than 10,000-ton cruisers will be considered small cruisers provided it is not necessary that their guns be different from those of the large cruisers.

Japanese Plan of July 6, 1929

	Surface Auxiliary Vessels	Submarines
Japan	300,000 tons (10,000-ton cruisers, 7)	70,000 round estimate
United States	450,000 (10,000-ton cruisers, 10)	
Britain	450,000 (10,000-ton cruisers, 10)	

Japanese Plan of July 13, 1929

Total Auxiliary Vessel Tonnage

Japan	310,000 tons
United States	454,000
Britain	484,000

Japanese Plan of July 18, 1929

Total Auxiliary Vessel Tonnage

Japan	315,000 tons (10,000-ton cruisers, 8; submarines, 70,000 tons)
United States	No proposal
Britain	484,000 tons (10,000-ton cruisers, 12 each for Britain and United States

British Plan of July 18, 1929

	Surface Auxiliary Vessels	*Submarines*
Japan	325,000 tons (10,000-ton cruisers)	60,000 tons
United States	No proposal	60,000
Britain	500,000 tons (10,000-ton cruisers, 12 each for Britain and the United States)	60,000

Note: 25% of total tonnage to be in superannuated vessels.

British Plan of July 28, 1929

	Overall Auxiliary Vessel Tonnage	*Submarines* *(Included in Overall Auxiliary Vessel Tonnage)*
Japan	385,000 tons (10,000-ton cruisers, 8)	60,000 tons
United States	No proposal	90,000
Britain	590,000 tons (10,000-ton cruisers, 12 each for United States and Britain)	90,000

Note: 25% of total tonnage to be in superannuated vessels.

SOURCE: JFM Archives.

TABLE 4

Preliminary Stages in the Development of the Japanese-American Compromise Plan at London Conference

1. American Proposal of February 5, 1930 (lower figures are the alternative plan)

	8-in.-Gun Cruisers	6-in.-Gun Cruisers	Destroyers	Submarines	Total
Japan	108,400 tons, 12 vessels	90,255 tons	120,000 tons	40,000 tons	358,655 tons
United States	180,000* / 150,000 — 18 / 15	147,000 / 189,000	200,000 / 200,000	60,000 / 60,000	587,000 / 599,000
Britain	146,800 / 176,000 — 15 / 18	192,200** / 150,200	200,000 / 200,000	60,000 / 60,000	599,000 / 587,000

*Japanese ratio to this figure is 60%
**Japanese ratio to this figure is 59.7%

2. Japanese Proposal of February 12, 1930 (upper figures are Plan A; lower figures are Plan B)

	8-in.-Gun Cruisers	6-in.-Gun Cruisers	Destroyers	Submarines	Total
Japan	108,400 tons, 12 vessels / 126,000 — 14	107,755 tons / 81,700	105,000 tons	77,900 tons	399,055 tons / 390,600
United States	150,000* / 180,000* — 15 / 18	189,000 / 147,000	150,000	81,000	570,000 / 558,000

*Japanese ratio to this figure is 70%

3. Japanese-British Conversations of February 18, 1930 (Saitō-Craigie) (provided the laying down of 3 of the 18 American 8-in. gun cruisers occurs in 1933 or later)

	8-in.-Gun Cruisers	6-in.-Gun Cruisers	Destroyers	Submarines	Total
Japan	108,400 tons, 12 vessels	98,000 tons	97,500 tons	52,729 tons	356,629 tons
United States	180,000* — 18	147,000	150,000	60,000	537,000
Britain	146,000 — 15	192,200**	150,000	60,000	549,000

*Japanese ratio to this figure is 66+%
**Japanese ratio to this figure is 64%

4. *Japanese-American Conversations of February 25, 1930 (Matsudaira-Reed)*

Japan	108,400 tons, 12 vessels	108,000 tons	90,000 tons	52,000 tons	258,400 tons	
United States	180,000*	143,500	150,000	60,000	533,500	*Japanese ratio to this figure is 67 + %
Britain	146,800	192,200**	150,000	60,000	549,000	**Japanese ratio to this figure is 66 – %

5. *Japanese-American Conversations of February 25, 1930 (Matsudaira-Reed); First Japanese Counterplan (Abo Plan)*

Japan	108,400 tons, 12 vessels	107,800 tons	105,000 tons	77,900 tons	399,000 tons	
United States	150,000*	189,000	150,000	81,000	570,000	*Japanese ratio to this figure is 70%
Britain	146,800*	192,200	150,000	81,000	570,000	

Note: United States and Britain permitted to reduce their 6-in.-gun cruiser tonnage by 42,000 tons and build three additional 8-in.-gun cruisers (30,000 tons). In that event Japan might reduce its 6-in.-gun cruisers by 26,100 tons and build 17,600 tons of 8-in.-gun cruisers.

6. *Japanese-American Conversations of March 2, 1930 (Matsudaira-Reed): Second Japanese Counterplan*

Japan	126,000 tons, 14 vessels	64,800 tons	105,000 tons	77,900 tons	373,700 tons	
United States	180,000*	143,500	150,000	60,000	533,500	*Japanese ratio to this figure is 70%

(Laying down to be delayed)

Note: Two of Japan's 8-in.-gun cruisers to be laid down only when American ones laid down here.

TABLE 4

Preliminary Stages in the Development of the Japanese-American Compromise Plan at London Conference

7. Japanese-British Conversations of March 3, 1930 (Saitō-Craigie)

The Japanese pointed out that, taking the highest figure proposed to the Japanese in the previous Japanese-American and Japanese-British conversations, the total tonnage was only about 7,000 tons short of 70% of the American tonnage.

8-in.-Gun Cruisers	108,400 tons, 12 vessels	
6-in.-Gun Cruisers	108,000	(suggested by the American negotiator)
Destroyers	97,500	(suggested by the British negotiator)
Submarines	52,729	
Total	366,629	

8. Japanese-American Conversations of March 7, 1930 (Wakatsuki-Stimson-Reed)

Japan	108,400 tons, 12 vessels	108,000 tons	90,000 tons	52,700 tons	359,100 tons
United States	180,000 18	143,400	150,000	60,000	533,500

These figures left the Japanese total tonnage slightly less than 15,000 tons short of a 70% ratio to the American tonnage. It was proposed that Matsudaira and Reed meet to discuss this point further.

9. Japanese-American Conversations of March 8, 1930 (Matsudaira-Reed)

Japan	108,400 tons, 12 vessels	118,415 tons*	95,000 tons	52,700 tons	374,515 tons
United States	180,000** 18	143,500	150,000	60,000	533,500

*The Japanese ratio to the comparable British tonnage is 68 + %.
**The Japanese ratio to this figure is 70 + %.

10. Japanese-American Conversations of March 10, 1930 (Matsudaira-Reed)

Japan	108,400 tons, 12 vessels	115,915 tons	95,000 tons	52,700 tons	374,515 tons

SOURCE: JFM Archives.

TABLE 5
Japanese-American Compromise Plan of March 12, 1930

	8-in.-Gun Cruisers		6-in.-Gun Cruisers	Destroyers	Submarines	Total
Japan	108,400 tons,	12 vessels	108,415 tons	97,500 tons	52,700 tons	367,015 tons
United States	180,000	18	143,500	150,000	52,700	526,200
Britain	146,800	15	192,200	150,000	52,700	541,700

SOURCE: JFM Archives.

TABLE 6
Japanese-American Compromise Plan of March 13, 1930

	8-in.-Gun Cruisers		6-in.-Gun Cruisers	Destroyers	Submarines	Total
Japan	108,400 tons,	12 vessels	100,450 tons	105,500 tons	52,700 tons	367,050 tons
United States	180,000	18	143,500	150,000	52,700	526,200
Britain	146,800	15	192,200	150,000	52,700	541,700

SOURCE: JFM Archives.

TABLE 7

Changes in Naval Strength Under the London Naval Treaty

	Actual Tonnage Before Conference	Tonnage Under Treaty	Increase or Decrease
Heavy Cruisers:			
Japan	108,400 tons	108,400 tons	—
United States	130,000	180,000 (150,000)*	+50,000
Britain	146,800	146,800	(+20,000)
Light Cruisers:			
Japan	98,415 tons	100,450 tons	+2,035 tons
United States	70,500	143,500 (189,000)*	+73,000 (+118,500)
Britain	217,111	192,200	−24,911
Destroyers:			
Japan	132,495 tons	105,500 tons	−26,995 tons
United States	290,304	150,000	−140,304
Britain	184,371	150,000	−34,371
Submarines:			
Japan	77,842 tons	52,700 tons	−25,142 tons
United States	82,582	52,700	−29,882
Britain	60,284	52,700	−7,584
Overall Tonnage:			
Japan	417,152 tons	367,050 tons	−49,717 tons
United States	573,386	526,200 (541,700)	−47,186 (−31,686)
Britain	608,566	541,700	−66,866

SOURCE: Navy Papers in JDA Archives.

*Figures in parentheses are those that would result if United States exercised its option to substitute light cruisers for heavy cruisers.

TABLE 8
Comparison of Japan's Original Demands with the Treaty Results

Original demands	70% heavy cruiser ratio	Existing submarine tonnage	Light cruisers and destroyers	70% overall tonnage ratio
Tonnage calculated on basis of original demands	126,000 tons (70%)	77,842 tons (148%)	164,498 tons (56.05%)	368,340 tons (70%)
Tonnage under treaty	108,400 tons (60.23%)	52,700 tons (100%)	205,950 tons (70.15%)	367,050 tons (69.75%)
Difference between treaty tonnage and tonnage demanded	−17,600 tons	−25,142 tons	+41,452 tons	−1,290 tons

SOURCE: Japan, Navy Ministry, "Sūmitsuin kankei shitsumon ōtō shiryō" (Materials upon Which To Base Responses to Questions That May Arise in the Privy Council), in *GSF*, p. 58.

Figures in parentheses are the ratios vis-a-vis the tonnage allowed America under treaty.

Notes

Full English-language titles, publication information, and Japanese characters may be found in the bibliography.

ONE

The London Naval Treaty, 1930

Introduction (Tiedemann)

1. For an analysis of East Asian international relations in the 1920s, see Akira Iriye, *After Imperialism: The Search for a New Order in the Far East, 1921–1931*. For the background of naval diplomacy in the 1920s and 1930s, the best work is Stephen Roskill, *Naval Policy Between the Wars*. However, this study is weak on the Japanese side, since it is based almost exclusively on Western sources and therefore views Japanese actions through the eyes of the European and American participants. The same reservation applies to Gerald E. Wheeler, *Prelude to Pearl Harbor: The United States Navy and the Far East, 1921–1931*. Four studies that use both Western and Japanese sources are: William Reynolds Braisted, *The United States Navy in the Pacific, 1909–1922*; Thomas H. Buckley, *The United States and the Washington Conference*; Ian H. Nish, "Japan and Naval Aspects of the Washington Conference," in William G. Beasley, ed., *Modern Japan: Aspects of History, Literature and Society*; and Roger Dingman, *Power in the Pacific: The Origins of Naval Arms Limitation, 1914–1922*.

2. The Japanese consistently exceeded the 10,000-ton displacement limit by about 3,000 tons and were thus able to design much better heavy cruisers than the Western countries.

3. Raymond G. O'Connor, *Perilous Equilibrium: The United States and the London Naval Conference of 1930*.

4. Horinouchi Kensuke, Yamagata Kiyoshi, and Unno Koshirō, *Kaigun gunshuku kōshō fusen jōyaku* (Naval Arms Reduction Negotiations and the Anti-war Pact).

5. Itō Takashi, *Shōwa shoki seiji shi kenkyū: Rondon kaigun gunshuku mondai o meguru sho seiji shūdan no taikō to teikei* (A Study of the Political History of the Early Shōwa Era: Cooperation and Opposition of Various Political Groups with Regard to the London Naval Conference Controversy).

6. Personal communication from a member of the study group.

7. See Sadao Asada, "Japanese Admirals and the Politics of Naval Limitation: Katō Tomosaburō vs. Katō Kanji," in Gerald Jordan, ed., *Naval Warfare in the Twentieth Century*, pp. 141–66; and Stephen E. Pelz, "Risō no teikoku: Shin chitsujo kensetsu e no Nihon gunjin no yume, 1928–1940" (Idealistic Empire: The Dreams of Japanese Military Men About the Construction of a New Order, 1928–1940), in Satō Seizaburō and Roger Dingman, eds., *Kindai Nihon no taigai taidō* (Modern Japanese Attitudes Toward the Outer World), pp. 155–86. For a discussion of the history of Japanese naval thinking, see Tsunoda Jun, "Nihon kaigun sandai no rekishi" (A History of Three Generations of the Japanese Navy), *Jiyū*, 11(2):138–69, February 1969. A good general survey of the Japanese navy is Ikeda Kiyoshi, *Nihon no kaigun* (The Japanese Navy). On the 70-percent-ratio question, see Suekuni Masao, "Teikoku kaigun to nanawari" (The Imperial Navy and the 70-Percent Ratio), in Bōeichō Senshishitsu (National Defense Agency, Military History Office), *Dai Tōa (Taiheiyō) sensō senshi sōsho* (The Greater East Asia (Pacific) War History Series), vol. 31: *Kaigun gunsembi 1* (Naval Armaments and Preparations for War 1); and Nomura Minoru, "Tai-Bei-Ei kaisen to kaigun tai-Bei naniwari shisō" (The Beginning of the War with America and Britain and the Navy's Ideas About the 70-Percent Ratio Toward America), *Gunji shigaku*, 9(2):23–24, September 1973.

8. For a discussion of this point, see Akira Iriye, "The Failure of Economic Expansion-

ism, 1918–1931," in Bernard S. Silberman and H. D. Harootunian, eds., *Japan in Crisis: Essays on Taishō Democracy.*

9. See also interesting material in Nomura Minoru, "Gunshuku mondai ni kansuru Hamaguchi shushō nisshi" (Prime Minister Hamaguchi's Diary Notes on the Arms Limitation Problem), *Gunji shigaku*, 12(3):74–81, December 1976.

10. For these developments, see Asada Sadao, "The Japanese Navy and the United States," in Dorothy Borg and Shumpei Okamoto, eds., *Pearl Harbor as History: Japanese-American Relations, 1931–1941*, pp. 225–59; Stephen E. Pelz, *Race to Pearl Harbor: The Failure of the Second London Naval Conference and the Onset of World War II*; and Nakamura Kikuo, *Shōwa kaigun hishi* (Secret History of the Navy during the Shōwa Era).

Essay (Kobayashi)

1. U.S. Department of State, *Foreign Relations of the United States: Diplomatic Papers* (hereafter FR), 1927, 1:13–14, 22–23.

2. Japan, National Defense Agency, Military History Office (hereafter JDA) Archives.

3. Saitō Shishaku Kinenkai, ed., *Shishaku Saitō Makoto den* (Biography of Viscount Saitō Makoto), 3:72–73.

4. Rolland A. Chaput, *Disarmament in British Foreign Policy*, pp. 169–70.

5. *Ibid.*, pp. 167, 172.

6. Henry L. Stimson and McGeorge Bundy, *On Active Service in Peace and War*, p. 164.

7. FR, 1929, 1:91–96.

8. Matsudaira to Tanaka, telegram of June 6, 1929, in Japan, Foreign Ministry (hereafter JFM) Archives.

9. Matsudaira to Tanaka, telegram of June 17, 1929, *ibid.*

10. Matsudaira to Tanaka, telegram of June 20, 1929, *ibid.*; FR, 1929, 1:121–28.

11. League of Nations, *Official Journal: Supplement No. 75, Records of the Tenth Ordinary Session of the Assembly, Plenary Meetings, Text of the Debates*, p. 34.

12. "Gumbi seigen mondai taisaku no ken" (Measures To Cope with the Arms Limitation Problem) and "Gumbi seigen ni taisuru teikoku no hōshin" (The Empire's Arms Limitation Policy), in JFM Archives.

13. Shidehara to Matsudaira, telegram of July 19, 1929, *ibid.*

14. Shidehara to Matsudaira, telegram of August 21, 1929, *ibid.*

15. Matsudaira to Shidehara, telegram of July 5, 1929, *ibid.*

16. Matsudaira to Shidehara, telegram of August 27, 1929, *ibid.*

17. Shidehara to Matsudaira, telegram of September 20, 1929, *ibid.*

18. JFM, *Nihon gaikō nempyō narabi ni shuyō bunsho* (Chronology and Major Documents of Japanese Foreign Relations), 2:137; Great Britain, Foreign Office, *Documents on British Foreign Policy, 1919–1939*, Second Series, 1:103–5.

19. JFM, *Nihon gaikō nempyō*, 2:138–39.

20. *Ibid.*, pp. 141–42.

21. JFM Archives.

22. Wakatsuki Reijirō, *Ōshū no tsukai shite* (My Mission to Europe), pp. 71–72.

23. Wakatsuki Reijirō, *Kofūan kaikoroku* (Memoirs Written at Kofūan), p. 355. The stages through which negotiations passed may be found in the appendix.

24. *Ibid.*, p. 356–57.

25. Delegates to Shidehara, telegram 202, March 12, 1930, JFM Archives, published

in Nihon Kokusai Seiji Gakkai, Taiheiyō Sensō Gen'in Kenkyūbu (Japan Association on International Relations, Study Group on the Causes of the Pacific War), ed., *Taiheiyō sensō e no michi: Bekkan shiryō hen* (The Road to the Pacific War: Supplementary Volume of Documents), pp. 9–10 (hereafter cited as TSM: *Bekkan*).

26. Delegates to Shidehara, telegram 208, March 14, 1930, *ibid.*, pp. 11–12.

27. Wakatsuki, *Kofūan*, pp. 363, 365.

28. Adachi Kenzō, *Adachi Kenzō jijoden* (Autobiography of Adachi Kenzō), p. 239.

29. Okada Taishō Kiroku Hensankai, ed., *Okada Keisuke*, p. 181.

30. Okada Keisuke, *Okada Keisuke kaikoroku* (Reminiscences of Okada Keisuke), p. 53; JDA Archives.

31. JDA Archives.

32. Reproduced in Ikeda Kiyoshi, "Rondon kaigun jōyaku ni kansuru Gunreibugawa no shiryō" (Navy General Staff Materials Related to the London Naval Treaty), *Hōgaku zasshi*, 15(4):102–26, March 1969, and 16(1):123–42, August 1969 (hereafter cited as *Katō Diary*).

33. *Ibid.*, 15:102.

34. *Ibid.*, pp. 104–7.

35. Katō Kanji, "Gunshuku shoken" (Views on Disarmament), item 515 in the Makino Nobuaki Papers, Kenseishi Shiryōshitsu (Constitutional Government History Archives), National Diet Library, Tokyo.

36. Katō Kanji Denki Hensankai, ed., *Katō Kanji taishō den* (Biography of Admiral Katō Kanji), pp. 891–92.

37. Katō to Takarabe, secret telegram 2, March 17, 1930, in Hori Teikichi, comp., "Shōwa go-nen shigatsu tsuitachi kaikun ni kansuru keiei" (Particulars Concerning the April 1, 1930, Return Instructions), in the Enomoto Shigeharu Papers, JDA Archives, published in TSM: Bekkan, pp. 16–17 (hereafter cited as Hori, Return Instructions).

38. "Okada Keisuke nikki" (Diary of Okada Keisuke), entry for March 23, 1930, published in *Gendai shi shiryō 7: Manshū jihen* (Source Materials on Contemporary History, 7; The Manchurian Incident) (hereafter GS 7), p. 5 (hereafter cited as *Okada Diary*).

39. Matsudaira to Shidehara, top secret telegram of March 15, 1930, in Hori Teikichi, comp., "Rondon kaigi seikun yori kaikun made no kikan shimpen zatsuroku" (Miscellaneous Personal Records Concerning the London Conference from the Request for Instructions Until the Dispatch of the Return Instructions). In the Enomoto Papers, reproduced in GS 7, p. 35 (hereafter cited as Hori, London Conference Records).

40. Wakatsuki, *Kofūan*, p. 356.

41. Hamaguchi Naikaku Hensanjo, ed., *Hamaguchi naikaku* (The Hamaguchi Cabinet), p. 155.

42. *Okada Diary*, entries for March 23, 1930, and March 17, 1931, GS 7, pp. 4–5, 28–29.

43. Sakonji to Yamanashi, navy disarmament secret telegram 57, March 23, 1930, in Hori, Return Instructions, TSM: *Bekkan*, pp. 24–25.

44. Sakonji to Yamanashi, navy disarmament secret telegram 59, March 25, 1930, *ibid.*, pp. 26–27.

45. Sakonji to Yamanashi, navy disarmament secret telegram 61, March 26, 1930, *ibid.*, p. 28; Wakatsuki, *Kofūan*, p. 356.

46. Wakatsuki to Shidehara, telegram 229, March 26, 1930, in Hori, Return Instructions, TSM: *Bekkan*, pp. 29–31.

47. Takarabe to Yamanashi, secret telegram 6, March 26, 1930, *ibid.*, pp. 27–28.

48. Abo to Yamanashi, secret telegram 4, March 29, 1930, *ibid.*, p. 33.

49. Harada Kumao, *Saionji kō to seikyoku* (Prince Saionji and the Political Situation), 1:31–32.

50. Sakonji to Yamanashi and Suetsugu, private secret telegram 1, March 16, 1930, in Hori, Return Instructions, TSM: *Bekkan*, p. 15.

51. Sakonji to Yamanashi and Suetsugu, private secret telegram 2, March 17, 1930, *ibid.*

52. Harada, *Saionji*, 1:27, 32.

53. Hori, London Conference Records, GS 7, p. 37.

54. Harada, *Saionji*, 1:17–19.

55. *Okada Diary*, entry for March 15, 1930, GS 7, p. 3.

56. Translator's note: Okada and Katō were both from Fuku prefecture.

57. Okada, *Kaikoroku*, pp. 42–43.

58. *Ibid.*, pp. 52–53.

59. Aoki Tokuzō, *Taiheiyō senso zenshi* (The Historical Background of the Pacific War), 1:30.

60. Abo to Katō, secret telegram 2, March 14, 1930, in Hori, Return Instructions, TSM: *Bekkan*, p. 14.

61. *Ibid.*

62. *Okada Diary*, entry for March 17, 1930, GS 7, p. 4.

63. Hori, Return Instructions, TSM: *Bekkan*, pp. 15–16.

64. *The Times* (London), March 18 and 19, 1930; delegates to Shidehara, telegram 219, March 19, 1930, JFM Archives. On March 20 Shidehara summoned William R. Castle, the American ambassador, to the Foreign Ministry and explained that the government had no knowledge of the "statement by the naval authorities." It represented, he said, the private views of certain navy officers and had been published by error. *Tōkyō Nichi-nichi shimbun*, March 21, 1930.

65. *Tōkyō Asahi shimbun*, March 22, 1930.

66. Shidehara to delegates, telegram 90, March 15, 1930, in Hori, Return Instructions, TSM: *Bekkan*, p. 14.

67. Shidehara to delegates, telegrams 93 and 95, March 19, 1930, *ibid.*, pp. 18–20.

68. See GS 7, pp. xxxiii–xxxiv; and "Sangatsu jūyokka zenken seikun (dai nihyakuhachi go den) ni kansuru taisaku" (Policy Toward the Delegates' Request for Instructions on March 14 [telegram 202]), *ibid.*, pp. 20–21.

69. "Zenken seikun ni taisuru kaikun an" (Proposed Draft for the Return Instructions To Be Sent in Response to the Delegates' Request for Instructions), *ibid.*, pp. 22–24.

70. "Kaikun an ni kansuru hikōshiki Gunji Sangikan Kaigi kiji" (Record of the Informal Meeting of the Supreme War Council Held in Connection with the Proposed Draft of the Return Instructions), *ibid.*, p. 24.

71. *Ibid.*, pp. 25–26; Hori, London Conference Records, GS 7, pp. 37–38.

72. *Ibid.*

73. *Ibid.*, p. 38.

74. *Okada Diary*, entry for March 27, 1930, GS 7, p. 6.

75. *Ibid.*, entry for March 28, 1930.

76. Hori, London Conference Records, GS 7, p. 38.

77. *Okada Diary*, entry for March 29, 1930, GS 7, p. 7.

78. Hori, Return Instructions, TSM: *Bekkan*, p. 39.

79. *Loc. cit.*

80. Hori, London Conference Records, GS 7, p. 39; *Okada Diary*, entry for March 31, 1930, GS 7, Okada, *Kaikoroku*, p. 54.

81. Hori, Return Instructions, TSM: *Bekkan*, pp. 37–38.

82. *Ibid.*, p. 38.

83. Yamanashi to Takarabe, secret telegram 24, April 1, 1930, *ibid.*, p. 43.

84. *Ibid.*, p. 50.

85. Yamanashi to Takarabe, secret telegram 21, March 31, 1930, *ibid.*, pp. 36–37.

86. Takarabe to Yamanashi, secret telegram 8, April 1, 1930, *ibid.*, p. 49.

87. Katō to Takarabe, Navy General Staff, secret telegram 3, April 2, 1930, *ibid.*, p. 49.

88. *Ibid.*

89. Aoki, *Taiheiyō sensō*, p. 43.

90. See Hori, Return Instructions, TSM: *Bekkan*, pp. 2, 56–63. On the navy documents, see n. 132 below.

91. Suzuki Kantarō, *Suzuki Kantarō jiden* (Autobiography of Suzuki Kantarō), pp. 275–76.

92. Hori, Return Instructions, TSM: *Bekkan*, pp. 33–34, 46–48.

93. *Ibid.*, p. 51.

94. *Okada Diary*, entry for April 22, 1930, GS 7, pp. 10–11.

95. Katō and Yamanashi to Takarabe, secret telegram 29, April 21, 1930, in Hori, Return Instructions, TSM: *Bekkan*, p. 51.

96. Harada, *Saionji*, 1:63.

97. Debuchi to Shidehara, telegram of April 13, 1930, JFM Archives.

98. Matsudaira to Shidehara, telegram of May 17, 1930, *ibid.*

99. Hori, Return Instructions, TSM: Bekkan, pp. 43–44.

100. "Sūmitsuin kankei shitsumon ōtō shiryō" (Materials upon Which To Base Responses to Questions That May Arise in the Privy Council), GS 7, pp. 79–80.

101. U.S. Congress, Senate, Committee on Foreign Relations, *Hearings on Treaty on the Limitation of Naval Armaments*, pp. 89–99, 101–21, 171–94.

102. *Ibid.*, pp. 25–26.

103. U.S. Department of State, *London Navy Treaty: Radio Address by the Honorable Henry L. Stimson, June 12, 1930*.

104. *New York Times*, July 23, 1930.

105. Great Britain, *Parliamentary Debates*, 239 *House of Commons Debates*, 5th Session, columns 1919–20.

106. *The Times* (London), April 23, 1930.

107. *Ōsaka Asahi shimbun*, January 14, 1930.

108. *Ibid.*, March 30, 1930.

109. *Jiji shimpō*, March 30, 1930.

110. *Ōsaka Asahi shimbun*, April 1, 1930.

111. *Tōkyō Nichi-nichi shimbun*, April 1, 1930; *Ōsaka Mainichi shimbun*, April 1, 1930.

112. *Jiji shimpō*, April 5, 1930.

113. *Ōsaka Asahi shimbun*, April 5, 1930.

114. Shidehara to Wakatsuki, telegram of April 2, 1930, JFM Archives.

115. JFM Archives.

116. *Ibid.*

117. *Tōkyō Asahi shimbun*, March 27, 1930.

118. JFM Archives.

119. For a detailed discussion, see Matsushita Yoshio, *Nihon gunsei to seiji* (Politics

and the Japanese Military System) and *Meiji gunsei shiron* (History of the Meiji Military System), vol. 2.

120. Hara Keiichirō, ed., *Hara Takashi nikki* (Diary of Hara Takashi), 9:467–68; Takakura Tetsuichi, *Tanaka Giichi denki* (Biography of Tanaka Giichi), 2:346–48.

121. Dai Nihon Teikoku Gikai Shi Kankōkai, ed., *Dai Nihon Teikoku Gikai shi* (Records of the Imperial Japanese Diet), 13:50–56.

122. *Ibid.*, 15:784.

123. Harada, *Saionji*, 1:42.

124. *Ibid.*

125. Reprinted in Minobe Tatsukichi, *Gikai seiji no kentō* (A Study of Parliamentary Politics), pp. 99–106.

126. *Tōkyō Asahi shimbun*, May 2, 3, 4, 1930, reprinted in Minobe, *Gikai seiji*, pp. 106–16.

127. *Ōsaka Mainichi shimbun*, May 1, 2, 3, 4, 5, 1930. Dr. Gorai Kinzō and Professor Nakano Tomio, both of Waseda University, argued, in the *Kokumin shimbun* (May 8, 1930) and the *Tōkyō Nichi-nichi shimbun* (May 3–11, 1930), respectively, that the cabinet's decision regarding the return instructions was not a violation of the right of military command. On the other hand, Drs. Ninagawa Shin, Soejima Giichi, and Matsumoto Shigetoshi maintained that it was a violation.

128. Harada, *Saionji*, 1:42.

129. Hori Teikichi, comp., "Rondon kaigi to tōsuiken mondai" (The London Conference and the Right of Military Command Problem), Enomoto Papers, published in TSM: *Bekkan*, pp. 63–71.

130. *Ibid.*, p. 69.

131. Hori, Return Instructions, TSM: *Bekkan*, p. 55.

132. Japan, Navy General Staff, "Seifu kaikun kettei happu no keiei nado ni kansuru sankō shorui sōfu no ken" (The Transmission of Materials Related to Events at the Time of the Issuance of the Government's Decision on the Return Instructions), included in "Gunreibu sakusei kaikun hatsurei zengo no kijira" (Account Produced by the Navy General Staff Concerning the Circumstances at the Time of the Issuance of the Return Instructions), Enomoto Papers, published in TSM: *Bekkan*, pp. 58–59 (hereafter cited as NGS Account).

133. Hori Teikichi, comp., "Rondon kaigun jōyaku teiketsu keii" (Particulars Concerning the Conclusion of the London Naval Treaty), Enomoto Papers, published in GS 7, p. 99 (hereafter cited as Hori, Treaty Conclusion).

134. *Jiji shimpō*, April 24, 1930.

135. See the materials drawn from Japan, Army General Staff, First Section, "Shōwa go-nen Rondon kaigi kankei tōsuiken ni kansuru shorui tsuzuri" (File of Documents Concerning the Right of Military Command and the 1930 London Conference), JDA Archives, published in GS 11: *Zoku Manshū jihen* (The Manchurian Incident 2), pp. 3–100 (hereafter cited as AGS File). See also Segawa Yoshinobu, "Issen kyūhyaku sanjū-nen Rondon gunshuku kaigi kaisai to Nihon rikugun" (The Holding of the 1930 London Arms Limitation Conference and the Japanese Army), *Saitama Daigaku kiyō (Shakai Kagaku hen)*, No. 1, March 1966, pp. 1–9, and "Tōsuiken to Sambō Hombu—Issen kyūhyaku sanjū-nen Rondon gunshuku kaigi o chūshin to shite" (The Right of Military Command Problem and the Army General Staff—The London Disarmament Conference), *Bōei ronshū*, 5 (3):13–37, October 1966.

136. Harada, *Saionji*, 1:56.

137. JDA Archives.

138. JFM Archives.
139. Yamaura Kan'ichi, ed., *Mori Kaku*, pp. 671–72.
140. Harada, *Saionji*, 1:83.
141. JDA Archives.
142. Shidehara Heiwa Zaidan, ed., *Shidehara Kijūrō*, pp. 420–21.
143. *Katō Diary*, 15:114.
144. *Okada Diary*, entry for May 3, 1930, GS 7, p. 11.
145. *Katō Diary*, 15:114.
146. *Okada Diary*, entry for May 11, 1930, GS 7, pp. 12–13; Okada, *Kaikoroku*, p. 62.
147. NGS Account.
148. *Tōkyō Asahi shimbun*, April 27, 1930.
149. Kikuchi Gorō, *Rikken Seiyūkai shi* (History of the Seiyūkai) 7:217–18, Inukai sōsai jidai (Inukai's Presidency).
150. *Ibid.*, p. 223.
151. *Ibid.*, pp. 249, 251.
152. *Tōkyō Asahi shimbun*, April 26, 1930.
153. *Ibid.*
154. *Hōchi shimbun*, April 28, 1930.
155. *Tōkyō Asahi shimbun*, May 1, 1930.
156. *Tōkyō Nichi-nichi shimbun*, May 1, 1930.
157. *Jiji shimpō*, May 4, 1930.
158. *Tōkyō Asahi shimbun*, May 1, 1930.
159. *Ibid.*, May 2, 1930; *Jiji shimpō*, May 4, 1930.
160. *Tōkyō Nichi-nichi shimbun*, May 3, 1930.
161. AGS File, p. 52.
162. *Ibid.*, p. 53.
163. *Tōkyō Asahi shimbun*, May 4, 1930.
164. *Ibid.;* AGS File, pp. 54–55.
165. *Tōkyō Asahi shimbun*, May 3, 1930; *Tōkyō Nichi-nichi shimbun*, May 3, 1930.
166. *Tōkyō Asahi shimbun*, May 8, 1930.
167. *Ibid.*, May 6, 1930; AGS File, p. 50.
168. *Kokumin shimbun*, May 6, 1930; AGS File, p. 50.
169. *Tōkyō Asahi shimbun*, May 6, 1930.
170. *Jiji shimpō*, May 8, 1930; AGS File, p. 51.
171. *Tōkyō Asahi shimbun*, May 10, 1930.
172. *Ibid.*, May 11, 1930.
173. Kikuchi, *Seiyūkai*, 7:352–53.
174. *Tōkyō Nichi-nichi shimbun*, May 18, 1930.
175. JFM Archives. On the executive committee of the Gunshuku Kokumin Dōshikai were Lieutenant-General Baron Kikuchi Takeo and a number of other retired generals and admirals, Honda Kumatarō, Uchida Ryōhei, Kuzū Yoshihisa, Ōkawa Shūmei, Kita Reiki-chi, Nishida Mitsugu, and Iwata Ainosuke.
176. For instance, on April 21 the Seikyōsha published a 31-page pamphlet by Hirata Shinsaku entitled "The Danger to National Defense" *(Kokubō no kiki)*. Hirata argued that if the 70-percent ratio were abandoned, Japan either would have to knuckle under to the United States and give up Manchuria and Mongolia or would have to fight the United States with a navy doomed to defeat; that the 60-percent ratio approved by the government would not prevent war but rather would give rise to a war in which Japan would be

defeated and the nation ruined; that even if Japan were to repudiate the London Treaty, there would be no naval race; that the conclusion, in disregard of the navy chief of staff's opposition, of a treaty certain to lead to defeat in war was a violation of the right of military command and destructive of the constitution.

177. JFM Archives.
178. Ibid.
179. Harada, Saionji, 1:221.
180. Kodama Yoshio, Ware yaburetari (We Were Defeated), p. 38.
181. Okada Diary, entry for May 20, 1930, GS 7, p. 14.
182. Harada, Saionji, 1:47.
183. Okada Diary, entry for May 7, 1930, GS 7, p. 12. Translator's note: The term "grave affair" referred to the assassination of Chang Tso-lin, the Manchurian warlord, by a group of Japanese army men in 1928. The political repercussions of this event helped to bring down the Tanaka cabinet in 1929.
184. Harada, Saionji, 1:62, 63.
185. Hiranuma Kiichirō Kaikoroku Hensan Iinkai, ed., Hiranuma Kiichirō kaikoroku (Reminiscences of Hiranuma Kiichirō), p. 92.
186. Harada, Saionji, 1:65.
187. Ibid., p. 70.
188. Ibid., p. 110.
189. Koga to Arima, Minister's Secretariat secret telegram 38, April 30, 1930, in Hori, Return Instructions, TSM: Bekkan, p. 51.
190. Koga to Arima, Minister's Secretariat secret telegram 39, April 30, 1930, ibid.
191. Aoki, Taihieyō sensō, pp. 27–32.
192. JFM Archives.
193. Ibid.
194. Wakatsuki, Kofūan, p. 362.
195. Tōkyō Nichi-nichi shimbun, May 4, 1930; Harada, Saionji, 1:52.
196. Ōsaka Mainichi shimbun, May 18, 1930.
197. Tōkyō Nichi-nichi shimbun, May 19, 1930.
198. Tōkyō Asahi shimbun, June 19, 1930.
199. Harada, Saionji, 1:61.
200. JDA Archives; Harada, Saionji, 1:70.
201. Kusakari was by nature an excitable man. Among his papers was found one that read: "In the past there were two gods: Wake no Kiyomaro and Kusunoki Masashige; I am the third god." Kiyose Ichirō, Seiki (Spirit of Justice), p. 96. He was obviously not mentally normal. On July 12, 1930, the Aizu branch of the Patriotic Labor Party (Aikoku Kinrōtō) held a memorial service for Kusakari at Wakamatsu city. At that meeting Hirata Shinsaku and Nakatani Takeyo discussed the failure of the London Conference and the right of military command problem. A resolution was passed "expressing absolute opposition to the traitorous London Treaty." JFM Archives.
Translator's note: Wake no Kiyomaro and Kusunoki Masashige were regarded by many Japanese as heroes for their efforts to protect the throne from traitors during two critical periods in ancient and medieval Japan.
202. Hori, Return Instructions, TSM: Bekkan, pp. 54–55; Katō Diary, 15:113, 114. On April 22, 1930, Katō requested his brother-in-law Murakami.Ryūhei, principal of the Tōyō Girls Higher School, to revise the address to the emperor in which he intended to submit his resignation, and so a draft of the document was in existence around that time. Putting together what Hiranuma said with the existence at that time of the address to the em-

peror, it can be assumed that Katō's visit to Hiranuma on April 27 was for the purpose of showing him the address.

203. *Okada Diary*, entry for May 20, 1930, GS 7, p. 14.
204. *Ibid.*, entry for May 25, 1930, p. 32.
205. *Katō Diary*, 15:114.
206. Hori, Treaty Conclusion, GS 7, p. 95; GS 11, p. xix.
207. *Okada Diary*, entry for May 29, 1930, GS 7, p. 16.
208. *Katō Diary*, 16:124.
209. Aoki, *Taiheiyō sensō*, p. 45.
210. Harada, *Saionji*, 1:109.
211. Aoki, *Taiheiyō sensō*, pp. 49–53.
212. *Ibid.*, p. 56. On June 5 Suetsugu had given the emperor an interpretation of Articles 11 and 12 while delivering a scheduled informational lecture on a completely separate naval topic. *Ibid.*
213. Harada, *Saionji*, 1:85–86.
214. Aoki, *Taiheiyō sensō*, pp. 59–60; Harada, *Saionji*, 1:85.
215. *Okada Diary*, entry for June 23, 1930, GS 7, p. 20.
216. Aoki, *Taiheiyō sensō*, p. 66.
217. JDA Archives.
218. Okada, *Kaikoroku*, p. 46. Takarabe had been encouraged by Shidehara to take his wife along on the grounds that this was customary diplomatic usage. (JDA Archives.) At the Geneva Conference Admiral Saitō had been accompanied by his wife.
219. *Okada Diary*, entry for June 27, 1930, GS 7, p. 20.
220. *Ibid.*, entry for July 2, 1930, p. 21.
221. Harada, *Saionji*, 1:110; Aoki, *Taiyeiyō sensō*, p. 81.
222. *Okada Diary*, entry for July 3, 1930, GS 7, p. 21.
223. Harada, *Saionji*, 1:86–87.
224. *Okada Diary*, entry for July 5, 1930, GS 7, p. 22.
225. *Ibid.*, entry for July 6, 1930, p. 23.
226. *Katō Diary*, 16:136.
227. *Okada Diary*, entry for July 8, 1930, GS 7, p. 23.
228. Ogasawara Naganari, *Bannen no Tōgō gensui* (Fleet Admiral Tōgō in His Later Years), pp. 52–54; *Okada Diary*, entry for July 14, 1930, GS 7, p. 24.
229. *Ibid.*, entry for July 15, 1930, p. 24.
230. GS 11, p. xx; AGS File, pp. 64–66.
231. JDA Archives.
232. AGS File, p. 64.
233. *Ibid.*
234. *Ibid.*, pp. 64–66.
235. JFM Archives.
236. *Katō Diary*, 16:137.
237. *Okada Diary*, entry for July 7, 1930, GS 7, p. 23.
238. AGS File, pp. 67–68; Harada, *Saionji*, 1:123; *Okada Diary*, entry for July 8, 1930, GS 7, pp. 23–24.
239. *Ibid.*, entry for July 14, 1930, p. 24.
240. *Ibid.*
241. *Ibid.*
242. *Katō Diary*, 16:138.
243. Harada, *Saionji*, 1:114–15.

244. *Ibid.*, pp. 115, 118–19.
245. *Ibid.*, pp. 123–26.
246. JDA Archives.
247. *Okada Diary*, entry for July 21, 1930, GS 7, p. 25.
248. Harada, *Saionji*, 1:134; Aoki, *Taihieyō sensō*, p. 86; Hori, Treaty Conclusion, GS 7, p. 97; GS 7, p. xxxiii.
249. Harada, *Saionji*, 1:134; *Okada Diary*, entry for July 22, 1930, GS 7, pp. 25–26. The change in phraseology was approved that afternoon by the prime minister.
250. *Ibid.*
251. Aoki, *Taiheiyō sensō*, p. 86.
252. Hori, Return Instructions, TSM: *Bekkan*, pp. 55–56.
253. Harada, *Saionji*, 1:130.
254. Aoki, *Taiheiyō sensō*, p. 88; Hori, Return Instructions, TSM: *Bekkan*, p. 56; Hori, Treaty Conclusion, GS 7, pp. 96–97.
255. Harada, *Saionji*, 1:147; AGS File, pp. 69–70, 71.
256. Harada, *Saionji*, 1:139–40.
257. *Ibid.*, p. 145.
258. JFM, "Issen kyūhyaku sanjū-nen Rondon kaigun jōyaku Sūmitsuin chōsa giji yō-roku" (Digest of the Proceedings of the Privy Council Inquiry on the London Naval Treaty), in JFM Archives, pp. 132–48 (hereafter cited as JFM, Privy Council Inquiry).
259. *Ibid.*, pp. 149–54.
260. Part of the material for Kawai's questions had been privately supplied to him by the Army General Staff. When Kawai included in his questions the exact file numbers of telegrams, the Army Ministry cautioned the General Staff that this was impolitic. Since the army chief of staff and his vice chief feared that public attention would be attracted if they themselves warned Kawai about this matter, they arranged to have a caution delivered by General Minami Jirō, the commander of the Korea Army, who had arrived in Tokyo on September 3. JDA Archives.
261. JFM, Privy Council Inquiry, pp. 186–90.
262. *Ibid.*, pp. 197–99.
263. *Ibid.*, pp. 202–8.
264. *Ibid.*, pp. 209–10.
265. *Ibid.*, p. 213.
266. Harada, *Saionji*, 1:159–60.
267. Aoki, *Taiheiyō sensō*, pp. 95–96.
268. JFM, Privy Council Inquiry, p. 217.
269. *Ibid.*, pp. 224–28.
270. *Ibid.*, pp. 235–45.
271. *Ibid.*, pp. 258–62.
272. *Ibid.*, pp. 271–74.
273. Harada, *Saionji*, 1:168.
274. *Ibid.*, pp. 177–78.
275. Kikuchi, *Seiyūkai*, pp. 364–65.
276. *Tōkyō Nichi-nichi shimbun*, September 17, 1930.
277. JFM, Privy Council Inquiry, p. 275.
278. Harada, *Saionji*, 1:172.
279. *Ibid.*
280. *Tōkyō Asahi shimbun*, September 18, 1930.
281. *Okada Diary*, entry for September 20, 1930, GS 7, p. 27.

282. Inoue Junnosuke Ronsō Hensankai, ed., *Inoue Junnosuke den* (Biography of Inoue Junnosuke), pp. 612–23.

TWO

The Manchurian Incident, 1931

Introduction (Jansen)

1. Thus, in their *China Reader: Republican China,* Franz Schurmann and Orville Schell reprint the "Memorial" with the argument that "whether or not it is an authentic document actually written by Baron Tanaka . . . is irrelevant" (p. 178).

2. Akira Iriye, *After Imperialism: The Search for a New Order in the Far East, 1921–1931,* p. 156.

3. Quoted *ibid.,* p. 236.

4. *Ibid.,* p. 171.

5. Akira Iriye, "Chang Hsüeh-liang and the Japanese," *Journal of Asian Studies,* 20 (1):35, November 1960.

Essay (Seki)

1. Saigō Kōsaku, *Itagaki Seishirō,* p. 157; Yamaguchi Shigeji, *Higeki no shōgun Ishiwara Kanji* (The Tragic General Ishiwara Kanji), p. 96.

2. Matsuoka Yōsuke, *Kōa no taigyō* (A Grand Enterprise for the Development of Asia), pp. 77–78.

3. Manshū Seinen Remmei Shi Kankō Kai, ed., *Manshū Seinen Remmei shi* (History of the Manchurian Youth League), p. 3.

4. *Ibid.,* p. 21.

5. *Ibid.,* pp. 21–22.

6. *Ibid.,* p. 15.

7. *Ibid.,* p. 27.

8. *Ibid.,* p. 29.

9. Ōsaka Tai-Shi Keizai Remmei, *Sorempō to Shina-Manshū no kyōsan undō* (The Soviet Union and Communist Movements in China and Manchuria), p. 559.

10. *Manshū Seinen Remmei shi,* pp. 21, 34–35.

11. *Ibid.,* p. 6.

12. *Ibid.,* pp. 5–6.

13. *Ibid.,* p. 51.

14. *Ibid.,* p. 85.

15. *Ibid.,* p. 92.

16. Takagi Seiju, *Tōa no chichi: Ishiwara Kanji* (The Father of East Asia: Ishiwara Kanji), p. 21.

17. Katakura Tadashi, "Manshū jihen to Kantōgun" (The Manchurian Incident and the Kwantung Army), p. 44.

18. Inaba Masao, "Shōwa sensō shi kōza: Manshū jihen (1)" (Lectures on Shōwa War History: The Manchurian Incident, Part 1), p. 74.

19. *Manshū Seinen Remmei shi*, pp. 72–73.

20. Saigō, *Itagaki*, pp. 306–7.

21. Takamiya Tahei, *Gunkoku taihei ki* (Chronicle of a Military Nation), pp. 24–26.

22. *Ibid.*, pp. 21–22. Takamiya substitutes Araki Sadao for Tsuchihashi in the map incident. Araki has, however, denied this to the author, and Inaba Masao has it directly from Tsuchihashi that the order was in fact directed to him.

23. Inaba, "Manshū jihen (1)," p. 74; Hata Ikuhiko, *Gun fashizumu undō shi* (History of the Military Fascist Movement), p. 68.

24. Inaba, "Manshū jihen (1)," pp. 74–75; Hata, *Gun fashizumu*, p. 68.

25. Takamiya, *Gunkoku*, pp. 26–28; Inaba, "Manshū jihen (1)," pp. 74–75.

26. *Ibid.*, p. 74.

27. Ishiwara Kanji, *Sekai saishū sen ron* (On the Final World War), pp. 189–90.

28. See Tsunoda Jun, comp., *Ishiwara Kanji shiryō: Kokubō ronsaku hen* (Papers of Ishiwara Kanji: His Doctrine of National Defense), pp. 35–39 (hereafter cited as *Ishiwara shiryō*); also, Nihon Kokusai Seiji Gakkai Taiheiyō Sensō Gen'in Kenkyūbu, ed., *Taiheiyō sensō e no michi: Bekkan shiryō hen* (The Road to the Pacific War: Supplementary Volume of Documents), pp. 82–85 (hereafter cited as TSM: *Bekkan*).

29. Yamaguchi, *Ishiwara*, p. 106.

30. See no. 28.

31. Inaba Iwakichi (pseud. Inaba Kunzan), *Manshū hatten shi* (A History of the Development of Manchuria).

32. *Ishiwara shiryō*, pp. 40–45; TSM: *Bekkan*, pp. 86–89.

33. Maruyama Masao, *Gendai seiji no shisō to kōdō* (Thought and Behavior in Contemporary Politics), 2:272; and as translated in Ivan Morris, ed., *Thought and Behavior in Modern Japanese Politics*, pp. 159–63.

34. Ōsaka Remmei, *Kyōsan undō*, pp. 562–63.

35. *Ishiwara shiryō*, pp. 52–57; TSM: Bekkan, pp. 91–95.

36. Inaba, "Manshū jihen (1)," p. 77.

37. *Manshū Seinen Remmei shi*, p. 154.

38. *Ibid.*, p. 160.

39. Ōsaka Remmei, *Kyōsan undō*, pp. 564–65.

40. *Ishiwara shiryō*, pp. 48–49; TSM: Bekkan, pp. 90–91.

41. Koiso Kuniaki, "Koiso kaisō roku" (Koiso Memoirs), unpublished; found also in Koiso Kuniaki Jijoden Kankōkai, ed., *Katsuzan Kōsō* (pen name of Koiso Kuniaki), p. 496.

42. Takamiya, *Gunkoku*, pp. 16–17.

43. Koiso, *Katsuzan kōsō*, pp. 497–99.

44. Ōsaka Remmei, *Kyōsan undō*, pp. 566–67.

45. *Manshū Seinen Remmei shi*, p. 259.

46. Tanaka Kiyoshi, "Iwayuru jugatsu jiken ni kansuru shuki" (Note on the so-called October Incident).

47. Hashimoto Kingorō memoir.

48. Imamura Hitoshi, *Kōzoku to kashikan* (The Imperial Family and Noncommissioned Officers), p. 202.

49. *Man-Mō jijō*, November 25, 1930.

50. Japan, National Defense Agency, Military History Office (hereafter JDA Archives); Inaba, "Manshū jihen (1)," pp. 77–79; *Ishiwara shiryō*, pp. 52–57; TSM: *Bekkan*, pp. 91–95.

51. Kōmoto Daisaku memoir; Hirano Reiji, *Manshū no imbōsha: Kōmoto Daisaku no*

ummeiteki na ashiato (A Conspirator in Manchuria: The Life of Kōmoto Daisaku), p. 126.

52. "Okada Masukichi kaisō roku" (Memoirs of Okada Masukichi), *Shūkan yomiuri*, November 28, 1954.

53. Interview with Mugita Hirao, July 10, 1962.

54. Hirano, *Kōmoto*, pp. 132–34.

55. JDA Archives.

56. Tanaka, "Jugatsu jiken."

57. Ninomiya Harushige memoir. Katakura, however, claimed that there were four plans. Interview with Katakura Tadashi, December 19, 1959; also, Katakura, "Manshū jihen," p. 45.

58. Shidō Yasusuke, *Tetsuzan, Nagata chūjō* (Lieutenant-General Nagata Tetsuzan), pp. 165–66.

59. *Ibid.*, pp. 150–51, 166–67; Inaba, "Manshū jihen (4)," p. 71.

60. Ueda Shunkichi, "Gumbu kakushin kanryō no Nihon kyōsan-ka keikaku an, Shōwa demokkurashī no zasetsu (2)" (The Scheme of the Military and Renovationist Bureaucrats To Communize Japan: The Failure of Shōwa Democracy).

61. Katakura interview.

62. *Gendai shi shiryō 7: Manshū jihen* (Source Materials on Contemporary History, 7: The Manchurian Incident), pp. 134–38 (hereafter cited as GS 7).

63. *Ibid.*, pp. 139–44.

64. *Ishiwara shiryō*, pp. 58–68.

65. *Ibid.*, pp. 70–73; TSM: Bekkan, pp. 96–99.

66. GS 7, p. 145.

67. TSM: *Bekkan*, pp. 101–7.

68. Mugita interview.

69. *Ibid.*

70. *Ishiwara shiryō*, pp. 76–79; TSM: *Bekkan*, pp. 99–101.

71. Inaba, "Manshū jihen (3)."

72. *Manshū Seinen Remmei shi*, pp. 11–12.

73. *Ibid.*, p. 443.

74. *Ibid.*, p. 14.

75. *Ibid.*, pp. 457–58.

76. Kido affidavit to the International Military Tribunal for the Far East (hereafter IMTFE), in Kido Kōichi, *Kido nikki* (Kido Diary), pp. 5–6.

77. JDA Archives.

78. Kōmoto memoir.

79. Kitsukawa Manaku, *Arashi to tatakan tesshō Araki* (Braving a Storm: General Araki Sadao), p. 141.

80. The original has not been found in the JDA Archives. Although they differ slightly in places, versions and summaries can be found in the Hashimoto memoir, the Ninomiya memoir, and the Katakura interview.

81. Hashimoto memoir; Hashimoto Kingorō affidavit, Exhibit 2188, in Kyokutō Kokusai Gunji Saiban Kōhan Kiroku (Records of the IMTFE), in Japan, Justice Ministry, War Crimes Materials Office (hereafter cited as IMTFE Records.

82. JDA Archives.

83. *Ibid.*

84. Hashimoto memoir.

85. Harada Kumao, *Saionji kō to seikyoku* (Prince Saionji and the Political Situation), supplementary volume of documents: *Bekkan*, p. 355.

86. Hanaya Tadashi, "Manshū jihen wa kōshite keikaku sareta" (Thus Was Plotted the Manchurian Incident), p. 43.

87. Katakura, "Manshū jihen," p. 45.

88. Inaba, "Manshū jihen (3)," p. 69.

89. Imamura, *Kōzoku*, pp. 193–95; Mitarai Tatsuo, ed., *Minami Jirō*, pp. 241–45; Imamura Hitoshi, "Manshū hi o fuku koro" (The Outbreak of the Manchurian Incident), pp. 61–62.

90. Saigō, *Itagaki*, pp. 133–34.

91. Kido affidavit, *Kido nikki*, p. 6.

92. JDA Archives.

93. *Ibid.*

94. Harada, *Saionji*, 2:6, and *Bekkan*, p. 119.

95. JDA Archives.

96. *Ibid.*

97. Kikuchi Gorō, *Rikken Seiyūkai shi* (History of the Seiyūkai), 7:636–37, *Inukai sōsai jidai* (Inukai's Presidency).

98. *Tōkyō Asahi shimbun*, June 28 and July 1, 1931.

99. Tanaka, "Jūgatsu jiken."

100. Harada, *Saionji: Bekkan*, p. 356.

101. Kōmoto memoir.

102. *Manshū Seinen Remmei shi*, pp. 459–66.

103. *Ibid.*, pp. 468–69.

104. Ayusawa Toshio, *Dai Nihon Seisantō jūnen shi* (Ten-Year History of the Great Japan Production Party), p. 23.

105. *Manshū Seinen Remmei shi*, pp. 478–88.

106. Imamura, *Kōzoku*, p. 195.

107. Inaba, "Manshū jihen (3)," p. 70.

108. Mitarai, *Minami*, pp. 217–18.

109. Harada, *Saionji*, 2:18–19.

110. Inaba, "Manshū jihen (3)," p. 73.

111. Harada, *Saionji*, 2:25–26.

112. *Ibid.*, pp. 24–25.

113. Hashimoto memoir.

114. Shimizu Kōnosuke affidavit, Exhibit 157, IMTFE Records.

115. Harada, *Saionji*, 2:31–34.

116. Hiranuma kiichirō Kaikoroku Hensan Iinkai, ed., *Hiranuma Kiichirō kaikoroku* (Reminiscences of Hiranuma Kiichirō), p. 118.

117. *Ibid.*, p. 119.

118. Harada, *Saionji*, 2:55.

119. Hiranuma, *Kaikoroku*, p. 119.

120. Harada, *Saionji*, 2:26.

121. Tanaka, "Jugatsu jiken"; Hata, *Gun fashizumu*, p. 97.

122. Harada, *Saionji*, 2:33–34.

123. *Ibid.*, pp. 39–40.

124. *Ibid.*, p. 34.

125. *Ibid.*, *Bekkan*, p. 121.

126. *Ibid.*, 2:34.

127. *Ibid.*, pp. 35–39.
128. *Ibid.*, pp. 40–41.
129. *Ishiwara shiryō*, p. 82; TSM: *Bekkan*, p. 109.
130. "Nakamura taii jiken ni kanshi jikan yori Kantōgun sambōchō ate dempō" (Telegram from the deputy chief to the chief of staff, Kwantung Army concerning incident involving Captain Nakamura), in Japan, Foreign Ministry (hereafter JEM) Archives.
131. *Ishiwara shiryō*, pp. 83–84; TSM: *Bekkan*, pp. 110–11.
132. Hanaya, "Manshū jihen," pp. 43–44.
133. Koiso, *Katsuzan Kōsō*, p. 532.
134. Fujita Isamu affidavit, Exhibit 160, IMTFE Records.
135. Hashimoto memoir; Nakano Masao, *Sannin no hōka-sha* (Three Who Set Fire).
136. *Ibid.*, pp. 28–37.
137. The Fujita affidavit (see note 134), Hashimoto memoir (see note 135), and Kōmoto memoir (see note 51) differ slightly in their accounts of the amount and use of this money. The author has had to rely on his own judgment in selecting versions.
138. Japan, Army Ministry, *Mitsu dai nikki* (Confidential Great Diary), in Japan Defense Agency archives. (Editor's note: No more detailed location is provided in the original footnote.)
139. Navy Ministry, Legal Affairs Bureau, "Go-ichi-go jiken kohan ni okeru Hama Yūji shuki" (Memorandum by Hama Yūji at the May 15 Incident Trial), quoted in Hata, *Gun fashizumu*, pp. 82–84.
140. Wakatsuki Naikaku Hensankai, ed., *Wakatsuki naikaku* (The Wakatsuki Cabinet), p. 534.
141. Koiso, *Katsuzan Kōsō*, p. 528.
142. Yamaura Kan'ichi, *Mori Kaku wa ikite iru* (Mori Kaku Is Alive), p. 163.
143. *Ibid.*, p. 208.
144. *Ibid.*, pp. 210–11.
145. *Ibid.*, p. 204.
146. Mitarai, *Minami*, p. 224.
147. *Tōkyō Asahi shimbun*, August 19, 1931.
148. Harada, *Saionji*, 2:47.
149. *Rikken Seiyūkai shi*, 7:641.
150. *Ibid.*, pp. 642–44; Mitarai, *Minami*, pp. 222–23.
151. *Ibid.*
152. Hashimoto memoir.
153. Harada, *Saionji*, 2:42–44.
154. *Ibid.*, p. 122.
155. *Ibid.*, p. 46.
156. "Nakamura taii jiken ikken" (The Captain Nakamura Affair), JFM Archives.
157. *Tōkyō Asahi shimbun*, September 8, 1931.
158. "Nakamura ikken," JFM Archives.
159. Wakatsuki Naikaku Henseikai, ed. *Wakatsuki naikaku* (hereafter cited as *Wakatsuki naikaku*), p. 552.
160. *Tōkyō Asahi shimbun*, September 7, 1931.
161. *Manshū Seinen Remmei shi*, pp. 502–3.
162. "Nakamura Taii Sōnan Jiken" (The Captain Nakamura Accident Incident), in JFM Archives; same as microfilm no. S 42602, cited in Cecil Uyehara, *Checklist of Archives in the Japanese Ministry of Foreign Affairs*, p. 60 (hereafter cited as "Nakamura Taii Sōnan Jiken").

163. *Jiji shimpō*, September 8, 1931.

164. *Wakatsuki naikaku*, p. 544.

165. *China Year Book, 1931*, p. 1235. (Editor's note: This citation has been impossible to verify; however a summary of a speech of similar content given by Sze on December 10 appears in *China Year Book, 1932*, p. 640).

166. Kido affidavit, *Kido nikki*, p. 6.

167. Shigemitsu Mamoru, *Gaikō kaisōroku* (Diplomatic Reminiscences), p. 104.

168. *Tōkyō Asahi shimbun*, September 14, 1931.

169. *Jiji shimpō*, September 12, 1931.

170. *Ibid.*

171. Japan, Army General Staff, "Manshū jihen kimitsu sakusen nisshi" (Confidential Operational Journal of the Manchurian Incident), September 23, 1931, TSM: *Bekkan*, pp. 126–27; also quoted in Inaba, "Manshū jihen (4)."

172. There are slight discrepancies among Katakura's account in *ibid.*, Hanaya's in "Manshū jihen," p. 45, the Hashimoto memoir, and Nakano, *Sannin no hokasha*, pp. 53–55.

173. Telegram from Shidehara to Hayashi, September 5, 1931, Exhibit 3739, IMTFE Records.

174. Harada, *Saionji*, 2:48–49.

175. *Ibid.*, pp. 49–50.

176. *Ibid.*, p. 50.

177. *Ibid.*, p. 55.

178. *Ibid.*, pp. 52–53, 61.

179. *Ibid.* Saionji told Harada of Minami's audience with the emperor as they motored from Gotemba to Kyoto via Numazu on the 15th. Saionji speculated, in view of Minami's having taken the initiative at the meeting, that he had been forewarned of the reason for the audience by the military chamberlain or the chief military chamberlain. Harada, however, thought it more likely that Minami had spoken with Navy Minister Abō following the latter's audience on the 9th, which Saionji then agreed was probably the case. *Ibid.*, pp. 52–53.

180. *Ibid.*, p. 52.

181. *Ibid.*, pp. 53–54.

182. *Ibid.*, p. 58.

183. *Jiji shimpō*, September 14, 1931.

184. Harada, *Saionji*, 2:52.

185. Imamura, *Kōzoku*, p. 197.

186. *Jiji shimpō*, September 15, 1931.

187. Harada, *Saionji*, 2:62. However, the reference to "Supreme War Council" seems to be erroneous. In his memoir Hashimoto says that it was "the meeting of the Big Three division heads." The author has concluded that this was in reality a meeting of the principal officials of the Army Ministry and General Staff. The Supreme War Council met on the 16th.

188. Koiso, *Katsuzan Kōsō*, p. 532.

189. Harada, *Saionji*, 2:61–62.

190. Hashimoto memoir. Nakano, in his lively description (*Sannin no hokasha*, pp. 60, 62–63), states that Shigetō and Tōjō were also present, but his account is frequently contrived and cannot be trusted fully.

191. Hanaya, "Manshū jihen," p. 45.

192. Shidehara Heiwa Zaidan, ed., *Shidehara Kijūrō*, p. 466.

193. Minami Jirō interrogation, Exhibit 2207, IMTFE Records; also in Yomiuri Hō-teikisha (Yomiuri court reporters) *Nijū-go hikoku no hyōjō* (The Appearance of Twenty-five Defendants), pp. 31–32.

194. Koiso, *Katsuzan Kōsō*, p. 532; Harada, *Saionji*, 2:61.

195. Imamura, "Manshū hi o fuku koro," p. 62.

196. *Ibid.* Imamura says that he left on the 16th, but according to the train schedule effective then, his departure at any time other than 9:45 P.M. on the 15th was impossible.

197. *Jiji shimpō*, September 16, 1931.

198. According to Katakura's account, the telegram said, "Have Itagaki or Ishiwara meet him en route." According to Ishiwara, it read, "Have Itagaki or Ishiwara stay in Mukden."

199. *Jiji shimpō*, September 18, 1931.

200. *Ibid.*

201. *Ibid.*, September 17, 1931.

202. *Ibid.*, September 15, 1931.

203. *Ibid.*, September 16, 1931.

204. *Ibid.*, September 18, 1931.

205. Inaba, "Manshū jihen (3)," pp. 74–75.

206. *Ibid.;* "Nakamura Taii Sōnan Jiken," pp. 867–68.

207. Mugita interview.

208. *Ibid.*

209. *Man-Mō jijō*, no. 119, August 25, 1931, pp. 3–4.

210. Mugita interview.

211. Interview with Hayashi Kyūkirō, July 19, 1962.

212. Inaba, "Manshū jihen (3)," pp. 66–67. This is confirmed in other accounts; see, for example, Morishima Morito, *Imbō, ansatsu, guntō: gaikōkan no kaisō* (Intrigue, Assassination, and Swords: Reminiscences of a Diplomat), p. 48.

213. Fujimoto Haruki, *Ningen Ishiwara Kanji* (Ishiwara Kanji, the Man), pp. 78–79.

214. Ishiwara Kanji deposition, Exhibit 2584, IMTFE Records.

215. Interview with Mitani Kiyoshi, November 19, 1962; also interview with Kawashima Tadashi, November 20, 1962.

216. Saigō, *Itagaki*, p. 147.

217. *Ibid.*, pp. 149–51.

218. *Manshū Seinen Remmei shi*, pp. 402–6.

219. *Ibid.*, pp. 493–94.

220. *Ibid.*, pp. 496–97.

221. *Ibid.*, pp. 498–501.

222. *Ibid.*, p. 505.

223. *Ibid.*, p. 506.

224. Yamaguchi, *Ishiwara*, pp. 98–105.

225. Katakura interview.

226. Hirata Yukihiro affidavit, IMTFE Exhibit 2404.

227. *Wakatsuki naikaku*, p. 534.

228. "Nakamura Taii Sōnan Jiken," p. 224.

229. JDA Archives.

230. Inaba, "Manshū jihen (3)," p. 79.

231. JDA Archives.

232. TSM: *Bekkan*, pp. 111–12.

233. *Mantetsu chōsa geppō,* September 14, 1931, no. 112, p. 193.
235. *Ibid.,* pp. 279–81.
236. *Wakatsuki naikaku,* pp. 537–38.
237. *Ibid.,* pp. 539–40.
238. Hayashi interview.
239. "Nakamura Taii Sōnan Jiken." (Editor's note: no page citation in original.)
240. *Wakatsuki naikaku,* pp. 539–40.
241. TSM: *Bekkan,* pp. 111–12.
242. *Wakatsuki naikaku,* p. 540.
243. *Ibid.,* p. 538.
244. *Tōkyō Asahi shimbun,* September 6, 1931.
245. *Wakatsuki naikaku,* p. 543.
246. *Japan Chronicle,* September 7, 1931.
247. *Wakatsuki naikaku,* p. 544.
248. *Ibid.,* pp. 545–46.
249. *Ibid.,* p. 546.
250. "Nakamura Taii Sōnan Jiken," p. 631.
251. *Wakatsuki naikaku,* pp. 547–48.
252. JDA Archives.
253. Tōa Dōbunkai, ed., *Zoku tai-Shi kaiko roku* (Recollections of Our Activities vis-a-vis China, Continued), 2:1009; Hayashi interview.
254. Kōmoto memoir. According to Kōmoto, this was on September 9, but Hirano, *Kōmoto,* dates it the 7th.
255. Takeda Hisashi affidavit, Exhibit 2405, IMTFE Record.
256. "Nakamura Taii Sōnan Jiken," pp. 689–93.
257. Mitarai, *Minami,* p. 256; Morishima Morito affidavit, Exhibit 245, IMTFE Records; Ishiwara deposition, exhibit 2584, IMTFE Records; Katakura interview; Morishima, *Kaisō,* p. 49.
258. Hayashi interview.
259. Morishima, *Kaisō,* p. 49.
260. *The Report of the Commission of Enquiry of the League of Nations into the Sino-Japanese Dispute, September 4, 1932,* p. 117.
261. According to Mitani's memoir, Hashimoto's telegram arrived the evening of the 14th. Other sources, however, suggest that it more probably arrived on the 15th; Hanaya ("Manshū jihen," pp. 45–46) says it arrived on the 15th, but it is strange that he places Itagaki and Ishiwara at a meeting of the Special Service Agency on the 16th, when they should have been in Liaoyang. The apparent discrepancy may be reconciled by having the meeting start on the evening of the 15th and last until 2 A.M. on the 16th. Hanaya and Kawashima agree.
262. Kawashima and Mitani interviews.
263. Mitani memoir.
264. *Ibid.*
265. Katakura interview.
266. Morishima, *Kaisō,* pp. 46–47.
267. *Wakatsuki naikaku,* pp. 547–49.
268. *Jiji shimpō,* September 17, 1931.
269. JFM Archives, cited in Uyehara, *Checklist,* S 1.1.1.0-18, pp. 39–40.
270. "Nakamura Taii Sōnan Jiken," pp. 731–33.
271. *Ibid.,* pp. 770–73.

272. Hanaya, "Manshū jihen," p. 46.
273. Mitani memoir.
274. Ishiwara interrogation.
275. Yamaguchi, *Ishiwara*, pp. 112–13.
276. TSM: *Bekkan*, p. 112; Inaba, "Manshū jihen (4)," p. 68.
277. Mitani memoir.
278. Concerning the fact that Itagaki went to Pench'i to see Tatekawa, see Yamaguchi, *Ishiwara*, pp. 113–14; Hanaya, "Manshū jihen," p. 46. The author has based train arrival time on the schedule effective in September 1931.
279. Morishima, *Kaisō*, p. 49.
280. Hayashi interview.
281. Morishima, *Kaisō*, p. 49.
282. *Ibid.*, pp. 50–51.
283. Ishiwara deposition.
284. Hanaya, "Manshū jihen," p. 46.
285. Morishima affidavit; Morishima, *Kaisō*, pp. 51–52.
286. Kawashima interview.
287. Hanaya, "Manshū jihen," pp. 46–47; Kawashima interview.
288. Kawashima interview.
289. Kōmoto memoir.
290. Itagaki Seishirō affidavit, Exhibit 3316, IMTFE Records.
291. Hirata Yukihiro affidavit, Exhibit 2404, IMTFE Records; Shimamoto affidavit, IMTFE Records.
292. Morishima affidavit.
293. Katakura interview.
294. Takeda affidavit.
295. Ishiwara deposition.

THREE

The Extension of Hostilities, 1931–1932

Introduction (Iriye)

1. Robert H. Ferrell, *Frank B. Kellogg; Henry L. Stimson;* Elting E. Morison, *Turmoil and Tradition: A Study of the Life and Times of Henry L. Stimson;* Armin Rappaport, *Henry L. Stimson and Japan, 1931–1933;* Ueda Toshio, "Manshū jihen o meguru Nihon no gaikō" (Japanese Diplomacy and the Manchurian Incident), *Tōyō Bunka Kenkyūjo kiyō* (Memoirs of the Institute for Oriental Culture), no. 33 (March 1964), pp. 1–43; Ichimata Masao, "Kanshū teki jieiken no saiginmi" (A Reexamination of the Customary Right of Self-Defense), *Kokusaihō gaikō zasshi*, 64:1–39, July 1965; Takehiko Yoshihashi, *Conspiracy at Mukden: The Rise of the Japanese Military;* Usami Seijirō, "Manshū shinryaku" (The Invasion of Manchuria), *Nihon rekishi*, 20:211–53, 1963; Sadako N. Ogata, *Defiance in Manchuria: The Making of Japanese Foreign Policy, 1931–1932.*
2. Shimada Toshio, *Kantōgun* (The Kwantung Army).

Essay (Shimada)

1. Japan, Army General Staff (hereafter AGS), "Manshū jihen kimitsu sakusen nisshi" (Confidential Operational Journal of the Manchurian Incident), in Nihon Kokusai Seiji Gakkai, Taiheiyō Sensō Kenkyūbu (Japan Association on International Relations, Study Group on the Causes of the Pacific War), ed., *Taiheiyō sensō e no michi* (The Road to the Pacific War) (hereafter cited as TSM): *Bekkan* (Supplementary Volume of Documents), p. 113.

2. Documents on the Korea Army episode are mostly taken from AGS, Second Section, "Chōsen-gun shireikan no dokudan shuppei to chūōbu no kore ni taishite toreru shochi ni tsuite" (The Expedition Ordered by the Korea Army Commander on His Own Authority and the Attitude of the Supreme Command), in *Gendai shi shiryō* (hereafter GS): 7 (Source Materials on Contemporary History 7: The Manchurian Incident), pp. 428–35.

3. *Ibid.*, pp. 429–31.

4. AGS, "Manshū jihen shi, 5; Manshū jihen ni okeru gun no tōsui (an)" (Draft History of the Manchurian Incident, vol. 5: Military Command in the Manchurian Incident), in GS 11 (The Manchurian Incident, 2), pp. 311–12.

5. Regarding the origins of the Manchurian Incident, see TSM, vol. 1, part 3, ch. 3 and 4.

6. AGS, "Manshū jihen shi, 5."

7. AGS, "Chōsen-gun shireikan," pp. 429–30.

8. *Ibid.*, p. 432.

9. Katakura Tadashi, "Manshū jihen kimitsu seiryaku nisshi" (Secret Political Journal of the Manchurian Incident), in GS 7, p. 188.

10. AGS, "Chōsen-gun shireikan," p. 433; AGS, "Manshū jihen kimitsu sakusen nisshi."

11. AGS, "Chōsen-gun shireikan," pp. 434–35.

12. AGS, "Manshū jihen shi, 5."

13. AGS, "Manshū jihen kimitsu sakusen nisshi."

14. Katakura, "Manshū jihen," p. 184.

15. AGS, "Manshū jihen kimitsu sakusen nisshi," separate file on the Chientao question; Harada Kumao, *Saionji kō to seikyoku* (Prince Saionji and the Political Situation), 2:81 (entry for October 2, 1931).

16. AGS, "Manshū jihen shi, 5."

17. AGS, "Manshū jihen kimitsu sakusen nisshi."

18. *Ibid.*; Harada, *Saionji*, 2:73 (entry for September 28, 1931).

19. AGS, "Manshū jihen kimitsu sakusen nisshi."

20. AGS, "Kantōgun shireikan reika shobutai no sakusen kōdō ni kanshi sono ichibu o sambōsōchō ni oite kettei meirei goinin no ken kiroku" (A Record of the Imperial Authorization to the Chief of Staff To Order Part of Kwantung Army Units' Operational Movements), in GS 7, pp. 440–41.

21. AGS, "Manshū jihen shi, 5."

22. GS 7, p. 443.

23. In contrast to Imamura, Endō Saburō, who returned from Manchuria on November 3, strongly urged an expedition to northern Manchuria. His pleas from Manchuria were ignored.

24. Katakura, "Manshū jihen," pp. 242–44.

25. AGS, "Manshū jihen shi, 5."

26. GS 7, pp. 436–47.

27. Katakura, "Manshū jihen," pp. 244–45.

28. GS 7, pp. 438–39.
29. Katakura, "Manshū jihen," pp. 245–46.
30. AGS, "Manshū jihen shi, 5."
31. Katakura, "Manshū jihen," pp. 258–60.
32. GS 7, pp. 447–48.
33. Katakura, "Manshū jihen," p. 275.
34. AGS, "Manshū jihen kimitsu sakusen nisshi."
35. Katakura, "Manshū jihen," pp. 276–77.
36. This number constituted more than 40 percent of the Northeastern Border Defense Army's total troop strength of 268,000. The Kwantung Army had naturally taken into consideration the fact that Chang's army in Manchuria had been cut almost in half.
37. AGS, "Manshū jihen shi, 5."
38. Henry L. Stimson, The Far Eastern Crisis, p. 53.
39. Katakura, "Manshū jihen," p. 206.
40. AGS, "Manshū jihen kimitsu sakusen nisshi."
41. AGS, "Kantōgun no Ryōsei ni taisuru kōdō ni kanshi" (Concerning the Kwantung Army's Action West of the Liao), in GS 7, pp. 455–56.
42. AGS, "Manshū jihen kimitsu sakusen nisshi."
43. AGS, "Manshū jihen shi, 5."
44. Shidehara Heiwa Zaidan, ed., Shidehara Kijūrō, pp. 483–89.
45. Katakura, "Manshū jihen," pp. 304, 318, 352.
46. AGS, "Manshū jihen kimitsu sakusen nisshi," separate file on the Harbin episode.
47. Shanhai Nippō Sha, comp., Shanhai jihen (The Shanghai Incident), pp. 12–18; the Shanghai Municipal Council's report on the incident was published in 1933.
48. Shanhai Kyoryū Mindan (Japanese Shanghai Residents Association), ed., Shanhai jihen shi (History of the Shanghai Incident), pp. 73, 83–84.
49. Shanhai Nippō Sha, Shanhai jihen, pp. 34ff.
50. Shanhai Kyoryū Mindan, Shanhai jihen, pp. 16ff.
51. Tanaka Ryūkichi, "Shanhai jihen wa kōshite okosareta" (The Origins of the Shanghai Incident), in Bessatsu Chisei 5: Himerareta Shōwa shi (Secret History of the Shōwa Era: Chisei special issue), December 1956, pp. 181–86.
52. Shanhai Nippō Sha, Shanhai jihen, pp. 64ff.
53. Shanhai Kyoryū Mindan, Shanhai jihen, pp. 51ff.
54. Harihara Shigeki and Kashiwa Masahiko, Shanhai jihen gaikō shi (A Diplomatic History of the Shanghai Incident), pp. 15–23.
55. Concerning the "outer roads," see Shimada Toshihiko, "Shanhai ekkai dōro o meguru kokusai ronsō" (International Disputes Concerning Shanghai's Outer Roads), Musashi Daigaku ronshū, 4, no. 2.
56. W. C. Johnstone, The Shanghai Problem, p. 272; Stimson, Crisis, p. 120; P. J. Treat, "Shanghai: January 28, 1932," Pacific Historical Review, 9:337–43, September 1940.
57. Shanghai Municipal Council report.
58. Based on documents in Japan, National Defense Agency, Military History Office Archives.
59. AGS, "Manshū jihen kimitsu sakusen nisshi."
60. Ibid.
61. Shimada Toshihiko, "Shōwa shichi-nen Shanhai teisen kyōtei seiritsu no keii" (The Shanghai Armistice Agreement of 1932), Ajia kenkyū, 3, no. 4, January 1957.
62. Harihara and Kashiwa, Shanhai jihen, pp. 5–6.
63. Stimson, Crisis, p. 140.

64. Harada, *Saionji*, 2:200–203 (entries for January 26 and February 16, 1932).

65. Shimada Toshihiko, "Shanhai teisen kyōtei shimpan mondai" (Violation of the Shanghai Ceasefire Agreement), *Musashi Daigaku ronshū*, 3(1):60–110, December 1955.

66. Katakura, "Manshū jihen," pp. 196–97, 200–201.

67. Ugaki Kazushige, *Ugaki Kazushige nikki* (Diary of Ugaki Kazushige), entry for October 1, 1931.

68. Harada, *Saionji*, 2:93, 96–97 (entries for October 25 and November 5, 1931).

69. Cabinet and Privy Council meetings as recorded in AGS, "Manshū jihen kimitsu sakusen nisshi."

70. Ishiwara's memorandum entitled "Man-Mō mondai no yukue" (The Outlook for the Manchurian-Mongolian Question), drafted on December 2, 1931, still referred to the possible establishment of a Japanese protectorate over Manchuria. This document is included in AGS, "Manshū jihen kimitsu sakusen nisshi," pp. 160–61.

71. TSM: *Bekkan*, p. 147.

72. GS 7, pp. 227–30.

73. *Ibid.*, pp. 248–56.

74. Japan, Foreign Ministry, *Nihon gaikō nempyō narabi ni shuyō bunsho* (Chronology and Major Documents of Japanese Foreign Relations), 2:186.

75. TSM: *Bekkan*, pp. 171–72.

Glossary

Abe Nobuyuki 阿部信行
Abo Kiyokazu (Kiyotane) 安保清種
Adachi Kenzō 安達謙蔵
Akiyama Yoshifuru 秋山好古
Amakasu Masahiko 甘粕正彦
Andō Masataka 安東昌喬
Andō Rikichi 安藤利吉
Arai Kentarō 荒井賢太郎
Arai Masao 新井匡夫
Araki Sadao 荒木貞夫
Arima Ryōkitsu 有馬良橘
Arima Yutaka 有馬寛
Chang Ching-hui 張景惠
Chang Ch'ün 張群
Chang Hai-p'eng 張海鵬
Chang Hsueh-liang 張學良
Chang T'ing-shu 張廷樞
Chang Tso-hsiang 張作相
Chang Tso-lin 張作霖
Chang Tsung-ch'ang 張宗昌
Cheng Hsiao-hsu 鄭孝胥
Chiang Kai-shek (Chieh-shih) 蔣介石
　（中正）
Chiang Kuang-nai 蔣光鼐
Chiang Tso-pin 蔣作賓
Chō Isamu 長勇
Debuchi Katsuji 出淵勝次
Den Kenjirō 田健次郎
Doihara Kenji 土肥原賢二
Egi Tasuku 江木翼
Eguchi Teijō 江口定条
Endō Saburō 遠藤三郎
Feng Yü-hsiang 馮玉祥
Fujii Hitoshi 藤井斉
Fujimura Toshifusa 藤村俊房
Fujita Isamu 藤田勇
Fukuda Hikosuke 福田彦助
Fukuda Masatarō 福田雅太郎
Fukuoka Seiichi 福岡誠一
Fushimi-no-miya Hiroyasu (Prince)
　伏見宮博恭
Futagami Hyōji 二上兵治
Godō Takuo 伍堂卓雄
Gorai Kinzō 五来欣造
Hama Yūji 浜勇治

Hamaguchi Osachi (Yūkō) 浜口雄幸
Han Fu-chü 韓復榘
Hanai Takuzō 花井卓蔵
Hanaya Tadashi 花谷正
Hara Shūjirō 原脩次郎
Hara Takashi (Kei) 原敬
Harada Kumao 原田熊雄
Hashimoto Kingorō 橋本欣五郎
Hashimoto Toranosuke 橋本虎之助
Hata Eitarō 畑英太郎
Hata Shinji 秦真次
Hata Shunroku 畑俊六
Hatoyama Ichirō 鳩山一郎
Hayashi Daihachi 林大八
Hayashi Kyūjirō 林久治郎
Hayashi Senjūrō 林銑十郎
Hayashi Yoshihide 林義秀
Hirajima Toshio 平島敏夫
Hiranuma Kiichirō 平沼騏一郎
Hirata Seihan 平田正判
Hirata Shinsaku 平田晋策
Hirata Yukihiro 平田幸弘
Hishikari Takashi 菱刈隆
Honda Kumatarō 本多熊太郎
Honjō Shigeru 本庄繁
Hori Teikichi 堀悌吉
Hotta Masaaki 堀田正昭
Hsi Hsia 熙洽
Hsiung Shih-hui 熊式輝
Huang Ch'iang 黄強
Hyakutake Haruyoshi 百武晴吉
Ichiki Kitokurō 一木喜徳郎
Ikeda Nagayasu 池田長康
Imada Shintarō 今田新太郎
Imamura Hitoshi 今村均
Imamura Nobujirō 今村信次郎
Inaba Iwakuchi (Kunzan) 稲葉岩吉
　（君山）
Inoue Ikutarō 井上幾太郎
Inoue Junnosuke 井上準之助
Inoue Kiyosumi 井上清純
Inoue Nisshō 井上日召
Inoue Saburō 井上三郎
Inukai Tsuyoshi (Ki) 犬養毅
Ishii Kikujirō 石井菊次郎

Ishimitsu Maomi 石光真臣
Ishimoto Kantarō 石本鑟太郎
Ishiwara Kanji 石原莞爾
Isogai Rensuke 磯谷廉介
Isugi Nobutarō 井杉延太郎
Itagaki Seishirō 板垣征四郎
Itō Miyoji 伊東己代治
Iwakuro Hideo 岩畔豪雄
Iwata Ainosuke 岩田愛之助
Jung Chen 榮臻
Kagesa Sadaaki 影佐禎昭
Kanai Shōji 金井章次
Kanaya Hanzō 金谷範三
Kanda Masatane 神田正種
Kaneko Kentarō 金子堅太郎
Kan'in-no-miya Kotohito (Prince)
　閑院宮載仁
Kanno Shōichi 管野尚一
Kasaki Yoshiaki 笠木良明
Kashii Kōhei 香椎浩平
Kasuya Sōichi 糟谷宗一
Katakura Tadashi 片倉衷
Kataoka Shun 片岡駿
Katō Kanji 加藤寛治
Katō Takaaki (Kōmei) 加藤高明
Katō Takayoshi 加藤隆義
Katsura Tarō 桂太郎
Kawabe Torashirō 河辺虎四郎
Kawai Misao 河合操
Kawakami Seiichi 川上精一
Kawashima Naniwa 川島浪速
Kawashima Tadashi 川島正
Kawashima Yoshiyuki 川島義之
Kido Kōichi 木戸幸一
Kikuchi Shinnosuke 菊地慎之助
Kikuchi Takeo 菊地武夫
Kimura Eiichi 木村鋭市
Kita Ikki (Terujirō) 北一輝（輝次郎）
Kita Reikichi 北昤吉
Kiyoura Keigo 清浦奎吾
Kobayashi Seizō 小林躋造
Kodama Gentarō 児玉源太郎
Kodama Yoshio 児玉誉志夫
Koga Mineichi 古賀峰一
Kohiyama Naotaka 小日山直登

Koiso Kuniaki 小磯国昭
Kojima Masanori 児島正範
Kojima Sōjirō 児島惣次郎
Kōmoto Daisaku 河本大作
Kōmoto Suemori 河本末守
Kondō Nobutake 近藤信竹
Konoe Fumimaro 近衛文麿
Kuan Yü-heng 關玉衡
Kubota Yuzuru 久保田譲
Kuhara Fusanosuke 久原房之助
Kuo T'ai-ch'i (Quo Tai-chi) 郭泰祺
Kuratomi Yūzaburō 倉富勇三郎
Kurihara Tadashi 栗原正
Kuroda Nagashige 黒田長成
Kuroki Shinkei 黒木親慶
Kusakari Eiji 草刈英治
Kusunoki Masashige 楠正成
Kuwashima Kazue 桑島主計
Kuzū Yoshihisa 葛生能久
Li Li-san 李立三
Lo Chen-yü 羅振玉
Lo Wen-kan 羅文幹
Ma Chan-shan 馬占山
Maeda Yonezō 前田米蔵
Makino Nobuaki (Shinken) 牧野伸顕
Maruyama Masao 丸山眞男
Matsudaira Tsuneo 松平恒雄
Matsui Iwane 松井石根
Matsui Seisuke 松井清助
Matsuki Tamotsu 松木侠
Matsumoto Shigetoshi 松本重敏
Matsuoka Yōsuke 松岡洋右
Mazaki Jinzaburō 眞崎甚三郎
Mi Ch'un-lin 米春霖
Mikami Takashi 三上卓
Minami Jirō 南次郎
Mine Yukimatsu 峰幸松
Minobe Tatsukichi 美濃部達吉
Mitani Kiyoshi 三谷清
Mitani Takanobu 三谷隆信
Miura Takemi 三浦武美
Miyake Mitsuharu 三宅光治
Miyake Yūjirō (Setsurei) 三宅雄二郎
　（雪嶺）
Miyazaki Masayoshi 宮崎正義

Miyazaki Torazō (Tōten) 宮崎寅蔵
　（滔天）
Mizumachi Kesaroku 水町袈裟六
Mori Kaku (Tsutomu) 森恪
Mori Ren 森連
Mori Takeshi 森赳
Morioka Shōhei 森岡正平
Morishima Morito 森島守人
Mudaguchi Renya 牟田口廉也
Mugita Hirao 麦田平雄
Murai Kuramatsu 村井倉松
Murakami Ryūei 村上竜英
Muraoka Chōtarō 村岡長太郎
Mutō Akira 武藤章
Mutō Nobuyoshi 武藤信義
Nagae Ryōji 永江亮二
Nagai Matsuzō 永井松三
Nagai Ryūtarō 永井柳太郎
Nagano Osami 永野修身
Nagata Tetsuzan 永田鉄山
Nagura Kan 名倉栞
Nakajima Shin'ichi 中島信一
Nakamura Ryōzō 中村良三
Nakamura Shintarō 中村震太郎
Nakano Ryōji 中野良次
Nakano Tomio 中野登美雄
Nakano Toraitsu 中野虎逸
Nakatani Takeyo 中谷武世
Nara Takeji 奈良武次
Nemoto Hiroshi 根本博
Ninagawa Shin 蜷川新
Ninomiya Harushige 二宮治重
Nishida Mitsugu 西田税
Nishihara Kamezō 西原亀三
Noda Kiyoshi 野田清
Noda Matao 野田又男
Noda Sukuo 野田耕夫
Nomura Kichisaburō 野村吉三郎
Obama Ujiyoshi 小浜氏善
Obata Toshishirō 小畑敏四郎
Obata Yūkichi 小幡酉吉
Ogasawara Naganari 小笠原長生
Ogata Katsuichi 緒方勝一
Ōgishi Yoriyoshi 大岸頼好
Ōhashi Chūichi 大橋忠一

Ōi Shigemoto 大井成元
Oikawa Koshirō 及川古志郎
Ōishi Yoshio 大石良雄
Okada Keisuke 岡田啓介
Okada Takema 岡田猛馬
Okamoto Ren'ichirō 岡本連一郎
Okamura Yasuji (Neiji) 岡村寧次
Ōkawa Shūmei 大川周明
Oku Yasukata 奥保鞏
Ono Masao 小野正雄
Ono Sanenobu 尾野実信
Ōsugi Sakae 大杉栄
Ōsumi Mineo 大角岑生
Ozawa Kaisaku 小沢開策
P'u Yi 溥儀
Saburi Sadao 佐分利貞夫
Sada Kōjirō 佐多弘治郎
Sagōya Tomeo 佐郷屋留雄
Saionji Kimmochi 西園寺公望
Saitō Hiroshi 斎藤博
Saitō Makoto (Minoru) 斎藤実
Sakano Tsuneyoshi 坂野常善
Sakata Yoshirō 坂田義朗
Sakonji Seizō 左近司政三
Sakuma Ryōzō 佐久間亮三
Sakuma Shin 佐久間信
Samejima Tomoshige 鮫島具重
Sasaki Sōichi 佐々木惣一
Satake Reishin 佐竹令信
Satō Yasunosuke 佐藤安之助
Sawamoto Yorio 沢本頼雄
Sengoku Mitsugu 仙石貢
Shang Chen 商震
Shibata Shin'ichi 柴田信一
Shibayama Kaneshirō 柴山兼四郎
Shidehara Kijūrō 幣原喜重郎
Shigemitsu Mamoru 重光葵
Shigetō Chiaki 重藤千秋
Shih Yu-san 石友三
Shimada Shigetarō 嶋田繁太郎
Shimamoto Masaichi 島本正一
Shimizu Kōnosuke 清水行之助
Shimizu Yaoichi 清水八百一
Shimomura Shōsuke 下村正助
Shiozawa Kōichi 塩沢幸一

Shirakawa Yoshinori 白川義則
Shiratori Toshio 白鳥敏夫
Soejima Giichi 副島義一
Sogō Shinji 十河信二
Suetsugu Nobumasa 末次信正
Suganami Saburō 管波三郎
Sugiyama Gen (Hajime) 杉山元
Suzuki Fujiya 鈴木富士弥
Suzuki Kantarō 鈴木貫太郎
Suzuki Kisaburō 鈴木喜三郎
Suzuki Sōroku 鈴木荘六
Suzuki Takao 鈴木孝雄
Suzuki Teiichi 鈴木貞一
Tai Chi 戴戟
Takabatake Motoyuki 高畠素之
Takagi Yoshito 高木義人
Takahashi Ibō 高橋伊望
Takahashi Kin'ichi 高橋金一
Takahashi Korekiyo 高橋是清
Takahashi Morio 高橋守雄
Takarabe Takeshi 財部彪
Takatsuka Gen'ichi 高塚源一
Takeda Hisashi 武田寿
Takeshita Yoshiharu 竹下義晴
Tamon Jirō 多門二郎
Tamura Tadashi 田村正
Tanaka Chigaku 田中智学
Tanaka Giichi 田中義一
Tanaka Kiyoshi 田中清
Tanaka Ryūkichi 田中隆吉
Tanaka Wataru 田中弥
T'ang Erh-ho 湯爾和
T'ang Yü-lin 湯玉麟
Tani Masayuki 谷正之
Taniguchi Naomi 谷口尚真
Tashiro Kan'ichirō 田代皖一郎
Tatekawa Yoshitsugu 建川義次
Terajima Kazuo 寺島一夫
Terauchi Masatake 寺内正毅
Ting Ch'ao 丁超
Tochinai Sojirō 栃内曽次郎
Tōgō Heihachirō 東郷平八郎
Tōjō Hideki 東条英機
Tōjō Tei 東条貞
Tokugawa Yoshichika 徳川義親

Tomita Tsunejirō 富田常次郎
Toyama Bunzō 外山豊造
Tōyama Mitsuru 頭山満
Ts'ai T'ing-k'ai 蔡廷楷
Tsang Shih-yi 臧式毅
Tsou Lu 鄒魯
Tsuchihashi Yūichi (Yūitsu) 土橋勇逸
Tsuji Masanobu 辻正信
Tsukamoto Seiji 塚本清治
Tsukuda Nobuo 佃信夫
Uchida Ryōhei 内田良平
Uchida Shinya 内田信也
Uchida Yasuya (Kōsai) 内田康哉
Ueda Kenkichi 植田謙吉
Uehara Yūsaku 上原勇作
Uematsu Kikuko 植松菊子
Ugaki Kazushige (Kazunari) 宇垣一成
Umezu Yoshijirō 梅津美治郎
Utsunomiya Tarō 宇都宮太郎
Wachi Takaji 和知鷹二
Wada Tsuyoshi 和田勁
Wakatsuki Reijirō 若槻礼次郎
Wake no Kiyomaro 和気清麿
Wan Fu-lin 萬福麟
Wang Chen-hsiang 王振祥
Wang Ching-wei 汪精衛
Watanabe Hideto 渡辺秀人
Watari Hisao 渡久雄
Wu Ken-hsiang 吳根香
Wu T'ieh-ch'eng 吳鐵城
Yabuki Shōzō 矢吹省三
Yamagata Aritomo 山県有朋
Yamagishi Hiroshi 山岸宏
Yamaguchi Jūji 山口重次
Yamakawa Kenjirō 山川健次郎
Yamamoto Gonnohyōe (Gombei)
　山本権兵衛
Yamamoto Hidesuke 山本英輔
Yamamoto Jōtarō 山本条太郎
Yamamoto Teijirō 山本悌二郎
Yamanashi Hanzō 山梨半造
Yamanashi Katsunoshin 山梨勝之進
Yamaoka Michitake 山岡道武
Yamaoka Shigeatsu 山岡重厚
Yamashita Tomoyuki 山下奉文

Yamaura Kan'ichi 山浦貫一
Yamawaki Masataka 山脇正隆
Yamazaki Takeshi 山崎猛
Yamazaki Tatsunosuke 山崎達之輔
Yang Yü-t'ing 楊宇霆
Yano Makoto 矢野真
Yasuoka Masaatsu 安岡正篤
Yen Hsi-shan 閻錫山

Yoshida Seichi 吉田静致
Yoshida Shigeru 吉田茂
Yoshimura Gō 吉村剛
Yoshizawa Kenkichi 吉沢謙吉
Yü Ch'en-ch'eng 于琛澂
Yü Chih-shan 于芷山
Yü Chung-han 于沖漢

Bibliography

I. Archives

Note: Major archival documents cited in the notes are listed separately in Section III below.

Japan, Foreign Ministry Archives. Cited as JFM Archives.

Japan, Justice Ministry, War Crimes Materials Office.

These archives contain the Kyokutō Kokusai Gunji Saiban Kōhan Kiroku 極東国際軍事裁判公判記録 (Records of the International Military Tribunal for the Far East). Cited as IMTFE Records.

Japan, National Defense Agency, Military History Office. Cited as JDA Archives. These archives contain:

Japan, Army Ministry. Mitsu dai nikki 密大日記 (Confidential great diary), part of the Dai nikki 大日記 (Great Diary) series, containing chronologically arranged secret army files for 1906–40, exclusive of military command matters.

Papers of Enomoto Shigeharu 榎本重治史料, portions of which have been reproduced in the *Gendai shi shiryō* series and in *Taiheiyō sensō e no michi: Bekkan shiryō hen* (see Section III below).

Papers of Ishiwara Kanji 石原莞爾史料, held in the Ishiwara family and JDA Archives (See under Tsunoda Jun in Section III below.)

Papers of Makino Nobuaki 牧野伸顕文書, held in the Kenseishi Shiryōshitsu 憲政資料室 (Constitutional Government History Archives), National Diet Library, Tokyo.

Okada Family Archives.

These contain: "Okada Keisuke nikki" 岡田啓介日記 (Diary of Okada Keisuke), which has been published in part in *Gendai shi shiryō 7*, pp. 3–34. Cited as *Okada Diary*.

II. Interviews

Hayashi Kyūjirō 林久治郎, former consul-general at Mukden, July 19, 1962.

Katakura Tadashi 片倉衷, former Kwantung Army staff officer, December 19, 1959.

Kawashima Tadashi 川島正, former Kwantung Army company commander, November 20, 1962.

Mitani Kiyoshi 三谷清, former military police commander at Mukden, November 19, 1962.

Mugita Hirao 麦田平雄, former army officer and head of Japan Airlines office at Dairen, July 10, 1962.

III. Published Works and Major Unpublished Materials Cited

Adachi Kenzō 安達謙蔵. *Adachi Kenzō jijoden* 安達謙蔵自叙伝 (Autobiography of Adachi Kenzō), edited by Izu Tomihito 伊豆富人. Tokyo: Shinjusha, 1960.

Aoki Tokuzō 青木得三. *Taiheiyō sensō zenshi* 太平洋戦争前史 (The Historical Background of the Pacific War), 3 vols. Tokyo: Gakujutsu Bunken Fukyūkai, 1953.

Asada, Sadao. "Japanese Admirals and the Politics of Naval Limitation: Katō Tomosaburō vs. Katō Kanji." In Gerald Jordan, ed. *Naval Warfare in the Twentieth Century*, pp. 141–66. London: Croom Helm, 1977.

—— "The Japanese Navy and the United States." In Dorothy Borg and Shumpei Okamoto, eds. *Pearl Harbor as History: Japanese-American Relations, 1931–1941*, pp. 225–59. New York: Columbia University Press, 1973.

Ayusawa Toshio 鮎澤俊男, *Dai Nihon Seisantō jūnenshi* 大日本生産黨十年史 (Ten-year History of the Great Japan Production Party). Tokyo: Dai Nihon Seisantō Hunbu, 1941.

Braisted, William Reynolds. *The United States Navy in the Pacific, 1909–1922*. Austin and London: University of Texas Press, 1971.

Buckley, Thomas H. *The United States and the Washington Conference*. Knoxville: University of Tennessee Press, 1970.

Chaput, Rolland A. *Disarmament in British Foreign Policy*. London: G. Allen and Unwin, 1935.

China Yearbook, 1931 (Editor's note: publishing data unavailable).

Dai Nihon Teikoku Gikai Shi Kankōkai 大日本帝国議会誌刊行会, ed. *Dai Nihon Teikoku Gikai shi* 大日本帝国議会誌 (Records of the Imperial Japanese Diet), 17 vols. and index vol. Tokyo: Dai Nihon Teikoku Gikai Shi Kankōkai, 1926–30.

Dingman, Roger. *Power in the Pacific: The Origins of Naval Arms Limitation, 1914–1922*. Chicago: University of Chicago Press, 1976.

Ferrell, Robert H. *Frank B. Kellogg; Henry L. Stimson*. Vol. 11 of *The American Secretaries of State and Their Diplomacy*. New York: Cooper Square Publishers, 1963.

Fujimoto Haruki 藤本治毅. *Ningen Ishiwara Kanji* 人間石原莞爾 (Ishiwara Kanji, the Man). Tokyo: Taichi Sangyōsha, 1959.

Gendai shi shiryō 7: Manshū jihen 現代史資料7 満洲事変 (Source Materials on Contemporary History 7: The Manchurian Incident). Tokyo: Misuzu Shobō, 1964. Cited as GS 7.

Gendai shi shiryō 11: Zoku Manshū jihen 現代史資料11 続満洲事変 (Source Materials on Contemporary History: The Manchurian Incident, 2). Tokyo: Misuzu Shobō, 1965. Cited as GS 11.

Great Britain, Foreign Office. *Documents on British Foreign Policy, 1919–1939*. Second Series, vol. 1. London: His Majesty's Stationery Office, 1947.

Haibara Shigeki 榛原茂樹 and Kashiwa Masahiko 柏正彦. *Shanhai jihen gaikō shi* 上海事件外交史 (A Diplomatic History of the Shanghai Incident). Tokyo: Kinkō-dō Shoseki, 1932.

Hamaguchi Naikaku Hensanjo 浜口内閣編纂所, ed. *Hamaguchi naikaku* 浜口内閣 (The Hamaguchi Cabinet). Tokyo: Hamaguchi Naikaku Hensanjo, 1947.

Hanaya Tadashi 花谷正. "Manshū jihen wa kōshite keikaku sareta" 満洲事変はこうして計画された (Thus Was Plotted the Manchurian Incident), *Bessatsu Chisei 5: Himerareta Shōwashi* 別冊知性5 秘められた昭和史 (Secret History of the Shōwa Era: *Chisei* Supplement No. 5), December 1956, pp. 40–50.

Hara Keiichirō 原奎一郎, ed. *Hara Takashi nikki* 原敬日記 (Diary of Hara Takashi), 9 vols. Tokyo: Kengensha, 1950–51.

Harada Kumao 原田熊雄. *Saionji kō to seikyoku* 西園寺公と政局 (Prince Saionji and the Political Situation), 8 vols. and supplementary volume of documents: *Bekkan*. Tokyo: Iwanami Shoten, 1950–52, 1956.

Hashimoto Kingorō 橋本欣五郎 memoir. Unpublished.

Hata Ikuhiko 秦郁彦. *Gun fashizumu undō shi* 軍ファシズム運動史 (History of the Military Fascist Movement). Tokyo: Kawade Shobō Shinsha, 1962.

Hirano Reiji 平野零児. *Manshū no imbōsha: Kōmoto Daisaku no unmeiteki na ashiato* 満洲の陰謀者河本大作の運命的な足あと (A Conspirator in Manchuria: The Life of Kōmoto Daisaku). Tokyo: Jiyū Kokuminsha, 1959.

Hiranuma Kiichirō Kaikoroku Hensan Iinkai 平沼騏一郎回顧録編纂委員会, ed. *Hiranuma Kiichirō kaikoroku* 平沼騏一郎回顧録 (Reminiscences of Hiranuma Kiichirō). Tokyo: Hiranuma Kiichirō Kaikoroku Hensan Iinkai, 1955.

Hori Teikichi 堀悌吉, comp. "Rondon kaigi seikun yori kaikun made no kikan shimpen zatsuroku" ロンドン会議請訓より回訓までの期間身辺雑録 (Miscellaneous Personal Records Concerning the London Conference from the Request for Instructions Until the Dispatch of the Return Instructions). In the Enomoto Papers, reproduced in *Gendai shi shiryō 7*, pp. 35–40. Cited as Hori, London Conference Records.

—— "Rondon kaigi to tōsuiken mondai" ロンドン会議と統帥権問題 (The London Conference and the Right of Military Command Problem). In the Enomoto Papers, reproduced in *Taiheiyō sensō e no michi: Bekkan*, pp. 63–71.

—— "Rondon kaigun jōyaku teiketsu keii" 倫敦海軍条約締結経緯 (Particulars Concerning the Conclusion of the London Naval Treaty). In the Enomoto Papers, reproduced in *Gendai shi shiryō 7*, pp. 88–100. Cited as Hori, Treaty Conclusion.

—— "Shōwa go-nen shigatsu tsuitachi kaikun ni kansuru keii" 昭和五年四月一日回訓ニ関スル経緯 (Particulars Concerning the April 1, 1930, Return Instructions). In Enomoto Shigeharu Papers, reporduced in part in *Taiheiyō sensō e no michi: Bekkan*, pp. 7–56. Cited as Hori, Return Instructions.

Horinouchi Kensuke 堀内謙介, Yamagata Kiyoshi 山形清, and Unno Koshirō 海野芳郎. *Kaigun gunshuku kōshō. fusen jōyaku* 海軍軍縮交渉. 不戦条約 (Naval Arms Reduction Negotiations and the Antiwar Pact). Vol. 16 of Kajima Heiwa Kenkyūjo 鹿島平和研究所, ed. *Nihon gaikō shi* 日本外交史 (Diplomatic History of Japan). Tokyo: Kajima Kenkyūjo Shuppankai, 1973.

Ichimata Masao 一又正雄. "Kanshū teki jieiken no saiginmi" 慣習的自衛権の再吟味 (A Reexamination of the Customary Right of Self-Defense), *Kokusaihō gaikō zasshi* 国際法外交雑誌, (July 1965) 64: 1–39.

Ikeda Kiyoshi 池田清. *Nihon no kaigun* 日本の海軍 (The Japanese Navy), 2 vols. Tokyo: Shiseidō, 1967.

Imamura Hitoshi 今村均. *Kōzoku to kashikan* 皇族と下士官 (The Imperial Family and Noncommissioned Officers). Tokyo: Jiyū Ajiasha, 1960.

—— "Manshū hi o fuku koro" 満洲火を噴く頃 (The Outbreak of the Manchurian Incident), *Bessatsu Chisei 5: Himerareta Shōwashi* 別冊知性5 秘められた昭和史 (Secret History of the Shōwa Era: *Chisei* Supplement No. 5), December 1956, pp. 60–71.

Inaba Iwakichi 稲葉岩吉 (pseud. Inaba Kunzan 稲葉君山. *Manshū hatten shi* 満洲

発展史 (A History of the Development of Manchuria.). Tokyo: Osakaya-gō Shuppanbu, 1915.

Inaba Masao 稲葉正夫. "Shōwa sensō shi kōza: Manshū jihen" 昭和戦争史講座満洲事変 (Lectures on Shōwa War History: The Manchurian Incident). Parts 1, 3, and 4, *Kokubō* 国防, Nos. 6, 8, and 9, 1962.

Inoue Junnosuke Ronsō Hensankai 井上準之助論叢編纂会, ed. *Inoue Junnosuke den* 井上準之助伝 (Biography of Inoue Junnosuke). Tokyo: Inoue Junnosuke Ronsō Hensankai, 1935.

Iriye, Akira. *After Imperialism: The Search for a New Order in the Far East, 1921–1931.* Cambridge, Mass.: Harvard University Press, 1965.

—— "Chang Hsüeh-liang and the Japanese," *Journal of Asian Studies* (November 1960): 20 (1): 33–43.

—— "The Failure of Economic Expansionism, 1918–1931." In Bernard S. Silberman and H. D. Harootunian. *Japan in Crisis: Essays on Taishō Democracy.* Princeton, N.J. Princeton University Press, 1974.

Ishiwara Kanji 石原莞爾. *Sekai saishū sen ron* 世界最終戦論 (On the Final World War). Tokyo: Ritsumeikan Shuppanbu, 1942.

Itō Takashi 伊藤隆. *Shōwa shoki seiji shi kenkyū: Rondon kaigun gunshuku mondai o meguru sho seiji shūdan no taikō to teikei* 昭和初期政治史研究ロンドン海軍軍縮問題をめぐる諸政治集団の対抗と提携 (A Study of the Political History of the Early Shōwa Era: Cooperation and Opposition of Various Political Groups with Regard to the London Naval Conference Controversy). Tokyo: Tōkyō Daigaku Shuppankai, 1969.

Japan, Army General Staff. "Manshū jihen kimitsu sakusen nisshi" 満洲事変機密作戦日誌 (Confidential Operational Journal of the Manchurian Incident), reproduced in *Taiheiyō sensō e no michi: Bekkan*, pp. 113–207.

—— "Manshū jihen shi, 5: Manshū jihen ni okeru gun no tōsui (an)" 満洲事変史満洲事変に於ける軍の統帥(案) (Draft History of the Manchurian Incident, Vol. 5: Military Command in the Manchurian Incident), reproduced in *Gendai shi shiryō 11*, pp. 299–523.

—— First Section. "Shōwa go-nen Rondon kaigi kankei tōsuiken ni kansuru shorui tsuzuri" 昭和五年倫敦会議関係統帥権ニ関スル書類綴 (File of Documents Concerning the Right of Military Command and the 1930 London Conference). In JDA Archives, reproduced in *Gendai shi shiryō 11*, pp. 3–100. Cited as AGS File.

Japan, Foreign Ministry. "Issen kyūhyaku sanjū-nen Rondon kaigun jōyaku Sūmitsuin shinsa giji yōroku" 一九三〇年ロンドン海軍条約枢密院審査議事要録 (Digest of the Proceedings of the Privy Council Inquiry on the London Naval Treaty). In JFM Archives. Cited as JFM, Privy Council Inquiry.

—— *Nihon gaikō nempyō narabi ni shuyō bunsho* 日本外交年表並主要文書 (Chronology and Major Documents of Japanese Foreign Relations), 2 vols. Tokyo: Hara Shobō, 1955; republished in 1965.

Johnstone, W. C. *The Shanghai Problem.* Stanford, Calif.: Stanford University Press, 1937.

Katakura Tadashi 片倉衷. "Manshū jihen kimitsu seiryaku nisshi" 満洲事変機密

政略日誌 (Secret Political Journal of the Manchurian Incident), *Gendai shi shiryō* 7, pp. 182–427.

—— "Manshū jihen to Kantōgun" 満洲事変と関東軍 (The Manchurian Incident and the Kwantung Army), *Gaikō jihō* 外交時報, No. 9, 1961, pp. 42–50.

Katō Kanji 加藤寛治. "Katō Kanji ikō" 加藤寛治遺稿 (The Literary Remains of Katō Kanji). Reproduced in Ikeda Kiyoshi 池田清. "Rondon kaigun jōyaku ni kansuru Gunreibugawa no shiryō" ロンドン海軍条約に関する軍令部側の資料 (Navy General Staff Materials Related to the London Naval Treaty), *Hōgaku zasshi* 法学雑誌 (March 1969), 15 (4): 102–26. (August 1969) 16(1): 123–42, Cited as *Katō Diary.*

Katō Kanji Denki Hensankai 加藤寛治伝記編纂会, ed. *Katō Kanji taishō den* 加藤寛治大将伝 (Biography of Admiral Katō Kanji). Tokyo: Katō Kanji Denki Hensankai, 1941.

Kido Kōichi 木戸幸一. *Kido nikki* 木戸日記 (Kido Diary). Edited by Kyokutō Kokusai Gunji Saiban Kenkyūkai 極東国際軍事裁判研究会. Tokyo: Heiwa Shobō, 1947.

Kikuchi Gorō 菊地悟郎. *Rikken Seiyūkai shi* 立憲政友会史 (History of the Seiyūkai), vol. 7: *Inukai sosai jidai* 犬養總裁時代 (Inukai's Presidency). Tokyo: Rikken Seiyūkai Shi Hensanbu, 1933.

Kitsukawa Manabu 橘川学. *Arashi to tatakan tesshō Araki* 嵐と闘ふ哲将荒木 (Braving a Storm: General Araki Tadao). Tokyo: Denki Hemponkai, 1955.

Kiyose Ichirō 清瀬一郎. "Seiki" 正気 (Spirit of Justice) (Editor's note: publication data unavailable).

Kodama Yoshio 児玉誉士夫. *Ware yabure tari* われ敗れたり (I Was Defeated). Tokyo: Kyōyūsha, 1949.

Koiso Kuniaki 小磯国昭. "Koiso kaisō roku" 小磯回想録 (Koiso Memoirs). Unpublished.

Koiso Kuniaki Jijoden Kankōkai 小磯国昭自叙伝刊行会, ed. *Katsuzan Kōsō* 葛山鴻爪 (Pen name of Koiso Kuniaki). Tokyo: Chūō Kōron Jigyō, 1963.

Kōmoto Daisaku 河本大作 memoir. Unpublished.

League of Nations. *The Report of the Commission of Enquiry of the League of Nations into the Sino-Japanese Dispute*, signed by members of the Commission on September 4, 1932, at Peiping. Geneva: League of Nations, Series A, League of Nations Publications, Political (1932), 7: 12, October 1, 1932.

—— *Official Journal: Supplement No. 75, Records of the Tenth Ordinary Session of the Assembly, Plenary Meetings, Text of the Debates.* Geneva: League of Nations, 1929.

Man-Mō jijō 満蒙事情 (Reports on Manchuria and Mongolia).

Manshū Seinen Remmei Shi Kankōkai 満洲青年聯盟史刊行会, ed. *Manshū Seinen Remmei shi* 満洲青年聯盟史 (History of the Manchurian Youth League). Mukden: Manshū Seinen Remmei Shi Kankō Iinkai, 1933.

Mantetsu chōsa geppō 満鉄調査月報 (South Manchuria Railway Research Monthly).

Maruyama Masao 丸山真男. *Gendai seiji no shisō to kōdō* 現代政治の思想と行動 (Thought and Behavior in Contemporary Politics), 2 vols. Tokyo: Miraisha, 1957. Part of this work has been translated into English as: *Thought and Behaviour in*

Modern Japanese Politics. Edited by Ivan Morris. New York: Oxford University Press, 1963.

Matsuoka Yōsuke 松岡洋石. *Kōa no taigyō* 興亜の大業 (A Grand Enterprise for the Development of Asia). Tokyo: Daiichi Kōronsha, 1941.

Matsushita Yoshio 松下芳男. *Meiji gunsei shiron* 明治軍制史論 (History of the Meiji Military System), 2 vols. Tokyo: Yūhikaku, 1956.

——— *Nihon gunsei to seiji* 日本軍制と政治 (Politics and the Japanese Military System). Tokyo: Kuroshio Shuppansha, 1960.

Minobe Tatsukichi 美濃部達吉. *Gikai seiji no kentō* 議会政治の検討 (A Study of Parliamentary Politics). Tokyo: Nihon Hyōronsha, 1934.

Mitani Kiyoshi 三谷清 memoir. Unpublished.

Mitarai Tatsuo 御手洗辰雄, ed. *Minami Jirō* 南次郎. Tokyo: Minami Jirō Denki Kankōkai, 1957.

Morishima Morito 森島守人. *Imbō, ansatsu, guntō: Gaikōkan no kaisō* 陰謀・暗殺・軍刀 ― 外交官の回想 (Intrigue, Assassination, and Swords: Reminiscences of a Diplomat). Tokyo: Iwanami Shoten, 1950.

Morison, Elting E. *Turmoil and Tradition: A Study of the Life and Times of Henry L. Stimson.* Boston: Houghton Mifflin, 1960.

Nakamura Kikuo 中村菊男. *Shōwa kaigun hishi* 昭和海軍秘史 (Secret History of the Navy During the Shōwa Era). Tokyo: Banchō Shobō, 1969.

Nakano Masao 中野雅夫 *Sannin no hōkasha* 三人の放火者 (Three Who Set Fire). Tokyo: Chikuma Shobō, 1956.

Nihon Kokusai Seiji Gakkai, Taiheiyō Sensō Gen'in Kenkyūbu 日本国際政治学会 太平洋戦争原因研究部 (Japan Association on International Relations, Study Group on the Causes of the Pacific War), ed. *Taiheiyō sensō e no michi: Bekkan shiryō hen* 太平洋戦争への道別巻資料編 (The Road to the Pacific War: Supplementary Volume of Documents). Tokyo: Asahi Shimbunsha, 1963. Cited as TSM: Bekkan.

Ninomiya Harushige 二宮治重 memoir. Unpublished.

Nish, Ian H. "Japan and Naval Aspects of the Washington Conference." In William G. Beasley, ed. *Modern Japan: Aspects of History*, pp. 67–80. London: Allen and Unwin, 1975.

Nomura Minoru 野村實. "Gunshuku mondai ni kansuru Hamaguchi shushō nisshi" 軍縮問題に関する浜口首相日誌 (Prime Minister Hamaguchi's Diary Notes on the Arms Limitation Problem), *Gunji shigaku* 軍事史学 (December 1976), 12(3): 74–81.

——— "Tai-Bei-Ei kaisen to kaigun tai-Bei nanawari shisō" 対米英開戦と海軍対米 七割思想 (The Beginning of the War with America and Britain and the Navy's Ideas about the 70-Percent Ratio Toward America), *Gunji shigaku* 軍事史学 (September 1973) 9(2): 23–34.

O'Connor, Raymond G. *Perilous Equilibrium: The United States and the London Naval Conference of 1930.* Lawrence, Kansas: University of Kansas Press, 1962.

Ogasawara Naganari 小笠原長生. *Bannen no Tōgō gensui* 晩年の東郷元帥 (Fleet Admiral Tōgō in His Later Years). Tokyo: Kaizōsha, 1934.

Ogata, Sadako N. *Defiance in Manchuria: The Making of Japanese Foreign Policy,*

1931–1932. Berkeley and Los Angeles: University of California Press, 1964.

Okada Keisuke 岡田啓介. *Okada Keisuke kaikoroku* 岡田啓介回顧録 (Reminiscences of Okada Keisuke). Tokyo: Mainichi Shimbunsha, 1950.

"Okada Masukichi kaisō roku" 岡田益吉回想録 (Memoirs of Okada Masukichi), *Shūkan yomiuri*, 週刊讀賣 November 28, 1954.

Okada Taishō Kiroku Hensankai 岡田大将記録編纂会, ed. *Okada Keisuke* 岡田啓介. Tokyo: Okada Taishō Kiroku Hensankai, 1956.

Ōsaka Tai-Shi Keizai Remmei 大阪対支経済聯盟 (Osaka China Economy League). *Sorempō to Shina-Manshū no kyōsan undō* ソ聯邦と支那満洲の共産運動 (The Soviet Union and Communist Movements in China and Manchuria). Tokyo: Shinkōsha, 1934.

Pelz, Stephen E. *Race to Pearl Harbor: The Failure of the Second London Naval Conference and the Onset of World War II*. Cambridge, Mass.: Harvard University Press, 1974.

—— "Risō no teikoku: Shin chitsujo kensetsu e no Nihon gunjin no yume, 1928–1940" 理想の帝国新秩序建設への日本軍人の夢一九二八――一九四〇 (Idealistic Empire: The Dreams of Japanese Military Men About the Construction of a New Order, 1928–1940). In Satō Seizaburō 佐藤誠三郎 and Roger Dingman, eds. *Kindai Nihon no taigai taido* 近代日本の対外態度 (Modern Japanese Attitudes Toward the Outer World), pp. 155–86. Tokyo: Tōkyō Daigaku Shuppankai, 1974.

Rappaport, Armin. *Henry L. Stimson and Japan, 1931–1933*. Chicago and London: The University of Chicago Press, 1963.

Roskill, Stephen. *Naval Policy Between the Wars*, 2 vols. London: Collins, 1968 and 1976.

Saigō Kōsaku 西郷鋼作 (pen name of Tamura Shinsaku 田村真作). *Itagaki Seishirō* 板垣征四郎. Tokyo: Seiji Chishikisha, 1938.

Saitō Shishaku Kinenkai 斎藤子爵記念会, ed. *Shishaku Saitō Makoto den* 子爵斎藤実伝 (Biography of Viscount Saitō Makoto), 4 vols. Tokyo: Saitō Shishaku Kinenkai, 1941–42.

Schurmann, Franz, and Orville Schell. *China Reader: Republican China*. New York: Knopf, 1967.

Segawa Yoshinobu 瀬川善信. "Issen kyūhyaku sanjū-nen Rondon gunshuku kaigi kaisai to Nihon rikugun" 一九三〇年ロンドン軍縮会議開催と日本陸軍 (The Japanese Army and the Holding of the 1930 London Disarmament Conference), *Saitama Daigaku kiyō (Shakai Kagaku hen)* 埼玉大学紀要（社会科学篇）(March 1966), no. 1, pp. 1–9.

—— "Tōsuiken to Sambō Hombu—issen kyūhyaku sanjū-nen Rondon gunshuku kaigi o chūshin toshite" 統帥権と参謀本部一九三〇年ロンドン軍縮会議を中心として (The Right of Military Command Problem and the Army General Staff—The London Disarmament Conference of 1930), *Bōei ronshū* 防衛論集 (October 1966), 5(3): 13–37.

Shanhai Kyoryū Mindan 上海居留民団 (Japanese Shanghai Residents Association). et. *Shanhai jihen shi* 上海事変誌 (History of the Shanghai Incident). (Editorial note: publishing data unavailable).

Shanhai Nippō Sha 上海日報社, ed. *Shanhai jihen* 上海事変 (The Shanghai Incident). Shanghai: Shanhai Nippō Sha Shuppanbu, 1932.

Shidehara Heiwa Zaidan 幣原平和財団, ed. *Shidehara Kijūrō* 幣原喜重郎. Tokyo: Shidehara Heiwa Zaidan, 1955.

Shidō Yasusuke 志道保亮. *Tetsuzan Nagata chūjō* 鉄山永田中将 (Lieutenant-General Nagata Tetsuzan). Tokyo: Senryūdō, 1938.

Shigemitsu Mamoru 重光葵. *Gaikō kaisōroku* 外交回想録 (Diplomatic Reminiscences). Tokyo: Mainichi Shimbunsha, 1953.

Shimada Toshihiko 島田俊彦. *Kantōgun* 関東軍 (The Kwantung Army). Tokyo: Chūō Kōronsha, 1965.

—— "Shanhai ekkai dōro o meguru kokusai ronsō" 上海越界道路をめぐる国際紛争 (International Disputes Concerning Shanghai's Outer Roads), *Musashi Daigaku ronshū* 武蔵大学論集, vol. 4, no. 2.

—— "Shanhai teisen kyōtei shimpan mondai" 上海停戦協定侵犯問題 (Violation of the Shanghai Ceasefire Agreement), *Musashi Daigaku ronshū* 武蔵大学論集, (December 1955), 3(1): 60–110.

—— "Shōwa shichi-nen Shanhai teisen kyōtei seiritsu no keii" 昭和七年上海停戦協定成立の経緯 (The Shanghai Armistice Agreement of 1932), *Ajia kenkyū* アジア研究 (January 1957), vol. 3, no 4.

Stimson, Henry L. *The Far Eastern Crisis: Recollections and Observations*. New York: Harper, 1936.

—— and McGeorge Bundy. *On Active Service in Peace and War*. New York: Harper, 1947.

Suekuni Masao 末国正雄. "Teikoku kaigun to nanawari" (The Imperial Navy and the 70-Percent Ratio). In Bōeichō Senshishitsu 防衛庁戦史室 (National Defense Agency, Military History Office). *Dai Tōa (Taiheiyō) sensō senshi sōsho* 大東亜(太平洋)戦争戦史叢書 (The Greater East Assia [Pacific] War History Series), vol. 31: *Kaigun gunsembi 1* 海軍軍戦備 (Naval Armaments and Preparations for War, 1). Tokyo: Asagumo Shimbunsha, 1969.

Suzuki Kantarō 鈴木貫太郎. *Suzuki Kantarō jiden* 鈴木貫太郎自伝 (Autobiography of Suzuki Kantarō), edited by Suzuki Hajime 鈴木一. Tokyo: Jiji Tsūshinsha, 1968.

Takagi Seiju 高木清寿. *Tōa no chichi: Ishiwara Kanji* 東亜の父・石原莞爾 (The Father of East Asia: Ishiwara Kanji). Tokyo: Kimbun Shoin, 1954.

Takakura Tetsuichi 高倉徹一. *Tanaka Giichi denki* 田中義一伝記 (Biography of Tanaka Giichi), 2 vols. Tokyo: Tanaka Giichi Denki Kankōkai, 1958–60.

Takamiya Tahei 高宮太平. *Gunkoku taiheiki* 軍国太平記 (Chronicle of a Military Nation). Tokyo: Kantōsha, 1951.

Tanaka Kiyoshi 田中清. "Iwayuru jūgatsu jiken ni kansuru shuki" 所謂十月事件に関する手記 (Note on the So-called October Incident), attached to *Shukugun ni kansuru ikensho* 粛軍に関する意見書 (Statement Concerning the Purification of the Army).

Tanaka Ryūkichi 田中隆吉. "Shanhai jihen wa kōshite okosareta" 上海事変はこうして起された (How the Shanghai Incident Occurred), *Bessatsu Chisei 5:*

Himerareta Shōwa shi 別冊知性5 秘められた昭和史 (Secret History of the Shōwa Era: *Chisei* Supplement No. 5), December 1956.

Tōa Dōbunkai 東亜同文会 (East Asia Common Culture Association), ed. *Zoku tai-Shi kaiko roku* 續対支回顧録 (Recollections of Our Activities Toward China, Continued), 2nd series, 2 vols. Tokyo: Tai-Shi Kōrōsha Denki Hensankai, 1941; reprinted by Hara Shobō, 1973.

Treat, P. J. "Shanghai: January 28, 1932," *Pacific Historical Review* (September 1940), 9(3): 337–43.

Tsunoda Jun 角田順, comp. *Ishiwara Kanji shiryō: Kokubō ronsaku hen* 石原莞爾資料国防論策篇 (Papers of Ishiwara Kanji: His Doctrine of National Defense). Tokyo: Hara Shobō, 1967.

—— "Nihon kaigun sandai no rekishi" 日本海軍三代の歴史 (A History of Three Generations of the Japanese Navy), *Jiyū* 自由 (February 1969), 11(2): 138–69.

Ueda Shunkichi 殖田俊吉. "Gumbu kakushin kanryō no Nippon kyōsan-ka keikaku an, Shōwa demokkurashī no zasetsu (2)" 軍部革新官僚の日本共産化計画案, 昭和デモクラシーの挫折(下) (The Military and Renovationist Bureaucrats' Plan To Communize Japan: The Failure of Shōwa Democracy II) *Jiyū* 自由, November 1960.

Ueda Toshio 植田捷雄. "Manshū jihen o meguru Nihon no gaikō" 満洲事変を繞る日本の外交 (Japanese Diplomacy and the Manchurian Incident), *Tōyō Bunka Kenkyūjo kiyō* 東洋文化研究所紀要 (Memoirs of the Institute for Oriental Culture) (March 1964), no. 33, pp. 1–43.

Uehara, Cecil H., comp., *Checklist of Archives in the Japanese Ministry of Foreign Affairs, Tokyo, Japan, 1868–1945*. Washington, D.C.: Photoduplication Service, Library of Congress, 1954.

Ugaki Kazushige 宇垣一成. *Ugaki Kazushige nikki* 宇垣一成日記 (Diary of Ugaki Kazushige). Tokyo: Asahi Shimbunsha, 1954.

U.S. Congress, Senate, Committee on Foreign Relations. *Hearings on Treaty on the Limitation of Naval Armaments*, 71st Congress, 2nd Session. Washington, D.C.: U.S. Government Printing Office, 1930.

U.S. Department of State. *Foreign Relations of the United States: Diplomatic Papers, 1927*, vol. 1. Washington, D.C.: U.S. Government Printing Office, 1942.

—— *Foreign Relations of the United States: Diplomatic Papers, 1929*. Washington, D.C.: U.S. Government Printing Office, 1943.

—— Publication No. 79. *London Naval Treaty: Radio Address by the Honorable Henry L. Stimson, June 12, 1930*. Washington, D.C.: U.S. Government Printing Office, 1930.

Usami Seijirō 宇佐美誠次郎. "Manshū shinryaku" 満洲侵略 (The Invasion of Manchuria), *Nihon rekishi* 日本歴史 (1963), 20: 211–53.

Wakatsuki Naikaku Hensankai 若槻内閣編纂会, ed. *Wakatsui naikaku* 若槻内閣 (The Wakatsuki Cabinet). Tokyo: Wakatsuki Naikaku Hensankai, 1931.

Wakatsuki Reijirō 若槻礼次郎. *Kofūan kaikoroku* 古風庵回顧録 (Memoirs Written at Kofūan). Tokyo: Yomiuri Shimbunsha, 1950.

—— *Ōshū ni tsukai shite* 欧州に使して (My Mission to Europe). Tokyo: Jitsugyō no Nihonsha, 1931.

Wheeler, Gerald E. *Prelude to Pearl Harbor: The United States Navy and the Far East, 1921–1931*. Columbia, Mo.: University of Missouri Press, 1963.

Woodhead, H. G. W., ed. *The China Yearbook, 1932*. Shanghai: North China Daily News and Herald, 1932.

Yamaguchi Shigeji 山口重次. *Higeki no shōgun Ishiwara Kanji* 悲劇の将軍石原莞爾 (The Tragic General Ishiwara Kanji). Tokyo: Sekaisha, 1952.

Yamaura Kan'ichi 山浦貫一, ed. *Mori Kaku* 森恪. Tokyo: Mori Kaku Denki Hensankai, 1940.

——— *Mori Kaku wa ikite iru* 森恪は生きている (Mori Kaku Is Alive). Tokyo: Takayama Shoten, 1941.

Yasutomi Shōzō 安富正造. *Kinsei gunshuku shikan* 近世軍縮史観 (A Historical View of Arms Limitation in Modern Times). Kokusai Remmei Kyokai sōsho 113 国際連盟協会叢書 113 (League of Nations Association Series 113). Tokyo: Kokusai Remmei Kyokai, 1932.

Yomiuri Hōteikisha 讀賣法廷記者, *Nijū-go hikoku no hyōjō* 二十五被告の表情 (The Appearance of the Twenty-five Defendants) (Editor's note: publication data unavailable).

Yoshihashi, Takehiko. *Conspiracy at Mukden: The Rise of the Japanese Military*. New Haven, Conn., and London: Yale University Press, 1963.

Young, John. *Checklist of Microfilm Reproductions of Selected Archives of the Japanese Army, Navy, and Other Government Agencies, 1868–1945*. Washington, D.C.: Georgetown University Press, 1959.

Yūshūkai 有終会. *Kaigun oyobi kaiji yōran* 海軍及海事要覧 (Handbook of Naval and Maritime Affairs). Tokyo: Yūshūkai, 1927.

Contributors

AKIRA IRIYE is professor and chairman of the Department of History, the University of Chicago. He received his B.A. from Haverford College and Ph.D. from Harvard University. He has also taught at Harvard University, the University of California at Santa Cruz, and the University of Rochester. He is the author of many books, including *After Imperialism: The Search for a New Order in the Far East, 1921–1931, Across the Pacific: An Inner History of American-East Asian Relations, Pacific Estrangement: Japanese and American Expansion, 1897–1911, The Cold War in Asia: A Historical Introduction, From Nationalism to Internationalism: American Foreign Policy to 1914,* and *Power and Culture: The Japanese-American War, 1941–1945.*

MARIUS B. JANSEN is professor of history and East Asian studies at Princeton University. His degrees are from Princeton (1943) and Harvard (1950). He taught at the University of Washington from 1950 to 1959 before taking his present post at Princeton, where he has been director of the East Asian studies program and chairman of the East Asian studies department. His publications relating to the themes in this volume include *The Japanese and Sun Yat-sen* (1954), *Japan and China from War to Peace: 1894–1972* (1975), and *The Thirty-three Years' Dream: The Autobiography of Miyazaki Toten* (jointly with Eto Shinkichi, 1982).

KOBAYASHI TATSUO is a leading specialist on the history of international relations in the interwar period. Born in 1916, he was graduated from the Law Faculty of Tokyo Imperial University in 1943 and began a university teaching career, first at Denki Tsushin University, then at Tokyo Kyoiku University, and finally at Kokugakuin University in Tokyo. In addition to collaborating on a general text, *Kindai Nihon gaikō shi no kenkyū* (Studies in the History of Modern Japanese Diplomacy) (Tokyo: Yuhikaku, 1956), he has written many essays on Japan's foreign relations; edited a number of significant documentary works, including the records of the Diplomatic Advisory Council, entitled *Suiusō nikki* (Tokyo: Hara shobo, 1966); and coedited several collections of important papers relating to the Manchurian Incident under the titles *Manshū jihen* (Manchurian Incident) (Tokyo: Misuzu shobō, 1964) and *Zoku Manshū jihen* (Manchurian Incident, supplement) (Tokyo: Misuzu shobō, 1965), being volumes 7 and 11 of Misuzu shobō's *Gendai shi shiryō* (Source Materials on Contemporary History) series.

SEKI HIROHARU is professor of international politics at the Institute of Oriental Culture, University of Tokyo and also professor of peace studies, Institute for Peace Science, Hiroshima University. He was educated at the University of Tokyo. His main publications include *Gendai Higashi Ajia Kokusai Kankyō no Tanjō* (The Birth of the Contemporary International Environment of East Asia) (1966), *Kiki no Ninshiki* (The Perception of International Crisis) (1969), *Kokusai Taikei Ron no Kiso* (Foundations of International Systems Theory) (1969), and *Chikyū Seijigaku no Kōsō* (A Conception of the Politics of Planet Earth) (1977).

SHIMADA TOSHIHIKO, a specialist on the history of Japanese-Chinese relations and a professor at Musashi University, was born in 1908 and died in 1975. He received his B.A. from Tokyo University in 1934. His writings include *Kantō Gun* (The Kwantung Army) (1965) and *Manshū Jihen* (The Manchurian Incident) (*Kindai no Sensō*, vol. IV, 1966). He contributed substantially to *Gendai Shiryō* (Contemporary Historical Documents) (1964); another of his essays, "Kahoku kōsaku to kokkō chōsei (1933 nen–1937 nen)," in *Taiheiyō sensō e no michi*, vol. 3 (1962), is largely translated as "Designs on North China, 1933–1937" in *The China Quagmire* (1983).

ARTHUR E. TIEDEMANN is professor of history and dean of social science at the City College of the City University of New York. He received his B.S.S. from the City College of New York in 1943 and his Ph.D. from Columbia University in 1959. His professional interest has centered on the interrelations in twentieth-century Japan among domestic politics, economic policy, and foreign relations. He is the author of, among other works, *Modern Japan: a Brief History* (2nd rev. ed. 1962), and editor of *An Introduction to Japanese Civilization* (1974).

Index

Studies of the East Asian Institute

THE LADDER OF SUCCESS IN IMPERIAL CHINA, by Ping-ti Ho. New York: Columbia University Press, 1962.

THE CHINESE INFLATION, 1937–1949, by Shun-hsin Chou. New York: Columbia University Press, 1963.

REFORMER IN MODERN CHINA: CHANG CHIEN, 1853–1926, by Samuel Chu. New York: Columbia University Press, 1965.

RESEARCH IN JAPANESE SOURCES: A GUIDE, by Herschel Webb with the assistance of Marleigh Ryan. New York: Columbia University Press, 1965.

SOCIETY AND EDUCATION IN JAPAN, by Herbert Passin. New York: Teachers College Press, 1965.

AGRICULTURAL PRODUCTION AND ECONOMIC DEVELOPMENT IN JAPAN, 1873–1922, by James I. Nakamura. Princeton: Princeton University Press, 1966.

JAPAN'S FIRST MODERN NOVEL: UKIGUMO OF FUTABATEI SHIMEI, by Marleigh Ryan. New York: Columbia University Press, 1967.

THE KOREAN COMMUNIST MOVEMENT, 1918–1948, by Dae-Sook Suh. Princeton: Princeton University Press, 1967.

THE FIRST VIETNAM CRISIS, by Melvin Gurtov. New York: Columbia University Press, 1967.

CADRES, BUREAUCRACY, AND POLITICAL POWER IN COMMUNIST CHINA, by A. Doak Barnett. New York: Columbia University Press, 1968.

THE JAPANESE IMPERIAL INSTITUTION IN THE TOKUGAWA PERIOD, by Herschel Webb. New York: Columbia University Press, 1968.

HIGHER EDUCATION AND BUSINESS RECRUITMENT IN JAPAN, by Koya Azumi. New York: Teachers College Press, 1969.

THE COMMUNISTS AND PEASANT REBELLIONS: A STUDY IN THE REWRITING OF CHINESE HISTORY, by James P. Harrison, Jr. New York: Atheneum, 1969.

HOW THE CONSERVATIVES RULE JAPAN, by Nathaniel B. Thayer. Princeton: Princeton University Press, 1969.

ASPECTS OF CHINESE EDUCATION, edited by C. T. Hu. New York: Teachers College Press, 1970.

DOCUMENTS OF KOREAN COMMUNISM, 1918–1948, by Dae-Sook Suh. Princeton: Princeton University Press, 1970.

JAPANESE EDUCATION: A BIBLIOGRAPHY OF MATERIALS IN THE ENGLISH LANGUAGE, by Herbert Passin. New York: Teachers College Press, 1970.

ECONOMIC DEVELOPMENT AND THE LABOR MARKET IN JAPAN, by Koji Taira. New York: Columbia University Press, 1970.

THE JAPANESE OLIGARCHY AND THE RUSSO-JAPANESE WAR, by Shumpei Okamoto. New York: Columbia University Press, 1970.

IMPERIAL RESTORATION IN MEDIEVAL JAPAN, by H. Paul Varley. New York: Columbia University Press, 1971.

JAPAN'S POSTWAR DEFENSE POLICY, 1947–1968, by Martin E. Weinstein. New York: Columbia University Press, 1971.

ELECTION CAMPAIGNING JAPANESE STYLE, by Gerald L. Curtis. New York: Columbia University Press, 1971.

CHINA AND RUSSIA: THE "GREAT GAME," by O. Edmund Clubb. New York: Columbia University Press, 1971.

MONEY AND MONETARY POLICY IN COMMUNIST CHINA, by Katharine Huang Hsiao. New York: Columbia University Press, 1971.

THE DISTRICT MAGISTRATE IN LATE IMPERIAL CHINA, by John R. Watt. New York: Columbia University Press, 1972.

LAW AND POLICY IN CHINA'S FOREIGN RELATIONS: A STUDY OF ATTITUDES AND PRACTICE, by James C. Hsiung. New York: Columbia University Press, 1972.

PEARL HARBOR AS HISTORY: JAPANESE-AMERICAN RELATIONS, 1931–1941, edited by Dorothy Borg and Shumpei Okamoto, with the assistance of Dale K. A. Finlayson. New York: Columbia University Press, 1973.

JAPANESE CULTURE: A SHORT HISTORY, by H. Paul Varley. New York: Praeger, 1973.

DOCTORS IN POLITICS: THE POLITICAL LIFE OF THE JAPAN MEDICAL ASSOCIATION, by William E. Steslicke. New York: Praeger, 1973.

THE JAPAN TEACHERS UNION: A RADICAL INTEREST GROUP IN JAPANESE POLITICS, by Donald Ray Thurston. Princeton: Princeton University Press, 1973.

JAPAN'S FOREIGN POLICY, 1868–1941: A RESEARCH GUIDE, edited by James William Morley. New York: Columbia University Press, 1974.

PALACE AND POLITICS IN PREWAR JAPAN, by David Anson Titus. New York: Columbia University Press, 1974.

THE IDEA OF CHINA: ESSAYS IN GEOGRAPHIC MYTH AND THEORY, by Andrew March. Devon, England: David and Charles, 1974.

ORIGINS OF THE CULTURAL REVOLUTION, by Roderick MacFarquhar. New York: Columbia University Press, 1974.

SHIBA KŌKAN: ARTIST, INNOVATOR, AND PIONEER IN THE WESTERNIZATION OF JAPAN, by Calvin L. French. Tokyo: Weatherhill, 1974.

INSEI: ABDICATED SOVEREIGNS IN THE POLITICS OF LATE HEIAN JAPAN, by G. Cameron Hurst. New York: Columbia University Press, 1975.

EMBASSY AT WAR, by Harold Joyce Noble. Edited with an introduction by Frank Baldwin, Jr. Seattle: University of Washington Press, 1975.

REBELS AND BUREAUCRATS: CHINA'S DECEMBER 9ERS, by John Israel and Donald W. Klein. Berkeley: University of California Press, 1975.

DETERRENT DIPLOMACY, edited by James William Morley. New York: Columbia University Press, 1976.

HOUSE UNITED, HOUSE DIVIDED: THE CHINESE FAMILY IN TAIWAN, by Myron L. Cohen. New York: Columbia University Press, 1976.

ESCAPE FROM PREDICAMENT: NEO-CONFUCIANISM AND CHINA'S EVOLVING POLITICAL CULTURE, by Thomas A. Metzger. New York: Columbia University Press, 1976.

CADRES, COMMANDERS, AND COMMISSARS: THE TRAINING OF THE CHINESE COMMUNIST LEADERSHIP, 1920–45, by Jane L. Price. Boulder, Colo.: Westview Press, 1976.

SUN YAT-SEN: FRUSTRATED PATRIOT, by C. Martin Wilbur. New York: Columbia University Press, 1977.

JAPANESE INTERNATIONAL NEGOTIATING STYLE, by Michael Blaker. New York: Columbia University Press, 1977.

CONTEMPORARY JAPANESE BUDGET POLITICS, by John Creighton Campbell. Berkeley: University of California Press, 1977.

THE MEDIEVAL CHINESE OLIGARCHY, by David Johnson. Boulder, Colo.: Westview Press, 1977.

THE ARMS OF KIANGNAN: MODERNIZATION IN THE CHINESE ORDNANCE INDUSTRY, 1860–1895, by Thomas L. Kennedy. Boulder, Colo.: Westview Press, 1978.

PATTERNS OF JAPANESE POLICYMAKING: EXPERIENCES FROM HIGHER EDUCATION, by T. J. Pempel. Boulder, Colo.: Westview Press, 1978.

THE CHINESE CONNECTION: ROGER S. GREENE, THOMAS W. LAMONT, GEORGE E. SOKOLSKY, AND AMERICAN-EAST ASIAN RELATIONS, by Warren I. Cohen. New York: Columbia University Press, 1978.

MILITARISM IN MODERN CHINA: THE CAREER OF WU P'EI-FU, 1916–1939, by Odoric Y. K. Wou. Folkestone, England: Dawson, 1978.

A CHINESE PIONEER FAMILY: THE LINS OF WU-FENG, by Johanna Meskill. Princeton: Princeton University Press, 1979.

PERSPECTIVES ON A CHANGING CHINA, edited by Joshua A. Fogel and William T. Rowe. Boulder, Colo.: Westview Press, 1979.

THE MEMOIRS OF LI TSUNG-JEN, by T. K. Tong and Li Tsung-jen. Boulder, Colo.: Westview Press, 1979.

UNWELCOME MUSE: CHINESE LITERATURE IN SHANGHAI AND PEKING, 1937–1945, by Edward Gunn. New York: Columbia University Press, 1979.

YENAN AND THE GREAT POWERS: THE ORIGINS OF CHINESE COMMUNIST FOREIGN POLICY, by James Reardon-Anderson. New York: Columbia University Press, 1980.

UNCERTAIN YEARS: CHINESE-AMERICAN RELATIONS, 1947–1950, edited by Dorothy Borg and Waldo Heinrichs. New York: Columbia University Press, 1980.

THE FATEFUL CHOICE: JAPAN'S ADVANCE INTO SOUTHEAST ASIA, edited by James William Morley. New York: Columbia University Press, 1980.

TANAKA GIICHI AND JAPAN'S CHINA POLICY, by William F.

Morton. Folkestone, England: Dawson, 1980; New York: St. Martin's Press, 1980.

THE ORIGINS OF THE KOREAN WAR: LIBERATION AND THE EMERGENCE OF SEPARATE REGIMES, 1945–1947, by Bruce Cumings. Princeton: Princeton University Press, 1981.

CLASS CONFLICT IN CHINESE SOCIALISM, by Richard Curt Kraus. New York: Columbia University Press, 1981.

EDUCATION UNDER MAO: CLASS AND COMPETITION IN CANTON SCHOOLS, by Jonathan Unger. New York: Columbia University Press, 1982.

PRIVATE ACADEMIES OF TOKUGAWA JAPAN, by Richard Rubinger. Princeton: Princeton University Press, 1982.

JAPAN AND THE SAN FRANCISCO PEACE SETTLEMENT, by Michael M. Yoshitsu. New York: Columbia University Press, 1982.

NEW FRONTIERS IN AMERICAN-EAST ASIAN RELATIONS: ESSAYS PRESENTED TO DOROTHY BORG, edited by Warren I. Cohen. New York: Columbia University Press, 1983.

THE ORIGINS OF THE CULTURAL REVOLUTION: II, THE GREAT LEAP FORWARD, 1958–1960, by Roderick MacFarquhar. New York: Columbia University Press, 1983.

THE CHINA QUAGMIRE: JAPAN'S EXPANSION ON THE ASIAN CONTINENT, 1933–1941, edited by James William Morley. New York: Columbia University Press, 1983.

FRAGMENTS OF RAINBOWS: THE LIFE AND POETRY OF SAITO MOKICHI, 1882–1953, by Amy Vladeck Heinrich. New York: Columbia University Press, 1983.

THE U.S.-SOUTH KOREAN ALLIANCE: EVOLVING PATTERNS OF SECURITY RELATIONS, edited by Gerald L. Curtis and Sung-joo Han. Lexington, Mass.: Lexington Books, 1983.